우루과이라운드

농산물 협상 4

우루과이라운드

농산물 협상 4

| 머리말

    우루과이라운드는 국제적 교역 질서를 수립하려는 다각적 무역 교섭으로서, 각국의 보호무역 추세를 보다 완화하고 다자무역체제를 강화하기 위해 출범되었다. 1986년 9월 개시가 선언되었으며, 15개 분야의 교섭을 1990년 말까지 진행하기로 했다. 그러나 각 분야의 중간 교섭이 이루어진 1989년 이후에도 농산물, 지적소유권, 서비스무역, 섬유, 긴급수입제한 등 많은 분야에서 대립하며 1992년이 돼서야 타결에 이를 수 있었다. 한국은 특히 농산물 분야에서 기존 수입 제한 품목 대부분을 개방해야 했기에 큰 경쟁력 하락을 겪었고, 관세와 기술 장벽 완화, 보조금 및 수입 규제 정책의 변화로 제조업 수출입에도 많은 변화가 있었다.

    본 총서는 우루과이라운드 협상이 막바지에 다다랐던 1991~1992년 사이 외교부에서 작성한 관련 자료를 담고 있다. 관련 협상의 치열했던 후반기 동향과 관계부처회의, 무역협상위원회 회의, 실무대책회의, 규범 및 제도, 투자회의, 특히나 가장 많은 논란이 있었던 농산물과 서비스 분야 협상 등의 자료를 포함해 총 28권으로 구성되었다. 전체 분량은 약 1만 3천여 쪽에 이른다.

2024년 3월
한국학술정보(주)

| 일러두기

· 본 총서에 실린 자료는 2022년 4월과 2023년 4월에 각각 공개한 외교문서 4,827권, 76만여 쪽 가운데 일부를 발췌한 것이다.

· 각 권의 제목과 순서는 공개된 원본을 최대한 반영하였으나, 주제에 따라 일부는 적절히 변경하였다.

· 원본 자료는 A4 판형에 맞게 축소하거나 원본 비율을 유지한 채 A4 페이지 안에 삽입하였다. 또한 현재 시점에선 공개되지 않아 '공란'이란 표기만 있는 페이지 역시 그대로 실었다.

· 외교부가 공개한 문서 각 권의 첫 페이지에는 '정리 보존 문서 목록'이란 이름으로 기록물 종류, 일자, 명칭, 간단한 내용 등의 정보가 수록되어 있으며, 이를 기준으로 0001번부터 번호가 매겨져 있다. 이는 삭제하지 않고 총서에 그대로 수록하였다.

· 보고서 내용에 관한 더 자세한 정보가 필요하다면, 외교부가 온라인상에 제공하는 『대한민국 외교사료요약집』 1991년과 1992년 자료를 참조할 수 있다.

| 차례

정 리 보 존 문 서 목 록					
기록물종류	일반공문서철	등록번호	2019080090	등록일자	2019-08-13
분류번호	764.51	국가코드		보존기간	영구
명 칭	UR(우루과이라운드) / 농산물 협상 그룹 회의, 1991. 전7권				
생 산 과	통상기구과	생산년도	1991~1991	담당그룹	다자통상
권 차 명	V.7 12월				

내용목차	* 2.26. TNC, Dunkel 사무총장 제안서 채택
	4.25. TNC, 농산물 그룹 의장에 Dunkel 선임
	6.12. Dunkel 현황 보고서 배포
	6.24. Dunkel 대안(optional paper) 제시
	8.2. Dunkel.대안(6.24.) 부록 배포
	11.21. Dunkel working paper 제시
	    - 11.25. Dunkel 작업문 초안 관련 농림부 장관 서한 발송
	12.13. Dunkel 의장 농산물 협상 협정 초안 배포
	    - 12.17. 민감품목 관세화 예외 인정 수정 제안 사무총장앞 서면 제출				

0001

발 신 전 보

번 호 : WJA-5462 911202 1847 ED 종별 :

WCN-1426 WGV-1741

수 신 : 주 일, 카나다 대사. 총영사 (사본 : 주 제네바, EC 대사)

발 신 : 장 관 (통 기)

제 목 : UR/농산물 협상

	분류번호	보존기간

1. 12.2자 매일경제 신문은 12.2자 일본 경제신문의 기사 내용을 인용, 귀주재국 정부가 표제 협상에서 논의되고 있는 예외없는 관세화에 대한 EC의 지지 입장 변화를 유도하기 위해 갓트 11조 2항 C 개정에 대한 종래 입장(순수입국에만 적용)을 완화하는 새로운 제안을 검토하고 있다고 보도함(상세 기사 내용 별첨 FAX 송부).

2. 상기 보도의 사실 여부등 관련사항 파악 보고바람.

첨 부 : 동 기사 (1매).   끝.   (통상국장 김 용 규)

		보 안 통 제	ᄱ

앙 고 재	91년 12월 2일 통상기구과	기안자 성명 농봉린	과 장 심의관	국 장	차 관	장 관

외신과통제

0002

日·加 「UR농산물」 새 提案검토

關稅化예외 範圍확대

EC協力 유도위한 布石

【東京=李雄燦특파원】우루과이라운드(UR)농산물협상과 관련, 일본정부와 캐나다정부는 농산물수입장벽에대한 관세화에 예외를 인정토록하는 새로운 제안을 검토하기 시작했다고 日本經濟新聞이 2일보도했다.

양국정부가 마련하고있는 안의 구체적 내용은 아직 밝혀지지 않고 있으나 현재 각국이 생산을 제한하고 있는 작물에 대해서 장개방에서의 예외를 인정하고 있는 가트 11조2항(C)의 규정 적용을 순수입국에 한정토록 하자는 종래의 제안을 수정, 적용대상국을 늘리는 박안이 유력하게 검토되고 있다는 이신문은 전했다.

그동안 양국정부는 「예외없는 관세화」 원칙을 저지하는 규정으로서 가트11조2항(C)의 적용기준을 강화△가공품과 원료와의 기준을 명확히 하고△생산제한조치가 실효성을 수반하고 있는가를 점검토

록 하자는 등의 안을 제시해 왔다.

양국이 새로운 방향의수정안마련을 추진하고 있는것은 이 규정의 적용을 순수입국에 한정한案에반발,수입국에 한정한案에반발,「예외없는 관세화」를 지지하는 쪽으로 기울어졌던 유럽공동체(EC)의 태도변화를 유도하기 위한전략의일환인 것으로보인다. 특히 日本정부는 EC측이 강점을 보이고 있는 유제품들을 관세화의 예외

목으로 상정,쌀에대한 관세화예외를 끌어낸 방침인 것으로 알려졌다.

가트의 11조2항(C)는 예외적으로 농산물의 수입수량제한을 인정, 그대상이 생산제한중인 작물과 동종의 산품일 것은 규정하고 있으나 더 이상의 세부항목은 제시되어 있지 않다.

매일경제 (91. 12. 2)

외 무 부

종 별 :

번 호 : JAW-6816   일 시 : 91 1203 2127

수 신 : 장관(봉기)

발 신 : 주 일 대사(일경)

제 목 : UR 농산물 협상

대:WJA-5462

대호, 12.2. 자 일본경제신문 보도 관련, 당관 김종주 농무관과 조태영 서기관은 12.3 "미야모토"농림수산성 국제경제과장을 면담하였는바, 동인의 발언요지를 다음 보고함.

   1. 기사 내용은 사실 무근으로서, 일본 정부가 기사 내용에 있는 것과 같은 제안을 검토한 적이 없음.

   2. 카나다의 낙농단체측이 11 조 2 항(C)의 적용 대상 확대를 희망하고 있다고는 듣고 있으나, 카나다 정부가 이러한 제안을 긍정적으로 검토하고 있다고 들은바가 없으며, 카나다측으로 부터 적용 대상 확대를 위한 수정제안 제출을 요청 받은 바 없음.

   3.(기사내용의 진위와는 관계없이, 11 조 2 항(C)의 적용 대상을 확대할 경우, 완전관세화 쪽으로 기운 EC 의 의견을 되돌릴수 있다고 보느냐는 질문에 대해) 현재 EC 국가들은 독일을 제외하고는 11 조 2 항(C)에 별로 관심이 없으므로, 동 조항 적용 대상확대를 통해 EC 의 완전관세화안 지지 입장을 되돌리기는 어렵다고 봄.

   가. EC 는 현재 기본적으로 국내 농산물 가격 인하를 통해 수출 보조금의 소요도 줄이고, 따라서 수출보조금의 재원으로 활용되어온 가변과징금도 낮춘다는 방향에서 협의가 진행되고 있는바, 이는 국내 생산제한을 통해 국내의 높은 가격을 유지하고, 이를 수입제한 철폐의 예외로 한다는 11 조 2 항(C)는 우선 순위가 떨어지는 의제가 되고 있으나, 다만, 일단 완전관세화를 하더라도 장래에 독일등 회원국들이 혹시 이조항을 필요로 하게 될지 모른다는 생각하에, 완전관세화와 모순되는 점에도 불구하고 11 조 2 항(C)는 그대로 둔다는(또는 명확화)입장인 것으로 알고 있음.

   4.11 조 2 항(C)는 물론 완전관세화안의 예외를 인정하는 효과가 있기는 하지만,

어디까지나 <u>부분개방의</u> 의무를 수반하고 있으므로로, 일본에 있어서 쌀등 기초 식량의 예외를 인정받는 수단은 <u>될수가 없음.</u> 이러한 점에서도 현재로서는 쌀등 기초식량에 대한 예외취급이 필요하다는 점을 강력히 주장하고, <u>완전관세화에 반대하는 국가의 수를 늘려 가는 것이 더욱 중요하다고 봄.</u>

　0 현재, <u>미 상원의원 60 명이 WAIVER 품목폐지에 반대하는</u> 서명을 하였다는 정보가 있는바, 미국으로서도 자체문제를 해결하지 못하는 상황에서 완전관세화안을 강력히 주장하기는 어려워 지지않을까 보고 있음. 끝.

　(대사 오재희-국장)

　예고:91.12.31.까지

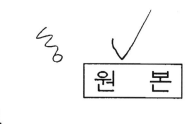

관리 번호	91-001

외 무 부

종 별 :

번 호 : CNW-1594　　　　　　　　　일 시 : 91 1204 1000

수 신 : 장 관(봉기,상공부)

발 신 : 주 캐나다 대사

제 목 : UR/농산물 협상

대 : WCN-1426

대호 매일 경제신문 보도의 사실여부등 관련사항 파악결과를 아래와 같이 보고함.

1. 주재국 외무통상부 MARIO STE-MARIE 부조정관(MTN BRANCH 농업부문)과의협의 결과

가. 예외없는 관세화에 대한 EC 의 입장 변화유도를 위해 주재국이 갓트 제11 조 2 항 C 개정에 대한 기존 입장을 변경, 새로운 제안을 할 계획은 현재로서는 없다고 동인은 밝혔음. 그러나 지난주 주재국 농민대표들이 제네바에서 주재국의 SUPPLY MANAGEMENT SYSTEM 를 존속케 할 목적으로 EC 회원국들에 대해 갓트 제 11 조 2 항 C 개정에 대한 입장을 완화할 용의가 있다고 밝혔으며 더욱이 동 농민대표들은 주재국 정부와의 사전 협의결과 정부로부터 긍정적인 반응을 얻고 EC 측에 이와 같은 제안을 한 것이라고 함.

나. 동인에 의하면 이러한 제안에 대해 EC 측으로부터 크게 호의적인 반응을 얻지는 못하였다함. 또한 상기 농문 대표들의 견해 표명은 주재국 정부의 입장과는 별개라고 동인은 밝히고 있으나 당관 평가로서는 정부측이 사전 협의를 가진 것으로 보아 주재국 정부가 SUPPLY MANAGEMENT SYSTEM 존속을 위해 EC 의 지지확보가 가능하다면 기본입장을 완화하는 새로운 제안을 할 용의가 있음을 시사해 주는 것이라고 봄.

다. 다만 동인도 주재국이 새로운 제안을 하는 경우에도 예외없는 관세화에대한 EC 의 입장 변화를 기대하기는 용이치 않을 것이라고 하면서 독일의 경우낙농업이 타 EC 국가(특히 프랑성, 덴마크등)에 비해 상대적으로 경쟁력이 저위에 있기 때문에 SUPPLY MANAGEMENT SYSTEM 존속을 지지할 가능성이 있으나 여타 국가에서는 큰 호응을 얻지 못할 것이라고 언급함.

통상국	차관	1차보	2차보	미주국	분석관	청와대	안기부	상공부

PAGE 1　　　　　　　　　　　　　　　　　　　　　　91.12.05　 05:08

　　　　　　　　　　　　　　　　　　　　　　　외신 2과 통제관 FI

2. MR. DOUGLAS ARTHUR(무역협회 고용 현지 컨설턴트)의 평가

가. 주재국이 EC 의 지지 확보를 위해 갓트 규정 개정에 대한 기존 입장을 완화하는 새로운 제안을 할 가능성을 배제할수는 없으나 예외없는 관세화에 대한미국의 입장이 확고부동하고 EC 도 UR 농산물 협상 타결을 위해서는 동 미국 입장에 동조할 수 밖에 없는 처지에 있는 것으로 카큭 정부가 평가하고 있기 때문에 협상 마지막 단계에 가서는 주재국의 낙농 가금류 및 계란에 대한 비관세 장벽은 결국 포기해야 한다는 인식이 내부적으로 평배하고 있는 것으로 감지된다고 동인은 언급

나. 또한 동인은 주재국 정부가 갓트 11 조 2 항 C 관련 새로운 제안을 할 가능성 보다는 동 제안으로 인해 EC 가 예외없는 관세화에 대한 기본 입장을 변경할 가능성은 더욱 희박한 것으로 본다고 전망. 끝

(대사-국장)

예고문 : 91.12.31. 까지

（미상원 2002,
UR협상방안 동의 (Fr. Track)에 대한
라당표시）

외 무 부

종 별 :

번 호 : GVW-2548

일 시 : 91 1204 1730

수 신 : 장 관(봉기, 경기원, 재무부, 농림수산부, 상공부)

발 신 : 주 제네바 대사

제 목 : UR/농산물 협상(미국 웨이버)

　　미 상원의원 59명이 유제품, 땅콩, 설탕, 면화등에 대하여 적용되고 있는 웨이버를 폐지하는데 반대하는 서명을 한 서한을 미 대통령에게 전달하였는 바 동 서한 사본을 별첨 FAX 송부함.

　　첨부: 미 상원의원 서한 사본 1부

　　(GVW(F)-0576). 끝

　　(대사 박수길-국장)

상원의경원: 1 oo 명
미의원두표수 = 다수 2 62구

통상국	장관	1차보	경기원	재무부	농수부	상공부

91.12.05　　09:30 WI

외신 1과　통제관

0008

주 제 네 바 대 표 부

번 호 : GVW(F) - *0576*   년월일 : *1204*   시간 : *1730*

수 신 : 장   관 (*통기, 경기원, 재무부, 농림수산부, 상공부*)

발 신 : 주 제네바대사

제 목 : *GVW-2548 첨부*

총 *1* 매(표지포함)

보 안 통 제	

외신과 통 제	

576-1-1

United States Senate

WASHINGTON, D.C. 20515

November 25, 1991

The President
The White House
Washington, DC 20500

Dear Mr. President:

The Agriculture Adjustment Act of 1933, as amended, provides a mechanism to allow the U.S. Government to take action that would limit the import of commodities which would undermine domestic farm support programs. Under the Agriculture Adjustment Act of 1933, Congress sought to maintain its constitutional right to legislate domestic farm programs. This authority was clearly set forth in Section 22 and states: "No international treaty heretofore or hereafter entered into by the United States shall be applied in a manner inconsistent with the requirements of this Section." 7 U.S.C. 624(f).

Since its inception, Section 22 has been used to stabilize at least 2 commodity programs. Currently this authority is operational for our cotton, dairy, peanut and sugar programs.

Under current GATT negotiations, with the unreasonable demands made by European Community negotiators, we feel that the willingness of the U.S. negotiators to unilaterally concede Section 22 is too high a price to pay for what little we apparently are to receive in return.

As the GATT negotiations draw to a close, we wish to reaffirm our strong support for this authority. We feel Section 22 should not be compromised in any final agreement.

Sincerely,

576-1-2

0010

The President
November 25, 1991

[signature]
B. Bennett Johnston

[signature]
Richard Shelby

[signature]
Quentin Burdick

[signature]
Sam Nunn

[signature]
Wyche Fowler, Jr.

[signature]
Jim Jeffords

[signature]
Bob Kasten

[signature]
Daniel K. Akaka

[signature]
Kent Conrad

[signature]
Conrad Burns

[signature]
Alfonse D'Amato

[signature]
Herb Kohl

[signature]
Section 22/Agriculture
Adjustment Act/GATT
Arlen Specter

[signature]
Barbara A. Mikulski

0011

536-7-3

The President
November 25, 1991

John Breaux

David L. Boren

Trent Lott

Johh Warner

David Pryor

Jesse Helms

Terry Sanford

Paul Wellstone

Daniel Inouye

Steve Symms

Frank Murkowski

Bob Graham

Quentin Burdick

Chuck Robb

576-9-4

0012

The President
November 25, 1991

Patrick Leahy

Strom Thurmond

Tom Harkin

Harris Wofford

Brock Adams

Dave Durenberger

Tom Daschle

Connie Mack

Joseph Lieberman

Larry Pressler

Timothy Wirth

Jack Garn

576-7-5   0013

The President
November 25, 1991

_____   _____
Al Gore   Orrin Hatch

_____   _____

_____   _____

_____   _____

_____   _____

_____   _____

576-1-6   0014

The President
November 25, 1991

James Exon

Trent Lott

Wendell Ford

Daniel Moynihan

Jeff Bingaman

Ernest Hollings

Dennis DeConcini

Connie Mack

Dale Bumpers

Pete Domenici

Harry Reid

Al Gore

Mitch McConnell

Christopher Dodd

0015

외 무 부

관리
번호 91-893

종 별 : 지 급

번 호 : ECW-1058   일   시 : 91 1205 1600

수 신 : 장관 (봉기,농림수산부,기정동문)

발 신 : 주 EC 대사

제 목 : GATT/UR 협상

대: WEC-0780

대호관련, 당관 이관용농무관은 EC 집행위 GUTH 농산물협상 담당과장및 12.4.
당지주재 일본대표부 HARAGUCHI 농무관을 각각 접촉한바 하기 보고함

    1. 지난주 일본 농림수산성 축산담당 부국장을 단장으로한 대표단이 EC 집행위를
방문, GATT 11-2-C 개정제안을 EC 가 지지해줄것을 요청한바 있음. 동 방문시 EC 는 :
순수입국 적용조항" 을 철회할 경우 긍정적으로 검토하겠다는 기존입장을 표명한바
있으며, 이에대한 일본의 확정적인 답변을 요청한바 있다고 함. 이에대해 일본측은 EC
가 먼저 동 조항 개정제안을 지지해 줄 경우 공동제안국들과 협의하여 동 적용조건
철회문제를 결정할수 있다는 입장을 보였다고 함

    2. 한편 일본이 동 적용조건을 철회하는 문제를 카나다와 협의한바 있느냐는
문의에대해 일본대표부 관계관은 구체적으로 아는바는 없으나 카나다는 당초제안을
변경할 의사가 없는것으로 알고 있다고 말하면서 EC 는 미국, 케언즈그룹이 강한
반대입장을 견지하고 있어 동 제안이 협상결과에 반영될 것인가에 의문을 갖고
있는것으로 안다고 덧붙임. 끝

    (대사 권동만-국장)

    예고: 91.2.31. 까지

통상국   장관   차관   1차보   2차보   구주국   경제국   외정실   분석관
정와대   안기부   농수부

PAGE 1   91.12.06   04:30
                                                    외신 2과 통제관 FM
                                                            0016

22   우루과이라운드 농산물 협상 4

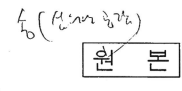

```
관리
번호  91-894
```

외 무 부

종 별 : 지급

번 호 : ECW-1064   일 시 : 91 1205 1800

수 신 : 장관 (봉기,경기원,재무부,농수산부,상공부,기정동문)

발 신 : 주 EC 대사 사본: 주 미,제네바-중계요망

제 목 : 갓트/UR 협상

연: ECW-1059

12.5. 표제협상 관련동향을 하기보고함

1. 미-EC 양자협상

가. MACSHARRY 집행위원 보좌관에 의하면 MACSHARRY 위원이 (12.7.) 워싱톤을방문, MADIGAN 미 농무장관과 농산물문제에 대해 협의를 하게 될것이라 함. 또한 동 보좌관은 MACSHARRY 위원의 말을 인용하여 12.4. 헤이그에서 가진 미-EC 접촉에서 부분적인 진전이 있었으며 특히 미국이 보조금 감축기간을 6 년간으로 하는 방안을 수락한 것으로 알고 있다고 말함

나. 동 보좌관은 워싱턴 회담에서는 양측이 계속 이견을 보이고있는, 1) 수출보조금 감축방법, 2) REBALANCING, 3) PEACE CLAUSE 및 4) GREEN BOX 요건에관한 사항이 논의될 것으로 보인다고 말함

2. 한편 당지언론에 의하면 BURDON 뉴질랜드 무역협상 장관이 표제협상이 실패로 끝날 가능성도 배제할수 없다고 말한것으로 보도함. 동인은 상금까지 동협상이 성공적으로 타결되기에는 충분한 진전이 없으며 특히 정치적 측면에서의 진전이 이루어지지 않고 있음을 지적함. 또한 동인은 EC 측은 이제까지 주장해온입장만을 고수하고 있으며 이러한 EC 측의 입장을 미국, 케언즈그룹및 여타협상 참여국들이 받아드릴 것으로 오해하고 있다고 비난하면서 UR 협상이 실패할 경우 동 협상의 성공을 기대하고 있는 협상국들로 부터 불가피하게 제기될 악영향 (INEVITABLE RECRIMINATION) 을 우려한다고 말함. 끝

(대사 권동만-국장)

예고: 91.12.31. 까지

통상국	장관	차관	1차보	2차보	구주국	정와대	안기부	
경기원	재무부	농수부	상공부	중계				

PAGE 1

분류번호	보존기간

발 신 전 보

WGV-1782   911207 1146 DU

번 호 : _____   종별 : _____

수 신 : 주   제네바   대사. 총/영사/

발 신 : 장 관 (통 기)

제 목 : UR/농산물 협상

1. 12.9부터 수시 개최될 가능성이 있는 UR/농산물 협상 회의 참가(자문) 및 농산물
    협상 관련 동향 파악등을 위해 최양부 농촌경제연구원 부원장을 파견하니 농산물
    협상 회의에 귀관 관계관과 함께 참석, 기존 입장 및 최부원장이 지참하는 쟁점별
    세부 입장에 따라 대처토록 조치바람.

2. 농산물 협상 진전상황에 따라 추후 김한곤 농림수산부 제2차관보를 본부대표로
    귀지 파견할 계획이니 참고바람.   끝.   (통상국장 김 용 규)

	1991.12.31
직위	성명

	보 안 통 제	

앙 고 재	91년 12월 7일	통상국 과	기안자 성명 홍병헌		과 장	심의관	국 장		차 관	장 관		외신과통제

0018

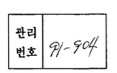

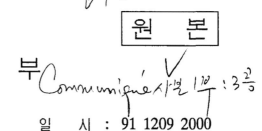

원 본

외 무 부

종   별 :

번   호 : GVW-2586   일   시 : 91 1209 2000

수   신 : 장관(봉기, 경기원, 재무부, 농림수산부, 상공부, 청와대, 경제수석)

발   신 : 주 제네바 대사   사본:주미,이씨,호주,카나다대사중계필

제   목 : UR/농산물 협상

대: WGV-1791

1. 케언즈 그룹 각료회의

가. 회의 개요

- 기간 및 장소: 12.8(일)-9(월) 기간중 당지에서 개최

- 참석자

0 호주: BLEWETT 대외무역성 장관

0 카나다: MAYER 농무장관

0 뉴질랜드: BURDON 무역협상장관

0 브라질: CABRERA 농무장관

0 알젠틴: REGUNAGA 농무장관

GUADAGNI 대외 경제성 장관

0 콜롬비아: CUBALLERO 농무장관

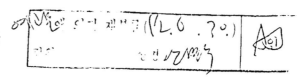

0 헝가리: MAJOR 국제경제성 차관

0 인도네시아: DJIWANDONO 무역성차관

0 태국: DEVAKULA 상무성차관

0 우리과이, 필리핀, 말련, 칠레, 폴란드, 휘지는 대사 또는 공사 참석

나. 회의결과

- 각료회의 참석 대표들은 12.8(일) 던켈총장을 면담, 협상 진전 상황과 향후 협상 계획에 대한 설명을 들었음. 동 보고에서 던켈 총장은 12.20 까지 전분야에 걸쳐 POLITICAL PACKAGE OF AGREEMENTS 를 만들겠다고 하였음.

- 동 각료회의 결과는 12.9(월) 하기 요지의 공동성명(COMMUNIQUE) 으로 발표되었음. (별첨 FAX 송부)

통상국	장관	차관	1차보	2차보	경제국	외정실	분석관	청와대
청와대	안기부	경기원	재무부	농수부	상공부			

O 최근 미.이씨간의 협상 타개 노력을 환영하지만 다자간 협상을 대체할수는 없으며, 협상결과에는 케언즈 그룹의 이익이 반드시 반영되어야 함.

O 던켈 총장의 작업문서에는 협상 타결에 필수적인 개념과 FRAMEWORK 가 포함되어 있지만 일부 개념이 아직 불분명함.

O 협상 결과 이행기간과 관련해서는 미.이씨간에의견이 접근되고 있는 5-6 년을 1 차적으로 약속(COMMITMENT)이 수반되어야 함.

O 기준년도, 삭감폭등에 대해서는 융통성을 가지고 협상에 참여하겠지만, 전품목에 대한 FORMULA 접근이 필요

O 구체적으로 시장접근 분야에서는 국경조치 제도변경

(REINSTRUMENTATION) 및 삭감, CMA 및 MMA 허용과 REBALANCING 의 반대

O 수출보조분야에서는 물량기준 및 금액기준 삭감과 신시장 및 신품목에 대한 수출보조 확대 방지

O 국내보조분야에서는 보조금의 실질적 삭감 및 생산과 연계된 보조금의 제도 변경

O 위생 및 검역 규제 조치는 부당한 무역장벽이 되지 않도록 규율

O 의미 있는 개도국 우대조치 인정

다. 평가

- 포괄적 관세화와 관련 카나다와 여타 케언즈그룹(특히 남미국가) 국가간의 현격한 입장 차이로 인하여 각료회의 개최 직전까지 논란이 많았는바, 동 각료회의 결과 공동성명에서는 포괄적 관세화 또는 예외없는 관세화라는 표현을 사용하지 않고 제도변경 (REINSTRUMENTATION) 이라고 표현함 (동 용어는 의장국인 호주가 DRAFT 에 의도적으로 사용, 11 조 2(C)관련 카나다와 여타국간 대결을 회피코자 하는데 그목적이 있었다함)

O 동 각료회의는 협상진전 사항 평가 및 조기 타결 촉구에 목적이 있었던 만큼 주요 쟁점에 대하여 회원국간의 이견 표출로 인한 부작용을 가능한 회피하면서 단합된 행동을 취하려고 한 때문으로 평가됨.

2. 최근 협상 동향 및 전망(당관 관계관이 케언즈그룹 각료회의장에서 탐문한 내용임)

- 12.8(일) 개최된, 미.이씨 농상회의에서는 주로 재균형화(REBALANCING)와수출보조금 문제가 논의되었으며 구체적인 타협안을 모색하고 있는 단계로 약간의 진전이 있었던 것으로 알려짐.

O MACSHARRY 이씨 농업집행위원은 12.9(월) 브랏셀로 귀임.

- 12.10(화) KATZ USTR 부대표와 CROWDER 농무차관이 브랏셀로 향발, 미.이씨간 고위 실무급 협의를 재개할 예정이며, 동회의가 사실상 년내 협상 타결 여부를 결정짓는 고비가 될것으로 전망됨.

- 12.12(목) MADIGAN 미농무장관이 브랏셀로 향발, 미.이씨간 농무장관 회담을 가질 전망임.

첨부: 케언즈그룹 각료회의 공동성명 1 부

(GVW(F)-0588). 끝

(대사 박수길-국장)

예고:92.6.30 까지

주 제 네 바 대 표 부

번 호 : GVR(F) - 0588   년월일 : 11 209   시간 : 2000

수 신 : 장   관 (동기.경기천, 재무부, 농림수산부, 상공부, 청와대 경제수석)

발 신 : 주 제네바대사   사본 : 주미. 주EC . 주로마, 주 카나다 대사

재 목 : 첨 부

총 3 매 (표지포합)

보 안 동 제	

외신과 동 제	

588 - 3 - 1

MINISTERIAL MEETING
CAIRNS GROUP
Geneva - Switzerland   9 December 1991

COMMUNIQUE

The Cairns Group met in Geneva on 8-9 December to review
developments in the Uruguay Round agriculture negotiations since
its last meeting at Manaus, Brazil in July 1991 and to consider
its approach to the final critical phase of the negotiations on
agriculture.

Ministers renewed their determination, maintained over five
years of joint effort, to achieve fundamental and irreversible
reform across all agricultural products. The Uruguay Round must
provide a turning point by beginning a sustained and credible
process to integrate agriculture fully into the general system
of GATT rules and disciplines.

Prior to their meeting, Cairns Ministers met with Mr Arthur
Dunkel, Chairman of both the agriculture negotiations and the
Trade Negotiations Committee at officials level. They received
his analysis of the current state of play on agriculture and on
wider Uruguay Round negotiations and were briefed on his plans
to achieve a political package of agreements in all areas by 20
December.

Ministers expressed their strong and continuing support for Mr
Dunkel's efforts to narrow differences and establish reform
mechanisms. They regard the concepts and framework contained in
the Dunkel November working papers as providing important
elements essential to an acceptable outcome, although there is a
need for greater precision in many areas and further development
of concepts.

Recalling that at their Manaus meeting they had urged G7
countries to exercise leadership in promoting domestic
agricultural reform and trade liberalisation through the Uruguay
Round, Cairns Ministers welcomed recent high-level efforts by
the United States and European Community to progress outstanding
agricultural issues. However, while bilateral discussions of
this kind can assist in narrowing differences over key issues,
they cannot substitute for the active participation of all
parties in genuine multilateral Uruguay Round negotiations.
Ministers made it clear that any acceptable outcome must address
the objectives of the Cairns Group.

Noting reports that recent EC/U.S. discussions have focussed on
cuts over a 5-6 year period only and of a lesser overall
magnitude than sought by the Cairns Group, Ministers recalled
that they had indicated their preparedness to participate in an
effective negotiation. However, a 5-6 year period could provide
only a first substantive step and it would need to be
supplemented by an unequivocal commitment to continue the
process of agricultural reform.

0023

十-88--3--2

2.

Moreover, any flexibility on the numbers depends both on the base periods involved and also on the scope, integrity and effectiveness of the framework disciplines that will govern multilateral, formula-based reductions in support and protection applied equitably across all agricultural products. In this regard, Ministers stressed that a meaningful agricultural outcome must include:

- reinstrumentation and reduction of border protection, assured increases in current market access and in minimum access levels (created where access has not been available in the past) and rejection of any increases in protection or other form of rebalancing

- substantial reductions in export subsidies in volume and value terms, along with secure disciplines to prevent their extension to new products or new markets

- the effective reduction and reinstrumentation of domestic support, including effective disciplines on all payments linked to production

- disciplines on sanitary and phytosanitary measures which ensure that unjustified barriers are not created or maintained

- meaningful differential and more favourable treatment to deal with the development needs of developing countries

Cairns Ministers emphasised that they would not accept any result that largely maintains under other guises existing levels of support, protection and trade distortion. They called upon those participants whose policies significantly distort world agricultural trade to demonstrate their commitment and the flexibility necessary to obtain a substantial and meaningful outcome.

They renewed their resolve that the Round could not and would not conclude, in whole or in part, without a substantial outcome on agriculture. For their part, Cairns Ministers recognised that such an outcome could be achieved only through a satisfactory and balanced overall package in the Uruguay Round. It is in clear acknowledgement of this that Cairns Group countries are participating actively and constructively across the Round.

Cairns Ministers expressed serious concern at the short time available to reach a political settlement and urged all Governments taking part in the Round to work expeditiously and constructively to achieve a satisfactory resolution. Ministers called in particular upon the major participants to accept their responsibilities at a moment when the world economy strongly needs the positive thrust of a successful conclusion to the Uruguay Round.

0024

6-88-3-3

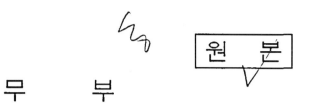

외 무 부

종 별 :

번 호 : GVW-2592

일 시 : 91 1210 1930

수 신 : 장 관(봉기,경기원,재무부,농림수산부,상공부)

발 신 : 주 제네바대사

제 목 : UR/농산물 협상(G-36)

　　1. 12.12(목) 11:00 표제 주요국비공식회의(G-36)가 개최될 예정임. 동회의시 논의예정인 삭감약속 계획서(LIST OFSPECIFIC COMMITMENTS) 초안 및 관련문서는 12.11(수)배포될 계획임.

　　2. 동 회의 소집 통지서 별첨 FAX 송부함.

　　첨부: UR/농산물 주요국 비공식회의 소집 통지서1부.끝

　　(대사 박수길-국장)

통상국　　2차보　　경기원　　재무부　　농수부　　상공부

PAGE 1

91.12.11　　09:15 WH

외신 1과 통제관

0025

주 제 네 바 대 표 부

번 호 : GVR(F) - 542   년월일 : 11210   시간 : 1P30

수 신 : 장 관 (통기, 경기원, 재무부, 농림수산부, 상공부)

발 신 : 주 제네바대사

제 목 : GVW-2542 회복

총 2 매 (표지포함)

보 안 통 제	회

외신과 통 재	

542-2-1

G A T T ·   F A C S I M I L E   T R A N S M I S S I O N

Centre William Rappard
Rue de Lausanne 154
CH-1211 Genève 21

Telefax: (022) 731 42 06
Telex: 412324 GATT CH
Telephone: (022) 739 51 11

TOTAL NUMBER OF PAGES   1
(including this preface)

Date: 10 December 1991

From: Arthur Dunkel
      Director-General
      GATT, Geneva

Signature

To:

Country	Representative	Fax No:
ARGENTINA	H.E. Mr. J.A. Lanus	798 72 82
AUSTRALIA	H.E. Mr. D. Hawes	733 65 86
AUSTRIA	H.E. Mr. W. Lang	734 45 91
BANGLADESH	H.E. Mr. M.R. Osmany	738 46 16
BRAZIL	H.E. Mr. C.L. Nunes Amorim	733 28 34
CANADA	H.E. Mr. G.E. Shannon	734 79 19
CHILE	H.E. Mr. M. Artaza	734 41 94
COLOMBIA	H.E. Mr. F. Jaramillo	791 07 87
COSTA RICA	H.E. Mr. R. Barzuna	733 28 69
CUBA	H.E. Mr. J.A. Pérez Novoa	758 23 77
EEC	H.E. Mr. Tran Van-Thinh	734 22 36
EGYPT	H.E. Mr. M. Mounir Zahran	731 68 28
FINLAND	H.E. Mr. A.A. Hynninen	740 02 87
HUNGARY	Mr. A. Szepesi	738 46 09
INDIA	H.E. Mr. B.K. Zutshi	738 45 48
INDONESIA	H.E. Mr. H.S. Kartadjoemena	793 83 09
ISRAEL	Mr. A. Perry	798 49 50
JAMAICA	H.E. Mr. L.M.H. Barnett	738 44 20
JAPAN	H.E. Mr. H. Ukawa	788 38 11
KOREA	H.E. Mr. Soo Gil Park	791 05 25
MALAYSIA	Mr. Supperamanian Manickam	788 09 75
MEXICO	H.E. Mr. J. Seade	733 14 55
MOROCCO	H.E. Mr. M. El Ghali Benhima	798 47 02
NEW ZEALAND	H.E. Mr. A.M. Bisley	734 30 62
NICARAGUA	H.E. Mr. J. Alaniz Pinell	736 60 12
NIGERIA	H.E. Mr. E.A. Azikiwe	734 10 53
PAKISTAN	H.E. Mr. A. Kamal	734 80 85
PERU	Mr. J. Muñoz	731 11 68
PHILIPPINES	H.E. Mrs. N.L. Escaler	731 68 88
POLAND	Mr. J. Kaczurba	798 11 75
SWITZERLAND	H.E. Mr. W. Rossier	734 56 23
THAILAND	H.E. Mr. Tej Bunnag	733 16 78
TURKEY	H.E. Mr. G. Aktan	734 52 09
UNITED STATES	H.E. Mr. R.H. Yerxa	749 48 94
URUGUAY	H.E. Mr. J.A. Lacarte-Muró	731 56 50
ZIMBABWE	H.E. Dr. A.T. Mugomba	738 49 54

You are invited to an informal consultation on agriculture to be held at 11 a.m. on Thursday 12 December in Room E of the Centre William Rappard. Attendance is restricted to two persons per delegation.

You are also advised that a non-paper entitled Draft Formats for Lists of Specific Commitments and Supporting Material, to assist in the discussions on Thursday, will be available in office 1028 (Mme Savoie) as from 10 a.m. on Wednesday 11 December 1991.

PLEASE NOTIFY US IMMEDIATELY IF YOU DO NOT RECEIVE ALL THE PAGES

** OUR FAX EQUIPMENT IS HITACHI HIFAX 210 (COMPATIBLE WITH
GROUPS 2 AND 3) AND IS SET TO RECEIVE AUTOMATICALLY **

0027

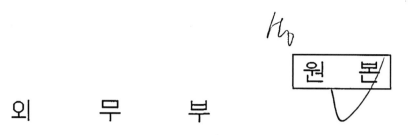

외 무 부

종 별 :

번 호 : AUW-1034

일 시 : 91 1211 1600

수 신 : 장 관(봉기)

발 신 : 주 호주대사

제 목 : UR 협상

    1. 주재국 BLEWETT 무역장관 주제하에 제네바에서 회의를 가진 CAIRNS 구룹은 UR농산 물협상에서 어떠한 결과가 나오더라도 이는 CAIRNS 구룹의 목적을 충족시켜야 한다는 내용의 성명서를 12.9 발표하였는바, BLEWETT장관은 동 회의후 기자회견을 통해 UR농산물 문제 협상에 있어 미국과 EC가 주역이며 이들사이의 이견조정이 가장중요한관건인 바, 지금까지 이들 사이에서 어떠한 돌파구가 마련되지 못하였으며 또한 협상의 붕괴(BREAKDOWN)도 없었다고 말하고, 금주 브라셀에서의 미-EC간의 회의의 결과가 UR협상 전체의 성공 또는 실패, 나아가서는 GATT자체의 앞으로의 장래를 좌우하게될것이라고 말함.

    2. 미-EC간 협상은 현재 우선 향후 5-6년간의 수출보조금 삭감문제에 초점을 두고 있는것으로 보도되고 있는것에 대해, 동장관은 앞으로 5-6년은 농산물 문제에 있어단지 첫번째의 중요한 진전의 계기를 마련할수 있을것이나 이러한 진전은 농업개혁의 과정을 계속한다는 분명한 약속이 수반되어야 한다고 말하고, 자신은 DUNKEL 총장에게 앞으로 국제농업무역을 손상시킬수 있는 BAD DEAL 보다는 차라리 NODEAL이 더좋다는 CAIRNS 구룹의 입장을 전달하였다고 말함.끝.(대사 이창범-국장)

통상국   2차보

91.12.11   14:54 WH

외신 1과 통제관

0028

관리 번호	91-816

외 무 부

종   별 :

번   호 : USW-6136   일   시 : 91 1211 1834

수   신 : 장 관(봉기, 경기원, 농수산부)

발   신 : 주 미국 대사

제   목 : UR 농산물 협상

　　　대: WUS-5610

　　　연: USW-5758, 5848, 6034, 6116

　　　1. KATZ USTR 부대표가 작 12.10 하원 농업위에서 UR 농산물협상의 최근 진전 상황에 관하여 증언한 발언 TEXT 를 별첨 송부함.

　　　2. 동 증언에서 KATZ 대표는 현재 협상이 민감한 단계에 있어 협상 내용을 세부적으로 밝히기는 곤란하다고 전제하면서도, 농산물 협상의 주요 쟁점별로 협상진행 현황을 설명하고 있음을 참고 바람.

　　　첨부: USWF-5484 (9 매). 끝.

　　　(대사 현홍주-국장)

　　　예고: 92.6.30. 까지

필 (1991. 12. 31.) 5

통상국 안기부	장관 경기원	차관 농수부	1차보	2차보	경제국	외정실	분석관	청와대

주 미 대 사 관

USR(F) : 5484 년월일 :   시간 :

수 산- : 장 관 (통기, 경기원, 능수산무)

발 신 : 주 미 대 사

제 목 : 청부 (9매)   (출처 :   )

보 안	
통 제	

(5484 - 9 - 1)

외신 1과	
통 제	

0030

HEARING OF THE HOUSE AGRICULTURE CMTE SUBJECT: AGRICULTURE TRADE
CHMN: REP. E. "KIKA" DE LA GARZA (D-TX)   WITNESS: JULIUS KATZ, DEPUTY
UNITED STATES TRADE REPRESENTATIVE   TUESDAY, DECEMBER 10, 1991
K-2-1 page# 1
    dest=hill,hsag,ustroff,usag,fortr,xfortr,gatt,trdpol,switz,eurcom,sugar
    dest+=untrdprc,japan,skor,fns10000,fns11182
    data

        REP. DE LA GARZA: (Sounds gavel.) The Committee will be in
order.

        We welcome all of you here. I'm starting on time. Members
will be coming in. As most of you know, the Congress is not in
session and members are flying in from their respective districts,
and some maybe as late as this morning. But I -- I want to impress
on all of our friends here that one of the reasons for this hearing,
of course, is we need the information. And I appreciate a
representative of the Trade Office being here, Mr. Katz, who's a
friend of many years. And I don't know I'd want to say how long you
and I have been here --

        MR. KATZ: It's a long time.

        REP. DE LA GARZA: -- Mr. Katz. But I -- we have had,
officially, a limited number of hearings -- July 29, September 29,
'86; February 28, '91. And periodically, we've had briefings, but
that's been Committee briefings, over a dozen this year alone with
Mrs. Hills, Secretary Madigan, Secretary Crowder, Ambassador Katz,
and I got concerned that people felt like there wasn't any input and
we weren't being briefed. We had been all along, but I decided that
the best thing at this time to do would be rather than to have the
Committee briefings, that we would have them as open hearings and we
will continue to do that, hopefully at least once a month, and so
that we might have publicly the developments in the Uruguay Round
and we very much appreciate the assistance of the Trade Office.

        Mr. Katz, Mr. Ambassador, I know that you will not be able to
stay for the entire hearing, as I understand you'll be leaving later
today for Geneva. But knowing of the time element that -- and how
long it takes to get from here to there, we've compiled the
testimony of the witnesses that are here today so that you might not
be -- I know that you'll be leaving as soon as we finish with your
testimony, but we'll give you copies so that you can take for your
night reading tonight and be appraised of what was said at the rest
of the hearing.

        And there are a number of other matters which I hope that we
can discuss today. For example, there is one, the sugar industry
testimony discusses a recent study done by the industry on European
Community support prices for sugar, and the concerns of the
administration on the validity of some of the figures cited.
There's also a concern expressed by one of the witnesses that the
industry advisory committee input on policy decisions has been --
has rarely been solicited, or when offered has generally been
ignored. Now, every time I meet with Mrs. Hills she assures me that
she has this advisory group and that they meet and they discuss.

0031

        And the subject of farmland tax assessments is raised also.
And this is a unique and certainly an interesting aspect that we
need to protect how such assessments will be treated in the Uruguay
Round. And there is also rumors and, as we know, this town leads the world
in rumor, but that, as a result of the recent bilateral meetings in
Brussels and the subsequent MacSharry-Madigan meeting this past
weekend, the European Community has put a proposal which differs
significantly from the previous position regarding deficiency
payments. And we will also like to know if you are aware of a
letter to President Bush signed by 66 or 67 Senators urging the
President not to be -- that Section XXII should not be compromised
in any final agreement. And I realize you may not be in a position
to address all these issues, but I mention them in passing in case
that you might. And we're always happy to have you here,
Ambassador, and we'll be happy to hear from you at this time.

        MR. KATZ: Thank you very much, Mr. Chairman. I welcome the
opportunity to appear before the committee to discuss the status of
the negotiations. Mr. Chairman, you have my full statement, and I
will excerpt it and request that the full statement be in the
record.

        REP. DE LA GARZA: That's agreeable and you may proceed as you
best see fit, Ambassador.

        MR. KATZ: Thank you. Thank you, sir. These negotiations are
now at a very delicate stage. In recent weeks, the momentum has
picked up considerably, but there remain some serious gaps in
positions and it is far from assured that an agreement can be
reached. And because of the sensitivity of the negotiations at this
moment, I hope that it will be understood that I cannot go into
great detail on the outstanding issues. But I'd like to describe
where we are in the process and to outline in general terms what the
main issues are in relation to the objectives that we have
previously discussed with the committee, and then I will certainly
be glad to answer questions, including the questions that you have
just raised.

        As the committee will recall, it was just a little more than a
year ago that the negotiations broke down in Brussels over the
refusal of the European Community, Japan, and Korea to agree to
negotiate specific reduction commitments in each of the three areas
of internal support, market access, and export subsidies. Since
that time, there has been a substantial effort by the Director
General of the GATT, who also serves as Chairman of the Agriculture
Negotiating Group, to agree upon a framework for the negotiations.
Agreement was reached earlier in the year that we would have
specific binding commitments in each of those three areas of
internal support and the two border measures. A great deal of
technical work has been accomplished since the spring in terms of
building on that outline, discussing what the specific means would be by
which reductions would take place, and some discussion of the reductions
themselves.

                        546K-9-3

                                                                        0032

HEARING OF THE HOUSE AGRICULTURE CMTE   SUBJECT: AGRICULTURE TRADE
CHMN: REP. E. "KIKA" DE LA GARZA (D-TX)   WITNESS: JULIUS KATZ, DEPUTY
UNITED STATES TRADE REPRESENTATIVE   TUESDAY, DECEMBER 10, 1991
K-2-1   page# 3

But clearly the issues are complex. They are highly political
in all countries. And in -- since the autumn there has been an
elevation of the issues to the political level. The negotiations --
the agriculture negotiations in particular -- were prominent on the
agenda of the US-EC summit at the Hague in early November when
President Bush met with the President of the EC Commission, Jacques
Delors, and the President of the Council for this six-month period
Dutch Prime Minister Lubbers. Secretary Madigan and Ambassador
Hills were also involved in those discussions. And at that meeting,
it appeared that we could come close to an understanding on the
magnitude of the reduction commitments, but we were far apart on
what those numbers would apply to. We could agree on what the
percentage would be, but there was still some question of percentage
of what?

Now since that time, we've had intensive discussions

CONTINUED

544-9-K

0033

HEARING OF THE HOUSE AGRICULTURE CMTE   SUBJECT: AGRICULTURE TRADE
CHMN: REP. E. "KIKA" DE LA GARZA (D-TX)   WITNESS: JULIUS KATZ, DEPUTY
UNITED STATES TRADE REPRESENTATIVE   TUESDAY, DECEMBER 10, 1991
K-2-2 page# 1
    dest=hill,hsag,ustroff,usag,fortr,xfortr,gatt,trdpol,switz,eurcom,sugar
    dest+=untrdprc,japan,skor,fns10000,fns11182
    data

    at all levels -- at the official level, at a senior official level,
    and at a political level. And at the moment, the bilateral talks
    between the US and the EC are the most critical part of this
    process, although we have been consulting closely with members of
    the Cairns group and other negotiating participants on a regular
    basis.

    Now, let me just summarize where we are with respect to the
    major outstanding issues. With respect to internal supports, the
    principal issue is to define which policies are subject to reduction
    commitments and which types of policies and programs are exempt from
    reduction commitments. There is broad agreement that such non-trade
    distorting policies as research, pest and disease control,
    environmental and conservation programs, resource retirement, crop
    insurance, and disaster assistance should not be subject to
    reduction commitments. There is a question, however, over whether
    direct income payments should be exempt. And in our view, such
    payments should be exempt only if they can be shown to be
    production-neutral.

    With respect to market access, we have general agreement with
    the EC and the Cairns group on comprehensive tariffication of all
    non-tariff measures as the primary instrument of reform of import
    policies. Such tariff equivalents would then be subject to formula
    reductions. We also agree that there should be the opportunity for
    access of at least 3 percent of domestic consumption initially and
    that this minimum access commitment should grow in subsequent years.
    What remains to be agreed upon is the precise method of
    tariffication, the amount of the formula reduction, and the precise
    terms of a price-based safeguard provision. Also pending resolution
    is the extent of the expansion for what we refer to as current
    access, that is, where access is currently above 3 percent of
    consumption.

    With respect to export subsidies, we've made substantial
    progress in reaching agreement on how to define export subsidies.
    We believe it is essential, however, that the reductions be assured
    in volume terms or volume and budget terms. We could not agree to
    budget limitations alone, and that is a major issue that remains
    open.

    With respect to the level of reductions, I don't think it's
    useful at this point to go into detail on that, but the press has
    reported discussion of percentages in the range of 20 to 30 percent
    over a period of five or six years. But the reason I don't think
    it's useful to dwell on those is that those percentages are not
    meaningful unless you know percentage of what, and that is what
    we're primarily engaged on at this point.

    With respect to other areas of the negotiations, there are

                    5484-9-5

                                                              0034

HEARING OF THE HOUSE AGRICULTURE CMTE SUBJECT: AGRICULTURE TRADE
CHMN: REP. E. "KIKA" DE LA GARZA (D-TX)   WITNESS: JULIUS KATZ, DEPUTY
UNITED STATES TRADE REPRESENTATIVE   TUESDAY, DECEMBER 10, 1991
K-2-2 page# 2

issues beyond those in the three areas mentioned above. There is a
-- first, there is our insistence on a continuation clause, and
since it is apparent that whatever agreement will not initially
cover more than a period of five or six years with a reduction of
somewhere around one-third, we are insistent on a commitment to
continue the liberalization process beyond the initial period. And
I'm encouraged to believe that we can get agreement on such a
commitment.

Another issue that has arisen is the desire of the community to
be assured that if there is an agreement and there is compliance
with the terms of that agreement, there will be no challenge of
their policies during the transition period. This issue has come to
be known as the peace clause. And while we are examining a number
of possible formulations, we are not prepared to forego??? any of
our GATT rights or domestic remedies to deal with situations that
are disadvantageous to our private sector interests.

Finally there remains the insistence of the European Community
on rebalancing. We have said again and again that we are opposed
to rebalancing. We continue to be insistent that we have no
interest in rebalancing. We just simply will not agree.

The issues that remain are significant, but they should not
overshadow the progress we have made. We have an agreement that
there will be reductions, significant reductions, in export
subsidies. Mr. Dunkel has made it clear that tariffication will
have to be comprehensive for all countries, for all commodities.
There is agreement on the need to maintain current access
opportunities and to ensure minimum access opportunities where no
access has existed in the past. All tariffs, including those
resulting from tariffication, will be reduced. Trade-distorting
internal supports will be reduced. While -- when the consensus on the
remaining issues is reached in agriculture and the other areas of the
Uruguay Round agenda, which we expect will be prior to Christmas, Arthur
Dunkel plans to prepare an overall text covering all of the negotiating
groups, including agriculture.

But even when the -- this log jam is broken, and hopefully it
will be over the next two weeks, much work will still remain before
an agreement text can be finalized. In particular, the market
access negotiations generally, that is beyond agriculture, have been
slowed awaiting movement in agriculture, and those need to be
completed.

The European heads of state have repeatedly expressed their
determination to successfully conclude the Uruguay Round talks by
the end of this year, which is now very close at hand. I'm hopeful
that we can reach an agreement on the core issues before Christmas,
but as I have said, success is not assured. While major differences
remain, the key players are at the table, discussing the key issues.
If commitment and hard work are the critical factors, we will
achieve a substantial and significant agreement. We are certainly
trying.

564-9-6

HEARING OF THE HOUSE AGRICULTURE CMTE SUBJECT: AGRICULTURE TRADE
CHMN: REP. E. "KIKA" DE LA GARZA (D-TX)   WITNESS: JULIUS KATZ, DEPUTY
UNITED STATES TRADE REPRESENTATIVE   TUESDAY, DECEMBER 10, 1991
K-2-2 page# 3

        As you know, Mr. Chairman, Under Secretary Crowder left last
night to go to Brussels today and continue talks there. Tonight I
leave for Geneva where I will join with Dick Crowder to continue our
discussions at the -- at a multilateral level.

        We've not set a deadline. We remain committed to the goal of
fundamentally reforming agricultural trade. We will not sacrifice a
substantial agreement for the sake of meeting a deadline. And in
conclusion, let me say that the Uruguay -- a good Uruguay Round
holds the potential for significant benefits for American
agriculture in this decade and on into the new century. Among other
things it would mean better rules for fair competition, reduced EC
export subsidies, and a stronger, more vigorous world economy with a
faster growing demand, a bigger pie. Secretary Madigan and
Ambassador Hills have outlined these benefits in some detail in
previous appearances before the committee.

        Mr. Chairman, the Congress is -- has been and is an essential
partner in this entire process, and we will continue to consult with
you to ensure that your concerns are fully addressed. We've also
consulted closely and frequently with the US agricultural private
sector, and I take note of your opening remark that some people are
dissatisfied. I don't understand the basis for that. I'd be glad
to have the particulars and pursue it. We spend almost as much time
in consultations with the Congress and the private sector as we do
negotiating, and that, in our view, is essential because we need to
bring the agreement back to the Congress and to be assured that any
agreement we negotiate can be approved.

        If we can achieve a good and fair agreement for American
farmers, it is worth fighting for, and that is exactly what we're
doing. Mr. Chairman, that concludes my statement. I would be
pleased to answer any questions of the committee. Thank you.

        REP. DE LA GARZA: Thank you very much, Ambassador, and we
appreciate your being here, and your mention of Secretary Crowder,
and Secretary Madigan informed me yesterday that he would be with
the President in Illinois during the day, and that Secretary Crowder
was already on the way to Brussels. And I can understand that, but
we appreciate very much that you're here, and you will be on the way
to Geneva.

        The question I have is, can you give us more than your
statement as to regards the timeframe? Is it really feasible to
expect before the end of the year, from your perspective, a final
solution?

        MR. KATZ: Well, yes, Mr. Chairman, I can conceive of a -- of
reaching an agreement on the main issues, on the core issues, on the
hard issues, which would make an agreement possible. We will not
have that reduced to writing, either on agriculture or on the other
issues which will continue for -- into the new year for one or two

                        5484-9-2

                                                            0036

HEARING OF THE HOUSE AGRICULTURE CMTE   SUBJECT: AGRICULTURE TRADE
CHMN: REP. E. "KIKA" DE LA GARZA (D-TX)   WITNESS: JULIUS KATZ, DEPUTY
UNITED STATES TRADE REPRESENTATIVE   TUESDAY, DECEMBER 10, 1991
K-2-2 page# 4

-- or perhaps a little longer -- one or two months or perhaps a little
longer. But what we are trying to do is really to unblock -- unblock the
negotiations and I think that an agreement is within reach. As I said to a
number of people yesterday, if it were a matter -- purely a matter of
rationality, if this were a completely rational world, it would be
inconceivable that we could not achieve agreement, but as we know, there
are other factors that intervene.

     REP. DE LA GARZA: You have been -- or you have made the
statement that better no agreement at all than a bad one. Are you
still of that opinion?

     MR. KATZ: Absolutely, Mr. Chairman. As a practical matter we
have always said that we had to have a large agreement rather if we achiev
it, will bring forth a good agreement. If we
can't achieve that hurdle rate the house of cards collapses. It
just can't be put together.

     REP. DE LA GARZA: We appreciate this position and I hope you
remind your colleagues periodically in the next several weeks.

     On page five of your statement you mentioned in regard to
tarrification, a price based safeguard provision. Could you explain
this concept in a little more detail?

     MR. KATZ: Yes, Mr. Chairman. Since we will be moving from a
situation of rather substantial protection in respect to a number of
commodities, we and other countries in the world, there is agreement
that there needs to be confidence on the part of farmers in all
countries that if there are sudden changes in circumstance of --
sudden movements of price which would put them at great jeopardy,
that there needs to be a way of dealing with that.

     You may recall that the European community suggested or
proposed a year ago that tarrification be accompanied with what --
by what they called a corrective factor, which would deal both with
price change and exchange rate changes. We felt that that could be
accomplished by a price based safeguard which would measure changes
in internal prices at the border, affected by changes in world
demand, or world production or extreme exchange rate volatility.
And we don't have the details of that completely agreed, but
essentially it would be based on variations in domestic prices, or
for some kind of a reference price.

     REP. DE LA GARZA: Ambassador, we have from time to time
mentioned, and I personally continue to insist that any disputes
under the sanitary and phytosanitary agreement will be settled
purely on scientific evidence and we had now recent activity that
went counter to that. What is our position? Can you elaborate on
that?

                        54p₭-9-₽

HEARING OF THE HOUSE AGRICULTURE CMTE   SUBJECT: AGRICULTURE TRADE
CHMN: REP. E. "KIKA" DE LA GARZA (D-TX)   WITNESS: JULIUS KATZ, DEPUTY
UNITED STATES TRADE REPRESENTATIVE   TUESDAY, DECEMBER 10, 1991
K-2-2   page# 5
    MR. KATZ: Yes. There is -- we are very far along on a
agreement to deal with sanitary and phytosanitary measures. I
didn't mention that in my statement, but that's actually one of the
four areas. I mentioned the three areas of internal support,
imports and exports, but there is a fourth leg of the agricultural
reform agreement we are seeking, and that is an agreement on
sanitary and phytosanitary measures, and very simply that agreement
would do what you have suggested. That is, it would assure in the
first instance that countries were free to regulate

                         CONTINUED

5484-9-9 End

0038

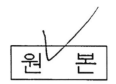

관리 번호	91-914

외 무 부

종 별 : 지 급

번 호 : ECW-1089   일 시 : 91 1211 1700

수 신 : 장관 (통기, 경기원, 재무부, 농림수산부, 상공부, 기정동문)

발 신 : 주 EC 대사   사본: 주 미, 제네바-중계요필

제 목 : GATT/UR 협상

연: ECW-1082

최근의 표제협상 동향을 하기 보고함

1. EC 의 동향

가. 12.10 MACSHARRY 위원의 EC 출입기자와 간담회시 언급요지

O 농산물 문제에대한 미-EC 간의 의견은 상당히 접근되고 있어 표제협상이 구체화되고 (SHAPE UP) 있는 단계이며 워싱턴회담에서 협의된 사항을 마무리 짓기위해 12.10 CROWDER 차관과 LEGRAS 총국장이 브랏셀에서 만났음

O 금주중 미-EC 의 농무장관간의 재회등 가능성을 배제하지는 않으며, 금주내 또는 내주초 양측 대표들은 제네바에 가서 주요 협상국들에게 양자협상 요지를 설명할 것임

O 미-EC 간에 해결되고 있지 않은 사항은 수출보조금과 REBALANCING 문제임

- REBALANCING 문제에대해 EC 는 당초 입장 내용을 수정 제의할 준비를 하고 있으며 그 주요내용은 당초 요구품목에서 대두와 OILMEALS 을 제외하여 CORN GLUTEN, CORN GERM MEAL, 고구마, 매니옥, CITRUS PELLETS 만을 대상으로 함으로서 REBALANCING 대상물량도 당초 60 백만톤에서 18 백만톤 수준으로 축소토록 하며, 수입물량을 18 백만톤 수준으로 동결하는 방안을 협의중임

- 수출보조금 감축에대한 미-EC 간의 쟁점은 감축방법에 있어 물량 또는 금액을 기준하느냐 문제이며 EC 는 양기준을 혼합하여 사용하는 방법을 협의중임

O GREEN BOX 및 PEACE CLAUSE 문제에대해 미-EC 간 대체적인 합의를 이루었으며 특히 CAP 개혁안에 포함되어 있는 HA 당 소득보조, PREMIUM 지급, 생산통제및 환경보전에 대한 소득보조등을 GREEN BOX 에 넣는 문제가 해결된 것을 만족스럽게 생각하며 미국의 DEFICIENCY PAYMENTS 도 GREEN BOX 대상에 포함되는데 별 문제가 없을것임

통상국 정와대	장관 안기부	차관 경기원	1차보 재무부	2차보 농수부	구주국 상공부	경제국 중계	외정실	분석관

PAGE 1

91.12.12   06:30

외신 2과 통제관 CA

0039

O 국내보조, 시장접근및 수출보조금 공히 93 년부터 6 년간 36% 씩 감축하는 방안이 합의될 가능성이 높으며 4-5 년후에 금번 협상의 결과를 재검토하는 문제에대해 EC 는 긍정적으로 검토할것임

나. 12.10 EC 정상회담 (EUROPEAN COUNCIL) 후 발표한 성명서에서 EC 정상들은 표제협상은 종결단계에 있음을 확인하고, 금년말까지 실질적이고 균형있는 협상전반에 대한 결과를 도출한다는 의지를 표명함. 그러나 동 성명서에는 농산물 분야에대한 새로운 제안 또는 양허방안은 언급하지 않았음

다. 12.10 화란및 벨지움 농민들은 EC 정상회담이 개최되고 있는 화란의 MAASTRICHT 에 모여, EC 의 CAP 개혁과 UR 농산물 협상에서 거론되고 있는 보조금감축에 반대하는 시위를 벌였으며, EC 회원국의 수도등 여러곳에서도 같은 시위가 있었음

라. 한편, EC 의 곡물무역협회는 REBALANCING 및 사료곡물의 쿼타제 폐지를요구하는 성명을 발표하였으며 특히 화란의 곡물무역협회는 화란산 배합사료 제조시 90% 이상을 타피오카등 곡물대체품을 사용하고 있어 REBALANCING 은 화란축산업에 막대한 지장을 초래한다는 점을 강조하면서 강경한 입장을 보이고 있음

2. 한편 12.10 당지언론에 의하면 YERXA 미국 GATT 담당대사는 제네바에서 가진 기자회견에서 향후 UR 협상은 EC 가 어떤 입장을 보이느냐에 달려 있다고 말하면서 미국은 농산물분야에서 EC 의 중요한 태도변화를 기대하고 있으나 아직까지 상당히 미흡하며, 워싱턴 회담결과로서는 미흡(BAD) 한 협상결과를 받아드릴수 없는입장이라고 말하면서 비록 미국도 보조금, 반덤핑및 써비스 분야등에서어려움이 있으나 12.20. 까지 정치적인 타결 (POLITICAL PACKAGE) 이 가능할 것이라고 전망함. 한편, 동인은 협상일정 문제에대해 관세양허, 써비스시장 개방방법등 실무적인 문제들이 해결되려면 6-8 주 정도가 소요될 것이라고 말하면서 협상 최종 합의문서 서명시기는 92.3 월경이 될것으로 전망함. 이와관련 12.9. 제네바에서 가진 기자회견에서 BLEWETT 호주 무역장관도 UR 협상의 최종시기는 92.3 월이 될 가능성이 있다고 밝혔다고 함. 끝

(대사 권동만-국장)

예고: 92.6.30. 까지

외 무 부

종 별 :

번 호 : GVW-2604

일 시 : 91 1211 2000

수 신 : 장 관(통기,경기원,재무부,농림수산부,상공부)

발 신 : 주 제네바 대사

제 목 : UR/농산물 협상

편 (1991. 12. 31)

　12.11(수) 16:00-18:00 개최된 표제 G-8 회의 관련 당관이 파악한 요지 하기
보고함.

　1. 동회의에는 KATZ 부대표(미국), MULLER 부총국장(EC), SHANNON 대사(카나다),
FIELD 차관(호주), 시와쿠심의관(일본), 후타니에미 대사(북구), GROSER
대표(뉴질랜드), 스탄카넬리 공사(알젠틴)당이 참석하였음.

　2. 동회의에서는 12.20 까지의 협상 일정이 주로 논의되었으며, 국내 보조중
허용정책(GREEN BOX) 과 특별 세이프가드가 일부 논의되었음.

　- 협상일정 관련 던켈 총장은 12.12 (목) 17:30- G-8 회의를 재개할 계획이며, 동
회의는 주말 (12.14-15)까지 계속하여 개최하고 필요한 경우 야간 회의도 할
것이라고 하였음. 또한 G-36 회의를 수시로 개최할 예정이라고함.

　- 12.12(목) 개최예정인 G-8 회의에는 이행기간중 각국의 약속 이행, 삭감약속의
방법(MODALITY OF CONCESSIONS), 위생 및 검역규제합의 초안, 순수입개도국을 위한
선언등 4 가지 문서가 제시될 것으로 알려짐.

　- 던켈 총장은 12.18(수)까지 최종합의 초안(FINAL DRAFT TEXT)을 작성하여12.20
TNC 회의때 제출할 계획임.

　0 동 최종합의 초안의 기초가 될 문서를 G-8 및 G-36 회의에서 논의하여 합의를
도출해 보고, 합의에 이르지못할 경우 의장책임으로 제시할 가능성이 큰것으로
전망됨.

　3. 동 회의에서 미국 및 이씨는 협의 진전 사항을 구체적으로 밝히기를 꺼렸으며,
던켈 총장은 이에 대해 불만을 나타내면서 가급적 제네바에서 협의가 진행되기를
희망하였다고 함.

　- 국내보조 및 특별 세이프가드등 SUBSTANCE 에 대한 논의는 TEXT 를 기초로

통상국	장관	차관	2차보	경제국	외정실	분석관	정와대	안기부
경기원	재무부	농수부	상공부					

PAGE 1

91.12.12　08:36
외신 2과　통제관 BS

0041

진행하자고 하여 깊은 논의가 없었다고 함. 끝.

　　(대사 박수길-국장)

　　예고 92.6.30 까지

외 무 부

종 별 :

번 호 : GVW-2596   일 시 : 91 1211 1130

수 신 : 장 관(통기, 경기원, 재무부, 농림수산부, 상공부)

발 신 : 주 제네바 대사

제 목 : UR/농산물 협상

12.11(수) 배포된 삭감약속 계획서 초안을 별첨 FAX 송부함.

첨부: 삭감약속 계획서 1부 (GVW(F)-595)

(대사 박수길-국장)

통상국   2차보   경기원   재무부   농수부   상공부

PAGE 1   91.12.12   10:08 WG

외신 1과 통제관

주 제 네 바 대 표 부

번 호 : GVW(F) - 585   년월일 : 11/11   시간 : 18 00

수 신 : 장   관 (동기, 평기원, 재무부, 농림수산부, 상공부)

발 신 : 주 제네바대사

제 목 : GVW-256 첨부

총 23 매(표지포함)

보 안 통 제	레

외신과 통 제	

0044

585-23-1

10 December 1991

Draft Formats for Lists of Specific Commitments and Supporting Material

The attached papers set out draft formats for the provision of lists of commitments and supporting material which are being made available for the consideration of participants and to assist in further work. They reflect the contents of the Draft Working Papers on Agriculture dated 21 November 1991. Like those Draft Working Papers they do not purport to be definitive.

0045

PART A: MARKET ACCESS COMMITMENTS

Table 1

AGRICULTURAL NEGOTIATIONS: LIST OF COMMITMENTS

MARKET ACCESS: name of country

Lists Relating to Ordinary Customs Duties, Including those Resulting from Tariffication

Tariff classification	Product description	Calendar/ marketing year applied	Base tariff level (Supporting Tables 1 and 2)	Other charges/ duties	Final tariff level	Other charges/ duties	Year of implementation of final tariff	Special safeguard applicability
1	2	3	4	5	6	7	8	9

0046

SPS-23 — 3

0047

Table 2

AGRICULTURAL NEGOTIATIONS: LIST OF COMMITMENTS

MARKET ACCESS: name of country

Lists Relating to Current Access to be Maintained via Tariff Quotas

Tariff classification	Product description	Calendar/ marketing year applied	Tariff quota quantity	In-quota tariff rate	Other terms and conditions
1	2	3	4	5	6

5PS-23-4

0048

Table 3

AGRICULTURAL NEGOTIATIONS: LIST OF COMMITMENTS

MARKET ACCESS: name of country

Lists Relating to Minimum Access to be Provided via Tariff Quotas

Product description	Tariff classification(s) encompassed in product description	Calendar/ marketing year applied	Initial tariff quota quantity (Supporting Table 3)	Initial in-quota tariff rate	Final tariff quota quantity (Supporting Table 3)	Final in-quota tariff rate
1	2	3	4	5	6	7

585-23-5

0049

PART B:　DOMESTIC SUPPORT COMMITMENTS

Table 4

AGRICULTURAL NEGOTIATIONS: LIST OF COMMITMENTS

DOMESTIC SUPPORT: name of country

Product-Specific Aggregate Measurements of Support

Product description	Calendar/ marketing year applied	Base product-specific AMS (Supporting Tables 4 to 8)	Annual commitment levels			
1	2	3	4	5	6	7...

TPS-23-6

0050

Table 5

AGRICULTURAL NEGOTIATIONS: LIST OF COMMITMENTS

DOMESTIC SUPPORT: name of country

Equivalent Commitments

Product description	Calendar/ marketing year applied	Base commitment parameter(s) (Supporting Tables 4,5 and 9)	Annual commitment levels			
1	2	3	4	5	6	7...

SPS-23-7

PART B: DOMESTIC SUPPORT

Supporting Table 4

AGRICULTURAL NEGOTIATIONS: SUPPORTING DATA

DOMESTIC SUPPORT: name of country

Policies Exempt from the Reduction Commitment

Policy name	Policy type	Description (including reference to criteria where appropriate)	Monetary value of policy	Data sources	Comments
1	2	3	4	5	6
(a) "general services"					
(b) "public stockholding for food security purposes"					
(c) "domestic food aid"					
(d) "decoupled income support"					
(e) "income insurance and income safety-net programmes"					
(f) "payments for relief from natural disasters"					
(g) "structural adjustment assistance provided through producer retirement programmes"					
(h) "structural adjustment assistance provided through land retirement programmes"					
(i) "structural adjustment assistance provided through investment aids"					
(j) "environmental programmes"					
(k) "regional assistance programmes"					

SPS-27-8

0051

0052

Table 6

AGRICULTURAL NEGOTIATIONS: LIST OF COMMITMENTS

DOMESTIC SUPPORT: name of country

Non-Product-Specific AMS

Base AMS (Supporting Tables 4,5 and 10)	Calendar/ marketing year applied	Annual commitment levels			
1	2	3	4	5	7...

SPS-27 -P

0053

PART C: EXPORT COMPETITION

Table 7

AGRICULTURAL NEGOTIATIONS: LIST OF COMMITMENTS

EXPORT COMPETITION: name of country

Export Subsidies: Budgetary Outlay Reduction Commitments

Product description	Calendar/ marketing year applied	Base outlay level (Supporting Table 11)	Annual commitment levels				Maximum ceiling quantity (where applicable) (Supporting Table 12)
1	2	3	4	5	6	7...	8

SPS-23 —10

Table 8

AGRICULTURAL NEGOTIATIONS: LIST OF COMMITMENTS

EXPORT COMPETITION: name of country

Export Subsidies: Export Quantity Reduction Commitments

Product description	Calendar/ marketing year applied	Base quantity (Supporting Table 12)	Annual commitment levels				Maximum ceiling outlays (where applicable) (Supporting Table 11)
1	2	3	4	5	6	7...	7

0055

Table 9

AGRICULTURAL NEGOTIATIONS: LIST OF COMMITMENTS

EXPORT COMPETITION: name of country

Other: Freeze Commitments

Product description	Calendar/ marketing year applied	Nature of commitments
1	2	3

SPS-27 —12

SUPPORTING MATERIAL

PART A: MARKET ACCESS

Supporting Table 1

AGRICULTURAL NEGOTIATIONS: SUPPORTING DATA

MARKET ACCESS: name of country

Tariff Equivalents: Tariff Equivalents Calculated Directly from Price Comparisons

Tariff classification	Product description	Current bound/ applied rate	Non-tariff measure tariffied	Internal price	External price	Quality/ variety adjustment	Tariff Equivalent specific	Tariff Equivalent ad valorem	Data sources	Comments
1	2	3	4	5	6	7	8	9	10	11
							(5-6 adjusted by 7)	(8/6)%		

(a) year 1 of the base period
(b) year 2 of the base period...
(c) average for product

SPS -27 -13

0057

Supporting Table 2

AGRICULTURAL NEGOTIATIONS: SUPPORTING DATA

MARKET ACCESS: name of country

Tariff Equivalents: Derived Tariff Equivalents for Transformed and Processed Products

Tariff classification	Product description	Current bound/ applied rate	Non-tariff measure(s) tariffied	Component product(s) tariff equivalent(s)	Proportion(s) of component product(s)	External price of derived product	Tariff Equivalent specific	Tariff Equivalent ad valores	Data sources	Comments
1	2	3	4	5	6	7	8	9	10	11
							$(5(s)*6(s))$	$(8/7)t$		

(a) year 1 of the base period
(b) year 2 of the base period...
(c) average for product

SPS-23-04

0058

Supporting Table 3

AGRICULTURAL NEGOTIATIONS: SUPPORTING DATA

MARKET ACCESS: name of country

Minimum Access Commitments

Product description	Tariff classification(s) encompassed in product description	Current access (product equivalent)	Consumption quantity	Initial new access quantity	Final new access quantity	Data sources	Comments
1	2	3	4	5	6	7	8
				(4°..8)-3	(4°..8)-3		

(a) year 1 of the base period
(b) year 2 of the base period...
(c) average for product

SPS-27 _15

0059

Supporting Table 5

AGRICULTURAL NEGOTIATIONS: SUPPORTING DATA

DOMESTIC SUPPORT: name of country

Policies Exempt from the Reduction Commitment - Special and Differential Treatment

Policy name	Policy type	Description	Monetary value of policy	Data sources	Comments
1	2	3	4	5	6

(a) "investment subsidies generally available to agriculture"

(b) "support to encourage diversion from the cultivation of illicit narcotics"

5PS-23 -16

Supporting Table 6

AGRICULTURAL NEGOTIATIONS: SUPPORTING DATA

DOMESTIC SUPPORT: name of country

Aggregate Measurements of Support: Market Price Support

Product description	Policy type(s)	Internal price	External reference price	Eligible production	Associated taxes/levies	Total market price support	Data sources	Comments
1	2	3	4	5	6	7	8	9
						$((3-4)*5)-6$		

(a) year 1 of the base period
(b) year 2 of the base period...
(c) average for product

0060

SPS-23-17

Supporting Table 7

AGRICULTURAL NEGOTIATIONS: SUPPORTING DATA

DOMESTIC SUPPORT: name of country

Aggregate Measurements of Support: Non-Exempt Direct Payments

Product description	Policy type(s)	Internal price	External reference price	Eligible production	Total price-related direct payments	Other non-exempt direct payments	Associated taxes/levies	Total direct payments	Data sources	Comments
1	2	3	4	5	6 $((3-4)*5)$	7	8	9 $(6+7-8)$	10	11

(a) year 1 of the base period
(b) year 2 of the base period...
(c) average for product

SPS-23-18

AGRICULTURAL NEGOTIATIONS: SUPPORTING DATA

DOMESTIC SUPPORT: name of country

Aggregate Measurements of Support: Other Product-Specific Support and Total AMS

Supporting Table 8.

Product description	Policy type(s)	Other product-specific budgetary outlays	Other product-specific support (include calculation details)	Associated taxes/levies	Total other product-specific support	Market price support (Supporting Table 6)	Non-exempt direct payments (Supporting Table 7)	Total AMS	Data sources	Comments
1	2	3	4	5	6 (3+4-5)	7	8	7 (6+7+8)	8	9

JPS -27 -1P

0063

Supporting Table 9

AGRICULTURAL NEGOTIATIONS: SUPPORTING DATA

DOMESTIC SUPPORT: _name of country_

Equivalent Commitments

Product description	Policy type(s)	Administered price	Production eligible to receive the administered price	Non-exempt direct payments	Other product-specific support	Data sources	Comments
1	2	3	4	5	6	7	8

(a) year 1 of the base period
(b) year 2 of the base period...
(c) average for product

SPS-23-20

Supporting Table 10

AGRICULTURAL NEGOTIATIONS: SUPPORTING DATA

DOMESTIC SUPPORT: name of country

Non-Product-Specific AMS

Policy type(s)	Non-product-specific budgetary outlays	Other non-product-specific support (include calculation details)	Associated taxes/levies	Total non-product-specific support	Data sources	Comments
1	2	3	4	5 (2+3-4)	6	7

(a) year 1 of the base period
(b) year 2 of the base period...
(c) average for product

SPS-27-21

Supporting Table 11

AGRICULTURAL NEGOTIATIONS: SUPPORTING DATA

EXPORT COMPETITION: name of country

Export Subsidies Subject to the Reduction Commitment: Budgetary Outlays

Product description	Direct export subsidies	Sales of stocks	Producer financed subsidies	Cost reduction measures	Internal transport subsidies	Subsidies on incorporated products	Total export subsidies	Data source	Comments including policy description
1	2	3	4	5	6	7	8	9	10

(a) year 1 of the base period
(b) year 2 of the base period...
(c) average for product

5P5-23-22

9900

Supporting Table 12

AGRICULTURAL NEGOTIATIONS: SUPPORTING DATA

EXPORT COMPETITION: name of country

Export Subsidies Subject to the Reduction Commitment: Export Quantities

Product description	Direct export subsidies	Sales of stocks	Producer financed subsidies	Cost reduction measures	Internal transport subsidies	Subsidies on incorporated products	Total export subsidies	Data source	Comments including policy description
1	2	3	4	5	6	7	8	9	10

(a) year 1 of the base period
(b) year 2 of the base period...
(c) average for product

SPS-27-23

발 신 전 보

WGV-1817   911212 1920 ED

번   호 : _____   종별 : _____

수   신 : 주   제네바   대사. 총영사/

발   신 : 장 관 (통 기)

제   목 : UR 농산물 협상

대 : GVW-2602

대호 관련, 금 12.12 개최된 관계장관 회의에서 농림수산부 제2차관보를 금주말경
귀지에 파견키로 하였으니 참고바람.   끝.

(통상국장   김 용 규)

성림   1991.12.31.

| 보 안
통 제 | ∿ |

양 고 재	91년 12월 12일	통상기구 과	기안자 성명 송봉헌		과 장 심의관 ∿	국 장 전결		차 관	장 관 JH

외신과통제

0067

발 신 전 보

WGV-1816   911212 1827 ED

번 호 :   종별 :

수 신 : 주   제네바   대사.총영사   (사본 : 주 엘지Cㅁ5ᄒ 대ᄡN-1457   WJA-5614   WUS-5683
                                                                주 카나다 대사

발 신 : 장   관 (통 기)

제 목 : UR/농산물 협상

1. 금 12.12 '야나기' 주한 일본 대사는 조경식 농림수산부장관을 방문, UR/농산물
    협상에서 논의되고 있는 포괄적 관세화(예외없는 관세화)에 반대하며 한국등 입장이
    같은 나라들과 향후 협상에서 공동 보조를 취해 나가기를 희망한다는 일본 정부
    입장을 전달함.

2. 이에 대해 농림수산부장관은 쌀에 대한 관세화는 물론 최소 시장접근도 받아들일 수
    없으며 아국 농업 여건상 개도국 우대 적용이 필요하다는 정부 입장을 설명하고,
    포괄적 관세화 관련 공동보조 필요성에 공감을 표시함.

3. 한편, 최근 Buchanan 카나다 온타리오주 농무장관은 현행 갓트 11조 2항 C의
    유지, 개선을 위해 양국간의 계속적인 협조가 필요하다는 요지의 서한(11.29자)을
    농림수산부 장관에게 발송한 바 있음을 참고바람.   끝.

(통상국장   김 용 규)

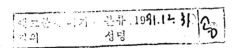

양고재	91년 12월 12일	통상 김규 과	기안자 성명 농봉헌	과 장	국 장	차 관	장 관	외신과통제

제2차관보 :   보안통제

외 무 부

종 별 : 지 급

번 호 : GVW-2617 일 시 : 91 1212 1900

수 신 : 장 관(봉기, 경기원, 재무부, 농수부, 상공부, 청와대경제수석)

발 신 : 주 제네바 대사

제 목 : UR / 농산물 협상(합의초안)

12.12(목) 당관이 입수한 표제협상 합의초안(DRAFTTEXT OF AGRICALTURE) 12.13(금) 배포 예정)을 별첨FAX 송부하니 지급 검토 회시바람.

첨부: 농산물 협상 합의초안 1부

(GVW(F)-0604).끝

(대사 박수길-국장)

통상국   2차보   청와대   경기원   재무부   농수부   상공부

91.12.13   06:33 FO

외신 1과 통제관

0069

주 제 네 바 대 표 부

번 호 : GVW(F) - 604   년월일 : 11/2/2 1P⁰⁰시간 :

수 신 : 장   관 (통기, 1경기원, 새너부, 농림수산부, 상공부) 청와띠경제수석

발 신 : 주 제네바대사

제 목 : GVW-2617 관련.

총 4P 매(표지포합)

보 안 봉 제	✓

| 외신파 통 제 | |

12.12.91

DRAFT TEXT ON AGRICULTURE

The participants,

Having decided to establish a basis for initiating a process of reform
of trade in agriculture in line with the objectives of the
negotiations as set out in the Punta del Este Declaration;

Recalling that the long-term objective as agreed at the Mid-Term
Review Agreement is to establish a fair and market-orientated
agricultural trading system and that a reform process should be
initiated through the negotiation of commitments on support and
protection and through the establishment of strengthened GATT rules
and disciplines;

Recalling further that the above-mentioned long-term objective is to
provide for substantial progressive reductions in agricultural support
and protection sustained over an agreed period of time, resulting in
correcting and preventing restrictions and distortions in world
agricultural markets;

Committed to achieving specific binding commitments in each of the
following areas: market access; domestic support; export
competition; and to reach an agreement on sanitary and phytosanitary
issues;

Noting that commitments under the reform programme should be made in
an equitable way among all participants, having regard to non-trade
concerns, including food security, and the need to protect the
environment, and to the agreement that special and differential
treatment to developing countries is an integral element of the
negotiations, and taking into account possible negative effects of the
implementation of the reform programme on net food-importing
developing countries;

Hereby agree, as follows:

0071

- 2 -

PART A

DRAFT URUGUAY ROUND AGREEMENT ON AGRICULTURE

Part I

Article 1 - Definition of Terms

In this Agreement, unless the context otherwise requires,

(a) the "Agreement on Modalities" refers to the Agreement on Modalities for the Negotiation of Specific Binding Commitments under the Reform Programme (Part B below);

(b) "AMS" and "aggregate measurement of support" refer to the aggregate measurement as defined in Annex 5 to the Agreement on Modalities;

(c) "equivalent commitments" are as defined in Annex 6 to the Agreement on Modalities;

(d) "budgetary outlays" or "outlays" includes revenue foregone;

(e) "transition period" or "implementation period" covers the period commencing on ... and ending on ...;

(f) "year" in relation to the specific commitments of a participant refers to the financial or marketing year specified in the Schedule of commitments relating to that participant.

0072

- 3 -

Article 2 - Product Coverage

This Agreement applies to measures maintained by participants in relation to the agricultural products listed in Annex 1 to the Agreement on Modalities.

Part II

Article 3 - Incorporation of Commitments

1.   The Schedules of market access concessions relating to participants together with such commitments on domestic support as are specifically referred to in market access concessions relating to individual products shall be Annexed to the Geneva (....) Protocol.

2.   Schedules of domestic support and export competition commitments in relating to participants shall be made an integral part of the legal instruments giving effect to the results of the Uruguay Round negotiations as constituting commitments limiting subsidization.

Part III

Article 4 - Market Access Commitments

1.   Market access commitments contained in Schedules negotiated under the Agreement on Modalities relate to bindings and reductions of tariffs, and to the consolidation of market access opportunities as specified therein.

2.   Except as provided for in Article 5 below market access commitments and concessions shall be governed by the relevant provisions of the General Agreement.

0073

- 4 -

Article 5 - Special Safeguard Provisions

1.   Any participant may impose an additional duty on imports of an
agricultural product which is the subject of a concession under paragraph 5
of the Agreement on Modalities if:

   (i) the volume of imports of that product entering the customs
        territory of the participant granting the concession during any
        marketing year (or ... month period for perishable or seasonal
        products) exceeds a trigger level equal to ... per cent of the
        corresponding average quantity during the three preceding
        marketing years (or periods) for which data are available or
        ... per cent of the minimum and current access opportunities,
        whichever is the greater[1]; or, but not concurrently,

   (ii) the price at which imports of that product may enter the customs
        territory of the participant granting the concession, as
        determined on the basis of the c.i.f. import price of the
        shipment concerned expressed in terms of its domestic currency
        falls below a trigger level equal to ... per cent of the
        corresponding average price or, if that price is not available, a
        reference price, during the preceding ... months (or ... days for
        perishable or seasonal products) period.

2.   Imports under a tariff quota established as part of the concession on
the product concerned on the basis of the modalities set out in paragraphs
11 to 15 of Annex 3 to the Agreement on Modalities shall be counted for the
purpose of determining the volume of imports required for invoking the
provisions of sub-paragraph 1(i) but imports under a tariff quota shall not
be affected by action taken under either paragraph 4 or paragraph 5 below.

---

[1]Recourse to this provision requires that the average quantity or
minimum and current access opportunities represent commercially significant
levels of imports.

0074

- 5 -

3.   Any supplies of the product in question which were _en route_ when the additional duty is imposed under sub-paragraph 1(i) above shall be exempted from any such additional duty provided that they may be counted in the volume of imports of the product in question during the following marketing year (period) for the purposes of triggering the provisions of sub-paragraph 1(i) in that year (period).

4.   Any additional duty imposed under sub-paragraph 1(i) above shall only be maintained until the end of the marketing year (or shorter period for perishable and seasonal products) in which it has been imposed, and may only be levied at a level which shall not exceed ... per cent of the level of the ordinary customs duty in effect in the year in which the action is taken.

5.   Any additional duty imposed under sub-paragraph 1(ii) above shall not be levied at a level which exceeds ... per cent of the difference between the c.i.f. import price and the trigger price as defined under that sub-paragraph up to a maximum of ... per cent of the level of the ordinary customs duty in the year in which the action is taken.

6.   Any participant taking action under paragraph 1(i) above, shall give notice in writing, including relevant data, to participants as far in advance as may be practicable and in any event within 10 days of the implementation of such action, and shall afford any interested participants opportunity to consult with it in respect of the conditions of application of such action.   Any participant taking action under paragraph 1(ii) above, shall give notice in writing, including relevant data, to participants within 10 days of the implementation of the first such action in any period and further notice for any following action taken which is based on a different value of the average c.i.f. import price or reference price.

7.   The operation of the special safeguard shall be carried out in a transparent manner.   To this effect, the volume of imports used to invoke safeguard action shall be publicly specified and available to the extent necessary to allow other participants to assess the likelihood of action

0075

- 6 -

being taken in advance of any such action; the c.i.f import price used to
invoke safeguard action shall be publicly available to the extent necessary
to allow other participants to assess the likely additional duty that may
be levied; and where used, the reference price used to the safeguard
action shall be publicly specified and available to invoke the extent
necessary to allow other participants to assess the likely additional duty
that may be levied. Where a reference price is used, the source of the
reference price shall only be changed in exceptional circumstances and
other participants concerned shall be notified.

8.   Action taken in conformity with the provisions of paragraphs 1 to 7
above shall not give rise to any claim for compensation.

9.   The provisions of this Article shall remain in force for the duration
of the reform process as determined under Article 19.

Part IV

Article 6 - Domestic Support Commitments

1.   The domestic support reduction commitments of each participant
contained in its Schedule of commitments shall apply to all of its domestic
support measures with the exception of domestic measures which are not
subject to reduction in terms of the criteria set out in Annex 4 to the
Agreement on Modalities. These commitments are expressed in terms of
Aggregate Measurements of Support and of equivalent commitments. The
constituent data and methods employed in the calculation of these
commitments shall be incorporated in to the Schedules of domestic support
commitments by reference to the relevant Tables of supporting material.

2.   Investment subsidies which are generally available to agriculture in
developing countries and input subsidies generally available to low-income
or resource-poor producers in developing countries shall be exempt from
domestic support reduction commitments which would otherwise be applicable
to such measures, as shall domestic support to producers in developing
countries to encourage diversification from growing illicit narcotic crops.

0076

- 7 -

3. Any participant shall be considered to be in compliance with its domestic support reduction commitments in any year where the sector-wide and product-specific AMS values for support, or the parameters of equivalent commitments, do not exceed the corresponding annual commitment levels specified in the Schedule of domestic support commitments of the participant concerned.

4. As long as domestic support subject to reduction does not exceed .. per cent of the total value of production of a basic product in the case of product-specific support, or of the value of total agricultural production for a sector-wide AMS, there shall be no requirement to undertake the reduction of that support. For developing countries the percentage under this paragraph shall be .. per cent.

Article 7 - Domestic Support General Disciplines

1. Each participant shall ensure that domestic support measures in force on ... 19.. which are not subject to reduction commitments are maintained on a continuing basis in conformity with the criteria set out in Annex 4 to the Agreement on Modalities.

2. Any domestic support measure referred to in paragraph 1 of this Article, including any modification to such a measure, and any measure that is subsequently introduced that cannot be shown to satisfy the criteria in Annex 4 to the Agreement on Modalities shall be included in the coverage of the relevant AMS or equivalent commitment and shall be subject to reduction under that commitment. Where no relevant AMS or equivalent commitment exists the support in question shall not exceed the de minimis level set out in Article 6(4).

3. The domestic subsidies listed in paragraphs .. to .. of Annex 4 to the Agreement on Modalities shall be considered as non-actionable for the purposes of general disciplines on subsidies and countervailing duties, but not otherwise, provided that such subsidies are in conformity with the general and specific criteria relating thereto as prescribed in that Annex.

0077

- 8 -

Part V

Article 8 - Export Competition Commitments

1. The Schedules of export competition commitments relate to budgetary outlays in respect of the export subsidies listed in paragraph 2 below and to quantities exported with such assistance as well as to commitments relating to limitations on the extension of export subsidies to certain products and/or markets as set out in the Schedules. A participant granting any export subsidy listed in paragraph 2 shall ensure that these commitments as specified in their Schedules are not exceeded in any year of the implementation period.

2. The following export subsidies are subject to reduction commitments under this Agreement:

   (a) The provision by governments or their agencies of direct subsidies, including payments-in-kind, to a firm, to an industry, to producers of an agricultural primary product, to a co-operative or other association of such producers, or to a marketing board, contingent on export performance.

   (b) The sale or disposal for export of publicly owned stocks at a price lower than the comparable price charged for the like product to buyers in the domestic market.

   (c) Subsidies on the export of an agricultural primary product which are financed from the proceeds of a levy imposed by virtue of governmental action, including the delegation of governmental taxing authority, on the primary product concerned or on the primary product from which the exported product is derived.

0078

- 9 -

(d)   The provision of subsidies to reduce the costs of marketing exports of agricultural primary products (other than widely available export promotion advisory services) including handling, upgrading and other processing costs, and the costs of international transport and freight.

(e)   Internal transport and freight charges on export shipments, provided or mandated by governments, on terms more favourable than for domestic shipments.

(f)   Subsidies on agricultural primary products contingent on their incorporation in exported products.

3.   Developing countries shall not be required to undertake reduction commitments in respect of the export subsidies listed in sub-paragraphs (d) and (e) of paragraph 2 above provided that these are not applied in a manner that would circumvent reduction commitments.

Article 9 - Prevention of Circumvention of Export Subsidy Reduction Commitments

1.   Subsidies contingent on export performance that are not listed in Article 8(2) of this Agreement shall not be applied in a manner which results in, or which threatens to lead to, circumvention of export subsidy commitments; nor shall non-commercial transactions be used to circumvent such commitments.

2.   Without prejudice to the generality of paragraph 1 above a _prima facie_ case of circumvention of budgetary outlay commitments shall be deemed to exist where it is established that:

(a)   subsidies contingent on exports which are not subject to reduction have been or are being resorted to at the national or sub-national level;   and

0079

- 10 -

(b) the volume of subsidized exports of the product concerned exceeds the volume of exports that could have been subsidized, or which can reasonably be expected to be subsidized, within the limits of the applicable product-specific budgetary outlay commitment level exclusively through such subsidy practices as are subject to the commitment alleged to have been circumvented.

3.   For the purposes of this Article, whether export credits, export credit guarantees or insurance programmes provided by governments or their agencies constitute export subsidies shall be determined on the basis of paragraphs (j) and (k) of Annex 1 to the Agreement (...) on Interpretation and Application of Articles VI, XVI, and XXIII of the General Agreement on Tariffs and Trade.

4.   Any participant which claims that exports in excess of a reduction or ceiling commitment level are not subsidized must establish that no subsidy contingent on exports, whether listed in Article 8 or not, has been granted in respect of the exports in question.

Article 10 - Incorporated Products

1.   Subsidies granted by governments or their agencies in respect of agriculture primary products contingent on their incorporation in exported products shall be prohibited unless aggregate budgetary outlays in respect of such subsidization are subject to separate reduction commitments.

2.   In no case may the per unit subsidy paid on an incorporated agricultural primary product exceed the per unit subsidy that would be payable on exports of the primary product as such.

0080

Article 11 - Provisions relating to International Food Aid

Exporting participants donors of international food aid shall ensure:

(a) that the provision of international food aid is not tied directly or indirectly to commercial exports of agricultural products to recipient countries;

(b) that all international food aid transactions, including bilateral food aid which is monetised, shall be provided in accordance with the FAO "Principles of Surplus Disposal and Consultative Obligations" including, in particular, the system of Usual Marketing Requirements (UMRs);

(c) that such aid shall be provided to the maximum extent possible in fully grant form or on the terms no less concessional than those provided for in Article IV of the Food Aid Convention 1986; and

(d) that an increasing proportion of such aid should be provided to the maximum extent possible through multilateral channels.

Part VI

Article 12 - Serious Prejudice

Subsidies that are being applied in conformity with reduction or ceiling commitments under the reform programme shall be subject to the requirement that they are not applied in a manner which causes serious prejudice to the interests of another participant in the sense of Article XVI:1 of the General Agreement, provided, however, that in any proceedings involving an allegation of serious prejudice against a participant applying subsidies in compliance with its commitments there shall be no evidential or other presumption adverse to that participant.

.0081

- 12 -

Part VII

Article 13 - Sanitary and Phytosanitary Measures

Participants agree to give effect to the Agreement on Sanitary and Phytosanitary Measures (Part C below).

Part VIII

Article 14 - Special and Differential Treatment

1.   In keeping with the recognition that special and differential treatment for developing countries is an integral part of the negotiation, special and differential treatment in respect of commitments shall be provided as set out in the relevant provisions of this Agreement and Schedules of commitments negotiated according to the Agreement on Modalities.

2.   Least developed countries shall not be required to undertake reduction commitments.

Part IX

Article 15 - Net Food-Importing Developing Countries

1.   Developed participants shall take such action as is provided for within the framework of the Declaration in Part D hereto, on the possible negative effects of the reform process on least-developed and net food-importing developing countries.

0082

- 13 -

2.   The Declaration shall form an integral part in the Final Act giving effect to the results of the Uruguay Round Negotiations.

Part X

Article 16 - Committee on Agriculture

A Committee on Agriculture Trade Reform open to all contracting parties shall be established to carry out the functions conferred on it under this Agreement or such other functions as may be deemed appropriate.

Article 17 - Review of the Implementation of Commitments

1.   The Committee established under Article 16 shall review progress in the implementation of commitments negotiated under the Uruguay Round reform programme.

2.   This review process shall be undertaken on the basis of notifications submitted by participants in relation to such matters and at such intervals as shall be determined by the Committee, as well as on the basis of such documentation as the Secretariat may be requested to prepare in order to facilitate the review process.

3.   In addition to the regular notifications submitted under paragraph 2, any new domestic support measure, or modification of an existing measure, for which exemption from the reduction commitment is claimed shall be notified promptly to the Committee. This notification shall contain details of the new or modified measure and its conformity with the agreed criteria as provided for in Tables ... and ... of the Attachment to Annex 2 to the Agreement on Modalities.

4.   In the conduct of the review process participants shall give due consideration to the influence of excessive rates of inflation on the ability of any participant to abide by its domestic support commitments.

0083

- 14 -

5.   The Committee established under Article 16 shall provide an opportunity for participants to raise any matter relevant to the implementation of commitments under the reform programme as set out in this Agreement.

6.   Any participant may bring to the attention of the Committee any measure which it considers ought to have been notified by another participant.

Article 18 - Consultation and Conciliation

1.   Each participant shall afford any other participant adequate opportunities for consultations with respect to any matter affecting the reform programme as set out in this Agreement.

2.   Failing a mutually agreed solution of any matter relating to the implementation of commitments undertaken under the reform programme, the matter may be referred to the Committee. The Committee shall review the facts involved with a view to making such recommendations or taking such other action as will encourage the participants concerned to reach a mutually satisfactory solution.

3.   The provision of the preceding paragraph shall be without prejudice to the right of a participant which considers that commitments under this Agreement have not been complied with to have recourse at any stage to the general GATT dispute settlement procedures.

4.   On the basis of the commitments undertaken in the framework of this Agreement, participants will exercise due restraint in the application of their rights under the General Agreement in relation to products included in the reform programme.

0084

- 15 -

Part XI

Article 19 - Continuation of the Reform Process

1.   Participants agree that the present Agreement constitutes the initial step of a reform process whose long term objective, as agreed at the Mid-Term Review Agreement, is to establish a fair and market orientated agricultural trading system.

2.   Participants shall accordingly meet at the appropriate level not later than ... to review the operation of this Agreement and to establish a programme for maintaining and extending the reform process in line with the long-term objective.

Part XII

Article 20 - Final Provisions

0085

- 16 -

PART B

DRAFT AGREEMENT ON MODALITIES FOR THE NEGOTIATION OF SPECIFIC BINDING COMMITMENTS UNDER THE REFORM PROGRAMME

1.   Specific binding commitments in the areas of market access, domestic support and export competition shall be negotiated in accordance with the modalities set out hereunder.

2.   The commitments under the reform programme shall apply to measures maintained by participants relating to products listed in Annex 1.

Reduction commitments:

3.   The following reduction commitments on market access, domestic support and export competition are agreed.

	Reduction commitment	Base period	Implementation period
Market Access	... per cent	19 - to 19 -	19 - to 19 -
Domestic Support	... per cent	19 - to 19 -	19 - to 19 -
Export Competition	... per cent	19 - to 19 -	19 - to 19 -

Specific Modalities: Market Access

4.   For agricultural products subject to ordinary customs duties only as at ..., the reduction commitment shall be implemented on the bound duty level or, in the case of unbound duties, the average level applied in the base period.

0086

- 17 -

5.   For agricultural products subject to border measures other than
ordinary customs duties as at ..., the reduction commitment indicated in
paragraph 3 shall be implemented on customs duties resulting from the
conversion of such measures ("tariffication"). The modalities of the
conversion and other related provisions, including those relating to
current access opportunities, and the establishment of minimum access
opportunities are set out in Annex 3.

6.   Ordinary customs duties, including those resulting from tariffication,
shall be reduced on average by ... per cent with a minimum rate of
reduction of ... per cent for each tariff line. Minimum access
opportunities shall represent in the first year of the implementation
period not less than ... per cent of corresponding domestic consumption in
the base period as specified in paragraph 3 and shall be expanded to reach
... per cent by the end of the implementation period. The reductions in
ordinary customs duties and expansion of access opportunities shall be
implemented in equal instalments.

7.   All customs duties, including those resulting from tariffication,
shall be bound. Specific binding commitments shall be negotiated on the
basis of the reduction commitment, base and implementation periods as
outlined in paragraph 3.

Specific Modalities: Domestic Support

8.   The reduction commitment shall apply to all domestic support with the
exception of policies exempted from reduction under Annex 4.

9.   Where any domestic support policy cannot be shown to satisfy the
criteria set out in Annex 4, it shall be subject to the reduction
commitment in paragraph 3. The reduction commitment shall be expressed and
implemented through Aggregate Measurements of Support (AMS) as defined in
Annex 5, or through equivalent commitments as defined in Annex 6 where the
calculation of an AMS is not practicable, and shall be implemented in equal
instalments.

0087

- 18 -

10. As long as domestic support which is subject to the reduction
commitment does not exceed ... per cent of the total value of production of
a basic product in the case of product-specific support or of the value of
total agricultural production for the sector-wide AMS, there shall be no
requirement to undertake the reduction of that support.

Specific Modalities: Export Competition

11. The export subsidies listed in Annex 7 shall be subject to budgetary
outlay and/or quantity commitments. These commitments shall be established
in accordance with the modalities prescribed in Annex 8.

12. Specific binding commitments shall include undertakings not to
introduce or re-introduce subsidies on the export of agricultural products
or groups of products in respect of which such subsidies were not granted
during the course of the base period. Undertakings may also include
commitments limiting the scope of subsidies on exports of agricultural
products as regards individual or regional markets. The products or
markets to which such undertakings apply shall be specified in the lists of
commitments on export competition.

Special and Differential Treatment

13. In keeping with the recognition that special and differential
treatment to developing countries is an integral element of the
negotiation, the provisions set out in paragraphs 14 to 20 below shall
apply in respect of developing countries.

14. Developing countries shall have the flexibility to select rates of
reduction in the areas of market access, domestic support and export
competition provided that the rate of reduction is no less than ... per
cent of that specified in paragraph 3. The implementation period may be
extended for developing countries by up to ... years.

0088

- 19 -

15. The least developed countries shall be exempt from the reduction commitments.

16. In the case of products subject to ordinary customs duties only as at ... developing countries shall have the flexibility to negotiate ceiling bindings on the basis of national offers.

17. In implementing the commitments on market access, developed countries will take fully into account the particular needs and conditions of developing countries by providing for a greater improvement of opportunities and terms of access for agricultural products of particular interest to these countries, including tropical agricultural products and products of particular importance to the diversification of production from the growing of illicit narcotic crops.

18. Special and differential treatment in respect of domestic support shall reflect the agreement by participants that government measures of assistance, whether direct or indirect, to encourage agricultural and rural development are an integral part of the development programmes of developing countries. Accordingly, policy measures specified below which may fall under the reduction commitment in paragraph 3 shall be exempt from reduction where implemented as part of agricultural and rural development programmes in developing countries:

   (a) investment subsidies which are generally available to agriculture;

   (b) domestic support to producers to encourage diversification from the growing of illicit narcotic crops;

   (c) input subsidies, whether in cash or kind, provided to low-income or resource-poor producers defined using clear and objective criteria, and which are available to all producers meeting these criteria;

0089

- 20 -

19. In addition to the exemptions listed above, and the general exemptions
from reduction commitments specified under Annex 4, special and
differential treatment shall apply to the <u>de minimis</u> provision concerning
reduction commitments on domestic support in paragraph 10 above. The
relevant threshold percentage for developing countries shall be
... per cent.

20. Developing countries shall not be required to undertake reduction
commitments in respect of the export subsidies described in Annex 7
paragraph 1(d) and 1(e).

<u>Lists of Commitments</u>

21. Lists of commitments together with related supporting tables, shall be
submitted in line with Annex 2 no later than ... . The lists as submitted
by participants shall constitute the basis for bilateral and plurilateral
negotiations leading to the establishment of definitive Schedules for each
participant not later than ... .

0090

- 21 -

Annex 1

PRODUCT COVERAGE

1.   This Agreement shall cover the following products as specified in participants' customs schedules:

(i)   HS Chapters 1 to 24 less fish and fish products, plus

(ii)	HS Code	29.05.43	(manitol)
	HS Code	29.05.44	(sorbitol)
	HS Heading	33.01	(essential oils)
	HS Headings	35.01 to 35.05	(albuminoidal substances modified starches, glues)
	HS Code	38.09.10	(finishing agents)
	HS Code	38.23.60	(sorbitol n.e.p.)
	HS Headings	41.01 to 41.03	(hides and skins)
	HS Heading	43.01	(raw furskins)
	HS Headings	50.01 to 50.03	(raw silk and silk waste)
	HS Headings	51.01 to 51.03	(wool and animal hair)
	HS Headings	52.01 to 52.03	(raw cotton, waste and cotton carded or combed)
	HS Heading	53.01	(raw flax)
	HS Heading	53.02	(raw hemp)

(iii) Any participant may extend its commitments to include additional products to those listed above, provided that other participants agree.

(iv) The foregoing shall not limit the product coverage of the Agreement on Sanitary and Phytosanitary Measures.

0091

- 22 -

· Annex 2

LISTS OF SPECIFIC COMMITMENTS

1.   Participants shall submit, not later than ..., lists of commitments
and supporting material established in line with the reduction commitments
(in paragraph 3 of the Agreement on Modalities) and modalities established
in relation to each area of the negotiation. The supporting material
shall, where specified, form an integral part of the specific commitments
to which it relates. These lists and the supporting material shall contain
information as indicated below and shall be communicated to the
Secretariat. Unless otherwise stipulated by the participant concerned,
lists shall be classified as secret documents and shall be made available
to other participants that have themselves submitted lists.

2.   The lists together with the supporting material shall be established
in line with the formats set out in the Attachment to the present Annex.
The Schedules shall include the following:

PART A: MARKET ACCESS COMMITMENTS

Section I: Commitments Relating to Products Subject, Prior to ....,
Ordinary Customs Duties Only

Headings:

1. Tariff item number
2. Description of products
3. Base and final rates of duty

0092

- 23 -

Section II: Commitments Relating to Agricultural Products Subject to
            Customs Duties Resulting from the Conversion, under this
            Agreement, of other Import Access Restrictions and
            Prohibitions

Headings:

    1. Tariff item number
    2. Description of products
    3. Base and final rates of duty
    4. Current access: quantity, rate of duty, other conditions
    5. Minimum access: quantity, rate of duty

PART B: DOMESTIC SUPPORT COMMITMENTS

Section I: AMS Commitments

Headings:

    1. Description of products
    2. Base period AMS: including reference to lists specifying method
        of calculation and constituent data
    3. Annual commitment levels for each year of the implementation
        period

Section II: Equivalent Commitments

Headings:

    1. Description of products
    2. Base period parameters (price/quantity/expenditure) subject to
        commitment
    3. Annual commitment levels for each year of the implementation
        period

0093

- 24 -

PART C: EXPORT COMPETITION COMMITMENTS

Section I: Product-Specific Reduction Commitments

Headings:

1. Description of products
2. Base level
3. Annual commitment levels for each year of the implementation
    period

Section II: Incorporated Products

Headings:

1. Description of products
2. Base level
3. Annual commitment levels for each year of the implementation
    period

Section III: Other Commitments

Attachment: Draft Formats for Lists of Specific Commitments and
             Supporting Material (not attached)

0094

- 25 -

Annex 3

MARKET ACCESS: AGRICULTURAL PRODUCTS SUBJECT TO
BORDER MEASURES OTHER THAN ORDINARY CUSTOMS DUTIES

Section A: The calculation of tariff equivalents and related provisions

1.   The policy coverage of tariffication shall include all border measures other than ordinary customs duties such as: quantitative import restrictions, variable import levies, minimum import prices, discretionary import licensing, non-tariff measures maintained through state trading enterprises, voluntary export restraints and any other schemes similar to those listed above, whether or not the measures are maintained under country-specific derogations from the provisions of the General Agreement[*].

2.   The calculation of the tariff equivalents, whether expressed as _ad valorem_ or specific rates, shall be made using the actual difference between internal and external prices in a transparent manner using data, data sources and definitions as specified in Annex 2. Data used shall be for the base period ... to ... .

3.   Tariff equivalents shall be established for all agricultural products subject to border measures other than ordinary customs duties:

   (i) tariff equivalents shall primarily be established at the four-digit level of the HS;

   (ii) wherever appropriate, as in the case of certain fruits and vegetables, tariff equivalents shall be established at the six-digit or a more detailed level of the HS;

---

[*]Measures maintained for balance-of-payments reasons or under general safeguard and exception provisions (Articles XII, XVIII, XIX, XX and XXI) shall not be subject to the relevant provisions of this text.

0095

604-4-26

- 26 -

(iii) for transformed and processed agricultural products, tariff
    equivalents shall generally be established by multiplying the
    specific tariff equivalent(s) for the agricultural input(s) by
    the proportion(s) in value terms or in physical terms as
    appropriate of the agricultural input(s) in the transformed and
    processed agricultural products.

4.　External prices shall be, in general, actual c.i.f. unit values for
the importing country.　Where c.i.f. unit values are not available or
appropriate, external prices shall be either:

(i)　appropriate c.i.f. values of a near country;　or

(ii)　estimated from f.o.b. values of (an) appropriate major
    exporter(s) adjusted by adding an estimate of insurance, freight
    and other relevant costs to the importing country.

5.　The external prices shall generally be converted to domestic
currencies using the annual average market exchange rate for the same
period as the price data.

6.　The internal price shall generally be the average wholesale price
ruling in the domestic market or an estimate of that price where adequate
data is not available.

7.　The initial tariff equivalents may be adjusted, where necessary, to
take account of differences in quality or variety using an appropriate
coefficient.

8.　Where a tariff equivalent resulting from these guidelines is negative
or lower than the current bound rate, the initial tariff equivalent may be
established at the current bound rate or on the basis of national offers
for that product.

6ч-4р-27

0096

- 27 -

9.   Where an adjustment is made to the level of a tariff equivalent which would have resulted from the guidelines provided above, participants may request consultations with a view to negotiating appropriate solutions.

10. The level of tariff equivalent resulting from tariffication shall constitute the base level for the implementation of reduction commitments on market access.

Section B: Requirements concerning the maintenance of current access opportunities

11. Current access opportunities on terms at least equivalent to those existing shall be maintained as part of the tariffication process. Current access opportunities shall be defined in terms of average annual import quantities for the base period ... to ... . Participants may request consultations with a view to negotiating increases in current access opportunities as part of the finalization of Schedules of commitments. Any such increases in access opportunities shall be provided on an m.f.n. basis.

12. For existing global or country specific quantitative restrictions, voluntary restraint agreements, voluntary export restraints, specific arrangements providing for imports with reduced import levies and like measures, current access opportunities shall be defined as the quantity of product permitted to be imported under those measures, whether or not that quantity was imported in the base period. Where imports exceeded the quantity of product permitted to be imported under those measures in the base period, the actual imported quantity shall be considered to be the current access opportunity.

13. For existing non-automatic import licensing, non-tariff measures maintained through state trading enterprises and like measures, current access opportunities shall be defined as the quantity of product imported during the base period.

604-4P-28

- 28 -

Section C: Requirements concerning the provision of minimum access opportunities

14. Minimum access opportunities shall be implemented on the basis of a tariff quota at a low or minimal rate and shall be allocated under the provisions of Article XIII.

15. Access opportunities under this commitment shall in general be provided at the 4-digit level of the HS and allocated to the tariff lines of internationally traded products. If another product category is used to implement the commitment the provisions of paragraph 6 of the Agreement on Modalities and paragraph 14 above shall still apply insofar as is practicable. Participants may request consultations on any matter affecting the implementation of this commitment with a view to negotiating appropriate solutions.

0098

- 29 -

Annex 4

DOMESTIC SUPPORT: THE BASIS FOR EXEMPTION FROM THE REDUCTION COMMITMENTS

1.   Domestic support policies for which exemption from the reduction commitments is claimed shall meet the fundamental requirement that they have no, or at most minimal, trade distortion effects or effects on production. Accordingly, all policies for which exemption is claimed shall conform to the following basic criteria:

   (i)   the support in question shall be provided through a publicly-funded government programme (including government revenue foregone) not involving transfers from consumers; and,

   (ii) the support in question shall not have the effect of providing price support to producers;

plus policy-specific criteria and conditions as set out below.

Government Service Programmes

2.   General services

   Policies in this category involve expenditures (or revenue foregone) in relation to programmes which provide services or benefits to agriculture or the rural community. They shall not involve direct payments to producers or processors. Such programmes, which include but are not restricted to the following list, shall meet the general criteria in paragraph 1 above and policy-specific conditions where set out below:

   (i)   research, including general research, research in connection with environmental programmes, and research programmes relating to particular-products;

0099

- 30 -

(ii) **pest and disease control**, including general and product-specific pest and disease control measures, such as early warning systems, quarantine and eradication;

(iii) **training services**, including both general and specialist training facilities;

(iv) **extension and advisory services**, including the provision of means to facilitate the transfer of information and the results of research to producers and consumers;

(v) **inspection services**, including general inspection services and the inspection of particular products for health, safety, grading or standardization purposes;

(vi) **marketing and promotion services**, including market information, advice and promotion relating to particular products but excluding expenditure for unspecified purposes that could be used by sellers to reduce their selling price or confer a direct economic benefit to purchasers; and

(vii) **infrastructural services**, including: electricity reticulation, roads and other means of transport, market and port facilities, water supply facilities, dams and drainage schemes, and infrastructural works associated with environmental programmes. In all cases the expenditure shall be directed to the provision or construction of capital works only, and shall exclude the subsidized provision of on-farm facilities other than for the reticulation of generally-available public utilities. It shall not include subsidies to inputs or operating costs, or preferential user charges.

0100

- 31 -

3. Public stockholding for food security purposes.

    Expenditures (or revenue foregone) in relation to the
accumulation and holding of stocks of products which form an integral
part of a national food-security programme. This may include
government aid to private storage of products as part of such a
programme.

    The volume and accumulation of such stocks shall correspond to
    predetermined targets related solely to food security and shall
    not be determined by annual production fluctuations. The process
    of stock accumulation and disposal shall be financially
    transparent. Food purchases by the government shall be made at
    current market prices and sales from food security stocks shall
    be made at no less than the current market price for the product
    and quality in question.

4. Domestic Food Aid

    Expenditures (or revenue foregone) in relation to the provision
of domestic food aid to sections of the population in need.

    Eligibility to receive the food aid shall be subject to a means
    test or other objective criteria related to need. Such aid shall
    be in the form of direct provision of food to those concerned or
    the provision of means to allow eligible recipients to buy food
    either at market or at subsidized prices. The volume of such aid
    shall not be determined by annual production fluctuations and
    food purchases by the government shall be made at current market
    prices. The financing and administration of the aid shall be
    transparent.

0101

- 32 -

5. Direct Payments to Producers

Support provided through direct payments (or revenue foregone) to producers for which exemption from reduction commitments is claimed shall meet the basic criteria set out in paragraph 1 above, plus specific criteria applying to individual types of direct payment as set out in paragraphs 6 to 13 below. Where exemption from reduction is claimed for any existing or new type of direct payment other than those specified in paragraphs 6 to 13, it shall conform to criteria (ii) to (vi) of paragraph 6 in addition to the general criteria set out in paragraph 1.

6. Decoupled income support

(i) Eligibility for such payments shall be determined by clearly-defined criteria such as status as a producer or landowner, factor use or income or production level in a defined and fixed base period.

(ii) The amount of such payments in any given year shall not be related to, or based on, the type or volume of production (including livestock units) undertaken by the producer in any year after the base period other than to reduce that production.

(iii) The amount of such payments in any given year shall not be related to or based on, the prices, domestic or international, applying to any production undertaken in any year after the base period.

(iv) The amount of such payments in any given year shall not be related to, or based on, the factors of production employed in any year after the base period other than to reduce the factors employed.

(v) No production shall be required in order to receive such payments.

- 33 -

(vi) Where such payments are related to the reduction of production or factor use, they shall not be related to the type or quantity of any remaining production or factor use undertaken by the producer, or the prices, domestic or international, applying to it.

7. Government financial participation in income insurance and income safety-net programmes

(i) Eligibility for such payments shall be determined by catastrophic income loss taking into account only income derived from agriculture, which exceeds a defined threshold of ... per cent of average income (excluding any payments from the same or similar schemes) in the preceding three-year period. Any producers meeting this condition shall be eligible to receive the payments.

(ii) The amount of such payments shall compensate for less than ... per cent of the producer's income loss in the year the producer becomes eligible to receive this assistance.

(iii) The amount of any such payments shall relate solely to income; it shall not relate to the type or volume of production (including livestock units) undertaken by the producer; or to the prices, domestic or international, applying to such production; or to the factors of production employed.

(iv) Where a producer receives in the same year payments under this paragraph and under paragraph 8 below for (relief from natural disasters), the total of such payments shall not exceed 100 per cent of the producer's total income loss.

604-4ρ-3½

0103

- 34 -

8. Payments (made either directly or by way of government financial participation in crop insurance schemes) for relief from natural disasters

   (i)   Eligibility for such payments shall arise only following a formal recognition by government authorities that a natural or like disaster (including disease outbreaks, pest infestations, nuclear accidents, and war on the territory of the participant concerned) has occurred or is occurring; and shall be determined by a catastrophic production loss which exceeds a defined threshold of ... per cent of the average of production in the preceding three-year period.

   (ii) Payments made following a disaster shall be applied only in respect of losses of income or of livestock, or land or other production factors due to the natural disaster in question.

   (iii) Payments shall compensate for not more than the total cost of replacing such losses and shall not require or specify the type or quantity of future production.

   (iv) Payments made during a disaster shall not exceed the level required to prevent or alleviate further loss as defined in criterion (ii) above.

   (v)   Where a producer receives the same year payments under this paragraph and under paragraph 7 above (income insurance and income safety-net programmes), the total of such payments shall not exceed 100 per cent of the producer's total income loss.

9. Structural adjustment assistance provided through producer retirement programmes

   (i)   Eligibility for such payments shall be determined by reference to clearly-defined criteria in programmes designed to facilitate the retirement of persons engaged in agricultural production, or their movement to non-agricultural activities.

604-pp-35

0104

- 35 -

(ii) Payments shall be conditional upon the total and permanent
retirement of the recipients from agricultural production.

10. **Structural adjustment assistance provided through land retirement
programmes**

(i) Eligibility for such payments shall be determined by reference to
clearly-defined criteria in programmes designed to remove land
from production.

(ii) Payments shall be conditional upon the retirement of land from
marketable agricultural production for a minimum of 10 years.

(iii) Payments shall not require or specify any alternative use for
such land which involves the production of marketable
agricultural products for whatever end use.

(iv) Payments shall not be related to either the type or quantity of
production or to the prices, domestic or international, applying
to production undertaken using the land remaining in production.

11. **Structural adjustment assistance provided through investment aids**

(i) Eligibility for such payments shall be determined by reference to
clearly-defined criteria in government programmes designed to
assist the financial or physical restructuring of a producer's
operations in response to objectively demonstrated structural
disadvantages.

(ii) The amount of such payments in any given year shall not be
related to, or based on, the type or volume of production
(including livestock units) undertaken by the producer in any
year after the base period other than to reduce that production.

604-4P-36

0105

- 36 -

(iii) The amount of such payments in any given year shall not be related to, or based on, the prices, domestic or international, applying to any production undertaken in any year after the base period.

(iv) The payments shall be given only for a limited period of time.

(v) The payments shall not mandate or in any way designate the agricultural products to be produced by the recipients except to require them not to produce a particular product.

(vi) The payments shall be limited to the amount required to compensate for the structural disadvantage.

12. Payments under environmental programmes

(i) Eligibility for such payments shall be determined as part of a clearly-defined government environmental or conservation programme and be dependent on the fulfilment of specific conditions under the government programme, including conditions related to production methods or inputs.

(ii) The amount of payment shall be limited to the extra costs or loss of income involved in complying with the government programme.

13. Payments under regional assistance programmes

(i) Eligibility for such payments shall be determined under a clearly-defined government programme of assistance to one or more specified geographical regions considered as disadvantaged on the basis of criteria clearly spelt out in law or regulation.

(ii) The amount of such payments in any given year shall not be related to, or based on the type or volume of production (including livestock units) undertaken by the producer in any year after the base period other than to reduce that production.

604-4-37

0106

- 37 -

(iii) The amount of such payments in any given year shall not be related to, or based on, the prices, domestic or international, applying to any production undertaken in any year after the base period.

(iv) Payments shall be available only to producers in eligible regions, but generally available to all producers within such regions.

(v) Where related to production factors, payments shall be paid at a degressive rate above a threshold level of the factor concerned.

(vi) The payments shall be limited to the extra costs or loss of income involved in undertaking agricultural production in the prescribed area.

604-4A-38

- 38 -

Annex 5

DOMESTIC SUPPORT: DEFINITION OF THE AGGREGATE MEASUREMENT OF SUPPORT

1.   An Aggregate Measurement of Support (AMS) shall be calculated on a
product-specific basis for each basic product (defined as the product at
the point of first sale) affected by: any non-border measure which acts to
maintain producer prices at levels above those prevailing in international
trade for the same or comparable products ("market price support");
non-exempt direct payments; or any other subsidy not exempted from the
reduction commitment ("other non-exempt policies"). Support which is
non-product specific shall be totalled into one non-product-specific AMS in
total monetary terms.

2.   Subsidies under paragraph 1 shall include both budgetary outlays and
revenue foregone by governments or their agents.

3.   Support at both the national and sub-national level shall be included.

4.   Specific agricultural levies, fees or taxes paid by producers shall be
deducted from the AMS.

5.   The AMS calculated as outlined below for the base period shall
constitute the base level for the implementation of the reduction
commitment on domestic support.

6.   For each basic product, a specific AMS shall be established, expressed
in total monetary value terms.

7.   The AMS shall be calculated at the point of first sale of the product
concerned. Policies directed at agricultural processors shall be included
to the extent that such policies benefit the producers of the basic
products.

0108

- 39 -

8.   Market price support: Market price support shall be calculated using the gap between a fixed external reference price and the effective administered price multiplied by the quantity of production eligible to receive the administered price. Budgetary payments made to maintain this gap shall not be included in the AMS.

9.   The fixed external reference price shall be based on ... - ... data and shall generally be the f.o.b. price for the product concerned in a net exporting country and the c.i.f. price for the product concerned in a net importing country in the base period. The fixed reference price may be adjusted for quality differences as necessary.

10. Non-exempt direct payments: Non-exempt direct payments which are dependent on the difference between the world price and an internal price shall be calculated using the gap between a fixed external reference price and the effective administered price multiplied by the quantity of production eligible to receive the administered price.

11. The fixed external reference price shall be based on ... - ... data and shall generally be the f.o.b. price for the product concerned in a net exporting country and the c.i.f. price for the product concerned in a net importing country in the base period. The fixed reference price may be adjusted for quality differences as necessary.

12. Non-exempt direct payments which are based on factors other than price shall be measured using budgetary outlays.

13. Other non-exempt policies, including input subsidies and other policies such as marketing cost reduction measures. The value of such policies shall be measured using government budgetary outlays or, where the use of budgetary outlays does not reflect the full extent of the subsidy concerned, the basis for calculating the subsidy shall be the gap between the price of the subsidised good or service and a representative market price for a similar good or service multiplied by the quantity of the good or service.

- 40 -

· **Annex 6**

DOMESTIC SUPPORT: THE DEFINITION OF
DOMESTIC SUPPORT EQUIVALENT COMMITMENTS

1.   Equivalent commitments shall be undertaken in respect of all products where market price support as defined in Annex 5 exists but for which calculation of this component of the AMS is not practicable. For such products the base level for implementation of the domestic support reduction commitments shall consist of a market price support component expressed in terms of equivalent commitments under paragraph 2 below, as well as any non-exempt direct payments and other non-exempt support, which shall be evaluated as provided for under paragraph 3. Support at both national and sub-national level shall be included.

2.   The equivalent commitments provided for in paragraph 1 shall be undertaken on a product-specific basis for all products at the point of first sale ("basic products") for which there is any non-border measure which acts to maintain producer prices at levels above those prevailing in international trade for the same or comparable products and for which the calculation of the market price support component of the AMS is not practicable. For those basic products, commitments in relation to market price support shall be made on the (administered) internal price and the quantity of production eligible to receive that price or, where this is not practicable, on budgetary outlays used to maintain the producer price.

3.   Where products falling under paragraph 1 above are the subject of non-exempt direct payments or any other product-specific subsidy not exempted from the reduction commitment, the basis for commitments concerning these measures shall be calculations as for the corresponding AMS components (specified in paragraphs 10 to 13 of Annex 5).

4.   Commitments shall affect the amount of subsidy at the point of first sale of the product concerned. Policies directed at agricultural processors shall be included to the extent that such policies benefit the

0110

- 41 -

producers of the basic products. Specific agricultural levies, fees or taxes paid by producers shall reduce the commitments by a corresponding amount.

0111

- 42 -

Annex 7

EXPORT SUBSIDIES SUBJECT TO REDUCTION COMMITMENTS

1.   The following export subsidies shall be subject to reduction
commitments:

(a) The provision by governments or their agencies of direct
subsidies, including payments-in-kind, to a firm, to an industry, to
producers of an agricultural primary product, to a co-operative or
other association of such producers, or to a marketing board,
contingent on export performance.

(b) The sale or disposal for export of publicly owned stocks at a
price lower than the comparable price charged for the like product to
buyers in the domestic market.

(c) Subsidies on the export of an agricultural primary product which
are financed from the proceeds of a levy imposed by virtue of
governmental action, including the delegation of governmental taxing
authority, on the primary product concerned or on the primary product
from which the exported product is derived.

(d) The provision of subsidies to reduce the costs of marketing
exports of agricultural primary products (other than generally
available export promotion advisory services) including handling,
upgrading and other processing costs, and the costs of international
transport and freight.

(e) Internal transport and freight charges on export shipments,
provided or mandated by governments, on terms more favourable than for
domestic shipments.

(f) Subsidies on agricultural primary products contingent on their
incorporation in exported products.

604-47-43

0112

- 43 -

Annex 8

MODALITIES OF EXPORT SUBSIDY COMMITMENTS

1.   Commitments to reduce budgetary outlays in respect of the export subsidies listed in Annex 7 or to reduce the quantity of exports of an agricultural product on which such subsidies may be granted, including ceiling commitments, shall be established in accordance with the provisions of this Annex.

2.   The expression "outlays" or "expenditure" shall, as appropriate, be taken to include "revenue foregone".

Budgetary Outlay Reduction Commitments

3.   The annual average of budgetary outlays in the base period relating to the export subsidies listed in Annex 7 in respect of an agricultural primary product or group of such products shall constitute the base outlay level for the product or group of products concerned.

4.   Base outlay levels reduced by equal instalments in each year of the implementation period shall represent the maximum level of expenditure that may be allocated or incurred during the implementation period in connection with the subsidies listed in Annex 7.

5.   Base outlay levels, as well as outlay commitments levels for each year of the implementation period, shall be specified in Schedules of export competition commitments.

0113

- 44 -

Export Quantity Reduction Commitments

6.   For the purposes of export quantity reduction commitments, the base
quantity shall be the annual average of the quantities of subsidized
exports of an agricultural primary product or group of such products in the
base period. For the purpose of establishing base quantities, subsidized
exports shall include exports in respect of which any export subsidy
referred to in Annex 7 or in Article 9(1) of the Uruguay Round Agreement on
Agriculture was granted during the base period.

7.   Base quantities reduced by equal annual instalments in the first and
each successive year of the implementation period shall constitute the
annual quantity reduction commitment level.

8.   The quantity commitment level relating to any particular year of the
implementation period shall represent the maximum quantity of an
agricultural primary product in respect of which export subsidies listed in
Annex 7 may be granted in that year. Base quantities and quantity
commitment levels for each year of the implementation period shall be
specified in schedules of export competition commitments.

Ceiling Commitments

9.   Ceiling commitments in relation to base level outlays or quantities
may be established in conjunction with reduction commitments.

10. In the case of outlay reduction commitments ceiling commitments shall
correspond to the annual average of the volume of subsidized exports in the
base period and represent the maximum quantity of subsidized exports that
may be financial in any year of the implementation period within the limits
of outlay reduction commitment levels. In the case of export quantity
reduction commitments the annual average of outlays in the base period
would constitute the ceiling commitment. Ceiling commitments shall be
specified in schedules of export competition commitments.

0114

Product Specificity of Commitments

11. Outlay and/or quantity commitment levels shall be established for all products or groups of products in any case where exports of such products are subsidized according to the measures listed in Annex 7, including, in particular:

(i)	Wheat and wheat flour	(ix)	Cheese
(ii)	Coarse grains	(x)	Bovine meat
(iii)	Rice	(xi)	Pigmeat
(iv)	Oilseeds	(xii)	Poultry meat
(v)	Vegetable oils and oilcakes	(xiii)	Sheepmeat
(vi)	Sugar	(xiv)	Eggs
(vi)	Butter and butter oil	(xv)	Wine
(vii)	Whole milk powder	(xvi)	Fruit
(viii)	Skim milk powder	(xvii)	Vegetables

12. This listing shall not preclude the scope for negotiating commitments on particular products within groups of products.

Incorporated Products

13. Base and annual commitment levels shall be established for aggregate budgetary outlays in respect of subsidies on agricultural primary products incorporated in exported products.

0115

604-4A-46

- 46 -

· PART C

AGREEMENT ON SANITARY AND PHYTOSANITARY MEASURES

(Separate document)

604-4/ - 47

0116

- 47 -

PART D

DRAFT DECLARATION ON MEASURES CONCERNING
THE POSSIBLE NEGATIVE EFFECTS OF THE
REFORM PROGRAMME ON NET FOOD-IMPORTING
DEVELOPING COUNTRIES

1.   Participants recognize that the progressive implementation of the
results of the Uruguay Round as a whole will generate increasing
opportunities for trade expansion and economic growth to the benefit of all
participants.

2.   Participants recognize that during the reform programme leading to
greater liberalization of trade in agriculture least developed and net
food-importing developing countries may experience negative effects in
terms of the availability of adequate supplies of basic foodstuffs from
external sources on reasonable terms and conditions, including short-term
difficulties in financing normal levels of commercial imports of basic
foodstuffs.

3.   Participants accordingly agree to establish appropriate mechanisms to
ensure that the implementation of the results of the Uruguay Round on trade
in agriculture does not adversely affect the availability of food aid at a
level which is sufficient to continue to provide assistance in meeting the
food needs of developing countries, especially least developed and net
food-importing developing countries. To this end participants agree:

(i)   to review the level of food aid established periodically by the
Committee on Food Aid under the Food Aid Convention and to
initiate negotiations in the appropriate forum to establish a
level of food aid commitments sufficient to meet the legitimate
needs of developing countries during the reform programme;

604-4P-48

0117

- 48 -

(ii) to adopt guidelines to ensure that an increasing proportion of
basic foodstuffs is provided to least developed and net
food-importing developing countries in fully grant form or on
appropriate concessional terms in line with Article IV of the
Food Aid Convention;

(iii) to give sympathetic consideration in the context of their aid
programmes to requests for the provision of technical and
financial assistance to least developed and net food-importing
countries to improve their agricultural productivity and
infrastructure.

4.   Participants further agree to ensure that any agreement relating to
agricultural export credits makes appropriate provision for differential
treatment in favour of least developed and net food-importing developing
countries.

5.   Participants recognize that as a result of the Uruguay Round certain
countries may experience short-term difficulties in financing normal levels
of commercial imports and that these countries may be eligible to draw on
the resources of international financial institutions under existing
facilities, or such facilities as may be established, in the context of
adjustment programmes, in order to address such financing difficulties. In
this regard participants take note of paragraph 37 of the report of the
Director General of the GATT on his consultations with the Managing
Director of the International Monetary Fund and the President of the World
Bank.

6.   The provisions of this Declaration will be subject to regular review
by the CONTRACTING PARTIES.

604-4P-4P

0118

외 무 부

원 본

종   별 :

번   호 : GVW-2619   일   시 : 91 1212 2300

수   신 : 장 관(통기,경기원,재무부,농수산부,상공부,청와대 경제수석)㎜

발   신 : 주 제네바 대사

제   목 : UR/농산물 협상

12.12(목) 개최된 표제 주요국 비공식 회의 (G-36)요지 하기 보고함.

(천농무관, 최농무관, 농경연 최부원장 참석)

1. 협상일정

- 던켈 총장은 12.13(금) 농산물 협상 합의 초안 (DRAFT TEXT ON AGRICULTURE)을 의장의 책임으로 배포할 것이며 동 합의초안은 11.21 배포된 작업문서와 내용상 대동 소이할 것이라고 하고, 동초안을 기초로 12.18 까지 합의 도출을 위한 협상을 진행시 키겠다고 하였음.

- 12.13(금) 오후 표제 주요국 비공식 회의 (G-36)가 개최되어 동 초안에 대한 검토가 시작될 것이며 동 회의는 수시로 개최될 예정이고 (REMAIN ON CALL)필요한 경우 쟁 점별 소그룹 회의와 TRANSPARENCY 확보를 위한 공식 회의도 개최될 것임을 시사하였음.

2. 삭감 약속 계획서 작성 양식 논의 요지

- 던켈 총장은 자료의 정확성과 일관성 확보를 위해 동 양식을 만들었으며, 11.21 배포된 작업문서에 기초하여 작성되어 있다고 하였음.

- 호주, 브라질, 콜롬비아 등 케언즈 그룹 국가는 표 1의 9항 특별 세이프가드 (SSG) 적용여부 난과관련, SSG 는 관세화 하는 품목에 대하여 한시적으로 적용하되 각국의 민감한 품목에만 적용할수 있도록 한정시켜야 한다고 주장하였음.

- 일본, 북구는 부표 4 허용보조 정책은 예시에 지나지 않는 만큼 '기타 허용정책' 난을 신설해야 한다고 주장하였음.

- WOLTER 농업국장은 표 2의 6항은 PREFERENTIALTREATMENT 등을 위해 있는 것이라고 설명함.

- 칠레는 품목 분류를 관세 항목별로 하여야한다고 주장함.

통상국   2차보   청와대   경기원   재무부   농수부   상공부

3. 기타 논의

- 태국은 농산물 협상 대상 품목에 수산물이 포함되지 않은데 불만을 표시하고, 동 협상분야에 포함되지 못할 경우에는 시장접근분야에서 협상이 되야 하지만 미국이 참치를 제외시키려 한다고 하면서, 수산물을 협상대상 품목에 포함시켜야 한다고 강조하였음.

- 호주는 케언즈 그룹을 대표하여 12.8-9 기간중 개최된 케언즈 그룹 각료회의 공동선언의 요지를 설명하였음.

- 아국은 협상이 TRANSPARENCY 부족에 불만을 표시하고 실질적 문제가 양자간에 논의되기 보다는 다자간 협상 테이블에서 논의되야 한다고 강조하였음.

또한 국내적으로 수용할수 없는 약속은 할수없다고 하면서 각국의 특별한 문제를 해결 해주어야 한다고 하였음.

O 던켈 총장은 개도국회의, G-36 , 공식회의등을 통해 최대한 TRANSPARENCY 를 확보하고 있으며, 특히 한국의 각종 대표단을 만나는데 많은 시간을 할애했다는 점을 강조하였음.

- 멕시코는 삭감 약속 계획서 양식과 관련 관세화 하지 않는 품목을 위한 표를 새로이 추가하자고 하였음.끝

(대사 박수길-국장)

관리번호	91-934

외 무 부

종 별 : 지 급

번 호 : ECW-1107   일 시 : 91 1213 1730

수 신 : 장관 (봉기, 경기원, 재무부, 농림수산부, 상공부)

발 신 : 주 EC 대사 사본: 주 미, 제네바-중계필

제 목 : GATT/UR 협상

마 필 (1991. 12. 31.) 3

연: ECW-1089

최근의 표제협상 동향을 아래 보고함

1. EC 의 동향

가. 12.12. MACSHARRY 위원은 EC 농업이사회 종료후 표제협상 관련 미-EC 의 접촉결과와 관련, 비록 PEACE CLAUSE, 감축기간 (6 년), 감축 또는 허용대상 보조의 구분문제에 대해서는 대체적인 합의점을 찾았으나 아직도 REBALANCING 과수출보조금 감축방법에 대한 견해차이가 있다고 말함. 동인은 아직까지 EC 측은 구체적으로 수출감축 물량을 제시한바가 없다고 말하고 전체 UR 협상 PACKAGE에대한 합의가 이루어져야 할것이라고 덧붙임

나. 한편, 당지 언론에 의하면, 표제협상이 막바지 단계에 돌입하면서 미-EC 는농업보조금 감축에 있어 감축 또는 허용대상 보조의 용어 정의문제가 중요요소로 부각되고 있으며, 이제까지 협상에서 사용되고 있는 GREEN, AMBER(YELLOW) 및 RED BOX 이외에 EC 측은 BLUE 또는 WHITE BOX 등의 새로운 용어를 고려하고 있다고 보도하면서 앞으로 협상국들은 자국이 시행하고 있는 농업보조가 협상결과에 의해 좌우되는 것을 최소화하기 위한 노력이 가중될 것이라고 함

다. MERMAZ 불란서 농무장관은 12.12. 농업이사회에서 미-EC 간 접촉시, EC측이 제시한 수출보조감축 내용이 무엇인가에 대해 민감한 반응을 보이면서 이에대한 문제가 동 이사회에서 공식적으로 논의될 것을 요구하고, 보조수출물량의감축결과는 6 년후에나 나타날수 있는 문제라고 말함

2. 미-EC 는 12.11. 브랏셀에서의 CROWDER 차관과 LEGRAS 총국장 회동 (동 회동후 LEGRAS 총국장은 와병으로 인해 제네바에 가지못함) 이후에도 MACSHARRY 위원이 12.11. 및 12.12 MADIGAN 미 농무장관과 전화를 통하여 협의한바 있으며, 12.11. 에는

통상국	장관	차관	1차보	2차보	외정실	분석관	청와대	안기부
경기원	재무부	농수부	상공부	중계				

PAGE 1   91.12.14   08:50
                                                     외신 2과   통제관 BD
                                                          0121

BUSH 대통령과 LUBBERS 화란수상이 전화통화로 UR 협상문제를 논의하는등 양측은
고위급 접촉을 계속, 마무리작업을 하고 있는 것으로 알려짐. 끝
　　(대사 권동만-국장)
　　예고: 92.6.30 까지

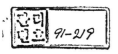

長官報告事項

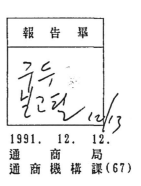

報 告 畢

1991. 12. 12.
通 商 局
通 商 機 構 課 (67)

題 目 : UR 協商 關聯 關係長官 會議(12.12) 結果

1. 會議 內容

　가. 政府代表團 제네바 派遣

　　○ 部處別로 別途로 必要에 따라 제네바에 派遣하되 農産物 分野의
　　　境遇에는 주 제네바 大使 建議대로 農水産部 次官補를 今週末頃 派遣

　나. 農産物 協商 對應 方案 (非公式 난상 討論)

　　○ 經濟企劃院, 商工部, 安企部는 92年 2月末 妥結 可能性과 國內政治
　　　日程을 考慮, 協商에 대한 對應方案을 미리 檢討하고, 事前에 適切한
　　　國內弘報를 實施할 必要性을 言及

　　○ 農水産部는 事前 對備가 不要하다는 立場 堅持

　　○ 外務部는 事前 對備가 어렵다는데 共感하나, 12.20. TNC 會議
　　　(首席代表 發言 文案等) 및 Bush 訪韓時의 具體的 對應 方案은 미리
　　　檢討되어야 함을 言及

　　○ 經濟企劃院은 UR 協商 動向에 대한 적절한 上部 報告 必要性을 提起한바,
　　　農水産部는 非公式으로 소상히 報告한 바 있다고 言及

　　○ 經濟企劃院은 92.1. 부시 大統領 訪韓時 쌀 市場 開放 問題와 關聯
　　　我側이 취할 立場에 대해 外務部에서도 檢討를 해야 한다고 言及

2. 國會 및 言論對策 : 該當 없음.　　　　　　　　　　　끝.

예 고 : 1992. 6. 30. 일반.

0123

외 무 부

종 별 :

번 호 : GVW-2621

일 시 : 91 1212 2300

수 신 : 장 관(봉기,경기원,재무부,농림수산부,상공부)

발 신 : 주 제네바 대사

제 목 : UR/농산물 협상(위생 및 검역규제)

12.15(일) 표제 협상 위생 및 검역 규제 회의가 개최될 예정인바 동 회의 소집 봉지서를 별첨 FAX 송부함.

첨부: 위생 및 검역규제 회의 소집 봉지서 1부. 끝(GVW(F)-608)

(대사 박수길-국장)

통상국   2차보   경기원   재무부   농수부   상공부

PAGE 1

91.12.14   10:27 WG

외신 1과 통제관

0124

주 제 네 바 대 표 부

번 호 : GVW(F) - *608*   년월일 *11212*   시간 : *2300*

수 신 : 장   관 (동기、기기원、과목부、행보닌부、영본)

발 신 : 주 제네바대사

제 목 : *GVW - 2621 관*

총   *2* 매(표지포함)

보 안 동 제	

외신과 동 제	

608 - 관

0125

GATT   FACSIMILE TRANSMISSION

Centre William Rappard   Telefax: (022) 731 42 06
Rue de Lausanne 154   ᴮ⁴/   Telex: 412324 GATT CH
CH-1211 Genève 21   Telephone: (022) 739 51 11

TOTAL NUMBER OF PAGES   1   Date: 11 December 1991
(including this preface)

From: Arthur Dunkel   Signature: a.Dunkel
       Director-General
       GATT, Geneva

To:			
ARGENTINA	H.E. Mr. J.A. Lanus	Fax No:	798 72 82
AUSTRALIA	H.E. Mr. D. Hawes		733 65 86
AUSTRIA	H.E. Mr. W. Lang		734 45 91
BRAZIL	H.E. Mr. C.L. Nunes Amorim		733 28 34
CANADA	H.E. Mr. G.E. Shannon		734 79 19
CHILE	H.E. Mr. M. Artaza		734 41 94
COLOMBIA	H.E. Mr. F. Jaramillo		791 07 87
EEC	H.E. Mr. Tran Van-Thinh		734 22 36
EGYPT	H.E. Mr. M. Mounir Zahran		731 66 28
FINLAND	H.E. Mr. A.A. Hynninen		740 02 87
HUNGARY	Mr. A. Szepesi		738 46 09
JAPAN	H.E. Mr. H. Ukawa		788 38 11
KOREA	H.E. Mr. Soo Gil Park		791 05 25
MALAYSIA	Mr. Supperamanian Manickam		788 09 75
MEXICO	H.E. Mr. J. Seade		733 14 15
MOROCCO	H.E. Mr. M. El Ghali Benhima		798 47 02
NEW ZEALAND	H.E. Mr. A.M. Bisley		734 30 62
SWITZERLAND	H.E. Mr. W. Rossier		734 56 23
THAILAND	H.E. Mr. Taj Bunnag		733 36 78
UNITED STATES	H.E. Mr. R.H. Yerza		749 48 80
URUGUAY	H.E. Mr. J.A. Lacarte-Muró		731 56 20

Consultations on the draft sanitary and phytosanitary agreement will be
held at the expert level on **Sunday, 15 December 1991**, beginning at 10 a.m. in
the Centre William Rappard. ————————————

PLEASE NOTIFY US IMMEDIATELY IF YOU DO NOT RECEIVE ALL THE PAGES

0126

** OUR FAX EQUIPMENT IS HITACHI HIFAX 210 (COMPATIBLE WITH
   GROUPS 2 AND 3) AND IS SET TO RECEIVE AUTOMATICALLY **

외 무 부

종 별 :

번 호 : GVW-2620   일 시 : 91 1212 2300

수 신 : 장 관(통기, 경기원, 재무부, 농림수산부, 상공부)

발 신 : 주 제네바 대사

제 목 : UR/농산물 협상

　　12.13(금) 개최 예정인 표제 주요국 비공식회의 (G-36) 소집 통지서를 별첨 FAX 송부함.

　　첨부: 농산물 협상 주요국 비공식 회의 소집 통지서1부 끝

　　(GVW(F)-607)

　　(대사 박수길-국장)

통상국   2차보   경기원   재무부   농수부   상공부

PAGE 1   91.12.14   10:27 WG
                                          외신 1과 통제관
                                                    0127

주 제 네 바 대 표 부

번 호 : GVW(F) - 607   년월일 : 11.12.12 23:00 시간 :

수 신 : 장   관 (동기、명기원, 재무부, 농림수산부, 상공부)

발 신 : 주 제네바대사

제 목 : GVW-2620 관련

총 2 매(표지포함)

보안통제 [필]

외신과통제

G A T T   F A C S I M I L E   T R A N S M I S S I O N

Centre William Rappard   Telefax: (022) 731 42 06
Rue de Lausanne 154   Telex: 412324 GATT CH
CH-1211 Genève 21   Telephone: (022) 739 51 11

TOTAL NUMBER OF PAGES   1   Date: 12 October 1991
(including this preface)

From: Arthur Dunkel   Signature
       Director-General
       GATT, Geneva

To: ARGENTINA   H.E. Mr. J.A. Lanus   Fax No: 798 72 82
     AUSTRALIA   H.E. Mr. D. Hawes   733 65 86
     AUSTRIA   H.E. Mr. W. Lang   734 45 91
     BANGLADESH   H.E. Mr. M.R. Osmany   738 46 16
     BRAZIL   H.E. Mr. C.L. Nunes Amorim   733 28 34
     CANADA   H.E. Mr. G.E. Shannon   734 79 19
     CHILE   H.E. Mr. M. Artaza   734 41 94
     COLOMBIA   H.E. Mr. F. Jaramillo   791 07 87
     COSTA RICA   H.E. Mr. R. Barzuna   733 28 69
     CUBA   H.E. Mr. J.A. Pérez Novoa   758 23 77
     EEC   H.E. Mr. Tran Van-Thinh   734 22 36
     EGYPT   H.E. Mr. M. Mounir Zahran   731 68 28
     FINLAND   H.E. Mr. A.A. Hynninen   740 02 87
     HUNGARY   Mr. A. Szepesi   738 46 09
     INDIA   H.E. Mr. B.K. Zutshi   738 45 48
     INDONESIA   H.E. Mr. H.S. Kartadjoemena   793 83 09
     ISRAEL   Mr. A. Perry   798 49 50
     JAMAICA   H.E. Mr. L.M.H. Barnett   738 44 20
     JAPAN   H.E. Mr. H. Ukawa   788 38 11
     KOREA   H.E. Mr. Soo Gil Park   791 05 25
     MALAYSIA   Mr. Supperamanian Manickam   788 09 75
     MEXICO   H.E. Mr. J. Seade   733 14 55
     MOROCCO   H.E. Mr. M. El Ghali Benhima   798 47 02
     NEW ZEALAND   H.E. Mr. A.M. Bisley   734 50 62
     NICARAGUA   H.E. Mr. J. Alaniz Pinell   736 60 12
     NIGERIA   H.E. Mr. B.A. Azikiwe   734 10 53
     PAKISTAN   H.E. Mr. A. Kamal   734 80 95
     PERU   Mr. J. Muñoz   731 11 68
     PHILIPPINES   H.E. Mrs. N.L. Escaler   731 68 98
     POLAND   Mr. J. Kaczurba   798 11 75
     SWITZERLAND   H.E. Mr. W. Rossier   734 56 23
     THAILAND   H.E. Mr. Tej Bunnag   733 36 78
     TURKEY   H.E. Mr. G. Aktan   734 52 09
     UNITED STATES H.E. Mr. R.H. Yerxa   749 48 94
     URUGUAY   H.E. Mr. J.A. Lacarte-Muró   731 56 50
     ZIMBABWE   H.E. Dr. A.T. Mugomba   738 49 54

     You are invited to an informal consultation on agriculture to be held at
5 p.m. on Friday 13 December in Room E of the Centre William Rappard.
Attendance is restricted to two persons per delegation.

        PLEASE NOTIFY US IMMEDIATELY IF YOU DO NOT RECEIVE ALL THE PAGES

          ** OUR FAX EQUIPMENT IS HITACHI HIFAX 210 (COMPATIBLE WITH
             GROUPS 2 AND 3) AND IS SET TO RECEIVE AUTOMATICALLY **   0129

외 무 부

종 별 :

번 호 : GVW-2632   일   시 : 91 1214 1930

수 신 : 장관(통기, 경기원, 재무부, 농림수산부, 상공부)

발 신 : 주 제네바 대사

제 목 : UR/농산물 협상(위생 및 검역규제)

　　표제 협상 위생 및 검역규제 합의 초안을 별첨FAX 송부함.

　　첨부: 위생 및 검역규제 합의 초안 1부. 끝

　　(GVW(F)-620)

　　(대사 박수길-국장)

통상국	차관	2차보	안기부	경기원	재무부	농수부	상공부

PAGE 1   91.12.15   08:50 ED

외신 1과 통제관

0130

주 제 네 바 대 표 부

번 호 : GVW(F) - 620   년월일 : 11214   시간 : 1800

수 신 : 장   관 (동기, 법기원, 재무부, 농림수산부, 상공부)

발 신 : 주 제네바대사

제 목 : GVW - 2632 천복

총 17 매 (표지포함)

보 안 통 제	화

외신과 통 제	

0131

The attached draft text is provided to focus the consultations of
sanitary and phytosanitary measures on 15 December. It is based on
MTN.GNG/NG5/WGSP/7. Deletions have been indicated by cross-hatching, while
modifications or additions are presented in bold type.

The draft agreement on sanitary and phytosanitary measures has been
prepared in the form of a Decision by CONTRACTING PARTIES. Should it be
decided that the final agreement will take some other legal form, it may be
necessary to modify or add additional provisions to the current draft text,
in particular with respect to dispute settlement, implementation and final
provisions.

Furthermore, should it be decided that the definition of sanitary and
phytosanitary measures for the purposes of the final agreement explicitly
includes measures taken for the protection of animal welfare and of the
environment, as well as of consumer interests and concerns, some further
adjustments to the text may be necessary, in particular with respect to
risk assessment.

0132

DECISION BY CONTRACTING PARTIES ON THE APPLICATION OF SANITARY AND PHYTOSANITARY MEASURES

The CONTRACTING PARTIES,

Reaffirming that no contracting party should be prevented from adopting or enforcing measures necessary to protect human, animal or plant life or health, subject to the requirement that they are not applied in a manner which would constitute a means of arbitrary or unjustifiable discrimination between countries where the same conditions prevail or a disguised restriction on international trade;

Desiring to improve the human health, animal health and phytosanitary situation in all contracting parties;

Noting that sanitary and phytosanitary measures are often applied on the basis of bilateral agreements or protocols;

Desiring the establishment of a multilateral framework of rules and disciplines to guide the adoption, development and the enforcement of sanitary and phytosanitary measures in order to minimize their negative effects on trade;

Recognizing the important contribution that international standards, guidelines and recommendations can make in this regard;

Desiring to further the use of harmonized sanitary and phytosanitary measures between contracting parties, on the basis of international standards, guidelines and recommendations developed by the relevant international organizations including the Codex Alimentarius Commission, the International Office of Epizootics, and the relevant international and regional organizations operating within the framework of the International Plant Protection Convention;

Recognizing that developing contracting parties may encounter special difficulties in complying with the sanitary or phytosanitary measures of importing contracting parties, and as a consequence, in access to markets, and also in the formulation and application of sanitary or phytosanitary measures in their own territories, and desiring to assist them in their endeavours in this regard;

Desiring therefore to elaborate rules for the application of the provisions of the General Agreement which relate to the use of sanitary or phytosanitary measures, in particular the provisions of Article XX(b)* ;

Decide as follows:

1.   This decision applies to all sanitary and phytosanitary measures which may, directly or indirectly, affect international trade. Such measures shall be developed and applied in accordance with the provisions of this decision.

---

*In this decision, reference to Article XX(b) includes also the chapeau of that Article.

620-1P-3

2.   For the purposes of this decision, the definitions provided in Annex A shall apply.

3.   The annexes are an integral part of this decision.

4.7.   ~~Nothing in this decision shall affect the rights of parties to the Agreement on Technical Barriers to Trade with respect to measures not within the scope of this decision.~~

Basic Rights and Obligations

4.   Contracting parties have the right to take sanitary and phytosanitary measures necessary for the protection of human, animal or plant life or health ~~within their territories, [including when appropriate measures more stringent than required by international standards, guidelines or recommendations,]~~ provided that such measures are not inconsistent with the provisions of this decision.

5.   Contracting parties shall ensure that sanitary and phytosanitary measures are applied only to the extent necessary to protect human, animal or plant life or health, are based on scientific principles and are not maintained against available scientific evidence.

6.   Contracting parties shall ensure that their sanitary and phytosanitary measures do not arbitrarily or unjustifiably discriminate between contracting parties where identical or similar conditions prevail, including between their own territory ~~[or parts thereof]~~ and other contracting parties. Sanitary and phytosanitary measures shall not be applied in a manner which would constitute a disguised restriction on international trade.

7.   Sanitary or phytosanitary measures which conform to the relevant provisions of this decision shall be presumed to be in accordance with the obligations of the contracting parties under the provisions of the General Agreement which relate to the use of sanitary or phytosanitary measures, in particular the provisions of Article XX(b).

Harmonization

8.   To harmonize sanitary and phytosanitary measures on as wide a basis as possible, contracting parties shall base their sanitary or phytosanitary measures on international standards, guidelines or recommendations, where they exist, except as otherwise provided for in this decision.

9.   Sanitary or phytosanitary measures which conform to international standards, guidelines or recommendations shall be deemed to be necessary to protect human, animal or plant life or health, and presumed to be consistent with the relevant provisions of this decision and of the General Agreement.

10. Contracting parties may introduce or maintain sanitary or phytosanitary measures which result in a higher level of sanitary or phytosanitary protection than would be achieved by measures based on the relevant international standards, guidelines or recommendations, if there

620-1P-4

0134

is a scientific justification, or as a consequence of the level of protection a contracting party determines to be appropriate in accordance with its obligations under paragraph 20. Notwithstanding the above, all measures which result in a level of sanitary or phytosanitary protection different from that which would be achieved by measures based on international standards, guidelines or recommendations shall not otherwise be inconsistent with the provisions of this decision.

Alternative 2

11. Contracting parties shall play a full part within the limits of their resources in the relevant international organizations and their subsidiary bodies, in particular the Codex Alimentarius Commission, the International Office of Epizootics, and in the international and regional organizations operating within the framework of the International Plant Protection Convention, to promote within these organizations the development and periodic review of standards, guidelines and recommendations with respect to all aspects of sanitary and phytosanitary measures.

12. The Committee on Sanitary and Phytosanitary Measures, as provided for in paragraphs 40 through 45, shall develop a procedure to monitor the process of international harmonization and coordinate efforts in this regard with the relevant international organizations.

Equivalence

13. Contracting parties shall accept the sanitary or phytosanitary measures of other contracting parties as equivalent, even if these measures differ from their own or from those used by other contracting parties trading in the same commodity, if the exporting contracting party provides evidence to the importing contracting party that objectively demonstrates to the importing contracting party that its measures achieve the importing contracting party's appropriate level of sanitary or phytosanitary protection. For this purpose, reasonable access shall be given, upon request, to the importing contracting party for inspection, testing and other relevant procedures.

14. Contracting parties shall, upon request, enter into consultations with the aim of achieving bilateral and multilateral agreements on recognition of the equivalence of specified sanitary or phytosanitary measures.

Assessment of Risk and Determination of the Appropriate Level of Sanitary or Phytosanitary Protection

15. Contracting parties shall ensure that their sanitary or phytosanitary measures are based on an assessment, as appropriate to the circumstances, of the risks to human, animal or plant life or health, taking into account risk assessment techniques developed by the relevant international organizations.

16. In the assessment of risks, contracting parties shall take into account available scientific evidence; relevant processes and production methods; relevant inspection, sampling and testing methods; prevalence of specific diseases or pests; ambient ecological [and environmental] conditions; and quarantine or other treatment.

17. In assessing the risk and determining the appropriate level of sanitary or phytosanitary protection, contracting parties shall take into account as relevant economic factors the potential damage in terms of loss of production or sales in the event of the entry, establishment or spread of a pest or disease, the costs of control or eradication in the importing contracting party, and the relative cost effectiveness of alternative approaches to limiting risks.

18. Contracting parties should, when determining the appropriate level of sanitary and phytosanitary protection, take into account the objective of minimizing negative trade effects.

Alternative/1/

/////Alternative/2/

19. With the objective of achieving consistency in the application of the concept of appropriate level of sanitary and phytosanitary protection against risks to human life or health, or to animal and plant life or health, each contracting party shall avoid arbitrary or unjustifiable distinctions in the levels it considers to be appropriate in different situations, if such distinctions result in discrimination or a disguised restriction on international trade. Contracting parties shall co-operate in the Committee on Sanitary and Phytosanitary Measures in accordance with paragraphs 40 and 41 of this decision, to develop guidelines to further the practical implementation of this provision. In developing the guidelines the Committee shall take into account all relevant factors, including the exceptional character of human health risks to which people voluntarily expose themselves.

20. {NOTE: paragraph combined with above}

21. Without prejudice to paragraph 9, when establishing or maintaining sanitary or phytosanitary measures to achieve the appropriate level of sanitary or phytosanitary protection, contracting parties shall ensure that such measures are the least restrictive to trade, taking into account technical and economic feasibility [///and/other/economic/considerations/and genuine/consumer/concerns/].

22. In cases where relevant scientific evidence is insufficient, a contracting party may provisionally adopt sanitary or phytosanitary measures on the basis of available pertinent information, including that from the relevant international organizations as well as from sanitary or phytosanitary measures applied by other contracting parties. In such circumstances, contracting parties shall seek to obtain the additional information necessary for a more objective assessment of risk and review the sanitary or phytosanitary measure accordingly within a reasonable period of time.

23. When a contracting party has reason to believe that a specific sanitary or phytosanitary measure introduced or maintained by another contracting party is constraining or has the potential to constrain its exports and the measure is not based on the relevant international standards, guidelines or recommendations, or such standards, guidelines or recommendations do not exist, an explanation of the reasons for such

620-1∤-6

sanitary or phytosanitary measure may be requested and shall be provided by
the contracting party maintaining the measure.

Adaptation to Regional Conditions, including Pest- or Disease-Free Areas
and Areas of Low Pest or Disease Prevalence

24. Contracting parties shall ensure that their sanitary or phytosanitary
measures are adapted to the sanitary or phytosanitary characteristics of
the area - whether a country, part of a country, or areas of several
countries - from which the product originated and to which the product is
destined. In assessing the sanitary or phytosanitary characteristics of a
region, contracting parties shall take into account, _inter alia_, the level
of prevalence of specific diseases or pests, the existence of eradication
or control programmes, and appropriate criteria or guidelines which may be
developed by the relevant international organizations.

25.. Contracting parties shall, in particular, recognize the concepts of
pest- or disease-free areas and areas of low pest or disease prevalence.
Determination of such areas shall be based on factors such as geography,
ecosystems, epidemiological surveillance, and the effectiveness of sanitary
or phytosanitary controls.

26. Exporting contracting parties claiming that areas within their
territories are pest- or disease-free or areas of low pest or disease
prevalence shall provide the necessary evidence thereof in order to
objectively demonstrate to the importing contracting party that such areas
are, and are likely to remain, pest- or disease-free or areas of low pest
or disease prevalence, respectively. For this purpose, reasonable access
shall be given, upon request, to the importing contracting party for
inspection, testing and other relevant procedures.

Transparency

27. Contracting parties shall notify changes in their sanitary or
phytosanitary measures and shall provide information on their sanitary or
phytosanitary measures in accordance with the provisions of Annex B.

Control, Inspection and Approval Procedures

28. Contracting parties shall observe the provisions of Annex C in the
operation of control, inspection and approval procedures, including
national systems for approving the use of additives or for establishing
tolerances for contaminants in foods, beverages or feedstuffs, and
otherwise ensure that their procedures are not inconsistent with the
provisions of this decision.

29. A contracting party operating a system for approval of the use of food
additives or for establishment of tolerances for contaminants in food,
feedstuffs or beverages shall ensure that such system is operated in a
manner consistent with the provisions of this decision. The contracting
party operating such a system may prohibit or restrict access to its
domestic markets for products based on the absence of an approval required
by the importing contracting party. However, in such circumstances and
where a relevant international standard exists, the importing contracting
party should, after preliminary determination, use the international
standard as the

620-1/- 2

0137

basis for permitting access until a final determination on approval has been made.

///// Alternative 1/

///// Alternative 2/

///// Alternative 3/

///// Alternative 4/

Technical Assistance

30. Contracting parties agree to facilitate the provision of technical assistance to other contracting parties, especially developing contracting parties, either bilaterally or through the appropriate international organizations. Such assistance may be, *inter alia*, in the areas of processing technologies, research and infrastructure, including in the establishment of national regulatory bodies, and may take the form of advice, credits, donations and grants, including for the purpose of seeking technical expertise, training and equipment to allow such countries to adjust to, and comply with, sanitary or phytosanitary measures necessary to achieve the appropriate level of sanitary or phytosanitary protection in their export markets.

31. Where substantial investments are required in order for an exporting developing contracting party to fulfil the sanitary or phytosanitary requirements of an importing contracting party, the latter shall consider providing such technical assistance as will permit the developing contracting party to maintain and expand its market access opportunities for the product involved.

Special and Differential Treatment

32. In the preparation and application of sanitary or phytosanitary measures, contracting parties shall take account of the special needs of developing contracting parties, and in particular of the least-developed ones.

33. Where the appropriate level of sanitary or phytosanitary protection allows scope for the phased introduction of new sanitary or phytosanitary measures, longer time-frames for compliance should be accorded on products of interest to developing contracting parties so as to maintain opportunities for their exports.

34. With a view to ensuring that developing contracting parties are able to comply with the provisions of this decision, the Committee on Sanitary and Phytosanitary Measures is enabled to grant to such countries, upon request, specified, time-limited exceptions in whole or in part from obligations under this decision, taking into account their financial, trade and development needs.

35. Contracting parties should encourage and facilitate the active participation of developing countries in the relevant international organizations.

620-19-8

321 P24   WOI   '91-12-15 03:13

0138

Consultations and Dispute Settlement

[Note: //Depending/on/the/form/of/this/agreement///it/may/be/necessary/to/make/specific/provisions/with/respect/to/dispute/settlement///If/the/agreement/takes/the/form/of/a/Decision/by/CONTRACTING/PARTIES//the/following/provisions/would/be/appropriate/

36. This/decision/shall/be/subject/to/the/provisions/of/Articles/XXII/and/XXIII/and/the/dispute/settlement/procedures/applicable/to/those/Articles/as/adopted/by/the/CONTRACTING/PARTIES/ Except as otherwise provided for in this decision, consultations and the settlement of disputes with respect to any matter affecting the operation of this decision shall be subject to the rules and procedures of Articles XXII and XXIII of the General Agreement, and the dispute settlement rules and procedures as adopted by the CONTRACTING PARTIES.

37. In a dispute under this decision involving scientific or technical issues, a panel should seek advice from experts chosen by the panel in consultation with the parties to the dispute. To this end, the panel may, when it deems it appropriate, establish an advisory technical experts group, or consult the relevant international organizations, at the request of either party to the dispute or on its own initiative.

38. Nothing in this decision shall impair the rights of contracting parties under other international agreements, including the rights to resort to the good offices or dispute settlement mechanisms of other international organizations or established under any international agreement.

39///In/cases/where/a/developing/contracting/party/is/involved/in/dispute/settlement/on/sanitary/or/phytosanitary/issues//the/GATT/Secretariat/shall/facilitate/the/provision/of/technical/and/legal/advice/and/information/to/it/

Administration

40. A Committee on Sanitary and Phytosanitary Measures shall be established to provide a regular forum for consultations. It shall carry out the functions necessary to implement the provisions of this decision and the furtherance of its objectives, in particular with respect to harmonization. To this end, the Committee shall encourage the use of international standards, guidelines or recommendations by all contracting parties and, in this regard, shall sponsor technical consultation and study with the objective of increasing coordination and integration between international and national systems and approaches for approving the use of food additives or for establishing tolerances for contaminants in foods, beverages and feedstuffs.

40bis The Committee shall encourage and facilitate ad hoc consultations or negotiations among its members on specific sanitary or phytosanitary issues. The Committee shall review the operation and implementation of this Decision three years after its entry into force, and thereafter as the need arises, and, where appropriate, propose modifications to the text of this Decision having regard, inter alia, to the experience gained in its implementation. The Committee shall reach its decisions by consensus.

620-1P-p

0139

41. The Committee shall maintain close contact with the relevant
international organizations in the field of sanitary and phytosanitary
protection, especially with the Codex Alimentarius Commission, the
International Office of Epizootics, and the Secretariat of the
International Plant Protection Convention, with the objective of securing
the best available scientific and technical advice for the administration
of this decision and in order to ensure that unnecessary duplication of
effort is avoided.

42. The Committee shall develop a procedure to monitor the process of
international harmonization and the use of international standards,
guidelines or recommendations. Such procedure should permit the clear
identification of which international standards, guidelines or
recommendations relating to sanitary and phytosanitary measures which the
Committee determines to have a major trade impact, are in practice used by
individual contracting parties as the basis for access to their markets.
The procedure should also permit the identification of the reasons for the
non-application by individual contracting parties of other international
standards, guidelines or recommendations which could have major trade
implications. This information should be kept up to date and reviewed
periodically by the Committee. ~~For this purpose the Committee should, in
conjunction with the relevant international organizations, establish a list
of international standards, guidelines or recommendations relating to~~

43. In order to avoid unnecessary duplication, the Committee may decide,
as appropriate, to use the information generated by the existing
procedures, particularly for notification, which are in operation in the
relevant international organizations.

~~44.   If a contracting party revises its position following its indication
of the use of a standard, guideline or recommendation as a condition for
import, it should provide an explanation for its change and to inform the
GATT as well as the relevant international organizations, unless such
notification and explanation is given according to the procedures of
Annex B.~~

45. The Committee may, on the basis of an initiative from one of the
contracting parties, through appropriate channels invite the relevant
international organizations or their subsidiary bodies to examine specific
matters with respect to a particular standard, guideline or recommendation,
including the basis of explanations for non-use given according to
paragraph 42 above.

Implementation

46. ~~[Contracting parties shall ensure that governmental authorities within
their territories comply with the relevant provisions of this decision.]~~
~~[Contracting parties shall ensure the observance of the provisions of this
decision by the regional and local governments and authorities within its
territory in accordance with Article XXIV.12 of the General Agreement.]~~
Contracting parties shall ~~also~~ take such reasonable measures as may be
available to them to ensure that non-governmental entities within their
territories, as well as regional bodies in which relevant entities within
their territories are members, comply with the relevant provisions of this
decision. In addition, contracting parties shall not take measures which

have the effect of, directly or indirectly, requiring or encouraging such regional or non-governmental entities to act in a manner inconsistent with the provisions of this decision.

Final Provisions

47.   [With/respect/to/existing/mandatory/legislation/inconsistent/with/this decision//this/decision/shall/enter/into/force/on/[plus/2/years]//With respect/to/all/other/sanitary/or/phytosanitary/measures//this/decision shall/enter/into/force/on/[plus/6/months]. Developing contracting parties may delay application of the provisions of this decision for 2 years following the date of entry into force of this decision until/[plus 2/years] with respect to their sanitary or phytosanitary measures affecting importation or imported products.

48///The/provisions/of/the/decision/shall/be/reviewed/and/revised/as appropriate/5/years/after/its/entry/into/force/ {NOTE: incorporated into paragraph 40bis.}

ANNEX A

Definitions[*]

For the purposes of this decision, the following definitions shall
apply:

1. Sanitary or phytosanitary measure - Any measure applied by a
contracting party to:

    -   t̶o̶ protect animal or plant life or health within its t̶h̶e̶
        territory o̶f̶/̶a̶/̶c̶o̶n̶t̶r̶a̶c̶t̶i̶n̶g̶/̶p̶a̶r̶t̶y̶ from risks arising from the
        entry, establishment or spread of pests, diseases,
        disease-carrying organisms or disease-causing organisms;

    -   t̶o̶ protect human or animal life or health within its t̶h̶e̶
        territory o̶f̶/̶a̶/̶c̶o̶n̶t̶r̶a̶c̶t̶i̶n̶g̶/̶p̶a̶r̶t̶y̶ from risks arising from
        additives, contaminants, toxins or disease-causing organisms, in
        foods, beverages or feedstuffs;

    -   t̶o̶ protect human life or health within its t̶h̶e̶ territory o̶f̶/̶a̶
        c̶o̶n̶t̶r̶a̶c̶t̶i̶n̶g̶/̶p̶a̶r̶t̶y̶ from risks arising from diseases carried by
        animals, plants or products thereof or from the entry,
        establishment or spread of pests; or

    -   t̶o̶ prevent or limit other damage within its t̶h̶e̶ territory o̶f̶/̶a̶
        c̶o̶n̶t̶r̶a̶c̶t̶i̶n̶g̶/̶p̶a̶r̶t̶y̶ arising from the entry, establishment or spread
        of pests.

NOTE: Sanitary or phytosanitary measures include all relevant laws,
        decrees, regulations, requirements and procedures including,
        inter alia, end product criteria; processing and production
        methods; testing, inspection, certification and approval
        procedures; quarantine treatments including relevant
        requirements associated with the transport of animals or plants;
        provisions on relevant statistical methods, sampling procedures
        and methods of risk assessment; and packaging and labelling
        requirements directly related to food safety; [m̶e̶a̶s̶u̶r̶e̶s̶/̶f̶o̶r̶/̶t̶h̶e̶
        p̶r̶o̶t̶e̶c̶t̶i̶o̶n̶/̶o̶f̶/̶a̶n̶i̶m̶a̶l̶/̶w̶e̶l̶f̶a̶r̶e̶/̶a̶n̶d̶/̶o̶f̶/̶t̶h̶e̶/̶e̶n̶v̶i̶r̶o̶n̶m̶e̶n̶t̶/̶/̶a̶s̶/̶w̶e̶l̶l̶/̶a̶s̶
        o̶f̶/̶c̶o̶n̶s̶u̶m̶e̶r̶/̶i̶n̶t̶e̶r̶e̶s̶t̶s̶/̶a̶n̶d̶/̶c̶o̶n̶c̶e̶r̶n̶s̶]. Requirements concerning
        quality, composition, grading, [c̶o̶n̶s̶u̶m̶e̶r̶/̶p̶r̶e̶f̶e̶r̶e̶n̶c̶e̶s̶/̶/̶c̶o̶n̶s̶u̶m̶e̶r̶
        i̶n̶f̶o̶r̶m̶a̶t̶i̶o̶n̶/ animal welfare, t̶h̶e̶/̶e̶n̶v̶i̶r̶o̶n̶m̶e̶n̶t̶ or ethical and moral
        considerations are not included in the definition of sanitary or
        phytosanitary measures.

2. Harmonization - The establishment, recognition and application of
common sanitary and phytosanitary measures by different contracting
parties.

---

[*] For the purpose of these definitions "animal" includes fish and wild
fauna; "plant" includes forests and wild flora; "pests" include weeds;
and "contaminants" include pesticide and veterinary drug residues and
extraneous matter.

620-1P - 12

0142

3. __International standa███, guidelines and recommendatio██__

- for food safety, the standards, guidelines and recommendations
  established by the Codex Alimentarius Commission relating to food
  additives, veterinary drug and pesticide residues, contaminants,
  methods of analysis and sampling, and codes and guidelines of
  hygienic practice;

- for animal health and zoonoses, the standards, guidelines and
  recommendations developed under the auspices of the International
  Office of Epizootics;

- for plant health, the international standards, guidelines and
  recommendations developed under the auspices of the Secretariat
  of the International Plant Protection Convention in co-operation
  with regional organizations operating within the framework of the
  International Plant Protection Convention;

- and, for matters not covered by the above organizations,
  appropriate standards, guidelines and recommendations promulgated
  by other relevant international organizations open for membership
  to all contracting parties, as identified by the Committee on
  Sanitary and Phytosanitary Measures.

4. __Risk assessment__ - The evaluation of the likelihood of __entry,
establishment or spread of pests or diseases within the territory of the
importing contracting party and the relevant potential biological and
economic consequences,__ [and/the/relevant/potential/biological/
environmental/and/economic/consequences] or the evaluation of the potential
adverse effects on human or animal health arising from additives,
contaminants, toxins or disease-causing organisms in foods, feedstuffs and
beverages.

5. __Appropriate Level of Sanitary or Phytosanitary Protection__ - The level
of protection deemed appropriate by the contracting party establishing a
sanitary or phytosanitary measure to protect human, animal or plant life or
health within its territory. (__Note__: Many parties otherwise refer to this
concept as the 'acceptable level of risk'.)

6. __Pest- or Disease-Free Area__ - An area, whether all of a country, part of
a country, or all or parts of several countries, as identified by the
competent authorities, in which a specific pest or disease does not occur.

__NOTE__: A pest- or disease-free area may surround, be surrounded by, or be
adjacent to an area - whether within part of a country or in a geographic
region which includes parts of or all of several countries - in which a
specific pest or disease is known to occur but is subject to regional
control measures such as the establishment of protection, surveillance and
buffer zones which will confine or eradicate the pest or disease in
question.

7. __Area of low pest or disease prevalence__ - An area, whether all of a
country, part of a country, or all or parts of several countries, as
identified by the competent authorities, in which a specific pest or

620-1/-13

disease occurs at low levels and which are subject to effective
surveillance, control or eradication measures.

0144

ANNEX B

Transparency of Sanitary and Phytosanitary Regulations

1.   Publication of regulations

1.1   Contracting parties shall ensure that all sanitary and phytosanitary regulations* which have been adopted are published promptly in such a manner as to enable interested contracting parties to become acquainted with them.

1.2   Except in urgent circumstances, contracting parties shall allow a reasonable interval between the publication of a sanitary or phytosanitary regulation and its entry into force in order to allow time for producers in exporting countries, and particularly in developing countries, to adapt their products and methods of production to the requirements of the importing country.

2.   Enquiry points

2.1   Each contracting party shall ensure that one enquiry point exists which is responsible for the provision of answers to all reasonable questions from interested contracting parties as well as for the provision of relevant documents regarding:

   (a)   any sanitary or phytosanitary regulations adopted or proposed within its territory;

   (b)   any control and inspection procedures, production and quarantine treatment, pesticide tolerance and food additive approval procedures, which are operated within its territory;

   (c)   risk assessment procedures, factors taken into consideration, as well as the determination of the appropriate level of sanitary and phytosanitary protection;

   (d)   the membership and participation of the contracting party, or of relevant bodies within its territory, in international and regional sanitary and phytosanitary organizations and systems, as well as in bilateral and multilateral agreements and arrangements within the scope of this decision, and copies of the texts of such agreements and arrangements.

2.2   Contracting parties shall ensure that where copies of documents are requested by interested contracting parties, they are supplied at the same price (if any), apart from the real cost of delivery, as to the nationals of the contracting party concerned.

---

*   Sanitary and phytosanitary measures such as laws, decrees or ordinances which are applicable generally.

3. Notification procedures

3.1 Whenever an international standard, recommendation or guideline does not exist or the content of a proposed sanitary or phytosanitary regulation is not substantially the same as the content of an international standard, recommendation or guideline, and if the regulation may have a significant effect on trade of other contracting parties, contracting parties shall:

(a) publish a notice at an early stage, in such a manner as to enable interested contracting parties to become acquainted with the proposal to introduce a particular regulation;

(b) notify other contracting parties, through the GATT Secretariat, of the products to be covered by the regulation together with a brief indication of the objective and rationale of the proposed regulation. Such notifications shall take place at an early stage, when amendments can still be introduced and comments taken into account;

(c) provide upon request to other contracting parties copies of the proposed regulation and, whenever possible, identify the parts which in substance deviate from international standards, recommendations or guidelines;

(d) without discrimination, allow reasonable time for other contracting parties to make comments in writing, discuss these comments upon request, and take the comments and the results of the discussions into account.

3.2 However, where urgent problems of health protection arise or threaten to arise for a contracting party, that contracting party may omit such of the steps enumerated in paragraph 3.1 of this Annex as it finds necessary, provided that the contracting party:

(a) immediately notify other contracting parties, through the GATT Secretariat, of the particular regulation and the products covered, with a brief indication of the objective and the rationale of the regulation, including the nature of the urgent problem(s);

(b) provide upon request to other contracting parties copies of the regulation;

(c) allow other contracting parties to make comments in writing, discuss these comments upon request, and take the comments and the results of the discussions into account.

3.3 Notifications to the GATT Secretariat shall be either in English, French or Spanish.

3.4 Developed contracting parties shall, if requested by other contracting parties, provide copies of the documents or, in case of voluminous documents, summaries of the documents covered by a specific notification in either English, French or Spanish.

620-1P-16

3.5 The GATT Secretariat shall promptly circulate copies of the notifications to all contracting parties and interested international organizations and draw the attention of developing contracting parties to any notifications relating to products of particular interest to them.

3.6 Contracting parties shall designate one single central government authority as responsible for the implementation, on the national level, of the provisions concerning notification procedures according to paragraphs 3.1, 3.2, 3.3 and 3.4 of this Annex.

4. General reservations

4.1 Nothing in this decision shall be construed as requiring:

(a) the provision of particulars or copies of drafts or the publication of texts other than in the language of the contracting party except as stated in paragraph 3.4 of this Annex; or

(b) contracting parties to disclose confidential information which would impede enforcement of sanitary or phytosanitary legislation or which would prejudice the legitimate commercial interests of particular enterprises.

0147

ANNEX C

Control, Inspection and Approval Procedures*

1.   Contracting parties shall ensure, with respect to any procedure to check and ensure the fulfilment of sanitary or phytosanitary measures, that:

  (a)   such procedures are undertaken and applied in a manner no less favourable for imported products than for like domestic products, and completed without undue delay, and, in the case of approvals for the use of food additives or of the establishment of tolerances for contaminants in food, beverages or feedstuffs, within two years after the receipt of a completed application.and ~~in/no/less/favourable/manner/for/imported/products/than/for/like domestic/products/~~

  (b)   the standard processing period of each procedure is published or that the anticipated processing period is communicated to the applicant upon request: when receiving an application, the competent body promptly examines the completeness of the documentation and informs the applicant in a precise and complete manner of all deficiencies; the competent body as soon as possible transmits the results of the procedure in a precise and complete manner to the applicant so that corrective action may be taken if necessary; even when the application has deficiencies, the competent body proceeds as far as practicable with the procedure if the applicant so requests; and that upon request, the applicant is informed of the stage of the procedure, with any delay being explained;

  (c)   information requirements are limited to what is necessary for appropriate control, inspection and approval procedures, including for approval of the use of additives or for the establishment of tolerances;

  (d)   the confidentiality of information about imported products arising from or supplied in connection with control, inspection and approval is respected in a way no less favourable than for domestic products and in such a manner that legitimate commercial interests are protected;

  (e)   any requirements for control, inspection and approval of individual specimens of a product are limited to what is reasonable and necessary;

  (f)   any fees imposed for the procedures on imported products are equitable in relation to any fees charged on like domestic

---

*   Control, inspection and approval procedures include, ~~inter alia~~, procedures for sampling, testing and certification.

(20-1P-18)

products or products originating in any other country and should
be no higher than the actual cost of the service;

(g) the same criteria should be used in the siting of facilities used
in the procedures and the selection of samples of imported
products as for domestic products so as to minimize the
inconvenience to applicants, importers, exporters or their
agents;

(h) whenever specifications of a product are changed subsequent to
its control and inspection in light of the applicable
regulations, the procedure for the modified product is limited to
what is necessary to determine whether adequate confidence exists
that the product still meets the regulations concerned;

(i) a procedure exists to review complaints concerning the operation
of such procedures and to take corrective action when a complaint
is justified.

2.   Where a sanitary or phytosanitary measure specifies control at the
level of production, the contracting party in whose territory the
production takes place shall provide the necessary assistance to facilitate
such control and the work of the controlling authorities.

3.   Nothing in this decision shall prevent contracting parties from
carrying out reasonable inspection within their own territories.

0149

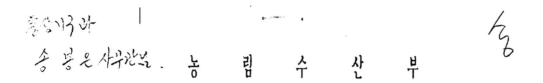

농 림 수 산 부

우 427-760 / 주소 경기 과천시 중앙동 1번지 / 전화 (02)503-7228 / 전송 503-7249

문서번호 동일 20650- 118

시행일자 1991.12.17   (3년)

(경유)

수신 외부부장관

참조

선결			지시		
접수	일자기간	1991. . . :	시결		
	번호		재·공		
	처리과		랍		
	담당사				

제목   UR 농산물협상 위생및 동식물검역규제 전문가회의

    1. UR 농산물협상 위생및 동식물검역규제 전문가회의가 '91.12.15일 스위스 제네바에서 개최될 전망입니다.

    2. 금차회의에서는 '91.11.20 브랏셀 UR 각료회의에 제출한 합의문초안중 미해걸 주요쟁점 분야에 대한 논의가 진행되어 거의 마무리될 전망이므로 금차회의에 주제네바 대표부 농무관이 참석, 아측입장을 최대한 반영하고자 별첨과 같이 훈령안을 시달코자 하오니 조치하여 주시기 바랍니다.

첨부 : 1. UR 농산물 협상위생및 검역규제 전문가회의대책 (안) 1부. 끝.

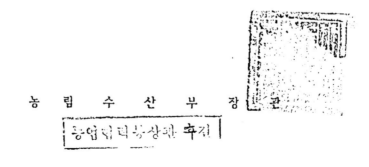

농 림 수 산 부 장 관

0150

UR 농산물협상/ 위생및 검역규제전문가회의 대책 (안)

1. 금차회의 성격과 전망

가. 금차회의는 위생및 검역규제작업단 회의결과에 따라 브랏셀 회의에 상정된 합의 초안(MTN GNG/WGSP/7, '90.11.20)을 토대로 협의가 진행될 예정임.

나. 상기 합의초안의 1) 국제기준보다 엄격한 조치인정문제, 2) 식품첨가제 사용및 잔류물질 허용기준의 수입국 승인문제, 3) 적용대상범위, 4) 지방정부의 규정준수 등의 미해결분야등이 중점적으로 논의될 것이 예상됨.

다. 현재 위생및 검역분야의 미합의사항은 '91.11.6-7 회의에서 일부분야에서 의견접근 이 이루어지고 있고 새로운 대안들이 제시되고있기 때문에 본 분야의 협의도 상당한 진전이 이루어질 전망임.

2. 아국 협상대응방안

가. 의장합의안은 북구, 일본, 아국등 수입국 입장이 상당부분 반영되어 있으나 최종 합의문에 별첨협상안에 근거하여 아국입장이 반영되도록 대처

- 국제기준보다 엄격한 위생및 검역규제조치 인정 명문화
- 식품첨가제 사용및 잔류물질 허용기준 승인시 수입국 승인절차 이행후 적용가능
- 지방정부도 중앙정부와 동일하계 합의분안 준수
- 동물복지, 환경보호, 소비자 관심사항(interests and concerns), 소비자선호, 소비자정보, 환경, 윤리및 도덕적 고려등을 적용대상에서 제외

나. 여타사항및 각국의 새로운 제안등에 대해서는 기존의 아국입장및 금차회의 검토 의견등을 토대로 적의 대처

0151

UR 농산물협상 위생및 검역규제 주요쟁점분야에 대한 협상안

1. 국제기준보다 엄격한 국내기준 인정 (제4조,제10조)

   (대안 1) 제4조의 괄호부분 "【국제기준, 지침 혹은 권고에 의해 요구되는 것보다 엄격한 규제조치를 취할 수 있다】 부분의 반영과 제10조의 첫번째 대안 채택 지지

   (대안 2) 제4조의 괄호부분 삭제불가피하면 제10조의 첫째대안을 수용

2. 위험도 평가시 고려사항 (제18조)

   (대안 1) 제18조 첫째대안및 둘째대안 모두삭제

   (대안 2) 첫째대안 내용중 "교역기회의 최대화에 유의해야한다"를 무역에 부정적영향을 최소화해야한다"로 수정제의한 EC안 수용

3. 식품첨가제, 잔류물질 허용기준등에 관한 수입국 승인제도

   (대안 1) 두번째 대안지지

   (대안 2) 두번째 대안채택이 어려울 경우 의장중재안 수용

4. 조화및 국제기준이용 감시절차 (제42조, 제44조, 제45조)

   (대안 1) 제42조, 제44조, 제45조 괄호부분 삭제

0152

5. 지방정부의 의무준수 여부 (제46조)

(대안 1) 지방정부도 중앙정부와 동일하게 합의문 준수의무 부여되어야 하므로 괄호부분 문안이 존치되어야 함.

6. 적용대상범위 (제16조, 제26조, Annex A)

(대안 1) 환경복지, 소비자이익과 관심사항, 동물복지등을 위생및 검역규제 적용대상 에서 제외되어야함.

7. 기타 쟁점분야

(1) 협의및 분쟁해결 관련사항 (제36조-제39조)

o 본조항은 GATT 분쟁해결 절차와 관련된 사항이며 본합의문 형식에 따라 포함여부가 결정될 사항임

o UR 협상결과에 따라 Total package 로 처리될 것이므로 예상되고 있음.

(2) 합의문 이행시기 (제48조)

o 본 합의문이 UR 협상의 Total package 로 처리될 경우 UR 협상결과에 따르게 되므로 이행시기 규정이 없어지게 될 것임.

(3) 합의문내용 재검토시기 (제49조)
o 괄호부문이 존치되어도 문제점이 없을 것으로 예상됨.

(4) 체약국 영토내의 위생및 검역규제적용 (제4조, 제6조)

위생및 검역규제는 한국가내에 상이한 규제기준 허용을 배제되어야 하므로 제4조, 제6조의 괄호부분 문안 존치되어야 함.

0153

관리
번호 91-928

외 무 부

종 별 :

번 호 : JAW-7020   일 시 : 91 1213 1824

수 신 : 장관(봉기)

발 신 : 주 일 대사(일경)   1991.12.31

제 목 : UR/농산물협상

대:WJA-5546

당관 김하중 참사관은 12.13(금) 오전 주재국 외무성 경제국 하라구찌 심의관과
만나 표제관련 의견 교환한바, 동 심의관의 발언 요지를 하기보고함.

1. 미.EC 간의 농산물 협상타결 전망

가. 미.EC 간의 교섭내용에 관해 여러 경로를 통하여 알아 보려고 노력하고있으나,
양측의 제한된 인원만이 교섭내용을 알고 있기 때문에 양측이 기본적으로 예외없는
관세화에 합의했다는 정도 이외의 내용에 댄하여는 알기가 어려운실정임.

나. 따라서 미.EC 협상이 어떻게 진전되고 있는지 정확히 모르는 상황이기 때문에
결과를 예측하기가 어려움. 다만 양측간에 이견이 상존하고 있고, 그 이견이 정치적
결단만에 의해 해결될수있는 것이기 때문에 쉽게 합의에 도달하지 않으리라고
전망되며, 타결가능성은 막연하지만 반반 정도라고 생각함.

2. 미국의 웨이버 철폐하는데 대하여 반대하는 세력이 있기는 하지만, UR 이
타결될 경우 거기서 생기는 이익이 더 크다고 판단이 되면 미국도 웨이버 문제를
양보할 가능성이 크다고 생각함.

3. 전망

가. 덩켈 사무총장이 제시한 협상 일정 관련, 상당한 어려움은 있겠지만, 12.20.
까지는 포괄적인 초안이 작성될 것으로 전망됨.

나. 다만 초안이 작성된다 하더라도 동 초안의 내용을 어떻게 정확하게 해석할
지에 관하여는 92.1.13. 부터 다시 협상을 진행하여야 하며, 그 과정에서 다시 상당한
논란이 있을 것으로 예상됨.

다. 그러나 12.20. 까지 작성될 초안은 향후 교섭의 중대한 토대를 제공한다는
점에서 매우 중요하며, 앞으로 12.28. 까지의 협상은 매우 힘들고 어려울 것으로

통상국	장관	차관	1차보	2차보	아주국	경제국	외정실	분석관
청와대	안기부							

생각함.

4. 일본의 대책

가. 일본으로서는 앞으로의 협상에 유리한 위치를 점하기 위해 12.18. 까지의 협상에 전력을 부구하여 임할 예정임.

나. 다만 쌀문제는 일본에서 정치 문제화되어 있기 때문에 아무도 동 문제에 대하여 해결방안을 제시하기가 어려운 상황이며, 미니멈 억세스를 하나의 대안으로 생각해 볼수 있기도 하겠지만 현재의 분위기로 보아 정부로서는 그와같은문제를 거론하기 조차 어려운 상황이기 때문에, 현재로서는 별다른 대안이 없이 협상에 임할 수 밖에 없는 것이 가장 큰 어려움임.

다. 또한 일본으로서는 UR 이 결렬되었을 경우 미국이나 EC 가 일본에게 그책임을 전가할 가능성이 있기 때문에 동 대책 마련에 부심하고 있음.

5. 당관 관찰

가. 최근 주재국 일부 언론에 일본 정부가 미니멈 억세스 방안을 준비하고 있는 것으로 보도된바 있고, 또한 주재국내에 부분개방 정도는 불가피한 것이 아니냐는 분위기가 상당히 확산되어 있는 것으로 보이는 점에서 일 정부는 부분개방선에서 타결을 짓고 싶은 생각이나, 미.EC 간에 어느정도 접근이 이루어지고 있는 지를 모르기 때문에 초조해 하고 있는 것으로 보임.

나. 따라서 일본으로서는 12.20. 작성 예정인 초안 관련, 일단 한국, 카나다등 유사한 입장에 있는 국가들과 긴밀히 협의하면서 교섭에 임하되, 만일의 경우 UR 이 결렬되었을때 이에 대한 비난을 받지 않기 위하여 세심한 주의를 할 것으로 관찰됨. 끝.

(대사 오재희-국장)

예고:91.12.31. 일반

외 무 부

종 별 :

번 호 : GVW-2635　　　　　　　　　　　　일 시 : 91 1213 1600

수 신 : 장관(통기, 경기원, 재무부, 농림수산부, 상공부, 청와대경제수석)

발 신 : 주 제네바 대사

제 목 : UR/농산물 협상

연: GVW-2610,1. 본직은 12.13(금) 09:00 카나다 대표부에서 개최된 연호 협의회에 참석 예외없는 관세화 저지를 위한 관계국간 공동 노력 방안 마련에 대하여 협의하였는바 요지 하기 보고함.(농경연 최부원장, 김농무관보 동석). 가. 동 협의회는 카나다 SHANNON 대사의 주재로, 본직 및 ROSSIER 스위스 대사, SEADE 멕시코대사, HUHTANIEMI 핀랜드 대사와 일본, 이스라엘, 노르웨이, 아이스랜드 및 EC 의 농산물 협상 대표가 참석하였음.

나. 동 협의회에 참석한 모든 나라가 11 조 2C 의 유지 및 개선 필요성에 공감하였으며, 이씨를 제외한 나머지 나라들은 예외없는 관세화 추진에 대하여 우려를 표명하고, 공동 보조를 취할 필요성이 있다는데 합의하였음.

- 카나다는 별첨 MESSAGE 를 공동 명의로 던켈 총장에게 전달하고 G-36 회의등에서 협의하는 방안을 제시하였음.(본직과 사전협의)

0 동 MESSAGE 는 포괄적 관세화 개념에 대한 예외인정을 주장하되 특히 갓트 11 조 2 항 개선에 촛점을 둔것임.

- 북구는 갓트 11 조 2 C 개선에 대한 카나다 입장은 지지하지만(순수입 조항은 반대) 예외없는 관세화의 반대 여부는 협상의 전체 PACKAGE 를 보아 판단할것이라고 하면서 우선 미국이 주장하는 LINEAR CUT 를 저지하는데 힘을 모아야 한다고 하였음.(예외 없는 관세화에 공동으로 반대하는데는 유보적 입장 표명) 카나다 제안에 대하여 PARA 2 의 마지막 부분(AND THAT 이하) 을 삭제하자고 제안하였음.

- 스위스는 갓트 11 조 유지개선에 매우 유용한 것이지만 모든 문제를 포괄하는 것은 아니라고 하면서 각국의 특수한 문제를 해결할 수 있는 방안을 찾아야 한다고 하였음.

- 멕시코는 공동보조의 필요성을 강조하면서 가입 의정서등 갓트에 근거가 있는

통상국	장관	차관	1차보	2차보	구주국	경제국	외정실	분석관
청와대	안기부	경기원	재무부	농수부	상공부			

PAGE 1　　　　　　　　　　　　　　　　　　　　　　　　　　　91.12.14　　05:39

외신 2과　통제관 FM

0156

수량제한을 유지할 수 있도록 표현을 수정하자고 하였음.

- 이씨는 11조 2항의 유지개선에 관심은 있으나 카나다측 제안에 참여할 수 없다고 하고, 특히 포괄적 관세화에 예외를 인정할 수는 없다고 거듭 밝혔음.

- 일본은 포괄적 관세화에 14개국이 반대하고 있고, 파키스탄과 페루가 반대의사를 가지고 있으며, 폴란드, 터키, 세네갈, 도미니카등이 신중이 검토하고 있다고 하면서, 1차적으로 갓트 11조 2항 유지개선을 위해 힘을 모아야 한다고 하였음.

- 본직은 동 협의회에 참석한 국가간의 공통점(COMMON GROUND)을 찾고 이를 기초로 예외없는 관세화 저지를 위한 공동전략을 모색해야 한다고 강조하고, 기 본적으로 갓트 11조 2(C)는 유지 개선되어야 하지만 그외에도 각국이 특수한 문제가 있는 만큼 이들을 반영해야 한다고 하고, 카나다 제안에 대하여 원칙적으로 지지하지만 PARA 2 세째줄 TARIFFICATION 다음에 "HAVING REGARD TO NON-TRADE CONCERNS, INCLUDING FOOD SECURITY" 를 삽입하자는 수정제안을 하였음.

특히 갓트 11조 유지개선도 중요하지만 예외없는 관세화 저지에 촛점을 둘 필요가 있으며, 관계국 대표가 함께 조속히 던켈 총장을 만나 공동입장을 전달하는 것이 효과적이라고 하였음.

다. 금일 협의를 기초로 카나다 대표가 수정 문안을 마련 금일 17:00 재회동 하여 구체적인 추진 방안을 협의키로 하였음.

2. 한편 본직은 예외없는 관세화에 대하여 보다 강력히 반대하고 있는 일본,서서, 멕시코대사와 회동(12.14.10:00 스위스 대표부) 상기 11조 2(C) 대책과 별도의 대책을 협의 추진하고 있음. 상황 진전 사항 추보 위계임.

첨부: MESSAGE 사본 1 부

GVW(F)-0610. 끝

(대사 박수길-국장)

예고:92.6.30 까지

주 제 네 바 대 표 부

번 호 : GVR(F) - 610   년월일 : 11-13   시간 : 1800

수 신 : 장   관 (동기, 1경기획, 계수부, 농림수산부, 상공부, 청와대 경제수석)

발 신 : 주 제네바대사

제 목 : " 훈령 "

총 2 매(표지포함)

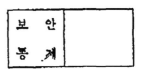

보 안	
봉 제	

외신과	
봉 제	

610 - 2 -

MESSAGE

IN THE MINISTERIAL DECLARATION AT PUNTA DEL ESTE AND
RECONFIRMED AT THE MID-TERM REVIEW, CONTRACTING PARTIES AGREED
THAT THE NEGOTIATIONS SHALL AIM INTER ALIA TO ACHIEVE
STRENGTHENED AND MORE OPERATIONALLY EFFECTIVE GATT RULES AND
DISCIPLINES ON AGRICULTURE.

WHILE SOME OF US HAVE OTHER REASONS FOR PROPOSING THAT THERE
SHOULD BE CAREFULLY CIRCUMSCRIBED EXCEPTIONS TO THE CONCEPT OF
COMPREHENSIVE TARIFFICATION THE FOLLOWING PARTICIPANTS ARE
UNITED IN THE VIEW THAT, CONSISTENT WITH THE AGREED OBJECTIVES
OF THE ROUND, GATT ARTICLE XI:2(C)(i) MUST BE STRENGTHENED AND
CLARIFIED AND THAT THE PROVISIONS OF THE DRAFT TEXT ON
AGRICULTURE BE MODIFIED TO EXCLUDE FROM TARIFFICATION TRADE
MEASURES TAKEN CONSISTENT WITH ARTICLE XI.

0159

외 무 부

110-760 서울 종로구 세종로 77번지　　　/　(02)720-2188　　　/　(02)725-1737

문서번호 통기 20644-

시행일자 1991.12.13.(　　　　)

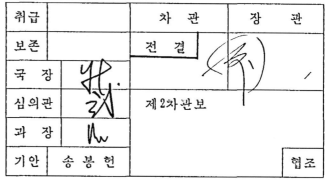

취급		차 관	장 관
보존		전 결	
국 장			
심의관		제2차관보	
과 장			
기안	송 봉 헌		협조

수신　　　　건 의

참조

제목　　UR 농산물협상 회의 정부대표 임명

　　　91.12.16 주간 스위스 제네바에서 수시 개최될 예정인 UR/농산물 협상 회의에
참가할 정부대표를 "정부대표 및 특별사절의 임명과 권한에 관한 법률" 에 의거 아래와
같이 임명할 것을 건의하오니 재가하여 주시기 바랍니다.

- 아　　　래 -

1. 회 의 명 ： UR/농산물협상회의

2. 회의기간 및 장소 ： 91.12.16 주간, 스위스 제네바

3. 정부대표

　　○ 농림수산부　　　　제2차관보　　　　　　　　김 한곤

　　○ 농림수산부　　　　농업협력통상관실 사무관　　　윤 장배

　　○ 주 제네바 대표부 관계관

4. 출장기간 ： 91.12.15-22

5. 소요경비 ： 소속부처 소관예산

6. 훈 령 ： 별첨 자료 참조　　　(끝)

외　무　부　장　관

0160

농 림 수 산 부

우 427-760 / 주소 경기 과천시 중앙동 1번지 / 전화 (02) 503-7227 / 전송 503-7249

문서번호 국협20644- 1178

시행일자 1991.12.13(년)

(경유)

수신 외무부장관

참조 통상국장

선결			지시	
접수	일자기간	19 . .	결재공람	
	번호			
	처리과			
	담당자			

제목 UR농산물협상 대표단 파견

---

    1. '91.12.11 던켈총장의 향후 협상일정 계획과 관련, 협상초안 제시이전 아국입장 관철을 위한 공식.비공식 활동추진을 위하여 다음과 같이 당부대표단을 파견코자 하오니 협조하여 주시기 바랍니다.

- 다 음 -

    가. 당부 대표단

구 분	소 속	직 위	성 명	비 고
대 표	농림수산부	제2차관보	김한곤	
"	농업협력통상관실	행정사무관	윤장배	

    나. 출장목적 : UR농산물협상 공식,비공식 활동 추진
    다. 출장기간 및 출장지
        0 '91.12.15 - 12.22(8일간), 스위스 제네바
    라. 소요경비 : 농림수산부 부담

첨부 : 1. 출장일정 1부.
        2. 협상 참가대책 1부. 끝.

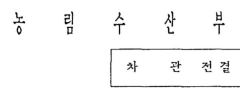

농 림 수 산 부

차 관 전 결

0161

출장일정 및 소요경비내역

가. 출장일정

'91.12.15(일) 12:40 서 울 발(KE 901)
               18:10 파 리 착
               20:45 파 리 발(SR 729)
               21:45 제네바 착

'91.12.16(월) - 12.20(금) : UR농산물협상 참석(공식,비공식 활동추진)

'91.12.21(토) 10:55 제네바 발(LH 1855)
               12:15 프랑크푸르트 착
               13:50 프랑크루르트 발(KE 916)

'91.12.22(일) 10:20 서 울 착

나. 소요경비

(1) 국외여비 : $8,539(1113-213)

구 분	차 관 보	윤장배 사무관
항 공 료	$4,355	$2,108
일 비	$ 30 x 8일 = $ 240	$20 x 8일 = $ 160
숙 박 비	$106 x 6일 =.$ 636	$66 x 6일 = $ 396
식 비	$ 50 x 7일 = $ 350	$42 x 7일 = $ 294
체재비계	$1,226	$ 850
합 계	$5,581	$2,956

12월 16일주간 UR농산물협상대책(안)

'90.12.11 TNC회의에서 던켈총장이 밝힌 협상일정에 따라 12월 20일까지 본격적인 협상이 진행될 것으로 예상되며 GATT를 중심으로 미·EC등 주요 협상주도국을 비롯하여 일본·캐나다와 캐언즈그룹 및 개도국등 모든 협상참여국이 자국입장 반영을 위하여 막바지 협상노력을 강화할 것으로 예상되는바, 기존의 아국입장(국협20644-1419, '91.12.7 참조)에 따라 대처하되 다음과 같은 방침하에 적의 대처하도록 함

- 다 음 -

① 시장개방분야에서 쌀등 기초식량등의 관세화 예외는 우리의 핵심적 관심사항인 만큼 포괄적인 관세화(Comprehensive Tariffication)에 반대입장을 강력히 제기하고 우리의 입장을 던켈 협상안에 반영하는데 주력할 것. 아울러 쌀에 대해서는 최소시장접근도 허용할 수 없음을 밝힐 것.

② 국내보조 분야에서는 구조조정등을 위한 농업부문 투자는 향후 자유화 확대과정에서 필요 불가결한 선행 조건임을 명백히 밝히고 허용가능 범위를 더욱 확대할 수 있도록 노력 할 것

③ 수출보조는 국제무역 왜곡의 근본원인임을 지적하고 국내보조나 시장개방 분야보다 분명한 감축계획이 제시되어야 함을 촉구 할 것

0163

④ 개도국우대 조치는 내용면에서 실질적인 우대조치가 획보되어야 하며, 영세한 우리 농업여건상 필히 아국에게 부여 되어야 함을 설명하고 아울러 개도국그룹의 활동에 적극 참여, 이러한 문제에 대한 공감대를 확산시키도록 할 것

⑤ 아국의 입장반영 노력과 병행하여 미국, EC, 케언즈그룹등의 움직임에 대한 정보수집 노력 강화 및 이러한 나라들에 대한 설득노력을 집중 시킬 것

⑥ 아울러 일본, 캐나다, 멕시코, 이스라엘, 스위스등 우리와 입장이 유사한(포괄적인 관세화 반대) 나라들과의 막바지 공동대응 노력을 강화 할 것

⑦ 던켈총장은 협상타결시한에 여유가 없다는 점을 이유로 미국등의 입장을 반영하여 무리한 협상타결을 시도할 가능성이 있음을 감안, 협상과정에서의 Transparency 확보에 최대한 노력 할 것

⑧ 기타 기술적 의제에 대해서는 기존입장에 따라 대처하되 헌지에서 대처하기 어려운 상황이 발생할 경우에는 본부에 청훈하여 대응토록 할 것

0164

외   무   부

110-760 서울 종로구 세종로 77번지   / (02)720-2188   / (02)725-1737

문서번호 통기 20644- *62***

시행일자 1991.12.13.(   )

수신   농림수산부장관

참조

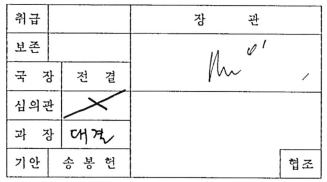

취급		장 관
보존		
국 장	전 결	
심의관	✕	
과 장	대결	
기안	송 봉 현	협조

제목   UR 농산물협상 회의 정부대표 임명

        91.12.16 주간 스위스 제네바에서 수시 개최될 예정인 UR/농산물 협상 회의에
참가할 정부대표가 "정부대표 및 특별사절의 임명과 권한에 관한 법률" 에 의거 아래와
같이 임명되었음을 알려드립니다.

                        - 아   래 -

    1. 회 의 명 : UR/농산물협상회의

    2. 회의기간 및 장소 : 91.12.16 주간, 스위스 제네바

    3. 정부대표(본부)

        ○ 농림수산부   제2차관보   김 한곤

        ○ 농림수산부   농업협력통상관실 사무관   윤 장배

    4. 출장기간 : 91.12.15-22

    5. 소요경비 : 소속부처 소관예산

    6. 출장 결과보고 : 귀국후 20일이내   (끝)

            외   무   부   장   관

발 신 전 보

WGV-1822   911213 1637 FL

번 호 : _____   종별 : _____

수 신 : 주   제네바   대사. 총영사//

발 신 : 장 관 (통 기)

제 목 : UR/농산물 협상

대 : GVW 2617

(귀지도착 : 12.15. 21:45 SR729편)

1. 12.16 주간 귀지에서 개최될 예정인 표제회의에 아래 본부대표를 파견하니 귀관
   관계관과 함께 참석토록 조치 바람.

    ○ 농림수산부   제2차관보   김 한곤

    ○ 농림수산부   농업협력통상관실 사무관   윤 장배

2. 금번 회의에는 기존입장에 따라 적의 대처하되, 현지에서 판단하여 대처하기
   어려운 상황이 발생할 경우에는 본부에 청훈하여 대처바라며, 일본, 카나다,
   스위스등 아국과 입장이 유사한 국가들과의 공동대응 노력을 강화 바람.

3. 대호 합의초안에 대한 임장은 검토되는대로 통보 하겠음. 끝.

(통상국장 김 용규)

	결재 1991.12.31	
	성명	

제2차관보 :

	보 안 통 제	

앙고재	91년 12월 13일	통상국과	기안자 성명 농봉현	과 장	심의관	국 장 전결	차 관	장 관

외신과통제

0166

면 담 요 록

1. 일시 및 장소

   ㅇ 91.12.13(금) 10:30 통상국장실

2. 면 담 자

   ㅇ 김용규 통상국장

   Christopher Butler 주한뉴질랜드대사

3. 면담요지(UR 문제)

   ㅇ 대 사

   - 다음주(12월20일)에 Dunkel 갓트사무총장은 UR 협상의 최종문안을 상정할
     예정인 바, 최근의 신문보도에 의하면 UR 협상에 임하는 한국의 입장,
     특히 쌀시장 개방문제에 있어서 약간의 변화가 있는듯 한데 이에 대해
     귀측 입장을 문의코자 귀하를 방문하였음.

   ㅇ 국 장

   - 쌀개방에 있어서 예외없는 관세화에 반대한다는 우리정부의 입장에는
     변화가 없음을 설명
   - 모든 원칙에는 예외가 없다는 것은 이상적(ideal)이나 현실은 그러하지
     못함과 한국에 있어서의 동 문제의 심각성 및 민감성을 지적
   - 우선 예외 없는 관세화에 반대하는 국가들과 공동보조를 취하여 다음주에
     상정 예정인 Dunkel 사무총장의 UR 협상 최종문안에 아측입장이 반영되도록
     노력 예정임을 설명
   - 한편 작일(12.12) 주한일본대사가 농수산부 장관을 예방, 쌀개방 문제에
     있어서 양국이 공동대처하기로 합의한 내용을 설명. 끝.

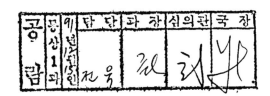

0167

발 신 전 보

WGV-1828   911214 1139 DU   종별 : 지급

번   호 :

수   신 : 주   제네바   대사. 총영사///

발   신 : 장   관 (통 기)

제   목 : UR ~~농산물~~ 협상

UR협상동향파악 및 금후 협상대책 협의를 위해

1. ~~금번회의시~~ 최혁 통상국 심의관을 본부대표로 추가 파견함.

2. 최심의관은 12.15(일) 21:45 SR 729 편 귀지 도착 예정임. 끝.

(통상국장   김 용 규)

일반문서로 재분류	1991. 12. 31

		보 안 통 제	

앙 고 재	91년 12월 14일	통상 국 과	기안자 성명		과 장	심의관	국 장		차 관	장 관	
			농법화								

외신과통제

0168

長 官 報 告 事 項

報 告 畢

1991. 12. 14.
通 商 局
通 商 機 構 課 (68)

題 目 : UR 農産物 協商 協定 草案

12.13 Dunkel 갓트 事務總長은 農産物協商 協定草案(draft text on agriculture) 을 配布한 바, 동 要旨, 評價 및 展望을 아래 報告 드립니다.

---

1. 農産物 協商 協定草案 內容

o 11.21 Dunkel 總長 자신이 配布한 農産物協商 討議文書(draft working paper)와 基本的으로 거의 동일 내용이나, 協定의 형태(前文, 本文, Annex)를 취함.

o 市場接近分野에서는 예외없는 關稅化를 採用과 最小 市場接近을

2. 評價 및 展望

o 農産物 協商에서의 美.EC 간 막후 절충을 촉진시키는 한편, 상금 Working paper 만 제시된 반덤핑, 投資等 여타 協商分野에서 12.20 까지 協定草案 도출을 도모하려는 의도로 評價

o 12.16 주간 주요 8개국, 36개국회의에서 동 協定草案을 논의한후 12.20 TNC 회의에 제출될 예정

 - 참여국간 合意 부재시 의장 자신의 책임하에 作成된 文書로 제출될 展望

o 동초안에대한 실질토의는 92.1.13 TNC 회의 이후로 예상

3. 言論 및 國會對策 : 별도조치 불요 (끝)

공람	통상기구과	담당	과장	심의관	국장	차관보	차관	장관
	91년12월16일	농병천						

0169

외 무 부

종   별 :

번   호 : GVW-2648   일   시 : 91 1214 1930

수   신 : 장관(봉기, 경기원, 재무부, 농림수산부, 상공부)

발   신 : 주 제네바 대사

제   목 : UR/농산물 협상

　　12.16(월) 10:00 표제 협상 개도국 비공식 회의가 개최될 예정임. 동 회의에는 아국 포함 22개국이 초청되었음. 동회의 소집통지서 별첨FAX 송부함.

　　첨부: 농산물 협상 개도국 비공식 회의 소집통지서 1부 끝(GVW(F)-621)

　　(대사 박수길-국장)

중아국　　차관　　2차보　　안기부　　경기원　　재무부　　농수부　　상공부

PAGE 1   91.12.15   08:50 ED

　　　　　　　　　　　　　　　　　　　　　　　　　외신 1과 통제관

0170

주 제 네 바 대 표 부

번 호 : GVW(F) - 62/   년월일 : 11214   시간 : 1800

수 신 : 장   관 (통기, 경기원, 재우부, 농림수산부, 상공부)

발 신 : 주 제네바대사

제 목 : GVW-2648 첨부

총 2 매 (표지포함)

보 안 통 제	히

외신과 통 제	

0171

G A T T   F A C S I M I L E   T R A N S M I S S I O N

Centre William Rappard   Telefax: (022) 731 42 06
Rue de Lausanne 154   Telex: 412324 GATT CH
CH-1211 Genève 21   Telephone: (022) 739 51 11

TOTAL NUMBER OF PAGES   1   Date: 14 December 1991
(including this preface)

From: Arthur Dunkel   Signature:
       Director-General
       GATT, Geneva

To: ARGENTINA   H.E. Mr. J.A. Lanus   Fax No: 798 72 82
      BANGLADESH   H.E. Mr. M.R. Osmany   338 46 16
      BRAZIL   H.E. Mr. C.L. Nunes Amorim   733 28 34
      CHILE   H.E. Mr. M. Artaza   734 41 94
      COLOMBIA   H.E. Mr. F. Jaramillo   791 07 87
      COSTA RICA   H.E. Mr. R. Barzuna   733 28 69
      EGYPT   H.E. Mr. M. Mounir Zahran   731 68 28
      INDIA   H.E. Mr. B.K. Zutshi   738 45 48
      INDONESIA   H.E. Mr. H.S. Kartadjoemena   793 83 09
      JAMAICA   H.E. Mr. L.M.H. Barnett   738 44 20
      KOREA   H.E. Mr. Soo Gil Park   791 05 25
      MALAYSIA   Mr. Supperamanian Manickam   788 09 75
      MEXICO   H.E. Mr. J. Seade   733 14 55
      MOROCCO   H.E. Mr. M. El Ghali Benhima   798 47 02
      NIGERIA   H.E. Mr. E.A. Azikiwe   734 10 53
      PAKISTAN   H.E. Mr. A. Kamal   734 80 85
      PERU   Mr. J. Munoz   731 11 68
      PHILIPPINES   H.E. Mrs. N.L. Escaler   731 68 88
      THAILAND   H.E. Mr. Tej Bunnag   733 36 78
      TUNISIA   H.E. Mr. Mohamed Ennaceur   734 06 63
      URUGUAY   H.E. Mr. J.A. Lacarte-Muró   731 56 50
      ZIMBABWE   H.E. Dr. A.T. Mugomba   738 49 54

You are invited to an informal consultation on agriculture to be held at
10 a.m. on Monday 16 December in the Green Room of the Centre William Rappard.
Attendance is restricted to two persons per delegation.

PLEASE NOTIFY US IMMEDIATELY IF YOU DO NOT RECEIVE ALL THE PAGES

** OUR FAX EQUIPMENT IS HITACHI HIFAX 210 (COMPATIBLE WITH
   GROUPS 2 AND 3) AND IS SET TO RECEIVE AUTOMATICALLY **   0172

관리
번호 91-839

외 무 부

종 별 : 지급

번 호 : GVW-2627 　　　　　　　　　일 시 : 91 1214 1300

수 신 : 장 관(봉기, 경기원, 재무부, 농림수산부, 상공부, 청와대경제수석)

발 신 : 주 제네바 대사

제 목 : UR/농산물 협상(G-36)

　　　　　　　　　　　　　　　　　편 (1991. 12. 31)

　12.13(금) 17:00-20:00 개최된 표제 주요국 비공식 회의(G-36) 요지 하기 보고함. (천농무관, 최농무관, 농경연 최부원장 참석)

　1. 합의초안 작성 배경 설명

　- 던켈 총장은 합의 초안이 4 개 부분으로 구성되어 있으며, A 부분이 본질적인 내용을 구성하고 B 부분(삭감방법)은 삭감약속, 예컨데 TE 계산 방법에 합의하여 TE 가 양허표(SCHEDULE)에 들어가게 되면 의미가 없어질 부분이라고 설명하였음.

　- 또한 동인은 동 합의초안에 숫자는 포함되어 있지 않는바, 12.20 까지 합의되지 않을 경우 의장 책임으로 넣을 것이며 동 숫자에 대하여 각국이 1.13 까지 수락여부등의 입장을 결정해야 한다고 하였음.

　2. 합의 초안 논의 요지

　- 던켈총장은 동 초안 B 부분 시장접근 부분부터 논의하자고 하였음.

　- 브라질, 콜롬비아, 알젠틴, 멕시코 등은 PARA 17 개도국 우대 부분이 불만이라고 하고 보다 구체적인 표현이 되어야 한다고 주장하였음.

　0 콜롬비아, 알젠틴 등은 열대산품에 대한 조기 이행, 시장접근 우대등이 포함되어야 한다고 주장하였음. 또한 A 부분 개도국 우대에 시장접근 분야는 포함되지 않았다고 불만을 표시하였음.

　0 던켈 총장은 시장접근 관련 개도국 우대가 양허표에 반영될수 있을 것이라고 답변함.

　- 던켈 총장은 PARA 16 은 자유화 품목에 대한 CEILING BINDING 가능성을 언급한 것이라고 설명하고, PARA 6 의 TARIFF LINE 에 대한 의미는 ANNEX 3 SECTION C 를 참고로 하면 된다고 답변하였음.

　0 " 포괄적 관세화" 단어가 사용되지 않은 의미를 니카라구아 대표가

통상국	장관	차관	1차보	2차보	외정실	분석관	청와대	안기부
경기원	재무부	상공부						

PAGE 1　　　예 의거 재분류(92.6.30.)　　　　　　　　　91.12.15 01:40

　　　　　직위　　　　성명　　　　　　　　　　　외신 2과 통제관 FL

　　　　　　　　　　　　　　　　　　　　　　　　　　0173

질문하였는바, 던켈 총장은 예외없는 관세화 표현을 ANNEX 3 PARA 3 첫째 문장에 분명히 명시했다고 답변함.

- 멕시코는 관세화 대상 품목에 문제를 제기하고 수정될 필요성을 주장하였으며, PARA 5 관련 86 년 이후 자유화 실적에 대한 CREDIT 인정문제를 제기하였음.

- 일본은 포괄적 관세화에 대한 기존 입장을 간단히 언급하고 PARA 4,5 에 대해서는 86 년 이후 자유화 실적에 대한 CREDIT 문제를 제기했으며, PARA 6 에서는 민감 품목에 대하여는 삭감폭과 MMA 설정시 특별취급이 인정되어야 한다고 하였으며, PARA 7 에서는 국제 유통이 많지 않은 품목의 경우 양허하는데 어려움이 있다고 하였음.

- 이스라엘은 예외없는 관세화에 대한 문제를 제기하고, 갓트 11 조의 유지개선을 주장하면서 ANNEX 3 FOOTNOTE 에 11 조도 포함시켜야 한다고 하였으며, PARA 6 관련해서는 관세화 품목의 경우 삭감 폭을 줄여야 한다고 하였음.

- 스위스는 PARA 6, 7 관련 FORMULA 삭감, 최저 삭감율, 전품목 양허등은 형평에 맞지 않는다고 하면서 예외없는 관세화 입장을 반대하는 나라가 완전히 고립되어 있는 것은 아니라고 주장하였음.

- 카나다는 11 조 2(C) 유지 개선 필요성을 주장하면서 동 품목은 관세화 예외로 인정되어야 한다고 하였음.

- 북구는 합의초안은 AMBITIOUS PACKAGE 라고 평가하고 이제는 전체적인 관점에서 판단하수 있는 싯점이 되었다고 하면서 포괄적인 관세화 인정시 민감품목에 대한 삭감폭과 이행기간면에서의 융통성이 필요하다고 하고, 전품목 양허, 최저시장 접근 등은 공산품 분야 협상과 비교할때 대단히 AMBITIOUS 하다고 하였음.

- 이집트는 포괄적 관세화에 문제가 있으며, 일부 예외 인정이 필요하다고 하면서 민감품목에 대한 장기 이행기간등 인정의 경우 동 개념을 고려할수 있다고 하였음.

- 아국은 예외없는 관세화는 이상에 치우친 접근법이라고 하면서 각국이 수용 가능한 현실적인 해결책을 찾아야 한다고 하고, 관세화 품목과 자유화 품목은 삭감폭 삭감방법등에 차이가 있어야 한다고 하였으며, 모든 품목의 양허는 곤란하고 R/O 접근 법에 의해 시장접근 확대와 양허 확대를 고려할수 있다고 하였음.

- 모로코는 포괄적 관세화에 대하여 종전 취해왔던 유보적 입장을 철회하고 모든 품목에 대한 관세화를 받아들인다고 하였으며, 개도국의 경우 양허폭에 대한 융통성 인정을 주장하였음.

- 이씨, 호주등 주요국은 발언이 없었으며, 미국은 개도국 우대에 대하여만간단히 언급함.

3. 던켈 총장은 12.15(일) 15:00 표제회의를 속개하여 시간제한 없이 국내 보조 분야부터 논의하자고 하였음.

- 동회의와는 별개로 12.14(토) 17:00 부터 개최되는 국내 보조 허용정책 문안작성 그룹(DRAFTING GROUP)에 아국이 초청되었음. 끝

(대사 박수길-국장)

예고 92.6. 30 까지

원 본

외 무 부

종 별 : 지 급

번 호 : GVW-2623   일 시 : 91 1214 1200

수 신 : 장 관(통기, 경기원, 재무부, 농림수산부, 상공부, 청와대경제수석)

발 신 : 주 제네바 대사

제 목 : UR/농산물 협상

12.13(금) 속개된 연호 협의회 요지 하기 보고함.

1. 카나다는 별첨 수정 MESSAGE 를 제시하고 각국의 지지여부를 물었음.

- 이씨는 서면 MESSAGE 에 공동 참여할수 없다고 하면서 다만 동 MASSAGE PARA 1 및 PARA 2 중간 부분 (갓트 11 조 강화 부분)은 회의에서 구두로 공감을 표명할수 있다고 하였음.

- 북구는 포괄적 관세화를 명시적으로 비판하는 내용에는 참하기 어렵다고 하였으며, 오지리는 이씨 입장을 지지하였음.

0 멕시코는 다소 미흡한점이 있지만 지지할수 있다고 하였고, 스위스도 지지의사를 표명하였으며, 일본 및 아국도 참여의사를 표명하였음.

2. 카나다는 12.15(일) 15:00 개최 예정인 G-36 회의 직전에 재회동, 결론을 짓자고 하고, 그때까지 각국의 입장을 정해줄것을 요청하였음.

첨부: 수정 MESSAGE 1 부

(GVW(F)-615)

(대사 박수길-국장)

예고 91.12.31. 까지

통상국	장관	차관	1차보	2차보	외정실	분석관	청와대	안기부
경기원	재무부	농수부	상공부					

주 제 네 바 대 표 부

번 호 : GVW(F) - *615*   년월일 : *11/21/&*   시간 : *1800*

수 신 : 장   관 (동기, 경기원, 재무부, 농림수산부, 상공부, 청와대 경제수석)

발 신 : 주 제 네 바 대 사

제 목 : " 전송 "

총 *2* 매(표지포함)

보 안	
통 제	

외신파	
통 제	

615-2-1

MESSAGE

[IN THE MINISTERIAL DECLARATION AT PUNTA DEL ESTE AND
RECONFIRMED AT THE MID-TERM REVIEW, CONTRACTING PARTIES AGREED
THAT THE NEGOTIATIONS SHALL AIM INTER ALIA TO ACHIEVE
STRENGTHENED AND MORE OPERATIONALLY EFFECTIVE GATT RULES AND
DISCIPLINES ON AGRICULTURE.]

WE BELIEVE THAT COMPREHENSIVE TARIFFICATION WITHOUT EXCEPTION
SHOULD NOT BE CONSIDERED AS THE ONLY WAY TO CONTRIBUTE TO THE
EXPANSION OF AGRICULTURAL TRADE. [WHILE SOME OF US HAVE OTHER
REASONS FOR HAVING PROPOSED THAT THERE SHOULD BE CAREFULLY
CIRCUMSCRIBED EXCEPTIONS TO THE CONCEPT OF COMPREHENSIVE
TARIFFICATION, THE FOLLOWING PARTICIPANTS ARE UNITED IN THE
VIEW THAT, CONSISTENT WITH THE AGREED OBJECTIVES OF THE ROUND,
GATT ARTICLE XI:2(C)(i) MUST BE STRENGTHENED AND CLARIFIED]AND
THAT THE PROVISIONS OF THE DRAFT TEXT ON AGRICULTURE BE
MODIFIED TO EXCLUDE FROM TARIFFICATION TRADE MEASURES TAKEN
CONSISTENT WITH ARTICLE XI.

0178

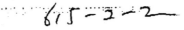

원 본

외 무 부

종 별 :

번 호 : GVW-2628 　　　　　　　　　　일 시 : 91 1214 1830

수 신 : 장 관(통기, 경기원, 재무부, 농림수산부, 상공부, 경제수석)

발 신 : 주 제네바 대사

제 목 : UR/농산물 협상

연: GVW-2635, GVW-2623

　　본직은 12.14 서서 대사, 멕시코 대사, 일본 농산물 협상 대표와 회동 별첨수정안(COMMUNICATION)을 작성하고 12.15 개최 예정인 표제 주요국 비공식 회의에서 농산물 합의 초안에 대한 공식 수정안으로 제출키로 논의하였음.

　　1. 동 수정안은 카나다 제안 XI 관련 MESSAGE 와는 별도 취급 제출키로 함.

　　2. 일본측은 동 수정안에 대한 참여 여부를 본국정부에 청훈하고 그 결과에따라 최종 입장을 밝히겠다함.(특히 XXI BIS 와 FOOTNOTE TO PARA 3 선택 누제)

　　3. 스위스, 멕시코는 동 수정안에 특별한 어려움이 없다고 했음.

　　4. 아국제안으로 FOOTNOTE TO PARA 3 를 반영하였음.

　　5. 동 수정안은 "예외없는 관세화"를 반대하는데 촛점을 두고 있으며, 많은동참 국가를 확보하는데 주력을 두고 있음. 특히 동 수정안 전문 마지막 PARA (ALL AGRICULTURAL PRODUCTS ,.,.. AND COMMITMENTS)는 아국 입장과는 일치 되지는 않으나 전반적인 균형문제를 고려한 것임.

　　6. 4 개국 회의는 12.15 14:00 에 재회동하여 각국의 최종 입장을 결정키로함.

　　연호 관련 카나다 제안에 대해서 12.15 14:30 에 재회동키로 함.

　　7. 카나다의 XI 관련 제안과 4 국 수정안에 대한 아국 입장을 지급 회신 바람.

첨부: 4 국 수정안 끝

(GVW(F)-616)

(대사 박수길-국장)

예고 92.6.30 까지

(1991. 12. 31)

통상국	장관	차관	1차보	2차보	외정실	분석관	청와대	안기부
경기원	재무부	농수부	상공부					

주 제 네 바 대 표 부

번 호 : GVW(F) - *616*   년월일 : *7/2-44*   시간 : *18∞*

수 신 : 장   관 (총기、경기단외계부、농림수산부、상공부、경제수석)

발 신 : 주 제네바대사

제 목 : "협 부"

총   2 매(표지포함)

보 안 통 제	
외신과 통 제	

616-2-1

Communication from..........................

In the Ministerial declaration at Punta del Este and reconfirmed at the mid-term review, contracting parties agreed that the negotiations shall aim inter alia to achieve strengthened and more operationally effective GATT rules and disciplines on agriculture.

We believe that comprehensive tariffication without exception should not be considered as the only way, or indeed in itself as an effective way to contribute to the expansion of agricultural trade. Broad based tariffication is a valuable instrument to prepare the ground for continuing negotiated improvements in agricultural market access. But it is access itself and not its instruments that is and must remain one of the three center pillars of the agricultural negotiations.

Having regard to non-trade concerns, including food security and the need to protect the environment, and in the end having due regard to bottom-line political, social and economic possibilities of contracting parties, there should be carefully circumscribed exceptions to the concept of comprehensive tariffication. All agricultural products which are not tariffied, will be the subject of access improvement negotiations [and commitments].

Therefore.......(name of signataries) propose the following:

1. In the light of the Panel decision from ... and consistent with the agreed objectives of the Round, GATT Article XI: 2(c)(i) shall be strengthened and clarified.

2. Annex 3, page 25 of the Draft Text on Agriculture from 12.12.1991 (english version) shall be amended as follows:

    -   Footnote linked to para 1:

        Measures maintained for BOP reasons or under general safeguard and exception provisions (Articles XI, XII, XVIII, XIX, XX and XXI [+ Article concerning basic foodstuffs as proposed as Article XXI bis in the Annex...] and other legal GATT - instruments negotiated under Article XXXIII) shall not be subject to the relevant provisions of this text.

    -   para 3:

        Tariff equivalents shall be established for all agricultural products subject to border measures as defined in para 1 here above other than ordinary customs duties:

    -   Footnote to para 3:

        For exceptionally sensitive agricultural products which should be carefully circumscribed, contracting parties may request a special derogation from tariffication as part of the finalization of schedules of market access commitments.

	분류번호	보존기간

발 신 전 보

WGV-1833   911215 2040 FO   종별: 초간급

번 호 :

수 신 : 주 제네바 대사. ~~총영사~~

발 신 : 장 관 (통기)

제 목 : UR농산물 협상

대= GUW -2628, 2623

1. 대호 4국 수정안에 전반적으로 동의하니 동제안에
   참여하기 바람.

2. 다만, XXI bis 와 Footnote to Para 3 가 모두
   반영되는 것이 바람직하나, 양자간 선택 문제가
   발생할 경우 상황에 따라 적의 대응바람.

3. 11조2항 C(i)관련 카나다 제안에 특별한 이견 없음.

(통상국장 김용규)

대 	1991. 12.31	合
	성명	

보 안 통 제	(서명)

앙 고 재	91년 12월 15일	통상 길 과	기안자 성명 농봉현		과 장 (서명)	국 장 전결	차 관	장 관 보결 (서명)	외신과통제

0182

관리 번호	9r-942

외 무 부

종 별 : 지급

번 호 : GVW-2659   일 시 : 91 1215 2130

수 신 : 장관(통기, 경기원, 재무부, 농림수산부, 상공부, 청와대경제수석)

발 신 : 주 제네바 대사

제 목 : UR/농산물 협상(공동제안)

대: WGV-1833

연: GVW-2623

1. 12.15(일) 14:00 스위스 대표부에서 개최된 연호 협의회에서 본직은 4 개국 공동제안문안에 동의하고 동제안에 참여할 것임을 밝혔음.

  - 동 제안문안중 첫번째 괄호(AND COMMITMENTS) 는 벗기기로 하였음.

  21 조 BIS 에 대한 괄호를 벗기는 문제는 일본이 재검토하기로 함.

  - 동 제안에 대하여 (아국) 및 (스위스) (일본) 이스라엘이 참여 의사를 표명하였고 멕시코는 현재 훈령을 기다리는 중이며, 이집트가 관심을 표명하고 있음.

  - 동 제안 관련 12.16(월) 08:30 재회동하여 최종 입장을 결정하기로 하였음

  - 스위스 대표는 12.15.15:00 개최된 주요국 비공식회의(G-36)에서 동제안을 제출할 계획임을 밝혔음.

2. 한편 동 14:30 개최된 11 조 개선 협의회에서 본직은 카나다 제안문안에대하여 참여의사를 밝혔음.

  - 카나다 제안에 참여의사를 밝힌 국가는 아국 및 카나다, 일본, 이스라엘, 노르웨이이며, 멕시코, 스위스와 핀랜드는 12.16 까지 확정적 답변을 주기로 함

  (스위스는 참여할 것으로 예상됨)

  - 아이슬랜드는 참여하지 않겠다고 하였고, 이씨는 종전 입장을 거듭 밝혔음. 오지리는 동 협의회에 참석치 않았으나 공동제안에 참여할 가능성은 적은 것으로 사료됨.

  - 동제안은 12.16(월) 오후 각국대사가 공동으로 던켈총장을 방문, 제출키로 하였음. 끝

통상국 안기부	장관 경기원	차관 재무부	1차보 농수부	2차보 상공부	외정실	분석관	청와대	청와대

PAGE 1

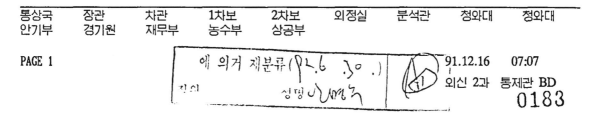

91.12.16   07:07
외신 2과   통제관 BD
0183

(대사 박수길-국장)
예고:92.6.30 까지

0184

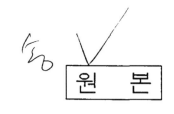

관리 번호	91-930

외 무 부

종 별 : 지 급

번 호 : GVW-2657   일 시 : 91 1215 2130

수 신 : 장관(통기, 경기원, 재무부, 농림수산부, 상공부, 경제수석)

발 신 : 주 제네바 대사

제 목 : UR/농산물 협상(G-36)

1. 12.15(월) 15:00-18:00 개최된 표제 주요국 비공식 회의(G-36)에서는 합의초안의 B 부분중 국내 보조분야에 대하여 논의하였는바 요지 하기 보고함. (천농무관, 최농무관, 농경연 최부원장 참석)

　가. 허용정책(GREEN BOX)

　- 정부의 일반서비스 사업에 대하여는 대부분 국가가 수용하는 분위기였음.

　0 인도는 식량안보를 위한 비축의 경우 수급상황에 따라서 생산량과 간접적연계가 불가피하다는 점을 지적하였음.

　0 아국은 농업하부 구조 정책에 경지정리(LAND CONSOLIDATION)가 포함되어야 한다고 주장하였음

　- 생산자에 대한 직접 지불정책에 대하여 개도국은 동 부분은 주로 선진국의 관심분야이므로 동 부분의 범위와 개도국 우대는 상호 관련된 문제라는 점을 지적하였음. 특히 케언즈그룹국가는 동 부분이 확대되고 융통성이 많아진데 우려를 표명하였음

　선진국들은 대체적인 만족을 표명하면서 일부 기술적 문제의 개선을 주장하였음.

　0 태국, 말련, 브라질, 콜롬비아, 인도등은 개도국 우대 부분이 개선되기는 했지만 아직 불충분하다고 주장하였음.

　0 헝가리 및 폴란드는 민영화에 따른 일시적 보조가 허용되야 한다고 주장함.

　0 아국은 기준년도 이후 농업을 새로이 시작하는 사람들에 대하여 보조금을 지급할수 없게하는 것은 형평의 문제가 있으며 이행상 어려움이 많다고 지적하였으며, 휴경(LAND RETIREMENT)보상은 10 년 이상의 경우에만 한정시키는 것은 부당하며 단기간 휴경하는 경우도 인정되야 한다고 하였음.

　0 이씨는 재해보상에 가축치료를 위한 지불을 포함시키고, 휴경보상의 경우는 매년

통상국	장관	차관	1차보	2차보		경제국	외정실	분석관
정와대	안기부	경기원	재무부	농수부	상공부			

PAGE 1

91-12.16   06:55

외신 2과 통제관 FM

0185

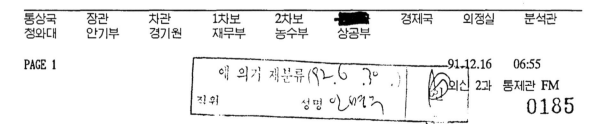

기준으로 인정해야 하며(YEARLY BASIS) 식품이외의 용도로 사용될 수 있어야 한다고 주장하였고, 지역개발 정책에 대한 DEGRESSIVE 조건을 없애야 하며, DECOUPLDE INCOME SUPPORT 의 다섯번째 조건을 없애자고 제안하였음.

O 북구, 스위스, 오지리등은 허용정책은 구조조정을 촉진할 수 있도록 설정되야 한다고 하였음.

O 일본은 전작계획을 설명하면서 휴경보상을 매년 기준으로 인정되야 한다고 주장하였음.

O 멕시코와 브라질은 동 초안 A 부분 7 조의 상계 가능성이 허용보조에 적용되는지를 지적하였음.

나. AMS

- 이씨는 국경조치효과의 배제, 품목별 특정 AMS(NON-PRODUCT-SPECIFIC AMS)등에 대하여 수용할 수 있음을 시사하면서, 국내의 가격차 계산시 국내가격은 개입가격을 사용하고, 품목특정 AMS 와 품목불특정 AMS 의 선택 가능성을 인정하자고 하였으며 생산봉제 효과 감안 필요성을 언급하였음.

- 동 초안 P39, PARA 8 둘째 문장에 대하여 WOLTER 농업국장은 2 중계산 방지를 위해 들어가 있다고 설명하였으며, 이씨는 개입정책에 수반되는 보관 및 관리 비용등을 가격차 계산에 추가하여 산입하지 않는다는 의미라고 설명하였음.

- 아국은 시장가격지지 계측에서 국경조치가 배제된데만족을 표시하고, 보다 효과적인 계측방법은 재정 지출액을 기준으로 하는 것이라고 하였음.

2. 동 회의는 12.16(월) 17:00 속개하여 동 초안 B 부분 수출보조분야와 A 부분에 대하여 논의하기로 하였음. 끝

(대사 박수길-국장)

예고:92.6.301 까지

PAGE 2

0186

UR/쌀시장 개방문제에 대한 대책(안)

91. 12. 14 (토)

0187

1. 금후 협상 일정
   (협상 타결 전제시)

91. 12. 20. 농산물 협정 포함 모든 협상분야에서 최종
   (TNC)   협정초안 (Draft Final Act 또는 Draft
             Final Agreements) 제시

92. 1. 13.   각 참가국의 최종협정 초안에 대한 입장표명 및
   (TNC)   동 초안을 기초로한 최종 협상 추진
             ― 시장접근, Service시장 양허등 양자협상
               병행함

92. 2월말   전분야에서 일괄타결안 마련
  또는 3월말   ― 농산물시장 양허표 포함

   "   참가국 통상 장관 회담 개최 및 Final
             Act 채택. 서명

93. 1. 1.   국내절차를 거쳐 협상결과를 비준한 나라
             간에 협정 발효 개시

95. 1. 1.   95. 1. 1. 이후에는 전혀 새로운 가입조건교섭부
             에만 참여 가능   0188
                                                  ①

2. 대안검토의 전제

o 농산물 협상에서 예외없는 관세화 (comprehensive
tariffication) 와 최소시장접근 (MMA) 허용안이
여타 모든 참가국의 수락을 받게되고, 아국만이
일체의 시장개방에 반대하는 유일한 나라로
고려되는 사태에 직면할 경우

o 농산물 뿐만아니라 모든협상분야에서 타결이
이루어져 Final Act 채택이 예상될 경우

3. 단계별 대책 및, 대안검토

(제1 단계조치)

o 아국이 국익대로에, 또한 국제적인 위치대로에
농산물협상이나 UR협상전체의 타결을
block 할수는 없기 때문에, "쌀시장에
대한 충분한 보호를 조건으로 consensus
안에 반대치 않는다"는 입장제시 0189
(consensus 안에 반대할 경우, 아국을 ②

제외하고 타결을 촉진하는 가능성은 크지 않으나,
국제적 비난과 압력은 감내하기 어려울 것임)

— 입장 표명시기가 대단히 중요함. 너무시기가
  늦는경우 조건교섭의 여지가 없어질 가능성이
  있음. (일본의 동향이 매우 중요)

— 조건은 협상시 아국의 운신의 폭을 가능적
  넓게하기위해 최대한 broad 하게 제시
  하되, 관계국이 조건자체도 못받겠다는
  반응을 보이지 않도록 유의

— 이 단계에서 정부의 입장변경을 국민에게
  잘 설명해야 할 것인바, 국내정치 상황은
  물론 대외관계도 충분히 고려하여 시행

(제2단계 조치)

  ㅇ 상기 조건을 근거로 관세화와 MMA 에 대한
    합의내용을 염두에 두어 쌀시장개방
    일정과 계획의 세부안에 대한 협상
    추진

0190
③

o 주협상대상국은 미국이 될것인바, 미-EC
  협상결과를 감안하고, NTC와 대개도국우대를
  최대한 활용하여 하기와 같은 아측안제시)

[제 1안] (미국등 수출국이 도저히 수용하기 어려운안)

- MMA ; 협정발효후 5년후 부터 허용
          허용총량은 1% 정도로하고 동결
- 관세화 ; 협정발효후 10년후 부터 시행
          관세감축폭은 일본수준의 1/2

[제 2안] (1안보다는 교서의 뜻을 보이는안이나, 여전히
          미국등의 수용이 어려운안)

— MMA ; 협정발효후 2-3년후부터허용
          허용총량은 1% 또는 일본의 1/2
— 관세화 ; 협정유효기간 최종년도(5-6년후)부터
          시행
          관세감축폭은 일본의 1/2 수준

[제 3안] (교서,타결을 전제로한 안)

— MMA ; 협정발효개시년도 부터 허용
— 관세화 ; 협정발효후 5년부터시행
  (허용총량, 감축폭은 융통성 있게)

0191
④

(제 3 단계 조치)

o 국내정치 일정을 고려, 상기 1·2안 을 고수
  하는경우, 협상시한내 (92.2~3월말) 타결에
  실패 예상

  ─ 따라서 농산물 양허표 와 Final Act 에
    쌀에 대한 양허내용은 포함될수 없게됨

o 이러한 상황에서 아국 1 나라, 쌀 1개품목
  때문에 Final Act 채택을 무작정
  지연시킬수 없을것이라는 점을 고려, 기합의된
  내용을 수록한 Final Act 는 그대로
  채택, 서명토록 하면서 쌀에 대한
  양허계획만을 예외적으로 추가협상을
  허용하여 그결과를 추가로 양허표에
  포함하도록 조치   0192

  ─ 이경우 추가협상 시한을 1~2 개월로
    한정할 가능성이 농후하며, 미국등은
    쌀에 대한 양허 없이는 Final Act 를 채택
    할수 없다는 강경한 입장을 보일 가능성이 ⑤

적지 않음.

— 아국으로서는 UR협상타결을 저지하지 않는다는
   기본입장을 명백히 하고 1~2개월내에 성실히
   교섭하여 타결을 추진하겠다는 정치적 의지
   표명이 불가피 한것임.

(제 4단계 조치)

ㅇ 상기 1~2개월간의 추가협상을 통해서도
   타결되지 않을경우 (아국이 정치적 고려
   때문에 의도적으로 타결을 미루는 경우 포함),
   아국은 추가적인 협상기간 연장 요청

   — 이를 위해서는 1~2개월간의 협상기간중
     아국이 의도적으로 협상을 결렬시키고
     있다는 인상을 주지 않도록 해야하며,
     어느경우에도 시장개방자체에 반대
     한다는 입장은 공개되어서는 안되도록
     유의 필요.

0193   ⑥

(제 5단계)

o 상기 4단계 아측의 추가협상기간 요청에
  대해 아래 상황이 예껀될수 있을것임.
  - 추가 협상기간 불인정 및. 행정상
    개방조건 impose
  - Final Act 서명효라 무효화 주장
  - 추가협상기간 조건부 재연장
    (협정이 93.1.1. 부터나 발효됨을 감안)
  - 추가협상기간 연장 (93.1.1 까지)

o 아측은 상기 첫가지 결정에 따라 협상을
  계속하면서 시간을 벌던기, 아니면
  쌀에대한 시장개방 유예 (5~10년후론)을
  일방적으로 발표하는 방안등 정치적
  결단을 내릴수 밖에 없을 것임.
  - 그결과는 예상키 어려우나, 쌀에
    대한 임여계획없이는 Final Act
                              0194   ②

서명초라가 없다고 하는 법적논쟁이 있을수 있고, 미국은 앙자적 보복조치를 발동할 것으로 예상. (합의된 농산물 협상 결과에 대응 prima facie violation case 임으로 분쟁해결절차 적용 대상이 되지 않을것임)

— 이단계에서는 미국의 보복 그자체보다는 국제사회에서 신인도(credibility)가 없는 나라라는 비난과 압력이 아국에 더욱더큰 부담이 될것이며,

— 가장 무서운 결과는 것르체제 밖으로 밀려나는 사태임. (Final Act 서명 초라가 무효화 될시 새로운 조건으로 재 가입해야함) 끝.

0195

最近 UR 協商 動向

(農産物 協商 中心)

1991. 12. 16.

通 商 機 構 課

0196

1. 最近 UR 協商 동향

   ○ 11.29. Dunkel 事務總長의 提議에 의해, 12.5부터 各 協商 分野別로 集中的
     協商 實施中

   ○ 12.11 非公式 TNC 會議에서 Dunkel 갓트 事務總長은 아래 要旨의 UR 協商
     終結 方案을 發表

     - 12.20 TNC에 協商 全分野에 걸친 包括的 最終 協商案 提示 豫定

       . 同 協商案은 가급적 合意文案이 되도록 할 것이나, 불가능한 경우
         議長 責任下에 協商案 提示

     - 각국은 12.20자 協商案을 UR 協商의 最終 結果로 간주하고 최고위층에서
       신중히 檢討해 줄것을 要望

     - 92.1.13 TNC를 開催 豫定인바, 그때까지 각국은 1.13 이후 수주내에
       協商을 終結할 수 있는 態勢를 갖출것을 要望

   ○ 12.12. Dunkel 事務總長은 農産物 分野의 最終 協定案을 提示

     - 關稅化 운칙에는 例外가 없으며, 最小 市場接近도 認定하는 方向으로 作成

   ○ 12.20까지는 모든 協商 分野에 걸쳐 어떤 形態로든 最終 協商案이 제시될
     것이며, 각국 정부는 92.1.13 TNC에서 이에 대한 立場을 밝힐 것으로 豫想

2. 美.EC間 막후 協商 動向

   ○ 11.9 頂上會談 以後 일부 쟁점에 대한 의견접근이 있었으나 11.20 農務次官級
     會議에서 核心爭點 이견 조정 失敗로 협의 一時 中斷

     - rebalancing, 輸出補助金 削減 方法等에 미합의

0197

o 兩側 頂上의 介入으로 12.3이후 양측간 協議가 繼續되고 있으나 核心爭點에
　관한 양측간 이견 尙存

　　- 12.3 이후 次官級 會議 수차례 開催

　　- 12.7-8 農務長官 會議

3. "例外없는 關稅化" 關聯 動向 및 우리의 對應 內容

o 지금까지의 農産物 協商 推移 및 美.EC間 協議 內容에 비추어 12.20자
　最終 協商案에는 "例外없는 關稅化"가 包含될 것으로 豫想

o 12.12 駐韓 日本 大使는 農水産部長官을 禮訪, "例外없는 關稅化"에 대한
　兩國 共同 對應 方案 協議

o 주 제네바 大使는 日本, 멕시코, 스위스, 이스라엘등과 基礎食糧 品目은
　關稅化 對象에서 除外한다는 內容의 共同 제안문 作成, 農産物 協商 會議에
　提出 豫定

o 주 제네바 大使는 또한 카나다, 日本, 이스라엘, 놀웨이, 멕시코, 스위스
　등과 함께 GATT 11조 2항(C) 改善 및 同 條項 該當品目은 關稅化의 例外로
　하는 內容의 共同 제안문을 作成, Dunkel 事務總長에 提出 豫定

o 제네바 現地 協商에 農林水産部 제2次官補 및 關係部處 局長級 代表를
　分野別로 派遣, 對處中.　　　　　　　　끝.

0198

長官報告事項

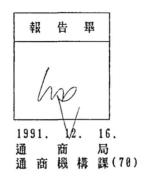

報告畢

1991. 12. 16.
通 商 局
通商機構課(70)

題 目 : UR/農産物 協商 關聯 我國 對應

12.13-15 주 제네바 大使는 日本, 카나다, 스위스등 例外없는 關稅化에 反對하고 있는 國家들의 제네바 現地 協商代表들과 連鎖 接觸, 共同 對處方案을 講究중인바, 現在까지의 推進 狀況을 아래와 같이 報告 드립니다.

---

1. 例外없는 關稅化 關聯 4個國 共同 提案

   ○ 我國, 日本, 스위스, 이스라엘 主導下에 關稅化에 대한 下記 例外 追加 方案 協議中

     - 加入 議定書上의 例外 (祖父 條項) 認定 및 食糧安保 關聯 갓트 21條의 追加 條項 新設을 통한 關稅化 例外 設定

     - 關稅化 協商 過程에서의 敏感品目에 대한 例外 認定

   ○ 12.16 同 提案文案을 最終 決定하여 36個國 非公式 會議에 提出 豫定

     - 멕시코, 이집트도 同 提案 參與에 關心 表明

2. 갓트 11조 2항 C 關聯 共同 提案

   ○ 갓트 11조 2항 C의 改善, 强化 및 同 條項 適用 品目의 關稅化 例外를 위해 카나다가 主導하고 있는 提案에 我國, 日本, 이스라엘, 놀웨이등이 參與 意思 表明

   ○ 12.16 同 提案을 Dunkel 갓트 事務總長에게 提出 豫定

3. 國會 및 言論對策 : 別途 措置 不要.   끝.

0199

長官報告事項

報 告 畢

1991. 12. 16.
通 商 局
通 商 機 構 課(70)

題 目 : UR/農産物 協商 關聯 我國 對應

12.13-15 주 제네바 大使는 日本, 카나다, 스위스등 例外없는 關稅化에 反對하고 있는 國家들의 제네바 現地 協商代表들과 連鎖 接觸, 共同 對處方案을 講究중인바, 現在까지의 推進 狀況을 아래와 같이 報告 드립니다.

---

1. 例外없는 關稅化 關聯 4個國 共同 提案

   ㅇ 我國, 日本, 스위스, 이스라엘 主導하에 關稅化에 대한 下記 例外 追加 方案 協議中

      - 加入 議定書上의 例外 (祖父 條項) 認定 및 食糧安保 關聯 갓트 21條의 追加 條項 新設을 통한 關稅化 例外 設定

      - 關稅化 協商 過程에서의 敏感品目에 대한 例外 認定

   ㅇ 12.16 同 提案文案을 最終 決定하여 36個國 非公式 會議에 提出 豫定

      - 멕시코, 이집트도 同 提案 參與에 關心 表明

2. 갓트 11조 2항 C 關聯 共同 提案

   ㅇ 갓트 11조 2항 C의 改善, 强化 및 同 條項 適用 品目의 關稅化 例外를 위해 카나다가 主導하고 있는 提案에 我國, 日本, 이스라엘, 놀웨이등이 參與 意思 表明

   ㅇ 12.16 同 提案을 Dunkel 갓트 事務總長에게 提出 豫定

3. 國會 및 言論對策 : 別途 措置 不要.   끝.

공람	통상기구과	91년 12월 16일	담당 송봉현	과장	심의관	국장	차관보	차관	장관

0200

외 무 부

종 별 :

번 호 : GVW-2678   일 시 : 91 1216 2000

수 신 : 장 관(통기,경기원,재무부,농수부,상공부,보사부)

발 신 : 주 제네바대사

제 목 : UR/농산물 협상(위생 및 검역규제)

연: GVW-2632

12.15(일) 14:30-15:30, 18:00-20:00 개최된 표제위생 및 검역규제 전문가 회의에서는 연호 합의초안을 기초로 단일 합의안을 만들기 위한 협상을 하였는 바, 요지 하기 보고함.(천농무관,김농무관보 참석)

1. 국제 기준보다 엄격한 국내 기준

- 미국, 이씨, 호주, 일본등 대부분 나라가 의장중재안 수용의사를 밝혔음.

- 알젠틴, 칠레, 콜롬비아등은 PARA 10 중간부분에 'PARA 19' 대신 'OARA 15-23'으로수정하자고 하였음.

- 아국은 동 LEUFM이 기본 권리(PARA 4)로서 인정되어야 한다고 강조하고, PARA 10 은타협안으로서 고려할수 있으나 OBLIGATION 부분이 빠져야 한다고 하였음.

2. 체약국 영토내의 위생 및 검역규제

- 충분한 논의가 없었는 바, 아국은 PARA 4 및6의 괄호내 문구가 삭제되서는 않된 다고 하였음.

3. 위험도 평가 고려 사항

- 케언즈 그룹은 의장 중재안에 불만을 표시하였음.

- 미국, 이씨, 일본, 북구등은 의장 중재안을 수락하였으며, 아국도 동 중재안을 수락할수 있다고 하였음.

4. 국제기준 이용 감시 절차

- 미국은 PARA 29 수정안을 제시하였음.(종전TEXT ALT 2 에 가까운 제안)

이씨는 미국 제안에 강한 불만을 표시하고, 의장중재안도 수용하기 어렵다고 하였음.

- 카나다 및 북구는 의장 중재안을 지지하였음.

통상국	2차보	보사부	경기원	재무부	농수부	상공부

PAGE 1

91.12.17   09:00 WH

외신 1과 통제관

0201

- 일본은 미국제안을 지지하였음.

5. 잔류 물질등 승인 절차

- 호주, 뉴질랜드 등 케언즈 그룹은 동 조항의 필요성을 주장하면서 의장 중재안을 지지하였음.

- 이씨는 의장 중재안에 불만을 표시하였음.

6. 개도국 이행 유예

- 미국, 이씨등은 개도국이 아무런 조치도 취하지 않을 가능성에 우려를 표명하였음.

- 태국, 알젠틴 등 개도국은 개도국에 대한 2년이상의 유예를 주장하였음. 끝

(대사 박수길-국장)

관리 번호 : 91-943

원 본

외 무 부

종 별 :

번 호 : GVW-2677

일 시 : 91 1216 1950

수 신 : 장관(봉기,경기원,재무부,농림수산부,상공부)

발 신 : 주 제네바대사

제 목 : UR/농산물 협상(개도국 그린룸 협의)

본직은 12.16(월) 10:00-13:00 개최된 표제협상 개도국 우대과년 그린룸 협의에 참석하였는바 요지 하기 보고함.(농림수산부 김한곤 차관보, 농경연 최부원장 동석)

1. 동 그린룸 협의에는 본직 포함 23 개 개도국 대사가 초청되었으며 농산물협상 합의 초안의 개도국 우대 부분에 대하여 논의되었음.

2. 수출 개도국은 가급적 세분된 관세항목별로 관세 삭감 약속을 하되 최저삭감율을 가급적 평균 삭감율에 가깝도록 하여야 하고, 현 시장접근 수준(CMA)은 단순히 유지되는 것으로 불충하며 반드시 확대되어야 한다고 주장하였음.

3. 본직은 아국이 개도국의 일원으로서 개도국 우대 내용에 많은 관심을 갖고 있다고 전제하고 아래 3 가지 아측입장을 밝힘

가. 개도국 우대가 국내 보조 부분에서는 많이 개선되었지만 시장접근 분야에서는 크게 미흡한바 시장접근 부분의 개도국 우대방안으로서 개도국에게 특히 민감한 품목에 대하여는 관세화에 대한 예외적 취급을 인정하는 조항이 반드시 반영되어야 함(동초안 ANNEX 3 PARA 3 참조)

나. 양허 품목과 관련, 협상을 통해 확대시키겠으나 전 품목을 양허하는 것은 곤란함.

다. 수입을 개방하는 품목에 대한 최저시장 접근(MMA) 수준을 설정하는데 있어서도 개도국 우대를 반영하여 선진국 보다는 적은 수준이 되어야 함.

4. 예외없는 관세화에 대하여 문제를 제기한 나라는 아국외에 멕시코, 파키스탄, 인도, 필리핀, 이집트등이었는바, 이들의 입장은 민감품목에 대한 예외인정 또는 이행상의 융통성 부여등을 주장하고 있어 그내용에 있어서 다소 상이한 것임.

5. 던켈 총장은 TNC 에 제출될 합의 초안은 현 합의초안 문안을 최대한 유지할 것이라고 언급하면서 금번 UR 협상에서 가장 중요한 것은 미국의 웨이버, 이씨의

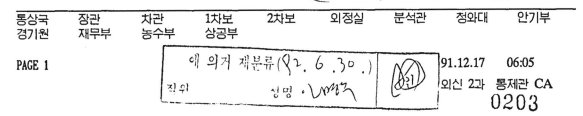

가변부과금 제도를 갓트 체제로 끌어들이는 것이며 이와 같은 개혁적 조치에 따른
비용은 어느정도 감수되야 한다고 하여, 포괄적 관세화 개념을 계속 유지하겠다는
뜻을 분명히 하였음. 끝

　　　(대사 박수길-국장)

　　　예고:92.6.30 까지

발 신 전 보

분류번호	보존기간

번   호 : WGV-1848   911217 1719   종별 : _____

수   신 : 주   제네바   대사. 총영사/

발   신 : 장 관 (통 기)

제   목 : UR/농산물 협상 _____

대 : GVW-2617

대호 던켈 사무총장이 제시한 협정초안에 대한 검토 자료를 별첨(FAX) 송부함.

첨 부 : 동 자료(7매).   끝.   (통상국장 김 용 규)

(WGVF -0390)

	보 안 통 제	⟋⟍

| 앙
고
재 | 91
년
12
월
17
일 | 통상국
과 | 기안자
성명
농봉헌 | | 과 장
⟋⟍ | 심의관
춘정흠 | 국 장
전여니 | | 차 관 | 장 관
⟋⟍ | | 외신과통제 |

0205

농 림 수 산 부

우 427-760 / 주소 경기 과천시 중앙동 1번지 / 전화 (02) 503-7227 / 전송 503-7249

문서번호 국협20644-1189

시행일자 1991.12.17(년)

(경유)

수신 외무부장관

참조 통상국장

선결			지시	
접수	일 자	19 . .	결재공람	
	기 간			
	번 호			
처 리 과				
담 당 자				

제목 UR/농산물협상 합의초안 검토

---

1. '91.12.13 배부된 UR농산물협상 Draft Text에 대한 당부 대책자료를 별첨과 같이 보내

드리오니 조치하여 주시기 바랍니다.

첨부 : UR농산물협상 Draft-Text대한 협상대책 1부.   끝.

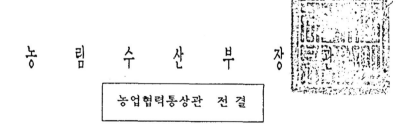

농 림 수 산 부 장

농업협력통상관 전결

0206

UR농산물협상 Draft Text(12.12)에 대한 협상대책

1. 기본 입장

O 던켈 Draft Text는 협상참여국간에 합의가 이루어지지 않은 것이며 전체적으로 수출국과 수입국의 입장이 균형되게 반영되지 않았음을 지적하고, 향후 공개적인 토의과정을 통해 수정 보완되어야 함을 분명하게 제기

O 각종 공식,비공식협의와 이해당사국과의 긴밀한 협의를 통하여 관세화예외 인정등 아래의 아국 핵심적 관심사항 반영에 주력

2. Draft 내용에 대한 분야별 입장

〈 국경보호 분야 〉

O 예외없는 관세화에 대한 수용불가 입장을 분명히 하고, 식량안보에 의한 쌀등 기초식품과 11조2항C에 의한 관세화예외를 반영하는데 주력

- 기초식품에 대한 식량안보 반영을 위해 일본, 스위스등과의 공동협력체제를 강화

- 11조2항C의 유지개선을 위해 캐나다를 중심으로 공동제안을 작성하는데 적극 참여

O 최소시장접근 보장은 원칙적으로 수용가능하다는 입장을 표명하되, 년도별 증량에는 반대하고 적용관세도 현행관세수준으로 하며, 쌀에 대해서는 최소시장접근을 허용할 수 없다는 기존입장으로 대응

0207

O 관세 양허 및 인하는 품목별 특수성을 고려하여 R/O방식이 채택되어야 하며,

  - 관세와 TE감축을 구분하되, 특히 관세인하는 관세협상에서의 감축수준과 같은 수준이

    되어야 함

O Special Safeguard에 대하여는 발동요건과 발동조치를 완화하는데 주력하고, 특히 국내산업

  보호를 위해 수량제한도 허용해야 한다는 입장을 제시

〈 국내보조 분야 〉

 O 허용대상정책의 범위확대와 조건완화에 주력하되, 특히 구조조정을 위한 투자지원을 한시적

   으로만 인정할 것이 아니라 지속적인 지원이 가능하여야 함

 O 국내보조 감축약속은 AMS를 기준으로 하되 인플레를 반영한 실질가치 기준으로 약속

   (Draft Text는 과도한 인플레만 반영하도록 하고 있음)

 O 감축대상정책중 시장가격지지는 국내외 가격차로 계산토록하고 있으나 정부재정지출 기준으로

   계산하여야 하며, 국경보호효과는 제외되어야 한다는 점을 분명히 제기

 O 국내보조에서 De Minimis 원칙을 설정하는 기준은 선진국의 감축이행년도 말 수준을 채택해야

   한다는 입장을 제시

〈 수출보조 분야 〉

 O 수출보조는 가장 무역왜곡적인 조치인 만큼 보다 엄격한 규제가 필요하며 국내보조와 국경

   보호에 우선하여 급격히 감축되어야 한다는 입장을 강력히 제기

 O 수출보조 감축기준은 금액과 물량을 동시에 적용함으로써 실질적인 감축이 있어야 한다는

   점을 강조

0208

〈 개도국우대 〉

0 개도국우대는 감축폭과 이행기간에서 모두 적용하되 개도국 정책의 목적과 성격을 고려하여

　별도의 우대원칙이 적용되어야 함을 강조

　　- 작목전환지원등이 반영되어야 하며

　　- 수출보조에 대한 감축예외 인정 뿐만아니라 수출보조분야에서도 De Minimis 원칙이 적용

　　되어야 한다는 점을 강조

0 개도국간을 차별하는데 반대입장을 제기하고 최빈개도국에 대한 감축의무를 면제하되, 여타

　개도국은 동일한 우대조치를 적용해야 한다는 점을 강조

〈 농업개혁의 지속문제 〉

0 농업개혁의 지속 또는 추가감축문제에 대하여는 장기이행기간등 개도국우대를 인정받아야

　할 필요성을 고려할 때 지속하는 방안을 선호하되 협상동향을 보아 신축적으로 대처

〈 약속이행 점검방법과 절차 〉

0 약속이행등과 관련된 농업위원회 설치, 이행점검방법, 분쟁해결절차등에 대하여는 기본적

　으로 특별한 이의가 없으나 농업생산과 교역의 특성상 공산품에 적용되는 규정보다는 완화

　되도록 하는데 주력하꼬, 명료하게 규정되어야 함을 제기

0209

3. 기타 사항

O GATT사무국은 12.20까지 최종협상안을 마련하기 위해 각 분야별로 Drafting Group을 운용할 계획으로 있는 바 동 그룹에 적극 참여하여 아국 입장을 반영시켜 나가는데 주력

O 기타 사항에 대하여는 기존입장에 따라 대처하되 현지에서 대응이 어려운 상황이 발생할 경우 청훈하여 대처

첨부 : UR농산물협상 Draft Text에 대한 아국입장

0210

UR농산물협상 Draft Text에 대한 아국입장

항목빌 (이건제기분야)	아 국 입 장	사 유
PART A 1) Article 3,1항	O "together with ...... to individual products" - 이 내용이 무엇을 의미하는지 명확히 할 필요가 있음 - 국내보조에도 양허의무를 부과하는 것이라면 수용곤란	O 국내보조와 수출보조의 감축약속은 현행 GATT규정과 약속이행의 탄력성을 고려할때 UR협상결과의 법적형태로 취급되어야 함 - GATT 제2조의 양허의무 배제
2) Article 5 O 1항(i)	O "any marketing year"를 "any marketing or calender year"로 수정 O "whichever is the greater"의 부가조건 삭제	O 실제 운용문제를 고려, 명확한 기간 개념정의 필요 O 협상결과의 의무부담은 MMA또는 CMA수준이므로 여기에 대한 불명확한 양적기준의 추가는 불필요
O 5항	O "as defined.... is taken" 삭제 〈 기타사항 〉 O trigger level의 완화와 피해구제에 충분한 발동조치 확보에 주력 O 수량규제는 허용되어야 한다는 아국 기본입장과 관련, 수입물량 및 가격변동폭이 일정수준 이상일 경우 잠정적인 물량규제 운용방안의 필요성을 제기하는 선에서 대응 O 항구적으로 운용	O 2중의 T.E인상한계 설정배제 O EC의 corrective Factor 반영 취지를 고려 O 제19조와 관련 논의현황을 주시

- 1 -

'0211

항목별(이견제기분야)	아 국 입 장	사 유
3) Article 6 0 3항	0 "sector-wide AMS"는 삭제	0 Product Specific AMS만 활용 (기존입장) - 품목별 할당방식 채택(협상 동향을 보아 탄력적 대응) ※ 감축대상 AMS와 품목특정 AMS와 sector-wid AMS로 구분되어 길 경우 De Minimis에 들어갈 가능성이 더 높을 수도 있다는 점도 고려하여 신축적으로 대응
4) Article 7 0 3항	0 Actionable한 경우, 수출보조와는 다른측면을 어떻게 고려 할 것인 지를 제기 ※ GATT 16조의 보조금 상계관세 규정은 수출보조에 대한 상계 관세를 규정한 것이고 국내보조 를 대상으로 한 것이 아님	
5) Article 8 0 2항(감축대상 수출보조의 정의)	0 Options Paper Addenda 10 3항b (deficiency payment)가 추가 되어야 할 것임을 제기	0 집행방법이 다를뿐 수출보조와 다를 바 없음
6) Article 9	0 circumvention에 대한 보다 더 명확한 판단기준 제시를 요구	0 circumvention에 대한 판단 기준이 모호하고 이의 위반시 구속력이 미약함
7) Article 17 0 4항	0 "excessive"을 "real"로 수정	0 실질 인플레율 반영
8) Article 18 0 3-4항	0 보다 더 명확한 개념정의 요구	0 동 규정이 의도하고 있는 내용을 파악 대처
9) Article 19 0 1항	0 "	0 서문에 제시된 기본목적으로 처리가능

- 2 -

항목별 (이견제기분야)	아 국 입 장	사 유
PART B		
1) 3항(기준기간)	○ 특히, 국내보조에 있어서 개도국의 기준기간은 최근연도 사용인정	○ MTR에서 개도국은 동결의무를 면제, 최근연도 사용이 허용되야 감축의무의 균형이 이루어질 수 있음
2) 4항	○ "in the case of unbound duties .... base period"를 "the level applied on 1 September 1986" 으로 수정	○ 아국의 관세인하 실적에 대한 credit가 배제될 수 있으며, 관세협상과 불균형 초래
3) 6항	○ "with a minimum rate of ..... each tariff line" 삭제 ○ "and shall be expanded.... implementation" 삭제	○ 품목별 최소감축목표 설정배제 - 평균감축목표도 관세협상그룹 합의목표를 초과할 수 없음 ○ MMA의 증량은 허용할 수 없음 - T.E감축으로 시장접근확대 가능
4) 7항	○ "all custom duties.... shall be bound"를 삭제하고 "Specific binding commitment"뒤에 "for customs duties including those resulting form tariffication" 추가	○ 모든품목의 양허 불가 - 관세협상에서도 양허품목의 확대만 논의되고 있으므로 전품목 양허는 곤란함
5) 11항	○ "budgetary outlay and / or quantity commitment"의 and/or 를 and로 확정	○ 수출보조 감축에 있어서 재정 지원과 보조물량 감축을 동시에 감축
6) 14항	○ "no less than.... per cent"를 축소하는데 주력(신진국 수준의 1/2 이내)	○ 개도국의 차등대우 배제 ○ 최대 범위내에서 개도국의 실정 에 따라 이행의무 선택

- 3 -

0213

항목별 (이견제기분야)	아 국 입 장	사 유

<u>Annex</u>
 	
1) Annex 2
  0 Part C
    section III
	0 other commitments에 다음사항을 구체화
	  1. Description of products on which export subsidies shall not be granted
	  2. Other
		0 Cease-Fire Commitment에 관한 약속표도 구체적으로 제시되이야 함

2) Annex 3 0 1항	0 관세화의 예외확보 문제에 대하여는 이해관계국과의 공동대응 전략에 따라 대응	
0 3항(iii)	0 다음과 같이 수정 (iii) for transformed and processed agricultural products, calculation would generally be made by multiplying the tariff equivalent(s) for the agricultural input(s) <u>or substitute(s)</u> by the proportion(s) of the agricultural input(s) <u>or substitute(s)</u> in the transformed and processed agricultural products.	0 대체품 가격기준으로 한 T.E산출 방법도 허용 - 동일상품이 없을 경우 대체 상품을 사용할 수 있도록 함
0 11항	0 "Participants may request..... m.f.n basis" 삭제	0 Current Access증량 협상권을 인정할 수 없음

- 4 -

0214

항목별 (이견제기분야)	아 국 입 장	사 유
0 14항	0 "at a low or minimal rate"를 다음과 같이 수정 "at the current bound rate or the normally applicable rates whicherer is the lower"	0 최소한 현행 실행관세수준 수용
3) Annex 4 0 1항	0 "no, or at most minimal" 삭제	0 어떤 정책이든 간접적인 효과가 없을 수 없고 진혀없는 정책은 부존재
0 2항(vi)	0 정책정의에 storage, transportation이 포함되는지를 clarify	0 아국 관심사항 추가
0 2항(vii)	0 정책정의에 land consolidation이 포함되는지를 clarifty	"
0 3항	1) "current market price"뒤에 "or administered price"를 추가	0 AMS계측과 동일기준 허용
	2) "at no less than the current market....."를 "in such a manner that the sales would not affect the domestic market price"로 수정	0 품질문제를 반영하고는 있으나 시중가격의 개념이 불명확하고 정책운용의 탄력성을 제약
	3) Predetermined targets결정의 주체, current market price는 전년도, 당해연도 또는 수년평균 연도를 사용할 것인지등을 clarify	0 자율성 확보에 중점 - 각국의 상이한 여건 고려
0 6항	0 신규 영농참여자에 대한 문제를 명확히 제기 - Base Period를 기준으로 한정 하고 있슴	0 모든 Direct Payment에 공통사항임

항목별 (이견제기분야)	아 국 입 장	사 유
0 7항 (i)	0 "taking into account .... agriculture" 삭제	0 재해손실은 농업손실뿐만 아니라 농가수익 손실이 그 대상이 되어야 함
(iii)	0 "relate 「solely」 to"의 "solely" 삭제	"
0 8항 (i)	0 "and shall be ..... period"를 "and be generally available to all agricultural producers in the designated disaster area" 로 수정	0 재해지역내의 모든 생산자를 보상대상으로 하여야 함
0 10항 (ii)	0 "for a minimum 10 years"삭제	0 단기 휴경의 경우도 허용정책에 포함
0 11항	0 (i)항과 (iv)항은 중복되므로 조정	
(v)	0 "designate the 「specific」 agricultural products"로 수정	0 엄격한 조건을 완화
4) Annex 5 0 1항	0 support which is.... in total monetary terms" 삭제	0 AMS의 본질적인 취지에 어긋남 - 다만, 협상추세에 따란 탄력적 대응
0 8항	0 8항을 다음과 같이 수정 - Market price support shall be calculated using govern- ment budgerary outlays paid to support the market price	0 제시된 계산방식은 국경보호를 통한 지지효과가 포함되이 있으며, 무역에 영향을 미치는 순수한 국내보조는 정부재정 지출임

- 6 -

0216

항목별 (이견제기분야)	아 국 입 장	사 유
0 9항	0 8항을 위와같이 수정할 경우 9항은 불필요	
0 10항 - 12항	0 10항을 다음과 같이 수정 "Non-exempt direct payment, including deficiency payment and like payments, shall be calculated using government budgetary outlays paid to prodcuer" - 11항 및 12항은 삭제	0 제시된 계산방식은 국경보호를 통한 지지효과가 포함되어 있으며, 무역에 영향을 미치는 순수한 국내보조는 정부재정 지출임
5) Annex 6 0 2항	0 "on the(administered) internal price..... where this is not practicable" 삭제	0 국내보조는 직접적인 재정지출이 감축대상이 되어야 함
6) Annex 7	0 Article 8항 검토의견 참조 0 조문구성 수정 , 8조2항의 감축 대상정책은 Annex로 처리	
7) Annex 8	0 5항에 draft working paper Annex 11의 1항을 추가하고 5항을 6항으로 함	0 원료 농산물의 수출보조를 시장 가격과 f.o.b 수출가와의 차이 내로 제한 포함

- 7 -

0217

외 무 부

종 별 : 지 급

번 호 : GVW-2676

일 시 : 91 12165 1950

수 신 : 장관(봉기,경기원,재무부,농림수산부,상공부,청와대 경제수석)

발 신 : 주 제네바 대사

제 목 : UR/농산물 협상

연: GVW-2659

1. 연호 공동제안 관련 12.16(월) 08:30 재개된 협의회에서 멕시코는 본국 훈령으로 참여할 수 없음을 밝혔고(멕시코의 예외없는 관세화 반대명문이 우리와상이하며, 특히 살리나사 대통령의 방미에 따른 미.멕시코 정상회담 결과가 영향을 미친 것으로 보임). 스위스는 갓트 33 조 예외조치에 대한 공동관심국인 멕시코가 참여하지 않을 경우 동 제안을 추진할 실익이 크지 않다는 소극적인 입장에 따라 4 개국 공동제안은 일단 무산되고 보다 많은 국가가 참여하고 있는 카나다측 제안에 공동 참여하면서, 각국의 개별적인 관심사항도 구체적으로 제기하는방안을 취하기로 하였음.

(멕시코 및스위스는 한국 및 일본과 공동보조를 취하는 정치적 대가가 너무크다고 판단한 것을 추측됨)2. 이에 따라 금 16(월) 15:00 본직 및 카나다, 이스라엘, 일본, 스위스, 노르웨이등 6 개국 대사가 던켈총장을 면담, 갓트 11 조 2항이 강화되어야 한다는 카나다측 제안을 서면 전달고 각국의 입장을 재삼 강조함.

- 동 기회에 본직은 아국은 동 조항 개선만으로는 불충분하며, 민감한 품목에 대한 관세화 예외가 반드시 인정되어야 한다는 점을 강조하였으며, 또한 던켈총장이 의장의 위치에서 어떤 것이 최선의 해결책인가를 판단하여 재량의 범위내에서 관심사항을 반영해 줌으로써 협상 결과가 정치적, 경제적, 사회적으로 이행가능한 내용이 되어야 할 것임을 재강조하였음.

- 던켈총장은 금일의 6 개국 DEMARCHE 가 마치 자기에게 주어지는 "최후봉첩" 같다고 전제하고 아국 및 스위스의 어려운 입장을 이해할 수 있다는 반응을 보이면서 반면 무역대국인 일본과 카나다의 태도에 대해서는 불만을 표시하였음.

- 동 총장은 또한 협상의 상대는 자신이 아니므로 미국, 케언즈 그룹등 국가를

통상국	장관	차관	1차보	2차보	외정실	분석관	청와대	안기부
경기원	재무부	농수부	상공부					

PAGE 1

직접 설득해야 할것이라는 입장을 재차 밝히면서 자기는 의장으로서 6 개국의 입장을 감안, 11 조 2(C) 의 삭제는 결코 제안하지 않겠다고 약속함으로써 일단 동 조항의 현상태로의 존치는 확실하게 되었음.

  3. 상기 2 항 관련 금 12.16(월) 17:00 개최된 표제 G-36 회의에서 먼저 카나다가 발언한후 일본, 아국, 스위스, 이스라엘, 놀웨이 순서로 지지 발언하였으며 아국은 동 11 조 개선지지 과정에서 아국의 입장은 단순히 11 조 2 항의 개선만으로 충족되는 것이 아니므로 합의초안 ANNEX 3 PARA 3 에 추가하여 FOOTNOTE 형식으로 아래와같이 개선할 것을 제안함

  " FOR EXCEPTIONALLY SENSITIVE AGRICULTURAL PRODUCTS WHICH SHOULD BE CAREFULLY CIRCUMSCRIBED, CONTRACTIING PARTIES MAY REQUEST A SPECIAL DEROGATION FROM TARIFFICATION AS PART OF THE FINALIZATION OF SCHEDULES OF MARKET ACCESS COMMITMENTS."

  4. 위와 같은 DEMARCHE 에 대하여 케언즈그룹을 비롯하여 많은 국가들은 관세화 예외 불인정의 입장을 재차 강조하고, 예외를 인정하면 PACKAGE 의 근본적인 근간이 붕괴됨을 강조함. 끝

  (대사 박수길-국장)

  예고:92.6.30 까지

PAGE 2

발 신 전 보

번　호 :

수　신 : 주　　제네바　　대사. 총영사//

발　신 : 장　관　（통 기）

제　목 : UR/농산물 협상

　　　　　　　　대 : GVW-2676

1. 대호, 4개국 공동 제안과 카나다 주동 11조 2(C) 관련 공동 제안이 동시에
　　검토되던중 카나다 안만이 채택 됨으로 인하여, 아국이 당초 이해관계국과의
　　공동 제안 추진을 통해 의도한바와는 달리 기초식량 또는 민감품목에 대한 예외
　　인정에 대하여는 관심이 ~~저조해지고 있는~~ 우리의 관심이고있는 반면 11조 2(C)에 대한 예외 인정
　　주장이 부각된 감이 없지 않음.

2. 예외없는 관세화와 관련, 아국으로서는 현시점에서 기초식량 또는 민감품목이
　　관세화의 예외로 인정되어야 한다는 점을 서면으로 분명히 제안해 두는 것이
　　중요하다고 판단되므로, 아국과 공동 제안이 가능한 국가들과 함께 ．
　　　　　　　우리의 입장을 어떤 형태로든 문서로 제시하는 방안을 검토, 조치
　　바라며, 이에 대해 특별한 의견이 있는 경우 보고바람.　　　　　　끝.

　　　　　　　　　　　　　　　　　　　　　　（차관　유종하）

0220

관리
번호 *91-949*

외 무 부

종 별 :

번 호 : SZW-0620

수 신 : 장 관(봉기)

발 신 : 주 스위스 대사

제 목 : UR 농산물 협상

일 시 : 91 1217 1800

대:WSZ-0494

연:SZW-0587

1. 연호관련, 스위스 정부는 현재 제네바 GATT, UR 협상 차원에서 윤곽이 밝혀지고 있는 농업협정 계획에 대한 예외조치를 획득하기 위하여 한국을 포함, 일본, 카나다, 이스라엘, 놀웨이 6 국이 공동데마쉐(DEMARCHES)를 취하고 있다고주재국 일간지 JOURNAL DE GENEVE 지가 12.17. 스위스 통신을 인용 보도하였음.

2. 동 보도에 의하면 스위스와 상기 5 국은 DUNKEL GATT 사무총장에게 농산품 수입장벽 통합관세화 분야에 대하여 적용을 배제하는 예외를 요청하는 한편 12.16. 자로 주요 농업국으로 구성된 36 국 그룹회의에 이와같은 예외신청을 제기하였다고함.

3. 동 관련기사는 정파편 송부하겠음. 끝

(대사 이원호-국장)

예고:91.12.31. 까지

통상국   장관   차관   1차보   2차보   분석관   청와대   안기부

PAGE 1

91.12.18   06:47

외신 2과 통제관 CA

0221

외 무 부

종   별 :

번   호 : GVW-2710   일   시 : 91 1218 1200

수   신 : 장 관(봉기, 경기원, 재무부, 농림수산부, 상공부, 보사부)

발   신 : 주 제네바대사

제   목 : UR/농산물 협상(위생 및 검역규제)

    12.17(화) 16:00 속개된 표제 위생 및 검역규제 전문가 회의에서는 합의초안 PARA 46과 47이 논의되었음.(최농무관, 김농무관보 참석)

    1. 개도국 우대(PARA 47)

    - 별첨 미국의 수정안에 대하여 이씨, 호주, 카나다, 북구, 일본등 대부분 국가가 지지하였음.

    - 우루과이, 브라질 및 멕시코는 미국 수정안을 수용할 수 있으나 UR 농산물 협상 전체의 개도국 우대와 연계시켜 검토해야 한다고 주장하였음.

    - 아국은 당초 위생 및 검역 규제분야는 여타분야와 달리 매우 기술적인 측면이 많으므로 개도국이 겪고있는 기술적 애로를 인정해야 한다고 하면서 당초 의장 문안(개도국에 차별없이 2년간 유예)을 지지한다고 하였으며 미국의 수정제안에 대해서는 검토할 용의가 있다고 하였음.

    2. 지방정부에 대한 적용(PARA 46)

    - 의장은 별첨 수정문안을 재시하면서 동문안은 TBT 합의 문안에 기초한 것으로서, 지방정부에 대하여 기본적으로 갓트 24조 12가 적용되지만 위생 및 검역규제 분야에서는 보다 구체적인 해석 기준을 제공하기 위한 것이라고 설명하였음.

    - 미국 및 카나다는 다소 불만을 표현하면서도 수용가능성을 시사하였고, 이씨는 완전한 적용이 필요하지만 타협안으로서 수용가능하다는 입장을 보였음.

    첨부: 미국 및 의장의 수정제안 각 1부

    (GVW(F)-0649).끝

    (대사 박수길-국장)

통상국	2차보	보사부	경기원	재무부	농수부	상공부	

PAGE 1   91.12.19   08:36 WH

주 제 네 바 대 표 부

번 호 : GVW(F) - 0648   년월일 : 11/2/18   시간 : 1200

수 신 : 장   관 (강관, 동기, 경기번, 재특북, 농련수산북, 상공북, 건사북)

발 신 : 주 제네바대사

제 목 : GUW-2710 첨부

총 4 매(표지포함)

보 안 봉 재	

외신과 봉 재	

16.12.91   Nordics

final

Draft "SPS3"

Annex I (pg 11)

4.   <u>Risk assessment</u> - The evaluation of the likelihood of entry,
establishment or spread of a pest or disease within the territory of an
importing contracting party according to the sanitary or phytosanitary
measures which might be applied, and of the associated potential biological
and economic consequences; or the evaluation of the potential adverse
effects on human or animal health arising from the presence of additives,
contaminants, toxins or disease-causing organisms in food, feedstuffs and
beverages.

0224

ANNEX I

17.12.91

의견

46. Contracting parties are fully responsible under this Decision for the observance of all of its provisions. Contracting parties shall formulate and implement positive measures and mechanisms in support of the observance of the provisions of this Decision by other than central government bodies.

46. Les parties contractantes sont pleinement responsables, en vertu de cette Décision, de l'observation de toutes ses dispositions. Les parties contractantes formuleront et mettront en oeuvre des mesures positives et des mécanismes destinés à favoriser l'observation des dispositions de cette Décision par les institutions autres que celles du gouvernement central.

46. En virtud de la presente Decisión, las partes contractantes son plenamente responsables de la observancia de todas las disposiciones. Las partes contractantes elaborarán y aplicarán medidas y mecanismos positivos que favorezcan la observancia de las disposiciones de la Decisión por las instituciones que no sean del gobierno central.

0225

6 4 p - 4 - 3

December 16, 1991

U S

FINAL COMPROMISE PROPOSAL AT THE LEVEL
OF THE SANITARY AND PHYTOSANITARY EXPERT GROUP

Paragraph 10 - Contracting parties may introduce or maintain
sanitary or phytosanitary measures which result in a higher
level of sanitary or phytosanitary protection than would be
achieved by measures based on the relevant international
standards, guidelines or recommendations, if there is a
scientific justification or as a consequence of the level of
protection a contracting party determines to be appropriate, in
accordance with the relevant provisions of paragraphs 15
through 23. Notwithstanding the above, ...

Paragraph 16 - ... prevalence or absence of specific diseases
or pests; relevant environmental conditions; and ....

Paragraph 29 - A contracting party operating a system for
approval of the use of food additives or for establishment of
tolerances for contaminants in food, feedstuffs or beverages
shall ensure that such system is operated in a manner
consistent with the provisions of this decision. The
contracting party operating such a system may, prior to
reaching a final approval determination based on a complete
application, prohibit or restrict access to its domestic
markets for products based on the absence of an approval
required by the importing contracting party. However, in such
circumstances and where a relevant international standard
exists, the importing contracting party should, after a
preliminary determination based on its review of data which
adequately demonstrate that the standard meets the importing
contracting party's acceptable level of protection, use the
international standard as the basis for permitting access until
a final determination on approval has been made.

Paragraph 47 - The least developed countries may delay the
application of the provisions of this decision for a period of
two years following the date of entry into force of this
decision with respect to their sanitary and phytosanitary
measures affecting importation or imported products. Developing
contracting parties may delay application of the provisions of
this decision, other than paragraphs 23 and 27, for 2 years
following the date of entry into force of this decision with
respect to their existing sanitary or phytosanitary measures
affecting importation or imported products where such
application is prevented by a lack of technical expertise,
technical infrastructure or resources

0226

647-4-4

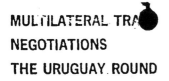
RESTRICTED

MTN.GNG/AG/W/6
18 December 1991

Special Distribution

Original: English

Group of Negotiations on Goods (GATT)
<u>Negotiating Group on Agriculture</u>

<u>ARTICLE XI:2(c)(i): STATEMENT BY CANADA, ISRAEL, JAPAN,
KOREA, NORWAY AND SWITZERLAND</u>

The following statement has been submitted by the above-mentioned
countries for circulation to participants in the agriculture negotiations.

———————

In the Ministerial Declaration at Punta del Este and reconfirmed at
the Mid-term Review, CONTRACTING PARTIES agreed that the negotiations shall
aim <u>inter alia</u> to achieve strengthened and more operationally effective
GATT rules and disciplines on agriculture.

We believe that comprehensive tariffication without exception should
not be considered as the only way to contribute to the expansion of
agricultural trade. While some of us have other reasons for having
proposed that there should be carefully circumscribed exceptions to the
concept of comprehensive tariffication, the following participants are
united in the view that, consistent with the agreed objectives of the
round, GATT Article XI:2(c)(i) must be strengthened and clarified and that
the provisions of the draft text on agriculture be modified to exclude from
tariffication trade measures taken consistent with Article XI.

GATT SECRETARIAT
UR-91-0181

0227

원 본

외 무 부

종 별 :

번 호 : GVW-2704   일   시 : 91 1218 1200

수 신 : 장관(봉기,경기원,재무부,농림수산부,상공부,청화대경제수석)

발 신 : 주 제네바 대사

제 목 : UR/농산물 협상(G-36)

    연: GVW-2676

    1. 12.16(월) 표제 G-36 회의는 연호 11 조 2 항 C 에 대한 공동 제안에 대한
논의에 이어 수출 보조 및 여타 분야에 대하여 논의하였는바, 요지 하기 보고함.

    (본직, 농림수산부 김차관보, 최심의관, 천농무관, 최농무관, 최부원장, 운사무관
참석)

    가. 수출 보조   필 (1991.12.31.

    0 미국은 수출 보조는 물량을 기준하여 감축해야 하며 재정 지출액은 보충적
기준으로 사용 가능하다는 입장을 제시하였으며 ANNEX 8 PARA. 11 수출 보조의
대상품목중 유지류와 유지막을 분리하고, 채소, 과일을 보다 세분화해야 하며,
생축(LIVE ANIMAL)과 담배를 추가할 것을 주장하였음.

    0 카나다, 브라질등 케언즈 그룹은 물량기준 감축과 단위당 보조액의 감축
TARGETING 금지를 강조하였음.

    0 EC, 스위스, 오스트리아는 재정 지출액을 기준으로 감축할수 있다는 입장을
제시하고 특히, EC 는 물량기준 감축은 기술적으로 불가능하다는 점을 강조하였음.

    0 멕시코, 이스라엘은 개도국의 경우 수출보조 분야에서 DE MINIMUS 원칙을
적용하고, 새로운 상품에 대한 수출 보조가 허용되어야 함을 제기하였음.

    0 인도, 파키스탄은 선진국 수출 보조의 완전 철폐가 이루어지지 않는한 전품목에
대한 관세양허는 불가하다는 입장을 강력히 주장하였음.

    0 아국은 수출 보조가 최우선적으로 해결되어야 할 과제임을 강조하고 물량과
금액이 동시에 감축되어야 하며, 시장접근에서 ANNEX 1 을 적용, 모든 품목을
포함하고 있으면서 수출 보조는 ANNEX 8 에서 품목범위를 별도로 제시한 것은
일관성과 균혀이 결여되어 있다는 점을 강조하고 모든 품목을 대상으로 해야 한다는

통상국	장관	차관	1차보	2차보	경제국	외정실	분석관	청와대
안기부	경기원	재무부	농수부	상공부				

애 의거 재분류(92.6.30.)
기의   성명 이명주

91.12.19   05:37
외신 2과 통제관 FM

0228

점을 제기하였음

0 일본은 수출 보조가 없는 나라와의 균형을 강조하고 새로운 상품에 대한 수출 보조는 명확히 금지되어야 한다는 점을 제기하였음.

　　나. 기타 사항

0 스위스는 동회의에서 DRAFT TEXT 에 대한 입장을 정리한 비공식 문서를 배포(별첨 참고)하고 관세화 예외에 33 조(가입의정서)의 포함, 특별 SAFEGUARD 발동시 국제가격 하락폭 만큼의 충분한 관세인상과 부패성있는 품목 PERISHERBLE PRODUCT 에 대한 융통성 부여, AMS 감축 약속시 인프레의 반영등을 강조하였음.

0 카나다는 동 스위스 제안과 관련, 특별 SAFEGUARD 의 항구화 및 100 % SNAP BACK 에 반대입장을 분명히 하였음.

2. 향후 협상 계획과 관련 던켈 총장은 18 일 밤까지 모든 협상 그룹의 TEXT 작성을 완료하는데 집중적인 노력을 할 것이나 비공식 협의는 계속해 나가야 겠다고 밝혔음.(추가적 회의 개최 여부에 대한 언급은 없었음.)

　첨부 DRAFT TEXT 에 대한 스위스 비공식 제안 1 부 끝

　(GVW(F)-647)

　(대사 박수길-국장)

　예고 92.6.30 까지

PAGE 2

0229

주 제 네 바 대 표 부

번 호 : GVW(F) - 0647   년월일 : 11218   시간 : 1200

수 신 : 장   판 (동기, 명가천, 재무부, 농린수산부, 상공부, 청와대경제수석)

발 신 : 주 제네바대사

제 목 : 첨부

총 4 매(표지포함)

보 안 통 제	께

외신과 통 제	

647-4-1

0230

SWISS DELEGATION　　　　　　　　　　Geneva, 15.12. 1991

COMMENTS TO THE DRAFT TEXT ON AGRICULTURE OF DECEMBRE 12 1991
(english version)

Without prejudice to our position concerning horizontal questions such as the followings:

- transitional periods,
- reduction formula for tariff reductions
- sequences for reduction steps
- binding commitments for tariffs
- notification and monitoring modalities
- minimal market access

which have to be dealt with in conformity wiht the Geneva (...) Protocol, we would like to submit the following proposals to the draft text on agriculture of decembre 12 1991:

1. Page 4, Footnote to Para 1 (i):

We propose to delete this footnote.

2. Page 5, Para 3:

We propose the following amendment:

"Any supplies of the product in question which were en route on the basis of a contract settled...."

3. Page 5, Para 5:

We propose the following wording:

" Any additonal duty imposed under sub-paragraph 1(ii) above shall not be levied at a level which exceeds the difference between the c.i.f. import price and the trigger price as defined under that sub-paragraph".　　*100 % Levy*

4. Page 5, Para 6:

We propose to delete the second sentence of this para (Any participant taking action under paragraph 1 (ii)....).

5. Page 6, Para 9:

We propose to delete this para.

641-K-2

0231

- 2 -

6. Page 7, Article 7, Para 3:

We propose the following wording:

"The domestic subsidies listed in Annex 4 to the....

7. Page 9, Para 2 (f):

We propose the following wording:

(...) in exported products, exceeding the difference between the domestic and world market price of the input.

8. Page 10, Para 1:

We propose the following amendment:

Subsidies granted (...) in exported products, exceeding the difference between the domestic and world market price of the input, shall be (...).

9. Page 13, Para 4, second line:

We propose to delete the words "of excessive rates".

10. Page 14, Para 4:

We propose to delete this para.

11. Page 17, Para 6, last line:

We propose the following amendment:

(...) shall be implemented in equal instalments, except as may be otherwise specified in a participant's schedule.

12. Page 17, Para 9, line six:

We propose the following amendment:

(...) shall be implemented in equal instalments, except as may be otherwise specified in a participant's schedule.

13. Page 20, Para 20:

We propose to delete this para. It is in contradiction to the General Agreement (availability to recourse to cvd).

641-쏘-3

0232

14. Page 25, Footnote to Para 1:

We propose the following wording:

*Measures maintained for balance-of-payments reasons or under general safegaurd and exception provisions (Articles XI, XII, XVIII, XIX, XX, XXI and other legal GATT-instruments negotiated under Article XXXIII) shall not be subject to the relevant provisions of this text.

15. Page 25, Para 3, second line:

We propose the following amendment:

(...) subject to border measures as defined in Para 1...

16. Page 33, Para 7 (ii), first and second line:

We propose to delete the words "less than ... per cent"

17. Page 35, Para 10 (ii), second line:

We propose a minimum of 5 years, instead of 10 years.

18. Page 35, Para 10 (iii), third line:

We propose to delete the words "for whatever end use".

19. Page 42, Para 1 (f):

We propose the following amendment:

(...) exceeding the difference between the domestic and world market price of the input.

20. Page 45, Para 13:

We propose the following amendment:

(...) exceeding the difference between the domestic and world market price of the input.

647-4-4

0233

관리
번호 91-216

원 본

외 무 부

종 별 : 지급

번 호 : ECW-1132

일 시 : 91 1218 1730

수 신 : 장관 (봉기, 경기원, 재무부, 농림수산부, 상공부)

발 신 : 주 EC 대사 사본: 주 미, 제네바-본부중계필

제 목 : GATT/UR 협상

연: ECW-1125

1. 12.17. 저녁 MADIGAN 미 농무장관은 EC 의 MACSHARRY 집행위원과 표제협상의 걸림돌이 되고있는 농산물 분야에대해 양자협상을 갖기위해 서둘러 브랏셀에 도착했음. 당초 동인은 12.21. 개최되는 미-EC 각료회의에 맞추어 하루전인 12.20. 당지를 방문할 것으로 알려졌으나, 미-EC 정상간의 전화접촉과 DUNKEL GATT 사무총장이 표제협상의 그룹별 의장 PAPER 제출시한을 12.18. 자정으로 설정한후, 동인의 브랏셀 방문일정을 바꾸었다 함

2. 한편, 12.18. 오전 양측 농무장관들은 회동한바, 회담결과에 대해서는 아직 알려지고 있지 않으나, EC 집행위 관계관들은 양인의 회담은 DUNKEL 총장이설정한 시한에 구애됨이 없이 미-EC 각료회의시 까지 계속될 것이며, 양측간에합의가 되지않은 수출보조감축 방법과 REBALANCING 문제가 집중 논의될 것이라함. 회담결과에 대해서는 EC 집행위 관계관등을 접촉한후 추보하겠음

3. 당지 언론에의하면 12.18. 불란서의 CRESSON 총리는 DUNKEL PAPER 에 농산물등 모든 분야에 EC 의 관심사항이 적절히 반영되지 않을 경우, 자국은 동 PAPER 를 검토하기 위해 개최되는 12.23. EC 일반이사회에서 이를 거부할 것이라고 밝혔다 함. 끝

(대사 권동만-국장)

예고: 92.6.30 까지

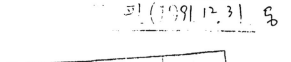

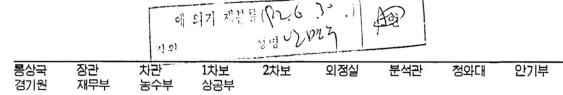

통상국	장관	차관	1차보	2차보	외정실	분석관	정와대	안기부
경기원	재무부	농수부	상공부					

PAGE 1

91.12.19 06:18

외신 2과 통제관 CA

0234

외 무 부

종 별 :

번 호 : GVW-2708   일 시 : 91 1218 1500

수 신 : 장 관(봉기, 경기원, 재무부, 농림수산부, 상공부, 청와대경제수석)

발 신 : 주 제네바대사

제 목 : UR/농산물 협상

연: GVW-2697

연호 김차관보의 던켈 총장 면담 결과를 하기보고함.

(김대사, 최심의관, 천농무관, 윤사무관 배석)

1. 김차관보는 한국은 쌀등 특수 품목에 대한 정치적 어려움 때문에 예외없는 관세화를 수용하기 어렵다는 점을 설명하고 12.20 최종협상안에 이와 같은 핵심적 관심사항이 반영되어야 한다는 것을 강조하였음.

2. 던켈 총장은 한국의 어려운 입장은 이해하며, 금일 오후에 한국의 수정제안 요청을 접수하였으며, 이를 검토해 보겠으나 특히 한개품목이라도 예외를 인정할 경우 미국의 설탕등 WAIVER 품목, 스위스의 치즈 및 EC 의 가변부과금등에 대한 예외도인정해야 한다는 문제가 있으므로 한국의 특수사정만 인정하기는 곤란하다고 말함.

특히 동 총장은 미국, EC 등 다른 국가들이 이미 기본적으로 예외없는 관세화에의견 접근하고 있음을 지적하면서 협상의 상대는 자신이 아니고 참가국이라고 말하였음.

3. 이에 대해 김차관보는 한국은 이제 구조조정의 착수단계에 있는 만큼 구조조정이 이미 완료된 미국, EC 와 동일한 선상에서 비교해서는 안된다는 점을 강조하였으나 던켈 총장은 한국은 OECD의 옵서버 참여를 신청할 정도의 경제력을 갖고 있는나라로서 선진국에 자동차등을 수출하고 있는점을 이해하고 임해야 한다고 지적하였음.

4. 던켈 총장은 이어 최소시장 개방은 완전개방을 의미하지 않으므로 예를 들면한국의 국내 쌀 소비량의 3 퍼센트를 개방한다면 550만톤중 165 천톤인바, 이는 경제적인 부담이 매우 적은 것이며 또한 관세화는 보호 장치가 완전히 없어지는 것이

통상국   2차보   청와대   안기부   경기원   재무부   농수부   상공부

PAGE 1

아니라고 하였으나, 김차관보는 이에 대해 3 퍼센트의 개방에 그치는 것이 아니고 궁극적으로는 모든 시장이 개방될수 밖에 없을것이라는 점을 강조하였음.

5. 끝으로 김차관보는 쌀 개방반대 1,000 만인서명운동 전개등 우리의 어려운 입장을 재차 강조하고 아국 요청의 반영을 당부하였음.

6. 참고로 던켈 총장은 만일 한국의 반대로 협상초안을 내지 못한다고 말할 때에다른 나라들이 어떻게 대처하겠는가를 생각해야 한다고 말하는 것으로 보아 금요일에 제시될 협상 초안에 예외없는 관세화를 포함하는 초안이 제시될 것으로 사료됨. 끝

(대사 박수길-국장)

관리 번호	91-24

외 무 부

종 별 :

번 호 : GVW-2697 　　　　　　　　　　일 시 : 91 1218 1000

수 신 : 장관(통기, 경기원, 재무부, 농림수산부, 상공부, 청와대경제수석)

발 신 : 주 제네바 대사

제 목 : UR/농산물 협상(서면제안)

　　　연: GVW-2676

　　　대: WGV-1850

　　　대호 서면제안 관련, <u>12.17</u>(화) 16:00 민감품목에 대한 관세화 예외가 인정되야 한다는 요지의 별첨 합의초안 수정 제안을 서면으로 던켈 총장에게 전달하였음.

　　　한편 동 12.17(화) 20:30 농림수산부 김한곤 차관보는 던켈 총장을 면담, 동 수정제안 제출 배경과 예외없는 관세화에 대한 아국 입장을 재강조하였음.

　　　첨부: 합의초안 수정 제안 및 관련 서한 1 부. 끝

　　　(GVW(F)-642)

　　　(대사 박수길-국장)

　　　예고: 92.6.30 까지

통상국	장관	차관	1차보	2차보	외정실	분석관	청와대	안기부
경기원	재무부	농수부	상공부					

PAGE 1 　　　　　　　　　　　　　　　　　91.12.18　　19:23

　　　　　　　　　　　　　　　　　　　외신 2과 통제관 BW

　　　　　　　　　　　　　　　　　　　　　　0237

주 제 네 바 대 표 부

번 호 : GVW(F) - 642   년월일 : 112.18   시간 : 18:00

수 신 : 장   관 (통기, 경기원, 재무부, 농림수산부, 상공부, 청와대경제수석)

발 신 : 주 제네바대사

제 목 : "천복"

총 3 매(표지포함)

보 안 통 제	천

| 외신과 통 제 | |

0238

642-7-1

PERMANENT MISSION OF THE REPUBLIC OF KOREA
GENEVA

17 December 1991

Dear Mr. Dunkel,

As you may recall, I put forward a specific proposal at the informal meeting of the group of 36 yesterday, reflecting the bottom line position of the Korean government aimed at seeking a derogation from tariffication concerning a few sensitive agricultural products of our vital concern.

Since yesterday's meeting was an informal one, I have been instructed by my government to submit a formal proposal as attached.

Your cooperation and assistance in this regard would be greatly appreciated.

Sincerely yours,

PARK, Soo Gil
Ambassador

H.E. Mr. Arthur DUNKEL
Director General
GATT
Centre William Rappard
154, rue de Lausanne
1211 - GENEVE 21

0239

642-3-2

December 17, 1991

Proposed Amendment to the Draft Text on Agriculture
of December 12, 1991

Korea proposes the following amendment to the Draft Text on Agriculture of December 12, 1991:

Footnote to paragraph 3, Annex 3 shall be added as follows:

"For exceptionally sensitive agricultural products which should be carefully circumscribed, participants may request a special derogation from tariffication as part of the finalization of schedules of market access commitments."

0240

642-3-3

관리
번호 91-960

외 무 부

종   별 :

번   호 : GVW-2711   일   시 : 91 1218 1900

수   신 : 장관(통기, 경기원, 재무부, 농림수산부, 상공부)

발   신 : 주 제네바 대사

제   목 : UR/농산물 협상

1. 12.18(수) 표제 협상 합의초안 수정제안을 갓트 사무국에 전달하였음.

(동 사본 별첨 FAX 송부함)

2. 김한곤 농림수산부 차관보는 동 12.18 BISLEY 뉴질랜드 대사 및 KAMAL 파키스탄 대사와 오찬(본직초대), 아국 농업의 어려운 실정을 설명하고 특히 쌀에 대해서는 관세화는 물론 최저시장 접근도 허용할수 없는 입장임을 강조하고 협조를 요청하였음.

첨부: 합의 초안 수정 제안 사본 1 부. (GVW(F)-650)

(대사 박수길-국장)

예고 92.6.30 까지

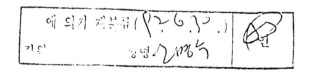

통상국   장관   차관   1차보   2차보   외정실   분석관   청와대   안기부
경기원   재무부   농수부   상공부

PAGE 1   91.12.19   07:32
                                                        외신 2과 통제관 BD
                                                              0241

UR(우루과이라운드) 농산물 협상 그룹 회의, 1991. 전7권(V.7 12월) 247

주 제 네 바 대 표 부

번 호 : GVR(F) -650   년월일 : 1.12.18   시간 : 1800

수 신 : 장   관 (통기, 명기5면, 2세속부, 홀린수산부. 상경부)

발 신 : 주 제네바대사

제 목 : ˋ 첸복 ˝

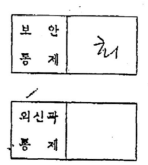

총 3 매(표지포함)

650-3-1

Proposals for amendment to the Draft Text on Agriculture
of December 12, 1991

In order to achieve a balanced, equitable final package
of results in the agricultural negotiation, Korea proposes
the following amendments to the Draft Text on Agriculture
of December 12, 1991 :

1. Page 17, paragraph 7 :
   - Delete first sentence.
   - Second sentence is amended as follows :
     "Specific binding commitments of all custom
     duties, including those resulting from
     tariffication shall be negotiated on the basis
     of the reduction commitment, base and
     implementation periods as outlined in paragraph
     3, through request and offer."

2. Page 18, paragraph 14 :
   - amend as follows :
     "Developing countries shall have the flexibility
     to select rates of reduction in the areas of
     market access, domestic support and export
     competition, and to select the level of minimum
     market access provided that the rate of
     reductions is no less than .... percent of that
     specified in paragraph 3. The implementation
     period may be extended for developing countries
     by up to .... years."

0243

3. Page 19, paragraph 16 :
   - add the following after the present sentence.
     "In the case of clearly defined sensitive products, such as basic foodstaples which are an integral part of the agricultural and rural development programmes, developing countries shall have the flexibility to negotiate specific binding commitments on market access indicated in paragraph 7 and in Annex 3 on the basis of national offer."

4. Page 25, Add a Footnote to paragraph 1 :
   "Measures maintained for balance of payments reasons or under general safeguard, exception provisions (Articles XI, XII, XVIII, XIX, XX, and XXI), shall not be subject to the relevant provisions of this text."

5. Page 25, paragraph 3 :
   - Add the following footnote to pargraph 3 : "For exceptionally sensitive agricultural products which should be carefully circumscribed, participants may request a special derogation from tariffication as part of the finalization of schedules of market access commitments.

6. Page 30, paragraph 2 (vii) :
   - Insert the following :
     dams and drainage, and land consolidation schemes, and infrastructural works....

650 -3-3

長官報告事項

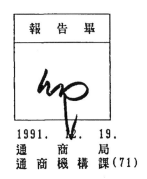
題 目 : UR/農産物 協商 關聯 我國 對應

12.17-18 주 제네바 代表部는 UR/農産物 協商 關聯 敏感品目에 대한 關稅化 例外 認定 提案과 12.12자 協定 草案 文案에 대한 修正 提案을 我國 單獨으로 Dunkel 갓트 事務總長 및 갓트 事務局에 각각 書面 傳達 하였는바, 關聯 事項을 아래와 같이 報告 드립니다.

---

1.   敏感品目에 대한 關稅化 例外 認定 提案 (12.17 提出)

  ○ 關稅化 協商 過程에서 敏感品目에 대한 關稅化 例外가 認定되도록 旣存 協定 草案上의 關稅化 例外(BOP, 國家安全 保障上의 例外) 項目에 別途 條項 新設 提案

2.   其他 修正 提案 (12.18 提出)

  ○ 上記 關稅化 例外 認定 內容에 追加하여 下記 我國 立場 提案

    - R/O 協商에 의한 關稅 및 TE 減縮

    - 最小 市場接近 水準에 대한 開途國 優待 規定

    - 開途國 農業 및 地域發展에 必須的인 基礎食糧等 敏感品目에 대한 市場接近 關聯 協商時 融通性 附與

    - 耕地 整理를 위한 國內補助는 許容補助로 分類

3.   國會 및 言論對策 : 當部 別途 措置 不要.   끝.

0245

長官 報告事項

報 告 畢

1991. 12. 19.
通　商　局
通 商 機 構 課(71)

題 目 : UR/農産物 協商 關聯 我國 對應

12.17-18 주 제네바 代表部는 UR/農産物 協商 關聯 敏感品目에 대한 關稅化 例外 認定 提案과 12.12자 協定 草案 文案에 대한 修正 提案을 我國 單獨으로 Dunkel 갓트 事務總長 및 갓트 事務局에 각각 書面 傳達 하였는바, 關聯 事項을 아래와 같이 報告 드립니다.

---

1. 敏感品目에 대한 關稅化 例外 認定 提案 (12.17 提出)

   ○ 關稅化 協商 過程에서 敏感品目에 대한 關稅化 例外가 認定되도록 既存 協定 草案上의 關稅化 例外(BOP, 國家安全 保障上의 例外) 項目에 別途 條項 新設 提案

2. 其他 修正 提案 (12.18 提出)

   ○ 上記 關稅化 例外 認定 內容에 追加하여 下記 我國 立場 提案

   - R/O 協商에 의한 關稅 및 TE 減縮

   - 最小 市場接近 水準에 대한 開途國 優待 規定

   - 開途國 農業 및 地域發展에 必須的인 基礎食糧等 敏感品目에 대한 市場接近 關聯 協商時 融通性 附與

   - 耕地 整理를 위한 國內補助는 許容補助로 分類

3. 國會 및 言論對策 : 當部 別途 措置 不要.　　　　　　끝.

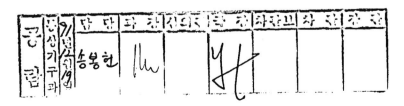

0246

외　무　부

종　별 :

번　호 : GVW-2744　　　　　　　　　일　시 : 91 1219 2000

수　신 : 장 관(봉기, 경기원, 재무부, 농림수산부, 상공부)

발　신 : 주 제네바 대사

제　목 : UR/농산물 협상

　　멕시코 및 이집트의 표제 협상 관련 제안을 별첨FAX 송부함.

　　멕시코는 예외없는 관세화에 대한 입장을 갓트문서로 배포되도록 사무국에 요청하
였고, 이집트는 순수입 개도국과 관련된 합의 초안수정 제안을 주요 협상 참여국에 FAX
로배포하였음.

　　첨부: 멕시코 및 이집트의 농산물 협상 제안 각1부. 끝

　　(GVW(F)-662)

　　(대사 박수길-국장)

통상국　　구주국　　경기원　　재무부　　농수부　　상공부

PAGE 1　　　　　　　　　　　　　　　　　　91.12.20　　21:01 FL

　　　　　　　　　　　　　　　　　　　　외신 1과　통제관

　　　　　　　　　　　　　　　　　　　　　　　　　0247

주제네바대표부

번 호 : GVW(F) - *662*   년월일 : *1121P*   시간 : *1P00*

수 신 : 장   관 (동기.경기원. 재무부. 농림수산부, 낭무부)

발 신 : 주 제네바대사

제 목 : *Gvw -2744*

총 *5* 매 (표지포함)

보 안 통 제	*훤*

외신과 통 제	

662-5-1

Egyptian comments on the Draft Text on Agriculture (12-12-91)

<u>Article (5)</u>, Page 4, footnote to paragraph 1 (1):
We propose to delete this footnote.

<u>Article (8)</u>, page 8, paragraph 1, we propose to delete the words " and / or markets "
in the fifth line.
- Paragraph 2 (b), we propose to add " except food aid transactions "
at end of the paragraph .

<u>Article (15)</u>,
- Paragraph 1: the word " Declaration " should be substituted by
" Ministerial Decision "
- Paragraph 2 should read : " The Ministerial Decision shall form an
integral part of this agreement ".
- A new paragraph "3" to be added as follows :
3. Given the negative effects of the reform process on them, net food-
importing developing countries should be given flexibility with
respect to reduction commitments in market access ares .

<u>Page 18</u>, <u>Paragraph 12</u>: We propose to delete the second sentence which reads " Under-
takings may also include commitments limiting the scope of subsidies
on exports of agricultural products as regards individual or regional
markets.". And to delete the words " or markets " from the third sentence
as such.

<u>Page 19</u>, paragraph 18" b" : We propose this paragraph should read as follows :
Domestic support to producers to encourage production diversification,
including from the growing of illicit narcotic crops.

<u>Page 45</u>
- Paragraph 11 : We propose to add cotton to the mentioned list.

Part D   Page 47, Draft Declaration.We propose to substitute the word " Declaration " by the word " Ministerial Decision."
- Paragraph 1. We propose to add " according to their various stages of
development.". at the end of the paragraph.
- Paragraph 2: We propose to add " due to possible rise in world food
prices", at the end of the paragraph.
- Paragraph 3 (I) : should read as follows :
" to review the level of food aid established periodicaly by the
committee on Food Aid under the Food Aid Convention and to initiate
negotiations in the appropriate forum with a view to ensure additional
level of food aid commitments sufficient to meet the legitimate needs
of NFIDCs and LDCs during the reform programme;

0249

Paragraph 3. (II) We proppose to add "/and " at the end of the third line.

Paragraph 3. (III) Should read as follows :
    To give full consideration on the context of their aid programme to
    requests for the provision of additional technical and
    financial assistance to least developed and net food-importing
    developing countries to improve their agricultural productivity and
    infrastructure.

Paragraph 4: Should read as follows :

    Participants further agree to ensure that any agreement relating to
    agriculture export credits, should provide for differential and more
    favourable treatment to least developed and net food-importing developing
    countries.
Paragraph 5: The first sentence should read as follows :
    Participants recognize that as a result of the Uruguay Round in general,
    and the reform process of the world trade in agriculture in particular,
    least developed countries and net food-importing developing countries
    may experience short-term difficulties in financing normal levels of
    commercial imports and that these countries may be eligible to draw
    on the resources of international financial institutions under existing
    facilities in the context of adjustment programmes, or under the time-
    bound window established during the reform process, in order to offset
    the negative effects thereof on these countries.

662-5-3

0250

COMMUNICATION FROM MEXICO

On the scope of tariffication

The Government of Mexico was one of the first participants in the Uruguay Round negotiations to fully endorse the concept of tariffication, as an expedient and valuable element in the agricultural negotiation.   Tariffs are more transparent than licensing systems or quantitative restrictions.   They also lend themselves more readily to negotiation.   Nevertheless, special circumstances may exist where general truths cease to apply, and the general goodness of tariffication is no exception to this.

Tolerance, accommodation and consensus are the basis of cooperation.   In most areas of the Round, both traditional and new, Mexico would prefer -or be in a position to agree- to more "pure" provisions, or more ambitious levels of commitments, than other participants can accept.   But we work on the conviction that ambition must be tempered by flexibility, and by mutual acceptance of the individually possible.   On no subject do we insist on pressing beyond the level of tolerance of any party in the negotiation.

Mexico's commitment to the market mechanism, to liberalization and to the letter and spirit of the GATT is wholly unquestionable.   Starting from the most multilaterally-committed terms any member had adopted upon its accession, the country has continued vigorously with its far-reaching program of economic reform across the board, inter alia going well beyond its GATT commitments through unilateral liberalization of all sectors, including agriculture.

Mexico negotiated, as a central element of its accession to GATT, a protocol that entitled it to retain non-tariff border measures on around 300 products, as a then-necessary instrument to help conduct the sector gradually towards a new day.   Acting on its own, the country in the meantime has eliminated 80% of those measures, negotiated only five years ago.

Mexico wants to continue decidedly with this process, and negotiate constructively in relation to access in all agricultural products: the country is ready to tariffy most of its remaining non-tariff instruments, negotiated and fully permitted under its protocol, and more importantly, to positively negotiate access in both its tariffied and non-tariffied products, as well as across-the-board tariff reductions.   The reason universal tariffication in the current Round poses fundamental problems to it is not at all to defend an unchanging situation. All the contrary: it is precisely because the country

0251

is engaged in a comprehensive, deep modernization of this sector of its economy, which goes well-beyond trade and internal price policy and will bring the sector fully into the new Mexico that its Government has striven to build over the last ten years.

Similar exceptions to those, limited ones, that Mexico demands have already been agreed for other measures, such as those taken under articles XII, XVIII, XIX and others, which like those that Mexico requires are not price-based and have both legal and substantive justification. Mexico, as a developing country with a thoroughly well-established readiness to assume its obligations, in the past and in the Round, in this and in all sectors, requires this limited, well-circumscribed measure of flexibility to support and not to avoid its movement forward.

In conclusion, it is with the greatest attention that the Mexican authorities will receive and read the document to be tabled on 20/12/91. Mexico expects finally to find due understanding to one of its few limitations in this negotiation. Mexico has already suggested how its concerns can be accommodated without disrupting the main thrust of this aspect of the negotiation. Mexico is respectful of other participants' economic or political constraints, and expects on that score full reciprocity.

관리
번호 *91-371*

원 본

외 무 부

종   별 : 지 급

번   호 : ECW-1155   일   시 : 91 1220 1920

수   신 : 장관 (봉기, 경기원, 재무부, 농림수산부, 상공부)

발   신 : 주 EC 대사 사본: 주 미, 제네바-중계필

제   목 : GATT/UR 협상

연: ECW-1149

1. 12.18-20 개최된 미-EC 간 농업보조금 문제에대한 양자간 합의도출에 일단 실패한 (BREAKDOWN) 것으로 알려짐. 12.20 오후 늦게까지 계속된 MACSHARRY 집행위원과 MADIGAN 농무장관간의 회담이 끝난후, EC 집행위 관계관은 동 회담에서 양자간 이견을 좁히는데 실패하였다고 전제하고, 이러한 실패가 일시적인 것인지 또는 합의도출이 아주 불가능한 것인지는 알수 없으며, 12.21. 개최되는 정례 미-EC 각료회담에서 이러한 상황이 호전될 가능성은 거의 없다고 말함. 한편, MADIGAN 장관은 동 회담성과에 대한 기자들의 질문에대해 무엇이라 답변해야 좋을지 모르겠으며, 아주 어려운 상황에 이르렀다고 언급함

2. 동 농무장관 회담과는 별도로 당지를 방문중인 HILLS 미 무역대표는 ANDRIESSEN 부위원장과 회담을 가진후 동 회담에서 UR 협상 전망에 대하여 자기로서는 낙관적으로 볼수 있는 입장이 아니라고 말함

3. 동건 양자회담 상세 결과및 12.21. 개최되는 미-EC 각료회담 결과에 대해서는 추보하겠음. 끝

(대사 권동만-국장)

예고: 92.6.30 까지

필 (1991.12 31.)

예 의기 개봉(92.6. 30.)
기안   성명

통상국	장관	차관	2차보	구주국	분석관	청와대	안기부	경기원
재무부	농수부	상공부	중계					

PAGE 1

91.12.21   06:11
외신 2과 통제관 FM
0253

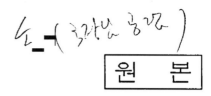

외 무 부

종 별 :

번 호 : GVW-2758   일 시 : 91 1220 1720

수 신 : 장관(통기, 경기원, 상공부, 재무부, 농림수산부, 청와대경제수석)

발 신 : 주 제네바 대사

제 목 : UR/농산물 협상(전체 비공식회의)

12.19(금) 11:00 개최된 표제 전체 비공식 회의에서 본직은 동 회의가 초안이 제시되기 직전에 개최되는 마지막 전체 회의라는 증요성을 감안하여 아국의 입장을 다시한번 강조하였는바 요지 하기 보고함.(농림수산부 김차관보, 외무부최심의관, 천농무관, 최농무관 참석)

1. 던켈 총장 언급요지

- 던켈 총장은 브럿셀 각료회의 이후 협상진행을 간략히 설명하면서 그동안 TRANSPARENCY확보에 노력해 왔음을 강조하였음.

- 특히 대안문서, ADDENDA, 작업 문서초안, 합의초안 순으로 제시된 문서의 성격과 특징을설명하면서 금일중에 제시될 예정인 최종합의초안(DRAFT AGREEMENT)은 최대한 형평을 유지한 것이므로 각국이 내용을 세밀히 검토하여 1.13. TNC 때 입장을 밝혀줄것을 요청하면서 즉각적, 감정적 반응을 자제해 달라고 당부하였음.

2. 각국 발언 요지

- 일본은 수출입국간, 협상 요소간, 여타 협상그룹간의 균형이 유지되어야 한다고하고 포괄적 관세화에 대한 깊은 우려를 표명하면서, 각국의 핵심 관심사항이 합의초안에 반영되어야 한다고 발언하였음.

- 카나다는 갓트 11조의 유지 개설 필요성과 예외없는 관세화에 대한 불만을 표명 하였음.

- 본직은 금일 제시될 합의초안이 균형되어야 하고 각국이 정치, 경제, 사회적으로수용 가능한 것이되어야 한다고 전제하고, 아국의 쌀문제는 쌀문화 권역국가의 특유한 역사 문화 전통의 불가결의 일부분으로서 단순한 경제 무역 차원을 초월하는 중요한 의미를 가짐으로 쌀은 결코 관세화의 대상으로 할수 없다는 아국의 기본입장을다시한번 강조하였음.

통상국	2차보	외정실	분석관	청와대	안기부	경기원	재무부	농수부
상공부								

PAGE 1   91.12.21   09:16 BX

외신 1과 통제관

0254

또한 공산품의 경우는 40년이상 다자간 협상을거쳐 현수준의 시장접근이 이루어졌음을 지적하면서 농산물의 경우 현실을 무시하고 너무 조급하게 개혁을 추진하면 오히려 부작용이 생기게 된다는점을 제기하면서, 특히 민감한 품목에 대해서는 관세화대상에서 제외될 수 있도록 합의초안에 융통성을 인정해 줄것을 요청하였음.

  - 스위스는 기존 입장을 간단히 언급하였고 멕시코는 예외없는 관세화를 수용하기 어렵다는요지의 COMMUNICATION 을 배포하였음을 발언하였음.끝

  (대사 박수길-국장)

외 무 부

종 별 :

번 호 : USW-6374   일 시 : 91 1220 1836

수 신 : 장 관(봉기,경기원,농수산부,경제수석) 사본:주제네바,주EC대사(직송필)(

발 신 : 주 미 대 사

제 목 : UR 협상

대: WUS-5781

12.20 자 INSIDE U.S. TRADE 지는 12.12 제네바에서 비공식으로 제시된 DUNKEL 사무총장의 협상안시안 내용을 설명하면서, 농산물등 주요 분야협상에 대한 주요국의 반응 및 동향을 아래요지로 보도하였는 바, 대체로 UR 타결전망이 점점 어두어지고 있음을 시사하고 있음.(보도내용별첨)

1. 농산물 협상안 시안 내용중 특이사항

. 전반적으로 EC 의 주장내용이 많이 반영됨. (PEACE CLAUSE 취지도입등)

. 미- EC 간 최대 쟁점인 각종 보조금의 GREENBOX 포함 문제는 원칙적으로 이러한 보조금을 엄격한 기준하에서 나마 GREEN BOX 에 포함시키는 방향으로 절충

2. 미국 농업계 반응

. AMERICAN FARM BUREAU FEDERATION 등 15개 농업관련 단체들은 12.18자 부시 대통령앞 연서서한을 봉하여, DUNKEL 총장 시안내용은 미국의 국익에 최선의 것이 못된다고 하면서 이를 거부할것을 촉구함.

. 반면에 곡물업자단체들은 동 협상안 시안이 만족할 만한 것은 못된다고 하면서도 최족적인 협상결과가 나올때 까지는 입장표명을 보류한다는 태도를 표명

3. 미국정부 반응

. HILLS 미 무역대표는 12.20 제시될 협상안이 부분적으로는 만족치 못하더라도, 불만스러운 부분을 모두 수정하려 하는 것은 합의도달을 불가능하게 만들 것이므로 가급적 협상안의 골격을 유지하면서 필수적인 수정만 해나가는 것이 바람직하다고지적, DUNKEL 총장의 괄호없는 협상안에 대한계속적 지지를 표명

4. EC 내 반응

. 프랑스는 DUNKEL 총장 협상안에 대한 반대의사를 분명히 하고 있으며,

통상국   2차보   청와대   경기원   농수부

PAGE 1   91.12.21   09:46 WG

외신 1과 통제관

0256

아일랜드도 이에 동조하고 있으나, 화란등은 동 협상안을 지지하고있는 것으로 알려짐.

. 여사한 EC 내 의견차는 12.23 EC 집행위회의시 집중적으로 협의될 것으로 예상됨.

. 한편, 프랑스는 명년말 미국의 대통령 선거를 거친 후에 UR 협상을 재론토록하고, 그 사이에 EC 도 CAP 개혁에 관하여 내부적 합의에 도달할 수 있지 않겠느냐하는 의견을 비공식적으로 타진하고 있는 것으로 알려짐.

5. 기타 협상분야 동향

. 미국은 기초통신분야를 UR 서비스협상의 예외로 한다는 종전의 입장을 수정상호주의에 입각하여 국내 기본통신분야에 대한 외국의 참여를 허용한다는 입장을 지난 12.18에 제시함.

. 이러한 서비스분야에서의 미측의 양보는 농산물분야에서의 미측의 입장을 강화시키기 위한 의도에서 취해진 것으로 분석되고 있음.

(대사 현홍주-국장)

USWF-5676 (11 매)

주 미 대 사 관

USW (F) : *5676*   년월일 :   시간 :

수 신 : 장   관 (통기, 통이, 통남) 사본, 차관보, 기개인, 제신부 | 보 | 안 |
                                                                      | 통 | 제 |

발 신 : 주 미 대 사

제 목 : UR 협상타결, 미국통신서비스분야에서 양보

USW (F) - 6374 참조   (출처 :   )

INSIDE U.S. TRADE - December 20, 1991

U.S. CONCEDES ON TELECOM SERVICES, BUSH LOBBIES EC LEADERS ON FARM REFORM

Administration efforts to ensure a successful conclusion of the Uruguay Round this week focused on pressuring the European Community at the highest political levels to make further concessions in agriculture, and included abandoning U.S. demands for an exemption of basic telecommunications services from a services agreement.

In addition, the U.S. apparently made concessions on the issue of regional development subsidies in the subsidies negotiations of the General Agreement on Tariffs & Trade, but continued to hold the line on changes to antidumping rules, U.S. private-sector sources said. Progress in the areas of antidumping and subsidies is related to the overall Uruguay Round deal, one informed source said. If the overall Uruguay Round deal as it emerges this week appears minimal to Congress, the pressure on the Administration to stonewall changes in the antidumping and subsidies laws will increase, he pointed out. Separately, U.S. industry sources reported a breakthrough in the standards area.

In addition, textile negotiators ended their efforts at striking a deal on Dec. 18 without resolving crucial issues. They did not reach agreement at the rate at which textile and apparel should be integrated into the GATT, and the extent to which access to the market should grow, according to a U.S. industry source. These decisions will be left to GATT director general Arthur Dunkel who is certain to make an offer that is more favorable to exporters than what was in the Chairman's draft text last year, according to the source.

The draft textile agreement, as it was forwarded to Dunkel, includes a safeguard provision and a provision on fighting quota fraud, he said. At the insistence of India and Pakistan it does not include a market access provision and stipulates that market access negotiations have to be conducted in the market access group.

Negotiators in that group reached an agreement on the protocol on market access that will be included in the final Uruguay Round draft agreement. The protocol will cover the deals of GATT members on cuts in tariffs and non-tariff barriers that will be negotiated in 1992. The agreement on tariffs stipulates that they will be cut in equal annual reductions starting Jan. 1, 1993 to be completed by Jan. 1, 1997, sources said.

(5176 - 11 - 1) | 외신 1과 | |
                       | 통   제 | |

0258

To break the impasse in the services negotiations, the U.S. formally offered on Dec. 18 to extend most favored nation treatment (MFN) to foreign telecommunications companies provided their home countries would allow competition in their international and domestic long-distance services. Until that time, the U.S. would maintain its derogation from MFN treatment of telecommunications suppliers, according to a Dec. 18 public statement. The offer is a clear challenge to the EC, Canada and Japan, which have been pressing the U.S. to drop its demand for an MFN derogation on basic telecommunications services. With the U.S., these three trading partners would constitute the critical mass of markets that would be needed to make the MFN concession offered by the U.S. meaningful, according to an informed source. However, an EC official said that the U.S. offer is totally unacceptable because the U.S. is asking the EC to change structures that are in fact similar to those in the U.S. The official pointed out that the only difference between U.S. and EC monopolies is that the networks in the EC are owned by governments while the U.S. structures are owned by shareholders.

The U.S. concedes that there would need to be a "reasonable transition" period for the telecommunications monopolies in these countries to make the structural changes necessary for allowing competition in domestic and international long-distance phone service as the U.S. does now, one source pointed out. This would have to include allowing foreign telecommunications firms to build their own networks and invest in foreign markets, he said. The U.S. government emphasized in a Dec. 18 public statement that foreign competition must be allowed in city-to-city and city-to-country long distance services.

The U.S. until recently had refused to extend this GATT principle to basic telecommunications services, arguing that it would lock in the current openness of the U.S. market while other countries keep their telecommunications markets closed. This is particularly true because the services agreement as it is now being negotiated permits monopolies, which in turn allows countries to escape the MFN principle and the obligation to negotiate market access commitments, according to U.S. sources. If the U.S. would apply the MFN principle without securing liberalization from other trading partners, it would actually serve as a disincentive for other countries to enter into negotiations. The Administration argued this point in a background statement released on Dec. 18 with a public statement announcing the change in the U.S. negotiating position.

The antidumping talks this week remained deadlocked because of Japanese insistence that trading partners make major changes in their laws, according to informed sources. One of their demands would exclude current U.S. practices of filing a case on products and on its parts with one antidumping petition, they said. Under the Japanese proposal, petitioners would have to file one petition for whole products, another new petition for its parts, they pointed out. But the U.S. and Japan also remain "miles apart" on a number of issues, such as cumulation calculations for finding injury, ending antidumping duties after five years, as well as averaging of production costs, they said. In addition, the U.S. found little support for its proposal on dispute settlement that stated countries could continue with their current practices if a code to the GATT was not explicit on a given subject. The proposal would have stipulated that dispute settlement panels only address what is explicitly stated in code provisions, closing the door to expansive interpretations of code provisions that have begun to emerge, sources said.

U.S. efforts to move ahead the agriculture negotiations with the EC seemed largely unsuccessful because of intense French pressure on the EC Commission, informed sources said. This led the Commission to backtrack in several areas, and the U.S. and other trading partners to focus their attention on the efforts of GATT director general Arthur Dunkel, they said. U.S. efforts also included calls by President Bush to European leaders as well as a Dec. 18 meeting between U.S. Agriculture Secretary Ed Madigan and EC Agriculture Commissioner Ray MacSharry, which was expected to be continued later in the week. The initial meeting at the request of MacSharry failed to narrow any of the major differences, despite intense efforts by the EC council president, EC and U.S. sources said.

President Bush called European Council president and Dutch Prime Minister Ruud Lubbers on Dec. 13, German Chancellor Helmut Kohl on Dec. 14, and British Prime Minister John Majors on Dec. 16, the White House announced this week. These calls centered on GATT, and all the leaders agreed on the need to achieve a successful Uruguay Round and reaffirmed their countries' efforts to do so, the Dec. 16 White House statement said. The announcement makes a separate reference to a call Bush made to French President Francois Mitterand on Dec. 15, and which raised the GATT negotiations as one of several issues. Mitterand and Bush also discussed the situation in the Soviet Union, the U.S. call for an international conference and the need to work for an end to the civil war in Yugoslavia, the announcement said.
By Jutta Hennig.

5676 - 11 - 2

0259

주 미 대 사 관

USW(F) :   년월일 :   시간 :

수 신 : 장   관 (통기. 통이. 통상) 사백. 상협. 경기원. 농수산부   보안
                                                              통제

발 신 : 주 미 대 사

제 목 : UR 협정안 단견.   (출처 :   )

-- INSIDE U.S. TRADE - December 20, 1991

HILLS SAYS DRAFT GATT AGREEMENT SHOULD NOT BE OPEN TO WHOLESALE CHANGES

U.S. Trade Representative Carla Hills this week said that a draft Uruguay Round agreement to be tabled today (Dec. 20) may "very well" be subject to some changes when trading partners return for a Jan. 13 meeting of the Trade Negotiations Committee. The U.S. will continue to consult with "each and every group" on the text as drafted by the top official of the General Agreement on Tariffs & Trade, Hills told reporters on Dec. 16.

She labeled the document as the secretariat's view of the "profile and content" of the Uruguay Round agreement, which she said would not contain brackets. But if one party tries to change the agreement drawn up by GATT director general Arthur Dunkel, the draft will unravel, she said. So the principle should be to try to keep it together, according to Hills. That message was repeated by a senior U.S. negotiator to industry sources in Geneva, who pointed out that some changes could be made to the text, but that it would be "very difficult" to do so, according to an informed U.S. private-sector source.

But at the same time, the Commerce Dept. was telling U.S. industry observers that the Dunkel text would mark the beginning of serious negotiations in the area of antidumping, according to the private-sector source. The antidumping talks this week were as deadlocked as they have ever been, sources said (see related story).

Other sources pointed out that there is a perception among GATT members that the Uruguay Round cannot survive if there are major modifications and negotiations on the text after the Jan. 13 TNC meeting. The critical issue in assessing the draft text will be to decide which of the aspects that U.S. industry dislikes are part of a deal struck by the Administration with trading partners that cannot be unraveled, and which of the provisions the industry opposes can be changed, one industry source pointed out.

Some sources speculated about the U.S. motive for giving Dunkel unprecedented power to shape the content of the trade agreement, especially in light of his willingness to take into account the concerns of

(5676 - 11 -3)   외신 1과 동   제

0260

developing countries. If the U.S. is already weary of the emerging final agreement, a Dunkel draft may offer the U.S. an easy excuse to walk away from a deal without taking the blame for ending the Uruguay Round, these sources speculated.

The Uruguay Round will be on the agenda of a U.S.-EC ministerial meeting scheduled under the U.S.-EC cooperation agreement for Dec. 21, but it may not include a detailed discussion of the draft agreement, because officials will not have been able to assimilate the contents of a paper that has come out the previous night, Hills said.

Hills offered an optimistic timetable for completing market access negotiations on goods and services. If negotiators reach a "rough framework" of an agreement in all 15 negotiating areas, and then turned their attention "entirely" to the access negotiations in the area of services, goods and agriculture, they could reach the kind of access commitments that would make an agreement meaningful economically, she said. Representatives of the services industry have argued that a deal must include actual increases in market access, but apparently have scaled back their expectations from earlier demands on what that constitutes. Hills said that she has always maintained that an "intense effort" in the market access area will take until January or February 1992. International sources said there would be a more realistic assessment on when these negotiations could be completed at the Jan. 13 TNC meeting.

Trading partners agreed this week that the market access concessions would go into effect over a four-year period, starting on Jan. 1, 1993. They would be implemented in equal annual rate reductions, with the full implementation achieved by Jan. 1, 1997, they said. In addition, the Uruguay Round 1992 Protocol to the GATT on market access stipulates that all concessions on non-tariff measures be considered "bound," which means changes could only be made with the consent and compensation of trading partners, sources said. Trading partners discussed the terms of the protocol in a Dec. 18 meeting of the market access group, they said.

The Administration has a "hurdle rate" with respect to every negotiating area in the Uruguay Round that has been established in consultations with Congress and the private sector, Hills said in the Dec. 16 briefing. If the Administration would go beyond that threshold, it will lose support, she said. Hills pointed out that there are 30 congressional staff members at the GATT negotiations and a congressional delegation attending the negotiations starting on Dec. 17. In addition, members of the agricultural policy advisory committee are in Geneva and they know what the issues on the table are and what is acceptable to the U.S. agricultural industry. *By Jutta Hennig*

5676 -11 -4

0261

주 미 대 사 관

USW(F) :   년월일 :   시간 :

수 신 : 장 관 (통기, 통이, 통삼, 경이)씨밀 상공부 겨개현

발 신 : 주 미 대 사

제 목 : 미농산물 업계, UR 농산물 협상안 배척촉구   (출처 :)
                                                  INSIDE U.S. TRADE - December 20, 1991

MAJOR FARM GROUPS URGE REJECTION OF GATT DEAL, OTHERS RESERVE JUDGMENT

The American Farm Bureau and several major farm organizations this week urged President Bush to reject an agriculture agreement based on a draft Uruguay Round trade pact being discussed in Geneva, because it would be detrimental to the interests of American agriculture, according to a Dec. 18 letter reprinted below. Without further concessions by the European Community, the draft agreement would lead to immediate cuts in U.S. income and tariff supports while postponing effective cuts for the EC and allowing its continued export subsidies, the letter said.

Other farm groups, including those representing grain producers, this week also acknowledged that the draft agriculture agreement as proposed will not bring about major gains in agriculture trade. Any increased access for the grain trade would come from the world market as a result of curbs of EC export subsidies. But they seemed willing to reserve final judgment until they know the exact numbers by which farm supports and subsidies are meant to be cut. Those numbers are likely to be much lower for market access than for export subsidies, as negotiators have apparently agreed to use different base periods and cuts for each of the three areas of farm reform, some sources said.

EC Commissioner Ray MacSharry as late as Dec. 18 told U.S. Agriculture Secretary Ed Madigan that the EC could only agree to reducing its subsidized wheat shipments to 15-million metric tons by the end of the agreement, that it needed to rebalance access for grain substitutes and that all its compensation payments to farmers envisioned to offset lower prices would have to be exempt from cuts, U.S. and EC sources said. U.S. and international sources this week insisted that the EC has hardened its position under French pressure, but EC sources said the positions of both sides had remained unchanged. After a Dec. 18 meeting, a U.S. official hinted that the U.S. had signaled willingness to make further concessions, but had been met with the "same old rhetoric" by the EC. However, both EC and U.S. sources conceded that the Dec. 18 meeting went past midnight and talks were scheduled to continue on Dec. 19.

The commodity groups withholding final judgment on the agreement are "less than pleased" about the structures and instruments as they are being set up under a potential farm agreement now being drawn up under the General Agreement on Tariffs & Trade, one informed source said. Nevertheless, the agreement could be defended as beginning the process of agriculture liberalization and placing farm trade under GATT rules, sources said. The U.S. government is not "totally happy" with the agreement as it is emerging, but would not walk away from the negotiating table in response to the draft agreement, according to Administration sources.

(5676 - 11 - 5)   외신 1과
                         통 제

0262

One official said the current situation is likely to be a repeat of the December 1990 Uruguay Round ministerial meeting, where the EC, Japan and Korea rejected a draft negotiating framework. Japan, Korea, Norway, Switzerland and Israel were in a group led by Canada that this week expressed opposition to the Dunkel text because it would force trading partners to convert their quotas to tariffs. In a Dec. 16 meeting of the G-36 agriculture group these countries argued that the agriculture text be changed to exclude from tariffication trade measures taken consistent with Article 11 of the GATT, according to international sources. The U.S. and Australia countered the arguments by saying that converting the quotas to tariffs was the only way to achieve market access, and the U.S. emphasized that it could not put up its section 22 quotas if other countries were not willing to take similar steps, sources said. The EC has agreed to tariffication, but there are allegations that it would move to inflate its resulting tariff-quota, U.S. sources charged.

U.S. industry objections seem to focus on a "very weak" provision to continue the reform process. The industry is also criticizing the agreement because there will be no additional access for goods that command more than 5% of a market at the beginning of the farm agreement, sources said. There are also provisions that appear to protect the EC from possible challenges to its rights to use export subsidies (see related story).

The Dec. 12 draft agreement was changed this week under intensive lobbying of GATT director general Arthur Dunkel by trading partners. Lobbying efforts began to shift to Dunkel after it became clear that the U.S. and the EC would not reach a breakthrough bilaterally, especially following U.S.-EC bilateral meetings on Dec. 9 & 10, that failed to produce any movement in the positions, sources said. The EC lobbied to achieve a minimal text, while the U.S. and Cairns group members focused on ensuring he · "would not pitch too low," informed sources said.

The farm group letter urging the rejection of the agriculture agreement was initiated by groups other than the Farm Bureau, which also issued a separate statement charging that the agreement's approach would affect U.S. farm income and tariffs more than those of the EC. "It provides no assured growth in trade beyond minimum access, and could effectively legitimize certain EC policies," American Farm Bureau President Dean Kleckner said in a Dec. 18 public statement.

The Dec. 18 letter is signed by 15 farm groups that differ from those that signed a November letter urging the Administration not to sign on to a bad farm agreement (*Inside U.S. Trade*, Nov. 8, p 22). Signatories to that letter were the National Assn. of State Dept. of Agriculture, National Assn. of Wheat Growers, National Barley Growers Assn., National Forest Products Assn., National Grain Sorghum Producers Assn., National Grange, North American Export Grain Assn., the United Fruit & Vegetable Assn. and the U.S. Feed Grain Council. *By Jutta Hennig*

567.6 11-6

0263

주 미 대 사 관

USW(F) :   년월일 :   시간 :

수 신 : 장 관 (통기, 통이, 통상) 사본 : 상공부. 경제원. 농수산부 본동 안제

발 신 : 주 미 대 사

제 목 : UR 농산물분야 협상 초안   *Inside, U.S. Trade*, 12/20
                                                   (출처:)

DUNKEL FARM DRAFT SHOWS WEAK COMMITMENT TO CONTINUE REFORMS

A draft agriculture pact proposed to be tabled by the top official of the General Agreement on Tariffs & Trade today (Dec. 20) is likely to offer a weak commitment to continue reforms beyond the initial Uruguay Round agreement. That assessment is based on a preliminary draft that GATT director general Arthur Dunkel provided to trading partners on Dec. 12 and partially reprinted below.

The so-called continuation clause in the Dec. 12 draft states that participants shall meet to "review the operation of this agreement and to establish a programme for maintaining and extending the reform process in line with the long-term objective" of establishing a fair and market-oriented agricultural trading system, according to a copy of the agreement obtained by Inside U.S. Trade. The Administration has emphasized that a strong commitment to continue the reforms is necessary because they are vital to achieving any long-term benefits.

In addition, the agreement seems to protect the European Community from challenges to its right to use subsidies. This gives in to the EC demand for the so-called peace clause, one source said. Article 12 of the draft agreement of Dec. 12 stated that subsidies applied in conformity with reduction or ceiling commitments made in a farm reform agreement should not be used in a manner that causes "serious prejudice" to the interests of other participants in the sense of GATT Article 16:1. This requirement is based on the condition that "in any proceedings involving an allegation of serious prejudice against a participant applying subsidies in compliance with its commitments, there shall be no evidential or other presumption adverse to that participant," according to the draft agreement.

The Dec. 12 version strictly defines the domestic supports that are not subject to cuts. It states that so-called green policies must have no or minimal trade-distorting effects or effects on production. In addition, they must be provided through a publicly funded government program (including government revenue foregone) not involving transfers from consumers. They also must not have the effect of providing price support to producers, and must meet policy-specific criteria and conditions set out in the draft, according to paragraph 1 of Annex 4 on domestic supports.

The EC objects to the Dunkel text partially because of the strict green box definitions, which some sources said would make the reform of the EC's Common Agricultural Policy impossible. Key member states, such as Germany, will not accept a system of direct payments meant to offset price cuts if they would have to be cut. One source speculated that the green box provisions were inserted under pressure from the Cairns group, and could be meant to motivate the U.S. and the EC to reach an agreement on which internal supports would have to be cut and which ones would be exempt from reductions.

The Cairns group emphasized in a communique issued after a ministerial meeting earlier this month the need for effective reduction of domestic support, including effective disciplines on all payments linked to production (Inside U.S. Trade, Dec. 13, p 20). But sources made it clear that the group's flexibility on what can be considered "green" policies exempt from reduction commitments will depend on the commitments made on export subsidy cuts and other core elements of an agreement.

(5676 - 11÷7)   외신 1과 통제

0264

The Cairns Group also wants to ensure that a farm deal does not provide one set of rules for export subsidies of grain and another set of disciplines for other commodities, such as beef. In addition, Australia is pressing that the Uruguay Round agreement honor its 1985 arrangement with the EC that the EC will not subsidize the sale of beef into designated East Asian markets. The Cairns Group as a whole reemphasized its demand that an export subsidy agreement would include a commitment not to extend export subsidies to new products and new markets, according to the communique.

Efforts to reach a compromise between the U.S. and EC on internal support payments earlier this month included a so-called "blue box" category designed exactly for the direct income payments that would be likely to emerge from the CAP reform, sources said. Under that plan, payments would not be cut if they were connected to a set aside program, had a set base for acreage and had a set yield, sources said. But that plan, which seemed to be active in EC-U.S. discussions in the first part of December, is not reflected in the Dunkel draft paper, nor is a so-called multi-tiered amber box that would have distinguished between internal supports that would have to be cut, and those that would only need to be capped (Inside U.S. Trade, Dec. 13, p 1).

5676-11-8

주 미 대 사 관

USW(F) :   년월일 :   시간 :

수 신 : 장   관 (통기.통이.탐삽경인) 싸복.상용복.경가린.농수산복 | 보   안 |
                                                                | 통   제 |

발 신 : 주 미 대 사

제 목 : 프랑스의 UR 협상초안 거부 예상   (출처 :   )

-- INSIDE U.S. TRADE - December 20, 1991

FRANCE TO FIGHT FOR REJECTION OF DRAFT URUGUAY ROUND AGREEMENT NEXT WEEK

The draft Uruguay Round agreement scheduled to be released today (Dec. 20) will face its first serious challenge at a Dec. 23 council meeting of European Community ministers, where the French government is expected to pressure members states to move toward rejecting the agreement, according to informed EC sources. French government officials, including President Francois Mitterand, this week left no doubt in internal meetings with EC Commission officials and with other member states that they will not accept an emerging draft agreement largely because of its agriculture provisions, these sources said.

France is likely to be joined in its opposition by Ireland, but the Dutch presidency and other member states seem to be leaning toward supporting the package, EC sources said. As a result, the likely conclusion of the council meeting on Dec. 23 under the best of circumstances will be the message that the EC will need further time to study the complex agreement. However, EC sources left little doubt that such a step opens the door to a rejection of the draft agreement, which will be phrased as the need to further negotiate it. There is some discontent among member states over parts of the deal other than agriculture, including services, but none that would lead to a move to kill the package, one EC source said. For example, Portugal may oppose the textile part of the agreement, but not enough to hold up the entire pact, the official said.

The Dec. 23 meeting is a general affairs council customarily attended by the foreign ministers. Commission officials expected that some member states will have their trade ministers present at the meeting, and the French delegation will include the French agriculture minister, sources said. French efforts last week to have all agriculture ministers attend the meeting was squashed by the Dutch Presidency, which made it clear that any issues arising from the draft agriculture agreement that had been distributed by the top official of the General Agreement on Tariffs & Trade would have to be raised between individual ministers and their respective heads of government, EC sources said.

France wants the Uruguay Round to pick up after the 1992 Presidential election in the U.S., according to informed sources. It signaled that in internal meetings with EC officials and other member states, despite warnings that the Uruguay Round could fail as a result of that delay, they said. In the meantime, the EC could discuss the reform of the Common Agricultural Policy, on which member states were not able to agree this year. A Dec. 11 & 12 council meeting did not move the approval process on CAP changes along and the issue is likely to be taken up at the next agriculture minister's council on Jan. 27 & 28, sources said.

(5676-11-9) | 외신 1과 |
                       | 통   제   : |

0266

The French government cannot accept the draft agriculture agreement as it is emerging, largely because it would restrict its subsidized grain exports too severely and would not allow curbing the imports of grain substitutes, informed sources said (see related story). The U.S. this week tried to modify the French position through a phone call between President Bush and French President Francois Mitterand on Dec. 15 and State Dept. efforts to have Germany pressure the French government, sources said. U.S. Trade Representative Carla Hills told reporters on Dec. 16 that it is possible, but not certain that there will be an Uruguay Round agreement. The French opposition had made the EC commission take a hard line in bilateral negotiations with the U.S., which started with a meeting by EC Agriculture Commissioner Ray MacSharry and U.S. Agriculture Secretary Ed Madigan on Dec. 18 and were expected to continue on Dec. 19, EC sources said.

Hills said that failure to strike a draft agreement by today (Dec. 20) may signal it will be impossible to do so in the future. If no draft agreement is reached, it would suggest that there are "insurmountable

hurdles" to reaching such a trade pact, Hills told reporters on Dec. 16. The failure could not be blamed on a lack of time, since the negotiations have been going on for five years, according to Hills.

She said she could not predict whether the negotiations in the General Agreement on Tariffs & Trade will produce an agreement that will represent the interests of U.S. industry sufficiently to present to Congress for approval. Separately, the president of the National Assn. of Manufacturers told reporters on Dec. 17 that he is skeptical a GATT agreement can be reached by Dec. 20, which NAM does not consider to mean the end of the entire Uruguay Round effort.

Hills said it would be "very difficult" to continue the Uruguay Round indefinitely, but implied that a final decision on how to proceed is not up to the U.S. alone. "The U.S. is only one of 108 nations that participate in the negotiations," Hills said. *By Jutta Hennig*

5676- 11- 10

0267

주 미 대 사 관

USW(F) :   년월일 :   시간 :

수 신 : 장   관 (통기·통이·통상)사본: 상업부.경제원.농수산부   보   안
                                                              통   제

발 신 : 주 미 대 사

제 목 : UR 녹산 동향   ,   (출처 :   )

-- INSIDE U.S. TRADE - December 20, 1991

BRAZILIAN AMBASSADOR WARNS OF DISTRACTIONS TO HIGH-LEVEL LOOK AT GATT ROUND

The Dec. 20 - Jan. 13 timeframe designated by the top official of the General Agreement on Tariffs & Trade (GATT) for contracting parties to decide whether they can accept a draft Uruguay Round agreement represents "a very narrow period" during which "high-level" political engagement is needed to achieve success, according to the Brazilian Ambassador to the U.S. Rubens Ricupero, a former representative to the GATT.

But there is a risk that the high-level political attention required to conclude the multilateral global trade talks during that 24-day period could be diverted by other factors, Ricupero warned an audience at the Brookings Institution on Dec. 13.

The disintegration of the Soviet Union could dominate the agenda of world leaders, as evidenced by U.S. Secretary of State James Baker's newly announced effort to organize relief efforts for the new commonwealth, Ricupero said. Moreover, European efforts to consolidate the results of the move toward continental political unification taken earlier this month at Maastricht, the Netherlands could divert the attention of European political leaders. And the rotation of the European Council presidency at the end of the year will remove the Dutch, who have played an active role in pressing for European movement on agriculture. The presidency will be taken over by Portugal, which have been very inactive in the Uruguay Round negotiations, he said. In addition, it should not be forgotten that important European players in any successful outcome of the Uruguay Round -- notably EC President Jacques Delors and EC Agriculture Commissioner Ray MacSharry -- have domestic political roles that do not necessarily coincide with such a positive outcome, Ricupero noted.

Consensus agreement on outstanding parts of the Uruguay Round negotiations is not likely this week, Ricupero said. He said that his judgment was based on very recent contact with associates in Geneva. They told him that a mood of expectation of results from U.S.-EC bilateral talks to break a year-long deadlock over agriculture had degenerated into a more pessimistic outlook after several weeks of negotiation had apparently failed to significantly narrow fundamental differences on five areas of disagreement: a "peace" clause protecting the EC from challenges to its policy instruments, continuation clause, base year, volume vs. budgetary outlay, and rebalancing to limit access for feed grain substitutes.

According to Ricupero, the GATT secretariat had recently tabled a paper spelling out how derogations from most-favored-nation (MFN) treatment should be handled in the services sector. According to the Brazilian ambassador, the paper says that all derogations should be reviewed after five years, at which time they could continue only if a two-thirds majority voted to let them. He noted that the provision "could cause a problem for a few countries."

5-676-11-11

외신 1과
통   제

외 무 부

종 별 :

번 호 : ITW-1814   일 시 : 91 1220 1135

수 신 : 장관(봉상,국기,농수부)

발 신 : 주이태리 대사

제 목 : UR 관련한 이태리 농림장관 주재회의

1. 이태리 농림장관 (MR.GORIA)은 12.19(목) 주이농무관단 대표들을 장관실에 초청, UR협상과 관련한 의견 교환을 위하여 면담형식의 회의를 개최하였음. 전체참석인원은   20여명으로 미국,카나다,네델란드,독일,영국,스위스,프랑스,스페인,아르헨티나,한국, 태국, 인도네시아 등이 참석하였으며 당관에서는 농무관,농무관보가 참석하였음.

2. 동회의에서는 미국, 아르헨티나, 오스트리아, 독일및 아국 대표등이 각국의 입장을 개진하였으며, 이어서 '고리아'장관의 견해 피력이 있었음.

3. 당관 농무관은 발언을 통하여 먼저 지난 11월 아국 농림장관의 이태리 방문시 고리아장관을 만나 UR 협상문제 및 양국 협조사항에 대한 의견을 교환코자 하였으나 일정상 만나지 못했음을 밝히고, UR과 관련, 아국의 입장으로서 협상에서 각국의 특수사정을 인정하여야 하며, 특히 우리나라의 쌀시장은 쌀의 경제적,사회적 비중을 고려할때 농업구조 조정이 이루어져 개방에서 오는 영향을 흡수할 수 있게될때까지는개방이 불가할 것임을 밝히고,따라서 현실적으로 예외없는 관세의 적용문제도 수용할 수 없음을 강조하였음.

또한 선진국의 수출 보조금은 크게 감소되어야 할것임을 지적하였고, UR 협상에대한 아국의 노력으로 지난 수년간 시장개방 노력에 적극 노력해왔음도 아울러 설명하였음.

4. 고리아 장관은 현재의 협상이 결론을 얻기에는 어려움이 있을 것으로 전망하고 있으나, 내년 미국대통령 선거전까지는 어떠한 형태이건 타결될것으로 의견 피력하였음.

또 동문제가 EC와 미국간의 대립이 중심이됨을 고려하여 G-7 정상회담을 통하여문제를 푸는 것도 고려할수 있을 것이라고 하였음. 또한 EC 외무장관 회담에서

통상국   2차보   국기국   농수부

91.12.20   21:15 DQ

외신 1과 통제관

0269

타결을 서두르고 있으나 농림장관의 입장에서는 수용하기 어려운 점이 많음을 아울러 밝혔음.

5. 고리아 장관은 회의후 개별 접촉시 UR협상에 임하는 아국입장을 충분히 이해한다고 말하였으며, 각국대표중 독일대표는 개별국 특수사정이 반영되고, 농민의 직접피해가 크지 않아야 협상이 실효를 거둘수 있을 것이라는 입장을 밝혔음.끝

(대사 김석규-국장)

외 무 부

종 별 :

번 호 : GVW-2766　　　　　　　　　일 시 : 91 1220 2000

수 신 : 장 관(통상국장)

발 신 : 주 제네바 대사(최혁 통상국 심의관)

제 목 : UR/농산물 협상그룹에서의 아국발언문

　　1. 금 12.20(금) 11:30-12:30 간 개최된 농산물협상그룹 마지막 회의시 박대사님이 행하신 발언문을 별첨 송부하니, 판단하시어 아국대표단이 쌀에 대한 관세화에 반대하는 아국의 입장을 협상결과에 반영시키기 위해 최종순간까지 최대한 노력하였다는 점을 홍보하는데 최대한 활용바랍니다.

　　2. 우리입장을 극명하게 나타내고 있으므로 필요하다면 FULL TEXT 를 번역하여 배포하는 것도좋을 것으로 생각됩니다.

　　첨부 상기 연설문 1부

　　(GVW(F)-0671)

통상국

PAGE 1

주 제 네 바 대 표 부

번 호 : GVR(F) - 067/   년월일 : 11220   시간 : 2000

수 신 : 장   관 (통상국장)

발 신 : 주 제네바대사

제 목 : GVW-2766 첨부

총 4 매(표지포함)

보 안 통 제	

| 외신파
통 제 | |

67/-4-1

0272

Statement made by
Ambassador Park at the Informal Meeting
on Agriculture on 20 December 1991

I wish to salute you for your eminent leadership in bringing us to where we stand now. We are indeed on the verge of concluding the long lasting negotiations, depending on how balanced and equitable the texts of agreement we will ~~have~~ soon.

In a matter of a few hours from now we will be presented with a consolidated texts of agreement in all the areas of the Uruguay Round negotiations.

It would be extremely risky or even wrong to make any judgement on the merits or demerits of the texts without undertaking an in-depth analysis of every word or sentence used in the texts.

It is therefore the intention of this delegation to offer its considered judgement on the texts at the TNC meeting on January 13, 1992.

However, Mr. Chairman, I would like to offer the following comments on the basis of reviewing the draft text on agriculture and subsequent development in agricultural negotiations, particularly because this meeting is ~~going to be~~ the last opportunity to express our view in this format before the text is produced.

Our basic position on the Uruguay Round ~~is~~ clear and loud. We want to see the Uruguay Round succeed as soon as possible. To this end, we will continue to remain a full cooperative participant.

Mr. Chairman,

As you are well aware, in the course of negotiations, my delegation has had one vital concern throughout, which we

1

671-4-2

expressed on every conceivable occasion, in our untiring efforts
to receive the support of fellow delegates and to win the heart ~~and mind~~
of the Chairman.

It is for this reason that we were deeply disappointed at
the presence of an Article providing for comprehensive
tariffication in the draft text on Agriculture.

There is one situation which this delegation wants to avoid
for the success of the Uruguay Round negotiation. That is the
situation in which basic political, economic, social capabilities
of contracting parties are ignored. This situation may compel
some contracting parties, like Korea, to assume politically an
impossible task. We tried hard to give this message clearly and
loudly, over the past five years, but unfortunately I have been
unsuccessful in getting this message across to you.

Mr Chairman,

In our view there is one essential element which is missing
from the draft text on agriculture. It does not take due account
of the country specific difficulties and political social
realities of some participating countries. The problem of rice
in my country is part and parcel of our culture, history, and
traditions, a significance that goes far beyond the dimensions
of trade and economy.

If a solution is imposed upon us which ignores the unique
nature of the rice culture in our part of the world, it would
place us in a serious dilemma.

The GATT is an institution charged with the responsibility
of ~~trade liberalization and expansion~~. Korea is among those
which has benefitted most from the multilateral trading system,
but I wish to underline the fact that it took more than 40 years
to achieve liberalization in the industrial sector to the extent
of the current degree. We are indeed torn between realism and

2

671 - 4 - 3

0274

idealism. If we try to achieve liberalization in agriculture too much and too rapidly by ignoring the realities it could be counterproductive. '

It is pragmatism and realism, not idealism, that should prevail in the end.

It is my sincere hope that the text of agreement on agriculture does not ~~neglect~~ _ignore more_ the vital concerns and interests of many countries which have expressed their preoccupation repeatedly in the past.

Just in case any one fails to understand our position on rice, I would like to emphasize the point _of our vital concern_ ~~once again~~: we would like to have enough flexibility in negotiating specific binding commitments on market access, so that exceptionally sensitive products should not be subject to tariffication.

This is the key factor upon which rests the ability of the Korean government to mobilize national support for the entire Uruguay Round package.

Thank you.

3

0275

12.20. UR/농산물 협상 비공식 회의시 박수길 주 제네바 대사 발언문

지금까지 협상을 이끌어 온 의장의 탁월한 지도력에 경의를 표하고자 합니다.
협상 참가국들이 곧 받게될 협정안이 얼마나 균형되고 형평에 맞는 것인가에
따라 그간 오랫동안 계속된 협상이 거의 종결되는 것입니다.
지금부터 수시간내에 모든 협상 참가국들에게 UR 협상 전분야에 대한 협정안이
주어질 것이므로 동 내용에 대한 심도있는 분석이 없이는 장.단점에 대한 평가를
내리는 것이 위험하거나 심지어 그릇된 것일수도 있습니다.

따라서, 92.1.13 TNC 회의에서 동 협정안에 대한 입장을 표명하고자 합니다.
그러나, 금번 농산물 협상 회의가 협정안이 제시되기 이전에 입장을 표명할 수
있는 마지막 기회이기 때문에 최근에 제시된 농산물 협정 초안과 그 이후에
전개된 농산물 협상 진전 현황에 근거하여 다음과 같은 논평을 하고자 합니다.
한국의 UR 협상에 대한 기본입장은 명확한 것입니다. 즉, 한국은 UR 협상의
조속한 성공을 희망하고 있으며 이를 위해 계속 협력해 나갈 것입니다.
의장께서 잘아시다시피 한국 대표단이 여타 협상 참가국의 지지를 얻고 의장의
이해를 구하기 위한 줄기찬 노력을 하면서 그간 협상 과정에서 기회 있을 때마다
일관되게 주장해 온 한가지 핵심 관심사항이 있습니다.
이러한 이유 때문에 최근 제시된 농산물 협정 초안에 포괄적 관세화 내용이
있는 것에 대해 극히 실망한 바 있습니다.

한국으로서는 UR 협상 성공을 위해 피하고자 하는 한가지 상황이 있는 바,
그것은 협상 참가국이 갖고 있는 기본적인 정치, 경제, 사회적 능력이 무시되는
상황이라 하겠습니다. 이러한 상황은 한국과 같은 몇몇 협상 참가국들로 하여금
정치적으로 감내하기 힘든 어려움을 강요하는 결과가 될 것입니다. 한국 대표단은
지난 5년동안 이러한 입장을 분명하고도 강력하게 전달하기 위해 최선을
다하였으나, 불행하게도 의장에게는 이러한 입장이 받아들여지지 않고 있습니다.

0276

의장,

농산물 협정 초안에는 반영되지 않고 있는 한가지 필수적인 사항이 있는 바,
그것은 개별국가의 특수한 어려움과 몇몇국가들의 정치, 사회적 어려움을 적절히
반영하지 못하고 있는 것입니다. 한국에 있어서의 쌀은 한국 문화, 역사, 전통과
불가분의 관계에 있으며 그 중요성은 무역과 경제적 측면을 훨씬 뛰어 넘는
것입니다.
한국이 갖고 있는 쌀에 대한 이와같은 특수성을 도외시한 협정안이 한국에게
강요된다면 한국은 심각한 딜레마에 빠져들게 되는 것입니다.

갓트는 세계무역의 자유화와 확대를 책임지고 있는 기구이며 한국은 이러한
다자무역체제의 혜택을 가장 많이 받아온 국가중의 하나인 것은 사실이나,
공산품 분야에서 지금과 같은 수준의 수입자유화를 달성하는 데도 40년이상이나
소요된 사실도 강조하고자 합니다.

우리는 이상주의와 현실주의 사이에서 분열되어 있으며, 현실을 도외시한채
농산물 분야에서 너무 대폭적이고 급격한 자유화를 달성하려 한다면 이는
부작용을 야기할 수도 있습니다. 이상주의가 아니라 결국 실용주의, 현실주의가
압도해야 할 것이며, 농산물 협정안에는 많은 국가들이 그간 계속해서 주장해온
핵심 관심사항을 무시해서는 안될 것입니다.

쌀에 대한 한국 입장을 이해하지 못하고 있는 국가가 있다면 다시한번 한국의
핵심 관심사항을 강조하고자 합니다. 즉, 시장접근 분야에서의 구체 약속을 위한
협상에서 극히 민감한 품목에 대해 관세화의 예외를 인정받기 위한 융통성을
인정받고자 한다는 것입니다.
방금 언급한 핵심 관심사항은 한국 정부가 전체 UR 협상 결과에 대한 국민적
지지를 얻을 수 있는 핵심 요소입니다.

감사합니다.

0277

UR/농산물 협상 최종 협정 초안 요지

1991.12.21.
통상기구과

1. 시장접근

   ○ 예외없는 관세화 및 모든 관세(TE 포함) 양허

   ○ TE 감축 기준년도, 감축기간 및 감축폭

     - '86-'88년 기준 '93-'99년간 36% 감축 (단, 품목별 최소 15% 감축)

   ○ 최소 시장접근

     - '86-'88년 평균 소비량 기준 이행 개시년도(93년) 3%, 이행 마지막
       년도(99년) 5%를 최소 시장접근으로 허용

2. 국내보조

   ○ 감축 기준년도, 감축기간 및 감축폭

     - '86-'88년 기준 '93-'99년간 20% 감축

   ○ 감축의무가 면제되는 de minimis 수준 (총생산액에 대한 보조 비율)

     - 선진국 : 5%

     - 개도국 : 10%

3. 수출보조

   ○ 감축 기준년도, 감축기간 및 감축폭

     - '86-'90년 기준 '93-'99년간 재정지출 기준 36% 및 물량기준 24% 동시 감축

4. 개도국 우대

   ○ 감축폭

     - 선진국 감축폭의 최소한 2/3 이상 감축 의무 부담

   ○ 감축기간

     - 최대 3년 연장 가능

5. 기 타

   ○ 92.3.1까지 양허 계획(country plan) 제출

   ○ 92.3.31까지 양자협상 완료.   끝.

0278

Statement by Mr. Arthur Dunkel
Chairman of the Trade Negotiations Committee
at official level

Geneva, Friday 20 December 1991

1.   I call to order this meeting of the Trade Negotiations Committee at official level.

2.   The purpose of this formal meeting of the TNC is to conclude the intensive consultations which, at the end of the Brussels meeting on 7 December 1990, Dr. Hector Gros-Espiell, Chairman of the Committee at Ministerial level, asked me to carry forward "until the beginning of next year". He meant, of course, 1991. The fact that we have almost reached the beginning of 1992 speaks for itself ...

3.   More specifically, the purpose of the meeting is to ask you to take note of the fact that before the end of today - 20 December - you will have available a complete and consolidated document bringing together the results of five years of effort. This document is the outcome both of intensive negotiation and of arbitration and conciliation: negotiation among you, the participants, and arbitration and conciliation by the Chairman when it became clear that, on some outstanding points, this was the only way to put before you a complete, consolidated text. It represents the global package of results of this Round. Even more importantly, it offers us, for the first time, a concrete idea of the scope and scale of the benefits of broad-based liberalization and strengthened multilateral rules which are within our grasp. In short; a promise given, a promise kept.

4.   This achievement has been reached thanks to you, the negotiators, and to the dedication and determination of the Chairmen. All have worked virtually non-stop for this result over the past days and nights.

- 2 -

5.   The document (MTN.TNC/W/FA), entitled "Draft Final Act Embodying the Results of the Uruguay Round of Multilateral Trade Negotiations", is ready, but for purely technical reasons - translation and printing - will be available in the three official languages of the GATT later this evening.

6.   This Committee will meet again on 13 January, with a view to concluding the Uruguay Round. And since the text is not yet in your hands, I will adjourn this meeting as soon as I have concluded my statement. Between now and 13 January, I expect - indeed, I know - that the package in its totality will be given the most serious and urgent consideration, at the highest political levels, in your capitals.

7.   In examining the Draft Final Act, governments will have to take into account a number of points:

    (i) First, the text is comprehensive. It seeks to strike the best possible balance across the board of the long negotiating agenda of this Round. It addresses all areas of the negotiations as laid down by the Punta del Este Declaration. It nails down and captures the very substantial progress we have made since January this year. All these factors make this document much more important than the one we sent to Ministers in Brussels last December.

    (ii) Second, however, the Final Act needs to be completed in one very important respect. It lacks the schedules of commitments that are still in the process of being negotiated in three major areas. I have in mind the results of the "Market Access Negotiations" in the various sectors of trade in goods; of the negotiations on specific commitments on internal support and export competition in agriculture; and of the negotiations on initial commitments on trade in services. These results will become available only on completion of the detailed and intensive negotiations in which delegations will have to engage early in the New Year. In this respect I would draw your attention to the statement of the Chairman of the Negotiating Group on Market Access which is being circulated in MTN.TNC/W/93.

.0280

66P-5-3

- 3 -

8.   Two further steps must be taken before the negotiations can be concluded. One is that the Group of Negotiations on Goods must conduct a final evaluation of the negotiations, in accordance with the mandate given by the Punta del Este Declaration. The other is that the entire body of agreements must be reviewed for legal conformity and internal consistency. This latter process is important and unavoidable - indeed, I am already aware that some technical corrections are required to ensure consistency in certain dispute settlement provisions. It should not, however, lead to substantive changes in the balance of rights and obligations established in the agreements.

9.   All this means that our work from January onwards will therefore have to be based on a global approach. And this means that the negotiating groups under the GNG now cease to exist. One exception will be the Market Access Group, since it is charged with the specific task of providing an obvious missing element of the Final Act. The GNS, of course, will remain in place and continue its responsibilities including the conduct of the machinery currently in place for conducting the negotiations on initial commitments in services. I must, however, immediately add that, as Chairman of the TNC, I will continue to count on the assistance of the Chairmen in their personal capacity.

10.   The Punta del Este Declaration clearly describes the Uruguay Round negotiations as a "single undertaking". As such, these negotiations are governed by the principle that nothing is final until everything is agreed.

11.   Once again, I am deeply grateful to my fellow chairmen for their support, and for their expertise and courage in carrying out this task. My appreciation and thanks also go to all my colleagues in the Secretariat without whom all this would not have been possible. As to the results, no one is infallible, and I would not for a moment expect all participants to be fully content with all the decisions which I have had to make. Nevertheless, you chose this route yourselves, in full awareness of the possible consequences involved, and there is no going back. As I have repeatedly stressed, the document I have tabled today forms a single

0281

66 p - s - 4

- 4 -

package, and it is as a package that it should be judged. Your evaluation should not therefore be hasty but well-considered and measured, looking to the future of the multilateral trading system and the opportunity it holds out for all our countries. I am confident that, if we continue to share the vision which brought us together in Punta del Este five years ago, your governments will judge the package favourably.

12. I know that the three weeks' break from now until the 13th January will not necessarily be a holiday. I would like to take this opportunity to convey my season's greetings to you and your families and express the wish that 1992 will go down in history as the year when the biggest of all multilateral trade negotiations were successfully concluded.

0282

66P-5-5

외 무 부

종 별 :

번 호 : JAW-7169   일 시 : 91 1222 1900

수 신 : 장 관(봉기,봉일,농림수산부장관)

발 신 : 주 일 대사(일경)

제 목 : UR 협상 초안에 대한 반응

12.21. 던켈 사무총장이 제시한 UR 합의초안에대한 주재국 반응을 우선 언론보도를토대로 다음보고함. (내주초 일 정부 접촉 예정)

1. 정부 및 정계반응

가. 가또 관방장관과 타나부 농림수산 대신은 11.21. 기자회견에서 예외없는 관세화를 반대하는 일본이 입장이 반영되지 않은데 유감을 표명하면서, 앞으로도 일본의 입장을 관철시키기 위해 계속 노력할 생각임을 명백히했음. (일 정부 및 자민당 내에서는 관세화를 통해 수입수량 제한을 전폐하면서, 수출보조금은 일부만 삭감하는것은 불공 평하다는 반응이 지배적인 것으로 알려지고 있음)

나. 한편, 와타나베 봉상대신은 '봉산성 관련분야에 대해서 거부할 이유는 없다'고 하면서 지적소유권, 분쟁처리 분야등 농업 이외의 분야에 대해서는 일측이 내심 만족하고 있음을 암시. (단, 반덤핑 규제의 강화가 불충분한 점 및긴급수입 제한의 차별적 적용이 그대로 남은점에 대해 일정부내에는 불만이 초래)

다. 일측으로서는 금번 합의 초안이 미. EC 등 주요국간의 의견이 충분히 조정되지 않은 상태에서 서둘러 작성된 것으로서 내년도 교섭개시시 단순한 기술적 문제의 구체협의 수준을 넘어 초안의 내용 자체가 변경될 가능서이 있는것으로 관측중.

라. 또한, 일본외에 미, EC 등 모두 금번 합의초안에 반발하고 있는 점에 비추어일측이 서둘러 정치적 결단을 내려야 할 필요는 없으며, 미. EC의 동향을 끝까지 본후 대응한다는 입장임. 일 정부 및 정계는 12.22. 저녁 정부. 자민당간 대책협의 및 12.25. 관계각료 간담회를 개최일본의 대응방침을 협의 예정이기는 하나, 상기미. EC의 반발등을 감안, 이 자리에서도 대책의 협의 보다는 각국의 동향 분석등 정보분석에 촛 점이 맞추어질 전망

0 한편, 일부에서는 미국 자체가 반발하고 있는이상 92.1월 부시 대통령 방일시는

통상국   2차보   아주국   통상국   외정실   정와대   안기부   농수부

PAGE 1   91.12.22   22:42 FN

일.미 양국이 UR 의 중요성에 인식을 같이하는 수준에 그칠 가능성이 있다는 낙관론도 보이고 있음.

마.한편, 일본의 야당들은 일제히 예외없는 관세화안이 제시된데 반대하는 입장을 표명

,2.일본 언론

가.합의 초안 수용 문제

1) 닛께이, 아사히, 산께이, 요미우리등 주요신문들은 12.22(월) 일제히 사설을통해 합의초안이 일부 만족스럽지 못한 면이 있더라도 일측으로서는 UR 실패시 초래되는 결과 및 국제사회에서의 일본의 위치를 고려하여 금번합의 초안의 토대 위에서UR 의 성공을 위해 노력해야 할것이라고 주장

2) 특히, 쌀시장 개방문제에 대해서는 금번제시된 조건(93-99년간 관세율 36프로삭감,미니멈 억세의 최고 3프로, 최후 5프로 인정)을 수용불가능한 어려운 조건은 아니라고 하면서 일정부의 적극적인 대응을 촉구

나.미. EC 의 대응 전망

1) 금번 합의 초안에 미국의 주장이 어느정도 반영되기는 하였지만, 농어보호의삭감율,삭감방식, 우회덤핑수출 방지면에서 미측의주장에 미흡한 점이 있고, 반면 통상법 301조와 같은 일방적 제재조치는 제한되게 된 점에서 의회 및 산업계의 반발이필지인 것으로 전망

2) EC 의 경우, 예산기준 수출보조금 삭감,농가소득 보상에 대한 예외 취급, 관세율재조정(REBALANCING) 등 EC 에 있어 매우중요한 점이 반영되지 않은 점 및 덤핑방지,긴급수입제한 분야에서도 EC 의 기대에 미흡하다는 점에서 금번 합의 초안을 수용 하기는 어려운 것으로 관측

3.재계반응

0 히라이와 경단련 회장등 재계 지도자들은 간접적인 표현이기는 하지만 모두 예외없는 관세화안의 수용등을 촉구하면서 일본 때문에 UR 이 실패했다는 결과가 되지않도록 일본이 대국적인 견지에서 UR 의 조기 타결을 위해 노력할 것을 요청.끝.

(대사 오재희-국장)

출 장 보 고 서

1991.12.15-22, 제네바

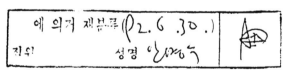

보고자 : 최혁 통상국 심의관

- 목   차 -

0286

1. 출장 개요

o 기 간 : 91.12.15(일)-12.22(일), 제네바

o 목 적 : UR 협상 최종 단계 현황 파악 및 92.1.13 이후 대책 협의

o 주요활동 사항

12.16(월)

09:00   주 제네바 대표부 정례 회의 참석

         (각 협상분야 진전 상황 파악)

13:00   Linden 갓트 사무총장 법률 자문 초청 오찬

         (12.20 제출 예정인 최종 협정안의 성격 및 92.1.13 이후

          협상 방향 타진)

17:00   농산물 36개국 비공식 회의

         (11조 6개국 그룹과의 공동 보조 및 예외없는 관세화에

          반대하는 아국 입장 표명)

12.17(화)

09:30   대표부, 본부대표 합동 대책회의

         (분야별 협상 진전 보고 및 12.20 이후 대책협의)

12:00   F. Rossler 갓트사무국 법률국장 면담

         (남북 물자교류, MTO, 301조 문제에 대한 의견 교환)

15:30   K. Broadbridge 사무국 차장보 면담

         (1.13 이후 협상 구조, 협상 일정, 한국인 사무국 채용

          문제 협의)

22:15   개도국 전체회의 참석

         (쌀에 대한 관세화 반대 입장 표명)

12.18(수)

13:00   뉴질랜드 및 파키스탄 대사 초청 오찬 참석

         (협상 현황 및 전망에 대한 의견 교환)

1

0287

15:00	Safeguards 주요국 협의 참석
	(QM 반대 입장 표명)
17:00	Dunkel 갓트 사무총장 면담 참석
	(쌀에 대한 시장개방의 어려움 설명 및 협상 결과 반영 요청)

12.19(수)

09:00	대책회의
	(12.20. 현지 및 본국에서의 홍보 대책 협의)
17:00	EC의 3개 체약국 대개도국 수혜 배제 의도 서한 송부에 대한 대책 협의 (싱가폴 대표부)

12.20(금)

11:00	EC의 대개도국 수혜 배제 관련 서한에 대한 정부 입장 통보 서한 전달
11:30	농산물 전체 참가국 비공식 회의
	(쌀에 대한 아국 입장 호소)
13:00	홍콩 D. Tsang 무역청장 초청 오찬 참석
	(QM 및 92.1.13 이후 협상 전망에 대한 의견 교환)
17:48	TNC 전체회의 참석

2. 관찰 및 평가

가. 아국대표단 활동

ㅇ 농산물에서 끝까지 기회있는대로 쌀에 대한 아국 입장 반영 노력

- 예외없는 관세화 반대 노력의 일환으로 11:2(C)에 근거한 관세화 예외 요청 그룹 구성 주도

- 예외적으로 민감한 품목에 대한 관세화 반대 그룹 형성 시도는 멕시코의 불참으로 좌절

2

0288

- 12.20 농산물 전체 참가국 회의에서 아국 입장 최종 정리하여 극명하게 표현하고 반영 호소

ㅇ 여타 주요 협상그룹에서도 마지막 순간까지 소그룹 협상에 참가하여 아국 입장 관철에 노력
 - Safeguards 에서의 QM 도입 반대국 (20개국 서명) 공동 demarche 주도
 - 보조금 협상에서의 개도국 분류 제안 제출
 - TRIPs에서의 IC 소장 완제품에 대한 지나친 규제 반대

ㅇ EC의 3개 체약국에 대한 대개도국 우대 배제 움직임에 대한 신속한 대응
 - 12.20자 EC 입장 반박 서한 송부, 조기 배포 요청
 - 카나다, 호주등 선진국에 대해 로비 전개
 - 3개 체약국과 협의, ASEAN 및 선발개도국을 포함한 개도국내 지지 세력 확보키로 합의

나. 12.20 최종 협정안(Package of Draft Agreements)의 성격

ㅇ 합의문서가 아닌 의장의 협정 초안이나, 최종 단계 협상에서 주요쟁점에 합의가 이루어짐으로서 전체적으로 합의 수준이 높아지고 타협안으로 제시된 미합의 부분이 크게 축소 되었음.
 - 거의 완전한 합의가 형성된 분야 : 분쟁해결, SVC Framework, 최종의정서, 시장접근 의정서
 - 미합의 쟁점이 1-2개로 좁혀진 분야 : Safeguards(19조), 보조금
 - 미합의 쟁점이 비교적 많은 분야 : 농산물, 반덤핑, TRIMs, TRIPs

ㅇ 금후 추가 협상이 필요한 분야는 구체적으로 명시됨(Footnote)
 - 시장접근 양허 협상, MTO 설립 조항, SVC/해운분야 부속서 및 분야별 MFN 일탈 범위, PPA 및 PA에 근거한 수입제한 철폐 기간등

ㅇ 따라서 추가 협상이 필요한 분야와 범위를 Footnote에 명시된 분야로 제한하고 있고, 그 이외의 모든 협상 결과는 Single undertaking에 의해 총체적 package로 검토하도록 요청받고 있음.

3

0289

다. 92.1.13 이후 협상 추진 방향 및 일정

    ㅇ 상기 최종 협정안의 성격에 비추어 금후 협상은 하기 두가지 track으로
      추진될 것으로 예상
      - 1st track : 12.20 제시된 일괄 협정 초안의 unraveling을 초래할 수
                         있는 수정을 피하면서 하나의 package로 수락토록
                         유도해 나가는 과정
      - 2nd track : 상기 track과 병행하여 시장접근 양허협상과 전체
                         package의 균형을 건드리지 않는 기술적 검토를 진행하여
                         92.4.15경 최종의정서 서명 추진

라. <u>예상되는 금후 협상 전망</u>

    ㅇ <u>협상 타결 여부</u> : 12.20 package에 대한 미국, EC의 평가에 따라
      좌우될 것인바, 양측 공히 또는 어느 일방이 이를 전체적으로 수락할 수
      없다는 입장을 표명할 경우 협상은 결렬을 면치 못할 것이라는 것이
      일반적인 평가임.
      - 그러나 미.EC가 결렬의 책임을 피하기 위해 어느 경우에도 협상 결과
        전체를 수락할 수 없다는 입장을 보이지는 않을 것임.

    ㅇ <u>추가 협상 여부</u> : 미.EC 태도에 따를 것이나 EC가 12.20 이미 농산물
      타결안을 수락할 수 없다는 1차적 반응을 보인바 있음에 비추워 농산물등
      일부 협상분야에서의 재협상을 요구해올 가능성이 크며, 미국도 농산물
      package 내용의 부실을 들어 재협상을 요구할 가능성이 있어, 양측이
      공히 여사한 반응을 보일경우 농산물 등에서 일부 추가 협상과 문안
      수정이 가능해질 수 있을 것임.
      - 그러나 미.EC가 기합의한 분야에서의 추가 협상은 없을 것임.

    ㅇ <u>미.EC를 제외한 여타 참가국의 예상되는 반응</u> : 분야별로 수락할 수
      없는 문제점을 지적하고 개선을 요구할 것으로 보이나, 일본, 카나다를
      포함 어느 참가국도 현실적으로 전체 package를 거부할 수는 없을
      것이라는 것이 현지의 분위기임.

4

0290

o 92.1.13 TNC 회의 전망 : 12.20 이후 3주간의 시일이 있으나, 년말 년시가 끼어 있어 충분한 검토가 어렵고, 여타국의 반응을 살펴려는 동향 때문에 어느나라도 12.20 package에 대해

- 확정적이거나 최종적인 입장을 제시치 않을 것이며,

- 특히 자국 관심분야에서의 문제점과 대안을 지적할 것이나

- 어느 경우에도 전체 package를 수락할 수 없다는 나라는 없을 것이나,

- 일부 나라는 문제점이 있기는 하나, 전체 package를 그대로 받을 수 있다는 나라도 있을 것으로 예견됨.

따라서 1.13이 결정의 날이 되지는 않을 것이며 package에 대해 consensus를 구축해 나가는 새로운 과정의 출발점이 될 것으로 보임.

마. 종합 관찰

o 금후 협상의 향방은 12.20 package에 대한 미.EC의 반응에 따라 크게 좌우될 것임.

o 현재로서 예상되는 미.EC의 반응은 하기와 같음.

- EC측이 농산물 협정안을 수락할 수 없다는 1차 반응을 보이고 있고 (보다 확실한 것은 12.23 EC 무역상/농상 합동 각료회의 결과를 보아야 함), 92.1.13전 미.EC간 농산물 추가 협상 계획이 없어 오는 1.13 TNC 회의시 EC측이 일단 농산물 협정안 수락을 거부하고 수정을 제의할 것으로 예견되고 있음.

EC측이 특히 수락에 어려움을 안고 있는 문제는 아래와 같음.

. 허용되는 국내 직접 소득지원 방식 문제(EC는 각국 실정에 맞게 운영하도록 각국에 위임할 것을 요청)

. 수출보조 감축을 예산과 물량 이중으로 감축하는 문제 (EC는 예산 감축 약속만 수락할 수 있다는 입장)

5

0291

- 미국으로서는 농산물 협정안이 다소 미측에 유리하게 되어 있으나, 국내보조 감축을 86-88년 기준 93-99년간 20%만 감축토록 하고 있는등 감축 수준이 낮기 때문에 농산물 package가 medium package로 평가될 가능성이 많고 미 의회 또는 업계의 지지를 확보하기가 어렵게 되는 dilemma를 안고 있음.

- 그러나 어느 경우에도 미.EC가 전체 협상을 결렬시키는 방향으로 몰고가지는 않을 것으로 보며, 92.1.13 이후에도 막후 협상을 속개 하여 입장 차이를 좁혀나가는 노력을 계속할 것으로 보임.

o 92.1.13 TNC 회의는 상기 미.EC의 입장에 비추어, 각국이 12.20 package에 대한 분야별 평가 결과를 밝히기는 하나 전체 package의 수락 또는 거부 입장은 유보하고 주요국 동향을 살피는 회의가 될 것으로 예상됨

o 상기 불투명한 전망에 비추어, 92.1.13 회의시 아국은 주요국 입장을 보아 대처하되 농산물 협정안(예외없는 관세화)에 대한 반대 입장등 협상 분야별 평가는 표명하되, 전체 package 수락을 거부 함으로써 협상 결렬의 책임을 안게되는 scapegoat가 되지 않도록 각별 유념할 필요가 있을 것임.

o 그러나 UR 협상이 타결되는 경우, 예외없는 관세화등 이미 미.EC가 합의하고 있는 부분은 사실상 더 이상 협상의 여지가 없음을 염두에 두고 대처해야 할 것으로 생각됨.

o 결론적으로,
- 미.EC가 협상을 성공시키거나 결렬시키는 관건을 쥐고 있으며,
- 1.13 이후 추가 협상 여부와 추가 협상 분야도 미.EC가 공히 합의하는 분야에서만 가능시되며
- 협상의 향방은 1.13 TNC 회의에서 결정되지 않고, 미.EC간 막후 협상과 양자간 양허 협상이 병행되어 가면서 서서히 판가름이 날 것으로 예상됨.

6

3. 금후 대책 건의

가. 최종 협정 초안 분석 평가

- 분야별 실익의 면밀한 분석 및 평가 작업 추진

- 상기 분야별 평가를 기초로 종합적인 실익 평가 (장-단기로 구분)

나. 주요국의 반응 파악

- 주요국 정부 반응외 의회, 업계 반응도 종합 필요
  (특히, 미국의 경우 의회 및 업계 반응)

다. 92.1.13 이후 협상 과정에 신중 참여

- 기본적으로 계속 협상의 성공적 타결에 협력하는 성실한 협력자라는
  인상을 부각시키면서

- 협상이 타결 방향으로 진전될 경우 관세화 문제로 고립되거나,

- 협상이 정체 또는 결렬 방향으로 가는 경우 관세화 문제로 협상
  결렬의 비난을 받지않도록 대처

라. 92년초 Bush 대통령 방한시 대처

- 어디까지나 UR 협상의 성공적 타결을 위한 협력자라는 이미지를
  부각시키면서,

- 쌀에 대한 시장개방의 어려움을 설명하고,

- 미측이 일부 시장개방을 요구해올 경우 시장개방을 위한 사전 준비로서
  구조 조정 기간이 필요함을 설득

7

마. 국내홍보

- 12.20 package 분석을 토대로 UR 협상의 타결이 종합적으로 아국에
  이익이 됨을 홍보해 나감으로서,

- 대외적으로는 쌀 때문에 야기된 아국에 대한 부정적 시각을 없애고,

- 대내적으로는 UR 협상 타결에 대비한 국민적 공감대 형성에 노력.

끝.

0294

UR 협상관련 12.20 Dunkel 제시 협정안에 대한 주요국 반응(농산물 중심)

1991.12.23.
통상기구과

1. 미국의 반응

   o C. Hills USTR 성명 및 발언 요지 (12.21.AFP 및 주 EC 대표부 보고)

   - Dunkel 사무총장의 협정안을 면밀히 분석예정 (AFP)

   - 미국의 UR 협상 목표 달성을 위해 Dunkel 총장 및 주요 교역 상대국들과의
     긴밀한 협의 노력 계속예정 (AFP)

   - 일부 분야에서는 consensus 를 반영하고 다른 분야에서는 논란의 여지를
     갖고 있는바, 의회 및 업계와 긴밀한 협의후 92.1.13.까지 문서로 입장
     제시 예정 (주 EC 대표부 보고)

   o Baker 국무장관 (12.22., UPI, AFP 연합)

   - 농산물 협상관련, 미.EC 양측은 전반적인 합의 도출에 실패 (UPI)

   - 수출 보조금 관련 Dunkel 협정안 수락 불가 (AFP 연합)

2. 일본의 반응

   o '카토' 관방상 발언요지 (12.21., AFP)

   - 예외없는 관세화 조항에 유감

   - 그러나, UR 협상 전체 package 에 대한 상세 평가는 세부 검토가
     필요하므로 시기 상조

   o '타나부' 농림수산상 발언 요지 (12.21., AFP)

   - UR/농산물 협상 관련 Dunkel 협정안은 수용 불가
     (Japan cannot accept it as it is.)

1

0295

o '와타나베' 통산상 발언요지 (12.22 주 일 대사관 보고)

   - 통산성 관련 분야에 대해서는 거부할 이유가 없음

     (다만, 반덤핑 규제 강화가 불충분한 점 및 safeguards 관련 선별
     적용이 남은 점에 대해서는 불만 상존)

o 일본의 향후 대책 전망 (12.22 주 일 대사관 보고)

   - 미.EC 가 금번 Dunkel 협정안에 모두 반발하고 있음에 비추어 일측이
     서둘러 정치적 결단을 내릴 것으로 보이지 않으며, 미.EC의 동향을
     끝까지 본후 대응할 것으로 전망

   - 92.1. 부시 방일시에는 일.미 양국이 UR 협상의 중요성에 인식을 같이하는
     수준에 그칠 가능성이 있다는 낙관론도 대두

3. EC의 반응 (12.22. 주 EC 대표부 보고)

o Lubbers 화란 (EC 의장국) 수상

   - 12.23. EC 일반 각료 이사회에서 Dunkel 협정안을 논의할 예정

o Andriessen EC 집행위 부위원장

   - 일차 검토 결과, 농산물 분야를 포함하여 동 협정안을 수락키 어려우며
     보다 신중한 검토가 필요

o MacSharry EC 농업담당 집행위원

   - 농산물 협상 관련 미.EC 양측간에는 이견이 상존하고 있으며, Dunkel
     협정안은 자신의 예상보다 훨씬 악화된 것으로 수출물량 감축 방식과
     허용보조의 조건등은 도저히 받아 들일 수 없음

   - 동 협정안을 명백히 거부하는 것은 아니나, EC 회원국들에게 수락을
     요청할 수 없는 형편임.

   - 미국과의 양자 협상계획은 상급없음.

2

.4. 호주의 반응 (12.23. 주 호주 대사관 보고)

   ㅇ Blewett 무역장관 기자회견 요지

     - 농산물 협정안은 호주가 희망해 온 정도의 진전된 내용은 아니나,
       농산물 교역을 장기간에 걸쳐 개혁할 수 있는 제도적 장치를 마련

     - EC의 반응은 그다지 부정적인 것으로는 보이지 않으며 상당히 온건한
       것이며, 호주의 공식 입장은 92.1.6 연방 각의에서 결정될 예정.

                                    끝.

WASHINGTON, D.C.   P.002

MEMORANDUM

FROM: Alan F. Holmer and Judith H. Bello

RE: Preliminary Analysis of Uruguay Round Package

DATE: December 23, 1991

Summary

As you know, the GATT Secretariat developed on December 20 a 451-page Uruguay Round "draft final act" that includes texts for most, but not all, agreements. Missing are the market access commitments for services and goods (both tariff and nontariff measures for goods). Negotiations are scheduled to reconvene in Geneva January 13. Privately, GATT Director-General Arthur Dunkel has told the U.S. the target date for concluding the negotiations is April 15.

The Administration's view is that these texts provide a constructive, tangible basis for further negotiations. With some key modifications, the Administration believes they could result in satisfactory agreements. The view of some in the Congress is more skeptical, and focuses on what the U.S. has not (yet) achieved, rather than what it has achieved. In particular, the absence of firm market access commitments by trading partners makes it difficult for Congress to be positive, even conditionally.

This memorandum provides our preliminary analysis of some of the major components of this package.

Agriculture

The agriculture negotiations have long been the greatest stumbling block to an acceptable agreement. Despite intense U.S.-EC negotiations this fall, the text that emerged from the GATT Secretariat is strongly opposed by not only France, but also the European Communities. The EC says it cannot accept either a complete severance of agricultural payments and farm production, or any limits on conditions of payments to farmers who retire or agree to "set aside" land from production.

Even though the U.S. statements about the text are generally positive, some U.S. special agricultural interests that have been protected by a combination of tariffs and quotas will oppose the text. In addition, the U.S. is disappointed that the draft final act sets more stringent limits on the outlays of export subsidies for, rather than the volume of exports of, farm goods. However, the GATT Secretariat appears to have tried to "split the difference" by including both limits on outlays (36 percent over six years) and volume (25 percent).

Moreover, both Japan and Korea will oppose the text, which calls for overall "tariffication" of agricultural import

5741 —B —2

0298

barriers (that is, conversion of nontariff barriers such as quotas to tariffs), with guaranteed minimum access to those markets (albeit only 3 to 5 percent) over a phase-in period. (However, if Japan and Korea must provide only such limited access to their protected markets, then presumably the U.S. will be able to limit access to its market for products protected under section 22 of the Agricultural Adjustment Act to similar levels.)

Japan in particular was regarded by the U.S. as most unhelpful in Geneva in a wide range of negotiations including, but not limited to, agriculture. Japan's unhelpful positions on many GATT issues are expected to be a key agenda item in President Bush's visit to Tokyo early in January. (The Uruguay Round also will figure prominently in his Seoul visit.)

Trade-Related Intellectual Property

The TRIPs agreement includes some important objectives of the United States, including a 20-year patent term and a prohibition of discrimination in patent practices, including compulsory licensing. However, it does not include any patent protection for pharmaceutical products "in the pipeline," as included in the recent Mexican intellectual property reforms. Further, it provides a long transition period -- up to 20 years -- for some developing countries to implement changes in their domestic patent practices to meet the new GATT obligations.

In addition to these critical patent deficiencies, the copyright provisions are considered unsatisfactory by the Motion Picture Association of America. In particular, the text in the draft final act does not prohibit the imposition of quotas on films based on their national origin, as currently imposed by the European Communities' current broadcasting directive.

Trade-Related Investment Measures

The TRIMs text in the draft final act prohibits some trade-related investment measures, such as local-content requirements and requirements to balance any imports with a commensurate level of exports. However, the text does not prohibit export performance requirements generally.

Safeguards

A "sleeper" in the negotiations continues to be the safeguards text, which includes substantial innovations. In particular, the draft final act prohibits voluntary restraint agreements, and permits a party substantially harmed by increasing imports to take safeguards actions for up to three years without any requirement to compensate adversely affected trading partners.

This change could increase significantly the use of section 201 of the Trade Act of 1974, as amended. This trade remedy authorizes the President to take action to promote

57 41 - 13 - 3

adjustment to import competition if the U.S. International Trade
Commission finds that increasing imports are a substantial cause
of serious injury to a U.S. industry. It has not been widely
used, however, at least in part because of Executive Branch
concern about the compensation the GATT currently requires to any
GATT party adversely affected by safeguards actions. The
elimination of the compensation requirement could transform
section 201 from a least favored to a most favored trade remedy,
since temporary relief would be not only consistent with GATT,
but "free" of any compensation requirement.

Dumping and Subsidies

Second only to agriculture in difficulty last week for
the GATT Secretariat was drafting the texts on subsidies and
dumping. Ultimately, the changes to the current GATT Subsidies
and Antidumping Codes are relatively modest compared to
interested parties' goals, but nonetheless bitterly
controversial. Reflecting deeply held views, for example, both
Senator Lloyd Bentsen and Congressman Dan Rostenkowski, Chairmen
of the Senate Finance and House Ways and Means Committees,
personally telephoned the Director-General last week to
communicate their serious opposition to any "weakening" of the
U.S. unfair trade laws.

The U.S. achieved some modest improvements intended to
prevent unfair traders from circumventing orders providing relief
under the antidumping or countervailing duty laws. On the other
hand, exporting nations seeking fundamental reform of these laws
obtained some reforms as well, including the following:

    o   A sunset provision requires termination of relief after
         five years, unless the administering authority
         determines that continued imposition of duties is
         necessary to prevent the continuation or recurrence of
         injury by dumped or subsidized imports.

    o   In dumping cases, prices "normally" must be compared on
         a weighted-average-to-weighted-average basis, or
         transaction-to-transaction basis. However, prices may
         be compared on a weight-averaged-to-transaction basis
         in specified circumstances (involving so-called
         targeted dumping).

    o   Regarding standing in antidumping cases, an
         administering authority must determine whether a
         petitioner represents an industry through an
         examination of support for, and opposition to, the
         petition. Thus, some producers' silence regarding
         their position on an antidumping petition cannot be
         construed as support for that petition.

    o   A dumping investigation must be terminated if the
         dumping margin is less than 2 percent ad valorem.
         (Currently, the U.S. de minimis level is 0.5 percent.)
         Likewise, it must also be terminated if the volume of

5141 - 13 -k

0300.

dumped imports or injury is negligible, defined in the
former case to mean less than 1 percent of the domestic
market for the like product, unless countries
individually accounting for less than 1 percent of the
domestic market collectively account for more than 2.5
percent. (Currently, the U.S. International Trade
Commission makes injury determinations on a case-by-
case basis, and does not use any mathematical threshold
for determining negligible imports.)

o   Likewise a countervailing duty investigation must be
    terminated if the subsidy level is found to be less
    than 1 percent. (Currently, the U.S. de minimis level
    is 0.5 percent.) It also must be terminated if the
    volume of subsidised imports or injury is negligible.
    Further, imports may not be cumulated from more than
    one country for purposes of injury determinations
    unless, for each country, the subsidy level is more
    than de minimis and the volume of imports is not
    negligible.

o   In constructing value in dumping cases, administering
    authorities must use actual data pertaining to
    production and sales in the country concerned unless
    they are unavailable, in which case the text prescribes
    a hierarchy of three types of information to be used.
    In no case may an administering authority resort to
    prescribed minima. (Currently the U.S. uses a minimum
    10 percent for general, selling and administrative
    expenses, and a minimum 8 percent for profit, in
    constructed value cases.)

o   In dumping cases, new exporters are entitled to an
    accelerated review determining their individual dumping
    margin, if any. Antidumping duties may not be assessed
    against their products until the review is completed,
    although liquidation of entries may be suspended and
    the posting of a bond required. (Currently under U.S.
    law, new exporters are subject to the "all other" rate,
    and have no opportunity to be reviewed until the next
    regularly scheduled administrative review.)

o   In dumping cases, administering authorities are
    authorized to use sampling in cases involving large
    numbers of producers and exporters, but only if it is
    statistically valid. Moreover, administering
    authorities may not discourage "voluntary" responses by
    producers/exporters.

Services

        The draft final text includes the General Agreement on
Trade in Services (GATS) and a few annexes (that is, on
telecommunications, financial services and air transport, and
exemptions from the most-favored-nation requirements of Article
II). Notably absent, however, are any market access and national

5141 — 13 — 5

treatment commitments under Articles XVI and XVII, respectively.

Generally, the GATS requires most-favored-nation (MFN) treatment and transparency, imposes broad conditions on domestic regulation, protects against the unauthorized disclosure of confidential information, broadly authorizes restrictions to safeguard the balance of payments, and provides general and security exemptions (along the lines of those provided in the GATT). It includes a non-application provision, but does not authorize sectoral non-application (that is, application to some, but not all, services and service providers).

Significantly, the Annex on Article II exemptions allows each party to take an indefinite exemption from the MFN obligation of Article II for specified services and service providers. "In principle," such exemptions "should not" exceed 10 years, but as a matter of law, each party is entitled to specify the date on which an exemption will terminate. However, regardless how far into the future a terminate date may be, each exemption is subject to review no later than five years after entry into force of the GATS, at which time the parties collectively shall "examine whether the conditions which created the need for the exemption still prevail" and decide on the date for any further review. Moreover, exemptions "shall be subject to negotiation in subsequent trade liberalizing rounds." The bottom line is that a party may specify exemptions from the MFN obligation of Article II, and those exemptions can be longer than 10 years.

Regarding financial services, uniquely there are two documents: an Annex on Financial Services, and an Understanding on Commitments in Financial Services. Apparently they result from efforts by the Secretariat to resolve a strong difference between financial officials of developed countries, who sought to define terms like "national treatment" with precision; and officials from developing countries, who argued that the GATS language should prevail over any inconsistent terms in the financial services annex.

The U.S. remains quite unsatisfied with either document. The U.S. was unable to achieve several key objectives, including sectoral non-application (that is, declining to apply the financial services commitments to specified countries, while applying GATS to other services and services providers); a good definition of national treatment, using the term equality of competitive opportunities; and assurances that decisions would be made by a financial committee composed of financial officials. The U.S. was able to achieve a prudential "carve-out" (that is, agreement that a party shall not be prevented from taking measures for prudential reasons).

Dispute Settlement

The draft final text includes provisions under negotiation for about a year that would put more teeth in dispute settlement proceedings of the GATT. Currently, a GATT panel

5741 - 13 -6

report lacks any legal|■rce until adopted by the GATT Council,
and a single party -- including a party to the dispute -- can
block such adoption.

The draft final text would create considerable momentum
for adoption of panel reports that could be difficult to stop.
Precisely opposite to the status quo, the draft final act calls
for automatic adoption of panel reports, unless a "consensus" of
countries (that is, more than one country) calls for
reconsideration and the Council then decides not to adopt the
panel report. Effectively, it creates a presumption of adoption,
whereas the current apparatus requires affirmative action for
adoption and permits a single party to block adoption altogether.

In the past, the U.S. viewed itself as a GATT plaintiff
most of the time. Currently, however, the U.S. appears as
frequently as a defendant as a plaintiff before the GATT. While
the proposed reforms benefit the U.S. as plaintiff, they
also make it harder to the U.S. to avoid GATT trade-liberalizing
decisions when it is a defendant as well.

Multilateral Trade Organization

Relatively little noticed to date but likely to be of
great significance, the draft final act contains provisions aimed
to make the GATT a far stronger organization. The GATT
originally was intended to be an International Trade Organization
(ITO), with powers roughly parallel to those of the World Bank
and International Monetary Fund. However, due to opposition from
the U.S. Senate, the ITO was abandoned and instead a less
ambitious, far more circumscribed GATT was created.

The provisions establishing a new Multilateral Trade
Organization essentially would restore the GATT organization to
its original concept. The concept is that the GATT structure
must be transformed to keep pace with its new responsibilities
for trade in services, investment, and the protection of
intellectual property as well as enhanced responsibilities in
traditional trade in goods.

5741-13-7

외 무 부

종 별 :

번 호 : FRW-2772   일 시 : 91 1224 1430

수 신 : 장 관(봉기)

발 신 : 주 불 대사

제 목 : UR 협상

대:WFR-2660

연:FRW-2732

1. 12.23(월) EC 봉상. 농업장관 회담은 DUNKEL 최종타협안이 "EC 의 이해가 공정히 반영되지 않았으므로 이를 수락할수 없으며, 수정되어야 할 것" 이라는 반대입장을 명백히 하고, 최종 평가는 동 협상안을 세부검토후 수립키로 결정함.

2. EC 측으로서는 동 타협안 내용 전반이 미측의 이해에 편중되어 있는데다, 특히 현재 논의중인 공동농업정책(CAP) 개혁취지가 제대로 반영되어 있지 않으며, 농산물 분야중 대농민 소득보장조치의 GREEN BOX 포함, REBALANCING, 수출보조삭감을 구체적 물량기준으로 표시하는 문제등에 있어 도저히 타협안을 수락할수 없다는 입장임.

3. 또한 EC 는 미국이 91.11. 미.EC 간 정상회담이후 각 협상분야에서 오히려 후퇴하는 인상을 주고 있다고 비난하고, 특히 DUNKEL 안은 미국의 일방적 보호조치(301 조)를 간접적으로 자제해 줄것을 요청하는 정도로 되어 있어 불만을 표함.

4. 당초 금번 회의는 UR 협상 관련, 불란서의 비타협적 입장을 다소 완화시키는 계기가 될것으로 전망하였으나, 궁극적으로 현안중인 CAP 개혁을 EC 차원의공동 UR 입장으로 확인하는 결과를 가져옴에 따라 불란서로서는 회의결과에 만족감을 표명함.

5. 이를 위해 불란서는 12.18 CRESSON 총리의 DUNKEL 안에 대한 사전 강력한 반대입장 표명과 함께 금번 회의에 STRAUSS-KAHN 상공장관, MERMAZ 농무장관, JEANNENEY 봉상장관(MINISTRE DELEGUE)으로 구성된 UR 관련 국내 수뇌진을 파견, 수락불가 입장을 적극 개진한 전략이 주효한 것으로 판단함.

6. 한편, 불란서는 92.1.13 이전 새로운 EC 봉상장관 회담 개최를 요구하였으나, 연호 불란서의 기본입장 및 전략에 비추어 EC 집행위에 92.1 월중 협상을 타개할 만한

통상국	장관	차관	1차보	2차보	구주국	경제국	외정실	분석관
정와대	안기부							

PAGE 1   91.12.25   02:26

외신 2과 통제관 FI

0304

새로운 MANDATE 를 부여하기는 어려울 것으로 관측됨. 끝.

(대사 노영찬-국장)

예고:92.6.30. 까지

1991.12.24.
통상기구과

DUNKEL 갓트 사무총장이 1.13 제시한 UR 협상의 최종 협상 문서에 대한
EC의 입장을 논의하기 위한 EC 일반 각료이사회가 각 회원국의 외무장관,
통상장관 및 농무장관들이 참석한 가운데 12.23(월) 브럿셀에서 개최된 바,
동 회의 종료후 발표된 성명을 별첨하니 참고하시기 바랍니다.

0306

COMMUNIQUE

GENERAL COUNCIL

23 DECEMBER 1991

- Recalling the conclusions of the European Council meeting in
  Naastricht, the Council stressed the importance of a
  successful conclusion of the Uruguay Round. A further
  opening up of markets and improvement of the rules and
  disciplines governing world trade are an indispensable
  element in the strategy to remedy the threat of world
  economic recession. More specifically the need for success
  is addressed by the beneficial effects an opening up of world
  trade will have on those countries that are in the process of
  transforming their economies into a more market oriented
  direction.

- The Council discussed the "Dunkel paper" on the basis of a
  first evaluation by the Commission. The Council shared the
  view of the Commission that at this stage a final assessment
  is premature. More time is needed to study the extensive and
  complicated text.

- Moreover the Council noted that a final assessment of the
  "Dunkel paper" is only possible after, and will be influenced
  by, the pending outcome of the outstanding specific
  negotiations planned for and resulting from the "Dunkel
  paper".

0307

- The Council's concerns focused on the proposed result on agriculture. Insofar as the "Dunkel paper" calls into question the foundation of the Community's agricultural policy, the paper is not acceptable and therefore has to be modified. Since the Community has embarked upon a far-reaching reform process of its agriculture policy, the proposed text was in particular evaluated in this light.

- Although the Council recognized that the paper contains some positive elements as it stands now, the Council is of the opinion that the paper is not balanced in total and therefore invites the Commission to negotiate further necessary improvements to it.

  Also genuine efforts from some major trading partners, especially US and Japan, should be obtained to ensure mutual advantages and to increase benefits to all participants.

0308

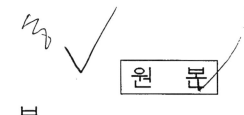

관리 번호	91-995

외 무 부

종 별 : 지급

번 호 : USW-6457　　　　　　　　　　　일 시 : 91 1226 1824

수 신 : 장관(통기)통이,미일,경기원,농수산부,외교안보,경제수석)

발 신 : 주 미 대사　　사본: 주 제네바,EC 대사(본부중계필)

제 목 : UR 농산물 협상 관련 동향

　　대 : WUS-5781,5778

　　연 : USW-6410,6435

　　당관 이영래 농무관및 서용현 서기관은 12.26 미 농무부 해외 농업처 SCHROETER 처장보 및 CRAIG THORN 다자 협력과 부과장을 면담, UR 협상관련 미측 동향을 타진한바, 동결과 하기 보고함.

　　1.DUNKEL 최종 협정안에 대한 미측 평가

　　가. 미 농무부측 견해

　　O SCHROETER 처장보는 DUNKEL 협정안은 농업부분에 관한한 훌륭하고, 긍정적(GOOD AND POSITIVE)이라고 평가하였으나, 미측이 동 협상안을 현재래로 수락할 생각인지 여부에 관한 아측 질문에 대하여는 아직 세부 내용에 대한 충분한검토가 이루어지지 않았으므로 논평할 계제가 못된다고 답변함.

　　O EC 를 위시한 다수의 참가국들이 동 협정안의 수정 필요성을 주장하고 있으며, HILLS 미 무역 대표도 부분적인 개선이 필요하다고 언급한 사실을 상기 시키면서 이러한 각국의 수정 요구를 수용키 위해서는 상당한 범위에서 동 협정안에 대한 수정이 불가피하지 않겠느냐는 아측 질문에 대하여 SCHROETER 처장보는 HILLS 대표가 동 협정안의 조정(ADJUSTMENT)을 언급했을뿐 수정을 주장한것은 아니라고 전제하면서, 비록 부분적인 것이라도 동 협정안 수정을 허용하면 각국의 연쇄적 수정 요구를 초래하여 결국 지난 5 년간의 협상 노력을 수포화시킬것이므로 농무부로서는 동 협정안은 재 협상(RENEGOTIATION) 의 대상이 아닌 TAKE-IT-OR-LEAVE-IT 의 성격을 갖는것으로 본다고 언급함.

　　O 동인은 동 협정안의 조정을 어떤 범위까지 추진할것인지의 문제는 USTR 이 결정할 문제이나, 동 협정안에 의해 불 이익을 받을 일부 분야의 이해 관계와동 협정안

통상국 정와대	장관 정와대	차관 경기원	1차보 농수부	2차보 중계	미주국	통상국	외정실	분석관

PAGE 1　　　　　　　　　　　　　　　　　　　　　　91.12.27　　10:34

외신 2과　통제관 CA

0309

수정시도시 전체 UR 협상 실패 초래 가능성이라는 대국적 이해를 교량해서 결정되어야 할것이라고 언급함.

O 동 협정안에 대한 EC 및 일본의 반대 입장 표명에 대하여, 동 처장보는 EC 측 반대에는 진정한 반대와 국내 정치용 반대가 반반씩 포함되어 있을것이라고 면서, EC 도 농산물 분야에는 반대하지만 서비스등 여타 부문에는 긍정적 입장을 보이고 있는바, 결국 각국이 부분적으로는 불만이 있더라도 UR 성경이 가져올 총체적 이득을 감안하여 동 협정안에 접근해 올것으로 기대한다고 말함.

나. 미 각계의 대응 방향에 관한 관찰

O 미 농업계중 AMERICAN FARM BUREAU 와 NATIONAL CATTLEMENS ASSOCIATION 등에서는 DUNKEL 협정안이 과거의 협상안 보다는 개선되었으나 보조금 삭감 분야에서 미흡하며 좀더 연구 검토가 필요하다는 입장을 표한데 이어, 곡물및 축산물수출 관련 농업 단체들도 대체로 AFB 와 유사한 입장을 표명하였으며, WAIVER 를 받고 있는 낙농, 땅콩, 설탕업계등은 국내 지원 정책의 불이익을 고려하여 계속 반대 입장을 견지하고 있음.

O 미 농무부는 DUNKEL 협정안에 대해 일응 만족하고 있는것으로 보이며, 국지적인 이해 관계 때문에 동 협정안에 대한 수정을 시도하는것은 오히려 대국적인 이득을 해롭게 한다는 논리를 내세워 일부 농업계의 반대를 설득하고 나아가 USTR 에 대해서도 DUNKEL 협정안 수정 시도를 가급적 삼가하도록 압력을 넣고 있는것으로 보임.

O 따라서 미측이 동 협정안을 큰 수정없이 받아들일수 있느냐의 문제는 USTR 이 향후 동 협정안 국내 수용에 관건이될 미 의회와 흥행업계, 전자및 섬유 업계등의 반대를 여하히 무마할수 있느냐에 달려있다고 보이는바, 이와 관련하여미측은 보다 큰 이익을 위해 작은 이익의 희생이 불가피하다는 취지의 여론 캠페인을 전개할것으로 예상됨(별첨 JOURNAL OF COMMERCE 지 사설도 이러한 취지의의견을 개진)

2. 한국에 대한 개도국 우대 불적용 문제

O 아측이 대호 EC 의 한국, 홍콩, 싱가폴등에 대한 개도국 운개 배제 시도에 대한 미측 입장을 문의한데 대하여, THORN 부과장은 미국으로서도 이들 국가들은 사실상 선진국으로 취급하고 있다고 밝힘.

O 이에 대해 서 서기관은 GATT 하에서 개도국 조항을 두고 특별 대우를 부여하는 기본 취지가 이들 개도국들은 선진국과 동일 차원에서 GATT 상 의무를 이행할만한

국내적 여건이 마련되어 있지 않다는 고려에 입각한것임을 상기시키면서, 한국의 경우 특히 농업분야는 어느 개도국보다도 낙후한데다가 국내의 농업과 공업간 불균형 성장에 따른 문제점까지도 않고 있는 형편에서 단순한 소득비교등의 막연한 개념만 가지고 한국의 개도국 우대 적용 대상에서 배제시키려 하는것은 합리적이지 못함을 지적함.

   0 SCHROETER 처장보는 한국 농업의 어려움은 십분 이해한다고 하면서 다만 한국, 홍콩등의 개도국 우대 배제는 이러한 나라들의 전반적 경제력에 비추어 나온것으로 아나, 이에 대한 미측 입장은 아직 정해지지 않았다고 말함.

   첨부 USW(F)-5756
   (대사 현홍주-국장)
   예고:92.6.30 까지

PAGE 3

정 리 보 존 문 서 목 록

기록물종류	일반공문서철	등록번호	2020030100	등록일자	2020-03-12
분류번호	764.51	국가코드		보존기간	영구
명 칭	UR(우루과이라운드) / 농산물 협상, 1992. 전4권				
생 산 과	통상기구과	생산년도	1992~1992	담당그룹	
권 차 명	V.1 1-3월				
내용목차	* 4.10. 한국 국별 이행계획서 GATT 사무국 제출 - 사절단 대표: 김영욱 농림수산부 통상협력 2담당관 5.21. EC CAP(공동농업정책) 개혁안 타결 11.20. 미.EC oilseed 및 UR 농업보조금 협상 타결 12.7.-23. 농산물 협상 - 수석대표: 김광희 농림수산부 기획관리실장				

0001

원 본

외 무 부

종 별 : 지 급

번 호 : USW-0093   일 시 : 92 0108 1635

수 신 : 장관(봉기,봉이,경기원, 농수산부,상공부)사본;주제네바대사, 주 EC

발 신 : 주 미 대사대리 대사(본부중계필)

제 목 : UR 농산물 협상관련 동향

    대;WUS-15

    연;USW-25

    당관 이영래 농무관은 1.8 미 농무부 해외 농업처 다자 협력과의 GRUEFF 과장을 면담, 표제관련 동향을 타진한바, 동결과 요지 하기 보고함(CHILD 한국 담당관 동석)

    1.DUNKEL TEXT (농업부문)에 대한 평가

    O GRUEFF 과장은 DUNKEL TEXT 가 당초 미국이 제안했던 OFFER LIST 에 비해서는 미흡하나, 현실적인 제반 여건을 감안할때 기본적으로 받아들일수 있는 훌륭한 협정 초안이라고 하였음.

    O 다만, 동 협상안중에서 수출보조 부문(24 프로 수량 감축)과 시장 접근 부문(민감 품목의 15 프로 감축과 TRAIFF EQUIVALENT LEVEL 조정과정에서의 협의허용등)감축이 다소 미흡하므로 이의 수정을 요구할 계획이라고 언급함.

    2. 앞으로의 계획과 전망

    O 동과장은 USTR 이 DUNKEL TEXT 의 농업 부문은 물론 타부문도 일단은 긍정적으로 평가하고 있다고 하면서 일부 미흡한 부문에 대하여는 추가 협상을 벌려 3. 까지는 마무리 해야할것임.

    O 또한 EC 가 현재 DUNKEL 의 농업부문 TEXT 에 대하여 반대하면서 CAP REFORM 과 관련한 GREEN BOX 인정, REBALANCING 등 그동안 주요 쟁점 분야에 대하여 재 협상을 요구하고 있으므로 앞으로의 전망을 낙관적으로만 볼수는 없다고 많고 일본은 관세화와 MINIMUM MARKET ACCESS 를 받아들일것을 신중히 고려하고 있는줄 안다고 하면서 한국의 입장을 문의한데 대하여 아측은 최근 한. 미 정상의 기자 회견 내용을 설명하면서 농업부문중 쌀등 기초 식량에 대한 관세화는 정치. 경제적으로 수용하기 어렵다는점을 강조하였음.

통상국 농수부	장관 상공부	차관 중계	1차부	2차보	미주국	통상국	분석관	경기원

PAGE 1   92.01.09   07:33

3. 미 농무부는 1.7. 30 개 주요 농업 관련 단체들로 구성된 AGRICULTURAL POLICY ADVISORY COMMITTEE 를 개최하여 UR 에 대한 그동안의 협상 경과와 DUNKEL TEXT 에 대한 행정부의 견해를 밝히고 자문을 구한결과 참석했던 대부분의 업계에서는 기본적으로 긍정적인 반응을 보이면서 다만 앞으로 추가 협상의 경우 수출 보조와 시장 접근 분야에서 보다 많은 삭감이 이루어지도록 촉구하였다고함(낙농등 WAIVER 품목 관련 업계는 계속 반대)

4. 또한 연호 보고와갑이 미 하원 농업위 는 1.9 행정부(USTR, USDA) 와 주요 농업 관련 단체들의 참석하에 공개 청문회를 개최할 예정인바 행정부와 업계의 기본 입장을 포함한 청문회 결과등은 추보 예정임.

(대사 대리 김봉규-국장) 예고:92.6.30.까지

예고문에 재보류
92.6.30

PAGE 2

0003

외　무　부

종　별 :

번　호 : USW-0115　　　　　　　　　　　　일　시 : 92 0109 1844

수　신 : 장 관(봉기,봉이,미일,경기원,농수산부,상공부,경제수석)

발　신 : 주 미 대사　　　　사본: 주제네바대사,주 EC 대사-본부중계 @

제　목 : UR협상 관련 미하원 청문회

연: USW-0025

1. 미 하원농업위 (위원장: DE LA GARZA의원)는 금 1.9 KATZ USTR 부대표, CROWDER농무부 부차관등 미 행정부 인사와 11개 분야농업계 대표들을 증인으로 출석시킨 가 운데 연호 청문회를 개최한 바, 상기 행정부 인사 2인의 증언요지 및 주요 질의응답 내용을 아래보고함. (당관 이영래 농무관, 조태열 서기관참석)

　가. 증언요지(증언문 팩시편 별송)

(1) KATZ 부대표

. DUNKEL 텍스트는 일괄 합의되지 않는한 어떤 부분도 합의되었다고 볼수 없으며, 시장접근, 농어분야 국내지원 및 수출보조금관련 규정등 상당부문에 대한 추가 협상이 필요함.

. 미국을 포함, 대부분의 협상 참여국들이 동텍스트를 획기적인 것 (MILESTON)으로 받아들이리라 믿지만, 아직 동 텍스트에 대한 최종판단을 내리기는 어려울 것임. DUNKEL 초오장이 1.13 이후에 협상 일정을 정하지는 않았으나 TNC회의직후 시장접근 분야에 대해 주로 쌍무차원에서의 집중적인 협상이 재개될 것으로 기대함.

. DUNKEL 총장이 4월초까지는 협상을 타결코자할 것으로 기대하나, 그러한 일정이 현실적인것인지의 여부는 판단키 어려움. 미국은 단지 협상시한에 맞추기 위해 협상안 서명을 서두르지는 않을 것이며, 미국의 기대수준에 못 미치는 협상안은 결코 수락 하지 않을 것임.

(2) CROWDER 부차관

. DUNKEL 텍스트는 협상의 성공적 타결을 위한 FRAMEWORK 를 제공하고 있다고 보나, 아직 추가협상이 필요함.

통상국　　2차보　　미주국　　통상국　　청와대　　경기원　　농수부　　상공부

외신 1과 통제관

0004

. 미국은 향후 협상에서 현 텍스트상 미국이 불만스럽게 생각하고 있는 분야에서 아래와 같은 개선을 시도할 것임.

    - 농산물 자유화 교역 일정 단축

    - 수량면에서의 수출 보조 추가 감축

    - 시장접근 추가 확대

    - 가공제품 수출에 대한 수량 및 예산지출규제 (현 텍스트는 예산 지출 규제만 적용)

    - 여러분야에서의 개념 정의 명료화

    나. 주요 질의 응답내용

. DUNKEL 텍스트상 개도국 정의 유무에 관한 DE LA GARZA 위원장 질의에 대해, KATZ부대표는 현 텍스트에는 개도국 정의가 없다고 답변하고, 전통적으로 갓트 체제하에 서는 GSP수혜와 관련, 각국이 스스로 개도국을 자칭 (SELF-ELECTION) 해 왔으며 일반적인 개념 규정이 어렵다고 부언함. CROWDER 붕차관은 UR 협상과정에서 이 문제에 관한 업계의 우려를 충분히 개진하였다고 답함. 이에 대해, DE LA GARZA위원장은 특정분야에서의 미국의 주요경쟁국이 BORDERLINE AREA 에 있을 경우 미국에 끼칠 불이익에 대비, 개도국에 대한 명화고한 개념 정의가 필요할 것이라고 강조함.

. 갓트 22조 대상잖물의 관세화를 통해 미국은 설탕, 땅콩등 주요 업계 이익을 희생할 뿐 그에 대한 댓가는 없는게 아니냐는 PETERSON의원 (미-본타나) 질문에 대해, CROWDER부차관은 최소한의 시장접근을 보장 받는데 실익이 있다고 답변하고, 그 예로 일본과 한국의 쌀시장개방을 제시함.

. MARLENEE (공-본타나) 의원이 최종 협상안에 서명할 경우 의회가 관련 국내법을 동 협정에 일치시키기 위해 수정할 의무를 부담하는 것이냐고 질의한데 대해, KATZ 부대표는 갓트 협정은 자기집행적조약 (SELF-EXECUTING TREATY) 아 아니므로의회가 협정은 서명에 의해 구속받지는 않으나, 국내법과의 상충을 이유로 의회가 승인을 거부한다면 주요교역 상대구과의 마찰이 불가피하며 미국은 그로 인한 댓가를 치루어야 할 것 이라고 답변함. 동 부대표는 이어 DUNKEL 텍스트상각국은 국내법을 동 협정에 일치시 키기 위해 노력하여야 한다는 ' BEST EFFORTS' 조항이 있으며 이를 이행치 못할 경우 국제적 문제가 야기될것임을 강조하고, 행정부는 의회가 수용 할 수있는 선에서 협상 타결을 위해 최선을 다할것이라고 부언함. 이에 대해

PAGE 2

MARLENEE의원은 협상 결과 국내법을 수정해야 하는 상황이 발생한다면, 국내적으로 심각한 문제 (INTERNAL WARFARE) 가 야기될 것이라고 경고함.

. 1.13 이후의 협상 전망 (위원장 질의)에 대해 KATZ 부대표는 미국은 나름대로의 수정 요구리스트를 갖고 있으나 수정 가능 범위를 예측하기는 어렵다고 답변함.

. 최종 협상안이 NAFTA 에 미치는 영향 여부에관한 질의 (위원장)에 대해 KATZ 부대표는 아무런 영향이 업다고 답변하고, 미국은 완전한 선택의 자유를 갖고 있다고 부언함.

. 상기 이외에 설탕, 땅콩, 면화등 개별의원의 지역구 이해와 관련한 질의 답변및 UR협상후 갓트체제를 정식 다자무역기구 (MTO) 로 개편할 필요성 여부에 관한 논의가 있었음.

2. 농업계 대표들의 증언문은 파편 송부 예정임.

(대사 대리 김봉규-국장)

PAGE 3

주 미 대 사 관

USW(F) : 0145   년월일 : 920109   시간 : 1844

수 신 : 장   관 (통기.통이.미길.경기간.농수산부.상석부
발 신 : 주 미 대 사   경제수석 ; 사본 : 축제네바, EC 대사)

보통 / 안제   심사

제 목 : UR 협상관련 미 하원청문회 증언논 (14매) 출처 :   )
             (USW-0115 참거용)

(0145 - 14 - 1)

외신 1과
봄 제

0000

STATEMENT BY
JULIUS L. KATZ
DEPUTY UNITED STATES TRADE REPRESENTATIVE
BEFORE THE
COMMITTEE ON AGRICULTURE
HOUSE OF REPRESENTATIVES
JANUARY 9, 1992

Mr. Chairman:

I appreciate the opportunity to appear again before your Committee to discuss the status of the agricultural negotiations in the Uruguay Round and, particularly, the "draft final act" also known as the "Dunkel text".

Since Under Secretary Crowder will discuss the specifics of the agricultural text, it may be useful for me, Mr. Chairman, to place the agricultural negotiations in the broader context of the overall Uruguay Round package.

The "draft final act" released by the Director General of the GATT, Arthur Dunkel, on December 20 covers all issues in the Round. We commend the Director General for his untiring efforts to bring the Uruguay Round to a successful conclusion.

The draft agreement is an important step in the negotiations. The largest portion of the document reflects agreement by participants -- the result of five years of negotiation. Where there was no consensus among the participants, the chairmen of the respective negotiating groups presented their own texts. In those situations, the text

0145-12-2

represents the best judgement of the Chairman of the negotiating group and Mr. Dunkel of what might be acceptable to participants at the end of the day.

Early last month I reported on efforts that were underway in an attempt to break the agricultural logjam. Those efforts continued throughout the time leading up to the release of the Dunkel draft. Despite our persistent efforts, we were not able to come to a meeting of the minds with the European Community on several key issues in the agricultural negotiations. Hence, the draft text on agriculture represents Mr. Dunkel's attempt, as Chairman of the Agricultural Negotiating Group, to resolve those issues.

The entire draft agreement is complex and more than 450 pages in length. The Administration is in the process of carefully examining the entire text. We are in the process of consulting within the Executive Branch, with the Congress and with the private sector in assessing the draft, to determine what problems there might be and where clarification may be required.

Timing and Process

Nothing in the draft final act is agreed until everything is agreed, and in this connection, considerable work remains to be done with respect to the negotiations on market access for goods and services and the schedules for internal support and export subsidy commitments in agriculture. Only when these negotiations are completed can we assess the true worth of the entire package of agreements.

Mr. Dunkel's timetable for completing the negotiations calls for first reactions to the draft final act at the Trade Negotiating Committee meeting on January 13. We believe most participants, including the United States, will accept the draft text as a milestone in the negotiations but will not pass final judgment on the text.

Mr. Dunkel has not set out the exact schedule for the negotiating process beyond January 13. However, we expect to resume intensive, mostly bilateral, negotiations on market access shortly after the TNC meeting.

The draft agreement on agriculture calls for participants to submit their lists of commitments, together with related supporting data tables, no later than March 1. Mr. Dunkel calls for agreement on final schedules for agriculture for each participant no later than March 31.

I expect that Mr. Dunkel will seek to push the Uruguay Round "package' to a conclusion by early April. I do not know at this point whether such a timetable is realistic. The United States will not rush to sign an agreement just to meet a deadline.

0145-14-4

Indeed, we will not sign _any_ agreement unless the package meets our standards of substantial overall benefits to the United States.

Conclusion

One important element of that overall package must be fundamental reform of agricultural trade. A successful Uruguay Round agreement for agriculture must begin the process of meaningful agricultural reform consistent with the long-term objective of a fair and market-oriented agricultural trading system.

In many respects the agriculture text is a major step forward in our effort to establish solid international rules for trade in agricultural commodities. The weakness of such rules has been a major short-coming of the GATT for the forty-four years of its existence.

A good Uruguay Round agreement holds the potential for significant benefits for American agriculture in this decade and on into the 21st century. If we can achieve a good and fair agreement for American farmers, it is worth fighting for, and that is what we have been doing and will continue to do.

Mr. Chairman, Congress has been an essential partner in this entire process, and we will continue to consult with you to

0011

ensure that your concerns are fully addressed. We have also consulted closely and frequently with the U.S. agricultural private sector. We could not have come this far without the broad support we have received.

That concludes my statement, Mr. Chairman. I will be happy to respond to your questions.

0145-1K-6

0012

Statement by
Richard T. Crowder
Under Secretary
International Affairs and Commodity Programs
U.S. Department of Agriculture
Before the
House Committee on Agriculture
January 9, 1992

Mr. Chairman, members of the Committee, I appreciate this
opportunity to appear before you to discuss the current status of
the GATT multilateral trade negotiations on agriculture. First, I
want to thank you and other members of the Committee who came to
Geneva in December during that critical phase of the negotiations.
We benefited from your interest and your counsel.

We also were fortunate to have a large number of private
sector representatives in Geneva in December. We received valuable
advice from these representatives and reflected their issues and
concerns during the discussions preceding the publication of the
Dunkel text.

Since the opening of the Uruguay Round more than five years
ago, it has been a long, hard and, at times, frustrating road,
especially for the agricultural portion of these negotiations.
Today, we are hopeful that we can bring these talks to a conclusion
that will benefit U.S. farmers and agricultural trade worldwide.

0145-14-7

American farmers are among the most efficient in the world. Our goal in the Uruguay Round has been constant -- the reduction of trade distorting policies for freer and fairer global agricultural trade. Given a more open world trading system, our farmers will compete successfully and achieve higher incomes in an expanded world market.

The Uruguay Round discussions are now focused on the comprehensive draft released by the Director-General of the GATT, Arthur Dunkel, on December 20. While this paper is not a final document, it is the Director-General's attempt to strike a compromise across all of the negotiating groups. There are some pluses and minuses for all participants in all of the negotiating areas. This comprehensive document includes, of course, a draft text on agriculture.

In several areas, including agriculture, no consensus was achieved among the participants and Mr. Dunkel has now determined to propose his own solutions. Therefore, the draft represents his attempt to resolve many contentious issues. Our analysis of this document is continuing, but we believe that it provides a framework to bring the negotiations to a successful conclusion.

5

It is important to keep in mind there is no agreement with respect to anything in this draft until there is agreement with respect to the entire contents of this draft and the commitments of individual countries. Therefore, more negotiating must be done before we will be finished. Only then can we make definitive judgments of its benefits.

Mr. Chairman, with your permission I would now like to highlight the key components of the Dunkel text on agriculture and then respond to questions that you and other members of the Committee may have.

Overview of the Draft Text on Agriculture

The draft text calls for specific commitments to reduce export subsidies, internal supports and market access barriers. Reduction commitments are to be implemented over a six-year period, beginning in 1993. One year before the end of the implementation period, negotiations -- in accordance with a "continuation clause" -- will be initiated to continue the reform process. The text also establishes disciplines on sanitary and phytosanitary measures that will prevent countries from using these measures as disguised barriers to trade.

In addition, the enhanced GATT dispute settlement procedures developed in the Uruguay Round will apply to agriculture.

0145-1K-9

I will now briefly present an overview of each of the four major areas of the agricultural trade negotiations.

Export competition

There are both volume and budget disciplines on the use of export subsidies. The base period for determining subsidy reductions will be 1986-90. Reductions would be measured from the average level of export subsidies provided in that period. This means that for cases in which export subsidies have increased since the 1986-90 period, the reductions could be significantly greater than simple reductions from current levels.

Only direct export subsidies will be subject to reduction commitments. Internal support, such as deficiency payments and marketing loans, will not be subject to these commitments.

The volume of primary and first-stage processed products exported with subsidies will be required to be reduced by 24 percent. Other processed products will be subject to budgetary disciplines. Budgetary outlays on export subsidies for primary and processed products will be reduced by 36 percent.

0145-14-10

Market access

Market access would be increased by converting non-tariff barriers -- such as the EC's variable levy, the U.S. Section 22 quotas and the Japanese import ban on rice -- to tariffs which would then be subject to a reduction of 36 percent on average with a minimum rate of 15 percent for each tariff line.

All non-tariff market access barriers will be subject to this tariffication process, except for temporary safeguard measures under Article 19 of the GATT and balance of payment restrictions. The base period for tariffication will be 1986-1988.

Minimum access commitments at zero, or very low tariffs, will be set at 3 percent of domestic consumption in 1986-88 and expanded to 5 percent.

Current access for tariffied products that have imports above 5 percent of consumption will be maintained. Growth in the zero or low tariff access opportunity will be possible, but probably only through the request/offer process.

A special safeguard provision for tariffied products can be triggered either in response to import surges or low import prices.

*/ㅆ5- /ㅆ- //

6

Internal supports

Measures providing internal support, unless specifically exempted from reduction commitments, would be reduced by 20 percent between 1993 and 1999 from 1986 levels (using a 1986-88 fixed reference price).

The Aggregate Measure of Support (AMS) will be used to carry out reductions in domestic support for individual commodities as well as for sector wide programs. If support for a single commodity or for the sector wide programs is 5 percent or less, no further reductions are required.

Sanitary and phytosanitary measures

The sanitary and phytosanitary element of the agreement would provide meaningful disciplines to ensure that countries do not erect unjustified trade barriers under the guise of health concerns.

At the same time, the text on these measures explicitly recognizes the rights of countries to protect human, animal, and plant life and health through appropriate sanitary and phytosanitary measures.

The text also calls for such measures which impact on trade to be science-based, and it excludes various nonscientific considerations which had been opposed by the United States.

0145-1K-12

While encouraging the use of international standards, the agreement also recognizes the right of countries to use stricter standards.

The agreement includes the concepts of equivalency and pest- and disease-free areas. It also makes it clear that the sanitary and phytosanitary area will be covered by the GATT dispute settlement procedures.

As I mentioned earlier, the Dunkel text represents his attempt to bridge differences on a number of contentious issues. Therefore, there are a number of things in the text that are not as we would have liked. Let me point out some of them.

The language in the text does not liberalize agricultural trade in the near-term as much as the United States would like.

We would like to see greater reductions in export subsidies in quantity terms.

We would like to see opportunities for the expansion of current market access.

We would like to have quantitative and budgetary disciplines on exports of processed products. The draft text would apply only budgetary export disciplines to these products.

o/ᴇ5 — /4 — /3

There also are a number of areas in the text where the meaning is not clear.

Over the coming weeks we will be discussing these and other issues in Geneva. Once this process is completed, we will be in position to pass final judgment on the document.

That concludes my statement, Mr. Chairman. I would be glad to answer your questions and those of the other committee members.

--#--

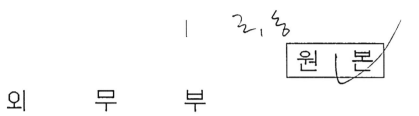

외 무 부

종 별 :

번 호 : GVW-0046   일 시 : 92 0109 1900

수 신 : 장 관(통기,경기원,재무부,농림수산부,상공부)

발 신 : 주 제네바대사

제 목 : UR/농산물 협상

1. 1.8(수) 최농무관은 WOLTER 농업국장을 면담,향후 협상 일정등에 대해 의견 교환한바 동인 언급 요지 및 제너바주재 각국 농업담당자와 접촉내용 하기 보고함.

　　가. WOLTER 농업국장

　- 향후 협상 일정 및 협상 전개방식에 대해서는1.9(목) 개최 예정인 그린룸 회의시 던켈 총장이 밝힐 것임. 협상 그룹별 협상은 없을 것이지만 TNC 형태의 일부 FINE TUNING 작업, 시장접근그룹, 서비스그룹, 법률문서화 작업그룹(LEGALDRAFTING GROUP)등 4개의 TRACK에 따라 협상이 전개될 것으로 예상됨.

　- 농산물 관련 3.1 까지의 감축 약속 계획 제출시한 및 3.31 까지의 양자 협상등의 일정은1.13.TNC 회의 결과와 관계없이 진행될 수밖에 없는 상황임.

　　나. 각국 동향

　- 대부분의 국가가 금주말 본국의 최종 평가가있을 것임을 시사

　- 카나다는 각국의 동향을 예의 주시하며 특히 EC, 일본의 동향에 관심 표명함.

　- 놀웨이는 북구로서 전체적 PACKAGE 는 받아들일수 있으나 농산물 분야에서 국경 조치(11조2항 C) 및 국내보조에 불만임.

　- 일본은 관세화 검토관련 외상발언에 대하여 정부의 공식입장의 결정이 아님을강조함.

　- 스위스는 기존 입장의 변경이 없음을 강조하고1.9(목) 중 3개도시(베른, 루체른등)에서 농민시위가 있을 예정이라고 함.끝

　　(차석대사 김삼훈-국장)

통상국　　2차보　　경기원　　재무부　　농수부　　상공부

UR(우루과이라운드)-농산물 협상, 1992. 전4권(V.1 1-3월)　**339**

長官報告事項

報告畢

1992. 1. 10.
通 商 局
通商機構課(3)

題 目 : UR/Dunkel Paper에 대한 美 下院 聽聞會 結果

1.9(木) Katz USTR 副代表, Crowder 農務部 ■次官等은 美 下院 農業委
聽聞會에서 UR/農産物 協商 關聯 Dunkel Paper에 대한 美 行政府의 立場을
證言한 바, 同 證言 要旨를 아래와 같이 報告 드립니다.

---

1. Dunkel paper에 대한 立場

   ○ ~~同 Paper에 대한~~ 內部 檢討를 ~~繼續~~中이며, 最終 立場은 下記 事項을 考慮하여
   決定할 方針

   - 農産物을 包含한 市場接近 分野에서의 讓許協商 結果

   - 輸出補助 減縮, 市場接近 機會 擴大 問題等에 대한 未備點 ~~補完~~ 토의

2. 1.13 TNC 會議 및 同 會議 以後의 協商 展望

   ○ 1.13 TNC 會議에서는 美國을 包含한 대부분의 國家들이 Dunkel Paper를
   協商의 基礎로는 받아들이되 最終 立場 表明은 하지 않을 것으로 展望

   ○ 1.13 以後에는 市場接近 分野에 대한 주로 兩者間의 集中的 協商이 展開될
   것으로 豫想

   ○ Dunkel 事務總長이 4月初까지 協商 終結을 推進할 것으로 豫想되나 同 協商
   日程이 現實的인 것인지는 현단계에서 不分明

   - 美國으로서는 만족할만한 package가 되지 않는한 同 協商 日程에
   구애받지 않을 方針.

3. 言論 및 國會對策 : 別途 措置 不要.   끝.

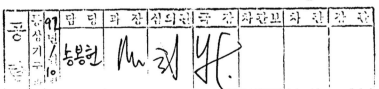

0022

長官報告事項

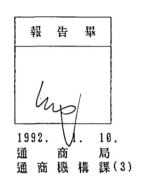

題 目 : UR/Dunkel Paper에 대한 美 下院 聽聞會 結果

> 1.9(木) Katz USTR 副代表, Crowder 農務部 次官等은 美 下院 農業委
> 聽聞會에서 UR/農産物 協商 關聯 Dunkel Paper에 대한 美 行政府의 立場을
> 證言한 바, 同 證言 要旨를 아래와 같이 報告 드립니다.

1. Dunkel paper에 대한 立場

   ○ 內部 檢討中이며, 最終 立場은 下記 事項을 考慮하여 決定할 方針

   - 農産物을 包含한 市場接近 分野에서의 讓許協商 結果

   - 輸出補助 減縮, 市場接近 機會 擴大等 未備點 討議

2. 1.13 TNC 會議 및 同 會議 以後의 協商 展望

   ○ 1.13 TNC 會議에서는 美國을 包含한 대부분의 國家들이 Dunkel Paper를
   協商의 基礎로는 받아들이되 最終 立場 表明은 하지 않을 것으로 展望

   ○ 1.13 以後에는 市場接近 分野에 대한 주로 兩者間의 集中的 協商이 展開될
   것으로 豫想

   ○ Dunkel 事務總長이 4月初까지 協商 終結을 推進할 것으로 豫想되나 同 協商
   日程이 現實的인 것인지는 현단계에서 不分明

   - 美國으로서는 만족할만한 package가 되지 않는한 同 協商 日程에
   구애받지 않을 方針.

3. 言論 및 國會對策 : 別途 措置 不要.   끝.

STATEMENT BY
JULIUS L. KATZ
DEPUTY UNITED STATES TRADE REPRESENTATIVE
BEFORE THE
COMMITTEE ON AGRICULTURE
HOUSE OF REPRESENTATIVES
JANUARY 9, 1992

Mr. Chairman:

I appreciate the opportunity to appear again before your
Committee to discuss the status of the agricultural negotiations
in the Uruguay Round and, particularly, the "draft final act"
also known as the "Dunkel text".

Since Under Secretary Crowder will discuss the specifics of
the agricultural text, it may be useful for me, Mr. Chairman, to
place the agricultural negotiations in the broader context of the
overall Uruguay Round package.

The "draft final act" released by the Director General of
the GATT, Arthur Dunkel, on December 20 covers all issues in the
Round. We commend the Director General for his untiring efforts
to bring the Uruguay Round to a successful conclusion.

The draft agreement is an important step in the
negotiations. The largest portion of the document reflects
agreement by participants -- the result of five years of
negotiation. Where there was no consensus among the
participants, the chairmen of the respective negotiating groups
presented their own texts. In those situations, the text

0145-1K-2

0024

represents the best judgement of the Chairman of the negotiating group and Mr. Dunkel of what might be acceptable to participants at the end of the day.

Early last month I reported on efforts that were underway in an attempt to break the agricultural logjam. Those efforts continued throughout the time leading up to the release of the Dunkel draft. Despite our persistent efforts, we were not able to come to a meeting of the minds with the European Community on several key issues in the agricultural negotiations. Hence, the draft text on agriculture represents Mr. Dunkel's attempt, as Chairman of the Agricultural Negotiating Group, to resolve those issues.

The entire draft agreement is complex and more than 450 pages in length. The Administration is in the process of carefully examining the entire text. We are in the process of consulting within the Executive Branch, with the Congress and with the private sector in assessing the draft, to determine what problems there might be and where clarification may be required.

Timing and Process

Nothing in the draft final act is agreed until everything is agreed, and in this connection, considerable work remains to be done with respect to the negotiations on market access for goods and services and the schedules for internal support and export subsidy commitments in agriculture. Only when these negotiations are completed can we assess the true worth of the entire package of agreements.

Mr. Dunkel's timetable for completing the negotiations calls for first reactions to the draft final act at the Trade Negotiating Committee meeting on January 13. We believe most participants, including the United States, will accept the draft text as a milestone in the negotiations but will not pass final judgment on the text.

Mr. Dunkel has not set out the exact schedule for the negotiating process beyond January 13. However, we expect to resume intensive, mostly bilateral, negotiations on market access shortly after the TNC meeting.

The draft agreement on agriculture calls for participants to submit their lists of commitments, together with related supporting data tables, no later than March 1. Mr. Dunkel calls for agreement on final schedules for agriculture for each participant no later than March 31.

I expect that Mr. Dunkel will seek to push the Uruguay Round "package" to a conclusion by early April. I do not know at this point whether such a timetable is realistic. The United States will not rush to sign an agreement just to meet a deadline.

0145-14-4

Indeed, we will not sign _any_ agreement unless the package meets our standards of substantial overall benefits to the United States.

Conclusion

One important element of that overall package must be fundamental reform of agricultural trade. A successful Uruguay Round agreement for agriculture must begin the process of meaningful agricultural reform consistent with the long-term objective of a fair and market-oriented agricultural trading system.

In many respects the agriculture text is a major step forward in our effort to establish solid international rules for trade in agricultural commodities. The weakness of such rules has been a major short-coming of the GATT for the forty-four years of its existence.

A good Uruguay Round agreement holds the potential for significant benefits for American agriculture in this decade and on into the 21st century. If we can achieve a good and fair agreement for American farmers, it is worth fighting for, and that is what we have been doing and will continue to do.

Mr. Chairman, Congress has been an essential partner in this entire process, and we will continue to consult with you to

0145-1K-5

ensure that your concerns are fully addressed. We have also consulted closely and frequently with the U.S. agricultural private sector. We could not have come this far without the broad support we have received.

That concludes my statement, Mr. Chairman. I will be happy to respond to your questions.

0145-1K-6

외 무 부

종 별 :

번 호 : GEW-0068

일 시 : 92 0110 1900

수 신 : 장관(통기)

발 신 : 주 독일 대사 사본:주 GV 대사(직송필)

제 목 : UR 협상동향

대:WGE-0004

연:GEW-2599

1. 대호관련, 당관 정문수 참사관이 금 1.10. 경제부 UR 농산물담당 KIESOW부과장을 면담, 파악한 내용 요지를 아래보고함.

　　가. 주재국 입장수립

　　- 주재국 정부는 금 1.10. 오전 KOHL 수상주재 각의에서 원칙적으로 12.20. 던켈 사무총장제의 협정초안의 농산물분야문서에 대해 협상기초로서 이를 포기(거부)하지 않고 계속하여 교섭해 나간다는 방침을 결정했다함.

　　- 1.10-11. 간 브랏셀개최 EC 경제, 농업장관회의에서 EC 공동입장 조정윤곽이 들어날 것이라 함

　　나. 농산물 문서중 세부 쟁점사항

　　전반적으로 주재국 정부는, 농산물분야의 몇몇개 세부사항에 있어 KIECHLE 농업장관은 보다 강한 톤으로 입장관철을 주장하고 있는데 반해 MOELLEMANN 경제장관은 UR 협상 타결을 위해 보다 유연하고 전향적 태도를 취하고 있는바, 주재국이 문제시하고 있는 세부 쟁점사항은 아래임.

　　- 던켈총장 초안의 93-99 년간 36 프로 관세삭감안 관련, 주재국 농업부측은 충분한 대외농업보호 필요성에 입각한 연호 KIECHLE 농업장관의 요망사항(연호 1 항 "나"참조)이 충분히 반영되지 않아 특히 밀등 곡물과 설탕(무) 보호에 미치는 문제점을 심각히 제기하고 있는 반면, 경제부측은 동제안이 수용가능한 사항으로 간주한다 함.

　　- EC 측에서 대체곡물의 관세설정으로 요구하는 REBALANCING 요구에 대해서도, 농업장관은 중요성을 강조하는데 반해, 경제부측은 동내용은 91.10.9. UR 협상 방침에

통상국	장관	차관	1차보	2차보	구주국	경제국	외정실	분석관
청와대	안기부							

PAGE 1

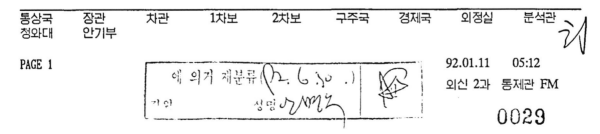

92.01.11　05:12

외신 2과　통제관 FM

0029

관한 각의 결정사항에 포함되어 있지 않은 점등에 비추어 양보가능한 사항을 본다함.

- 던켈총장의 GREEN BOX 안(협정초안 부속문서 2)이 대체적으로 연호 KIECHLE 농업장관 주장과 합치하고 있어 문제되지 않을것으로 보며, 다만 동초안 부속문서 2의 제 6 항(DECOUPLED INCOME SUPPORT) 내용 개선을 바라고 있으나, 중요 내용은 수용에 문제가 없을 것으로 본다함.

농업부측은 외면적으로는 GREEN BOX 범위확대를 주장하나, 내막적으로는 관련 초안내용이 불리한 방향으로 해석되거나 하지않고 그대로 채택되도록 보장하기 위한 입장강화에 진의가 있는 것으로 분석 한다함.

국내보조관련 EC 측이 크게 반대하고 있는 것으로 외지에 확대보도된 것은, RUBBERS 전 EC 의장이 91.12.30. 자로 DELORS 위원장 앞으로 GREEN BOX 범위확대를 요구하는 서한을 송부한데 연유한 것인바, 차기 EC 위원장 피선을 희망하는 동인이 던켈총장안 전반에 대해 반대하고 있는 프랑스의 환심을 사기위한 의도에서 나온것으로 분석한다함.

다. TNC 대표단 파편

EC 측 대표 참석과 별도로 주재국 대표단 파견은 없다함.

2. 한편 정참사관은, 식량 안보적 측면에서 아국의 쌀시장 개방의 어려움을 설명하고 이에 관한 주재국측의 측면지원 가능성을 재차 타진한바, 동인 반응은 아래와 같음.

- MOELLEMANN 경제장관은 한국을 포함한 모든 주요교역국가들이 UR 협상을 가능한한 조속히 매듭짓는데 우선적인 이해를 같이하고 있으므로 이를 위하여 모든 협상참가국의 건설적이며 객관적인 양보가 필수적이라는 입장을 견지하고 있음.

- 동장관이 91.11. 한국과 유사한 문제에 처한 일본방문시에도 동입장을 표방하는등 UR 협상타결에 전향적자세로 임하고 있음.

- 사견임을 전제로 던켈총장 초안이 예외없는 관세화를 목표로 하고 있음에 비추어 일부품목의 관세 예외반영 가능성은 현재로서는 희박한 것으로 봄

3. 동건 관련 EC 입장조정 동향등 진전사항은 1.15. 동인 오찬초청 접촉후 추보하겠음. 끝

(대사-국장)

예고:92.6.30. 까지

원 본

외 무 부

종 별 :

번 호 : USW-0296   일 시 : 92 0117 1845

수 신 : 장 관(통기, 경기원, 농림수산부) 사본:주제네바, 일대사(중계필)

발 신 : 주 미국 대사대리

제 목 : UR 협상

대: WUS-0218

1. 당관 이영래 농무관및 서용현 서기관은 1.17. 농무부 해외농업처 SCHROETER 부처장보와의 오찬기회에 시와꾸 일본 농산성 심의관의 방미협의 결과를 타진하였음.

2. SCHROETER 부처장보에 의하면, 작 1.16. 시와꾸 심의관이 CROWDER 농무차관과 면담하였으나 예외없는 관세화에 대한 일본의 반대입장을 재확인하였을 뿐, 뚜렷한 새로운 입장을 제시한바는 없었다함.

3. 동 부처장보는 일본을 중심으로 하여 최근 거론되고 있는 관세화의 FLEXIBILITY 라는 것은 결국 일본이나 한국의 쌀과 같은 민감한 품목에 대해서 관세화의 유예기간을 설정해 달라는 것으로 이해하고 있다고 하면서(시와꾸 심의관이 이를 직접 언급한 것은 아니라함), 국부적으로는 이러한 유예기간을 허용함으로써 관련국들이 국내정치적 민감성을 극복하고 UR 협상 결과를 수용하도록 유도하는데 도움이 될수도 있겠으나, 이는 DUNKEL TEXT 에 대한 실질적 수정의 선례가 될 수 있다는 측면에서 속단하기 어려운 문제라고 언급함. 끝.

(대사대리 김봉규-국장)

예고: 92.6.30. 까지

통상국 안기부	장관 경기원	차관 농수부	1차보 중계	2차보	미주국	외정실	분석관	정와대

외신 2과 통제관 BS

0031

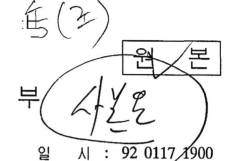

관리번호 92-69

외 무 부

종 별 :

번 호 : GVW-0122

일 시 : 92 0117 1900

수 신 : 장관(봉기, 경기원, 재무부, 농림수산부, 상공부, 경제수석)

발 신 : 주 제네바 대사

제 목 : UR/시장접근 협상

연: GVW-0110

1.17 DENIS 의장 주재로 개최된 표제협상 그룹 비공식 회의 토의 요지 아래보고함.(본직, 엄재무관, 최농무관 참석)

1. 향후 협상일정

- 의장은 지난 수일간 주요 참가국과 비공식 논의를 거쳐 합의된 별첨 향후협상일정(농산물을 포함한 모든 품목에 대한 시장접근 협상) 을 배포하면서 금일 회의는 동 협상 일정을 확정지을 목적으로 소집된 것이라 언급함.

- 주요 회의일정

0 시장접근 협상그룹은 ON CALL 상태로 필요할때 수시 개최

0 금일 회의부터 2.28 까지 협상 참가국간 양자, 복수국가간 다자간 협상을 계속함.

0 1.28-2.6, 2.20-2.28 사이에는 집중적인 협상 진행

0 2.7 에는 비공식 협상 그룹회의 개최

0 3.1 까지 협상 종료 및 그 결과 제시(농산물의 국내보조 및 수출 보조 포함)

0 3 월중순(3.15 경)에 협상 결과 평가

0 3.31. 각국의 양허 SCHEDULE 을 PROTOCOL 에 첨부

0 의장은 상기 협상 과정에서 개도국 우대원칙 특히 CREDIT 부여 방안에 대한 의장 GUIDELINE 이 존중되어야 함을 강조함. - 이에 대해 각국은 별다른 발언이 없었으며 다만 멕시코가 라틴 및 카르비안 국가를 대표하여 다음 요지의 발언이 있었고 칠레, 아르헨티나로 부터 지지 발언이 있었음.

0 협상 결과에 동 지역 수출 이익이 반영되어야 함.(특히 열대산품 및 천연산품에 대한 시장접근 개선)

0 개도국 우대 원칙이 존중되어야 하고 특히 양허폭 확대에 대한 CREDIT 가적절히

통상국	장관	차관	1차보	2차보	경제국	외정실	분석관	청와대
정와대	경기원	재무부	농수부	상공부				

PAGE 1

에 의거 재분류(92.6.30.)

성명

92.01.18   08:27

외신 2과   통제관 BD

0032

부여되어야 함.

0 개도국 관심품목은 관세인하 이행기간이 3 년이내 이어야 함.

- 브라질, 폐루는 모든 품목에 대하여 35 퍼센트 수준에서 일괄 BINDING 라는 수정 OFFER 를 제시키로 하였다 함.

2. 관찰 및 평가

가. 의장 제시 일정에 의한 농산물 협상의 원만한 진행 여부

- 금일 회의에서도 DENIS 의장은 연호 보고한바와 같이 농산물을 포함한 TRACK I 의 협상을 3.1 까지 종결짓고자 하는 의지를 천명하였으나 회의 종료후 EC, 일본, 북구등과 접촉한 결과 이들 국가들도 농산물 TEXT 에 대한 참가국간 합의 부족(TRACK 4 에 의한 추가 협상에서 수정되어야 할 부문이 상당히 있음을 암시)시일 촉박등의 이유를 들어 3.1 까지의 농산물 협상 종결에 문제점이있다는반응을 보였음.

- 그러나 금일 회의에서 농산물협상안에 불만을 갖고있는 EC, 일본등 모든참가국들이 의장의 작업계획에 아무런 반대를 표시하지 않았음에 비추어 의장이 제시한 일정에 따라 농산물을 포함한 모든 품목에 대한 협상이 양자간, 복수국가간 협상으로 진행될 예정이며 동 협상에 농산물 협상도 협상 상대국에 따라서는 깊이 있게 논의될 것으로 예상되므로(아국시장에 관심을 갖고있는 농산물 수출국은 동 협상 과정에서 아국의 COUNTRY PLAN 제시 여부에 불문하고 특정 품목에 대한 시장접근 개선을 요구할 가능성등) 내부적으로 이에대한 구체적인 대비책 마련이 요망됨.

나. 시장접근 협상(공산품)

- 시장접근 협상의 주요 걸림돌인 분야별 접근방식에 대한 미국과 EC 간의 의견차이가 현재까지 상존하고 있어(미국에 문의한 결과 별다른 진전이 없는 것으로 확인) 1.28 주간에 개최될 집중적 협상과정에서 품목 협상등 구체적이고 실질적인 협상이 전개될 것인지는 불투명하나 주요교역국으로 부터 양자협상 개최 요청이 반드시 있을것으로 예상되며 미국과는 1.29 양자 협상을 개최키로 합의하였는바, 동 협상에 대비하여 다음사항에 대한 사전 준비가 요망됨.

0 화학제품 관세조화 방안에 대한 아국의 입장정립

0 미국등 최근 새로운 REQUEST LIST 를 제시한 국가에 대한 협상 대책

0 비관세 OFFER 중 양허가능 부분의 선별 및 양허 불허 불가능할 부문에 대한 구체적인 설명자료

0 농산물이 포함됨에 따라 농산물 관세 OFFER 를 포함시켜 계산한 협상 상대국과의

PAGE 2

양허 균형 비교 분석

다. 대표단 구성 및 파견시기

 - 3.1 까지 협상을 실질적으로 종료하기 위한 마지막 노력인점을 감안하여 지금부터 진행되는 협상에는 본부 대표의 파견이 요망됨(미국은 본부대표가 이에당지에 체류중이며 일본은 1.27 도착 예정이라고 함)

 - 그 구성은 농산물이 동시에 논의됨에 따라 관련 부서 합동으로 대표단이 구성되어야 할것으로 사료됨.

 - 파견시기는 당관에서 주요국과 양자협상 일정을 1.28-1.31 사이로 추진하고 있음을 참고하여 결정바람.(동 일정이 확정되는 대로 추보 예정임)

   첨부: 향후 협상일정 1 부

   (GVW(F)-0027). 끝

   (대사 박수길-국장)

   예고:92.6.30 까지

주 제 네 바 대 표 부

번 호 : GVW(F) - 0027   년월일 : 2011 7   시간 : 1100

수 신 : 장   판 (통기·경제인·재무부·농림수산부·상공부·경제수석)

발 신 : 주 제네바대사

제 목 : 첨 부 :

총 2 매(표지포함)

보 안 봉 제	《署
외신과 몸 제	

27-2-1

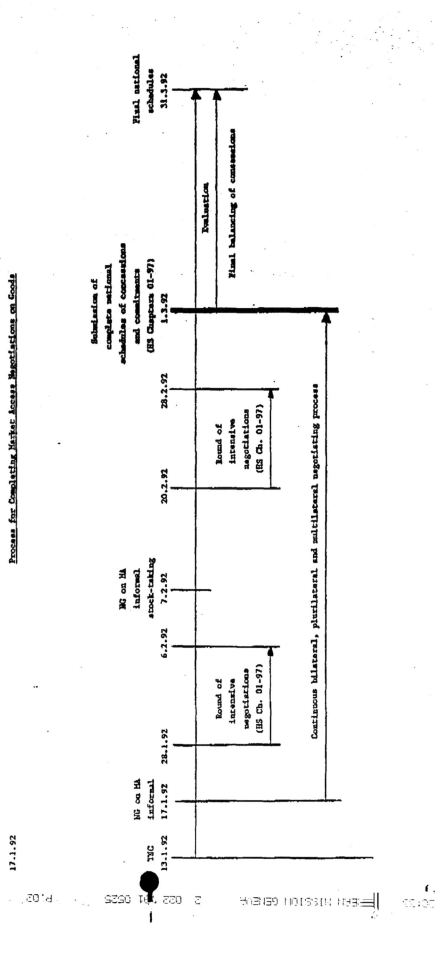

Process for Completing Market Access Negotiations on Goods

외 무 부

원 본

종   별 :

번   호 : GVW-0140   일   시 : 92 0120 2000

수   신 : 장 관(통기, 경기원, 재무부, 농림수산부, 상공부)

발   신 : 주 제네바 대사

제   목 : 서한송부

　　12.20 일자 UR협상 문서와 관련 미상원 MAXBAUCUS 무역소위원장이 HILLS USTR 에게 송부한 서한 사본을 참고로 별첨 송부함.

　　첨부: 상기서한(92.1.9자)
　　　　(GVW(F)-0031).끝
　　　　(대사 박수길-국장)

통상국　　2차보　　경기원　　재무부　　농수부　　상공부

92.01.21　08:15 WG
외신 1과　통제관

0037

외 무 부

종 별 :

번 호 : GVW-0142   일 시 : 92 0120 2000

수 신 : 장관(봉기,경기원,재무부,농림수산부,상공부)

발 신 : 주 제네바대사 사본:주미,주일,주EC대사본부중계필

제 목 : UR 농산물 협상 동향

　　당관 최농무관이 농산물 시장접근 협상(92.1.28-2.6), COUNTRY PLAN 제출 및 제 4 TRACK 등과 관련 주요국 관계관을 접촉한 결과를 하기 보고함.

　　1. 각국의 동향

　　가. 일본(하야시 참사관)

　　0 지난 15 일 미국과 이씨를 각각 방문한 시와꾸 농림수산성 심의관 및 아즈마 국제부장의 방문 목적은 제 4 TRACK 과 관련 중요 상대국인 미국과 EC 를 방문 일본 쌀의 관세화 예외인정을 요청하고 양국의 동향을 파악하기 위한 것임.

　　- 이씨 방문 결과(1.15 멜러 농업총국장차장과 면담)

　　. 이씨로서는 GREEN BOX, REBALANCING, 수출 물량 감축에 문제가 있어 수정이 필요하다고 보며

　　. 이씨의 공식 감축 약속 계획(OFFICIAL COMMITMENT LIST)은 이미 준비되어있으나 앞으로의 이사회에서 회원국의 동의를 얻는데 어려움이 있을 것으로 예상

　　. 금차 시장접근 협의시 이씨의 POSITION 은 지난 90.11 제출한 OFFER LIST가 중심이 될것이며

　　. 일본이 주장하는 "관세화 예외"는 각국의 동의를 얻기 어려울 것으로 봄.

　　- 미국 방문 결과(1.16 USTR 의 KATZ 부대표 및 CROWDER 농무차관)

　　. 미국으로서는 던켈 PAPER 를 협상의 기초로 인식하며 언제든지 이를 기초로양자, 다자간의 협의에 응할 것임.

　　. 일본의 쌀 관세화 예외인정은 받아들일수 없음.

　　. 4 월중순까지 협상이 완료되지 못할때는 미의회의 동의 절차에 어려움이 있음.

　　- 일본은 상기 출장 결과를 토대로 본국에서 제 4 TRACK 의 추진 전략을 검토하게 될것이며 그결과에 따라 지난해말 아국등과 공동제안한 바 있는 11 조 2C개선문제등을

통상국	장관	차관	1차보	2차보	외정실	분석관	정와대	안기부
경기원	재무부	농수부	상공부	중계				

PAGE 1

관계국과 다시 협의할 것으로 전망

- 미. 이씨 방문시 양국의 동의를 얻기 위한 타협안

(예: 미국에게 상당량에 해당되는 쌀의 시장개방 보장등)을 제시한바 없으며 미국과 이씨가 관세화 원칙을 고수하는한 타협안이 수용하기 어려울 것이브로관측

0 금 1.28 부터 시작되는 1 차 시장접근 협의에서는 개별 협의보다는 전반적인 문제와 각국의 관심사항 개진되는 정도가 될것으로 전망하고 던켈 TEXT 상의 불분명한 문제점도 논의될 가능성이 있으며 특히 양자 다자간의 협의 기초자료 미비 때문에 실질적인 협의는 어려울 것으로 예상

0 3.1 까지의 COUNTRY PLAN 제출시기도 국내적인 조정등 어려움이 예상되지만 GATT 사무국에는 최선을 다할 것이라고 하였다 함.

- 쌀등 주요 품목에 대한 TE 등의 처리문제가 제 4 TRACK 과 관련 협상이 종결된 상태가 아니며 정부기존 방침의 변경없이는 현재로서는 이를 COUNTRY PLAN 작성시는 아국과 일본이 90 년 국별리스트(C/L) 작성시와 같이 실무적인 사전협의를 하기로 하였음.

나. 카나다(HANSEN 참사관)

0 11 조 2C 와 관련된 제 4 TRACK 반영문제는 당분간 미.EC 간의 움직임을 지켜본후 결정할 계획임.

0 관세화 예외를 주장하는 낙농제품등 4 개 품목의 TE 를 감축약속 계획표(COUNTRY PLAN)에 포함시키는 문제는 본부에서 검토중이나 지난 90 년 국별리스트(C.L) 제출시 일단 제시는 하였던 점을 상기시킴

0 향후 시장접근 협의에서는 본질적 문제는 논의하기 어렵겠지만 적극 참여할 것임.

다. 스위스(MATYASSY 스위스 농업총국 협상담당과)

0 시장접근 협의에서 농산물은 기초자료가 없기 때문에 구체적 논의는 어려울 것으로 보나 적극 참여할 계획임.

0 던켈 TEXT 에 여러가지 요소(PARAMETER)들이 있어 작성에 상당시간 소요될 것이나 2 월말까지 제출하는데는 문제가 없을 것으로 봄.

0 관세화 대상품목의 감축 계획표 포함여부 및 제 4 TRACK 에 관한 방안은 현재 내부적으로 검토중에 있으며 11 조 2C 개선추진 문제등이 결정되면 아국과도 협의할 것임.

PAGE 2

0039

라. 이스라엘(PERRY 참사관)

0 협상자료 미비로 구체적 협의는 어렵겠지만 협상에는 참여할 것임.

0 감축약속 계획표는 초기단계이기는 하지만 최선을 다하여 준비할 것임.

0 제 4 TRACK 관련 이스라엘은 MAJOR PLAYER 가 아니기 때문에 다른나라(미.EC)의 동향을 지켜보면서 PROCESS 가 명확해지면 참여할 것임.

마. 멕시코(SOTO 참사관)

0 제 4 TRACK 관련 멕시코의 관심 사항 반영을 위한 적극적인 움직임을 하고 있지는 않으나 향후 진행을 보아 가면서 반영 방안을 모색할 것임.

0 관세화 대상품목의 TE 를 감축약속 계획표에 반영하는 문제는 본국정부에서 검토중이나 사견으로는 어려울 것으로 예상

2. 평가

0 일단 내주로 예정된 시장접근 협상에서 농산물에 관하여는 본격적인 실질협상은 어려울 것으로 보이지만 모든 참가국이 적극적으로 참여할 것으로 예상됨.

0 3.1 까지의 감축약속 계획표 제출시한 관련 일부 국가는 국내의 기술적 어려움을 제기하고 있지만 대부분 시한내 제출할 준비가 될것으로 전망됨.

0 제 4 TRACK 관련 일본 이외는 대부분 관망하는 상태로서 특히 미국과, EC의 동향을 주시하고 있는 것으로 관측됨.

0 특히 대부분의 국가가 향후 협상 전망과 자국의 입장 반영 여부등에 대하여 조심스러운 입장을 취하면서도 앞으로의 협상에는 적극 참여하겠다는 의사를 밝히는 것에 비추어 볼때 향후 협상 과정에서 자국이 비협조적인 국가로 지목받는 것을 최대한 피하려는 것으로 관측됨.

0 아국도 이와같은 관점에서 시장접근 협상에 적극적으로 참여하면서 관심국가와의 양자 협상에 대비하여 가능한 범위내에서 구체적인 사전준비가 요망됨. 끝

(대사 박수길-국장)

예고:92.6.30 까지

발 신 전 보

분류번호	보존기간

번   호 : WJA-0242   920120 1837   DW총번 :

수   신 : 주   일   대사. 총영사//   (사본 : 주 제네바 대사)   WGV -0106

발   신 : 장   관   (통 기)

제   목 : UR/농산물 협상

외신보도에의하면

　1.20자 ~~국내 일간지는~~ 1.19. '와타나베' 귀주재국 외상이 지방유세에서 "예외없는 관세화에 반대하고 있는 나라는 일본, 카나다등 7개국 뿐으로 일본이 외톨이가 되는 것은 곤란하며, 남은것은 관세율 몇%로 할 것이냐의 문제뿐"이라고 언급 하였음을 보도한 바, 동 내용 사실 여부 및 일 정부 입장 파악, 보고바람.   끝.

(통상국장   김 용 규)

외 무 부

종   별 :

번   호 : GVW-0141   일   시 : 92 0120 2000

수   신 : 장관(봉기, 경기원, 재무부, 농림수산부, 상공부)

발   신 : 주 제네바대사

제   목 : UR/농산물 협상

　　　대: WGV-0106(92.1.20)

　　　연호 관련 당관 최농무관이 주제네바 일본대표부 하야시 참사관과 접촉 동
보도내용의 사실 여부를 확인한바, 동인은 아직까지 본국정부로 부터 입장 변경에
대한 어떠한 통보도 받은바 없다고 하면서 대호 일본 외상의 발언은 비공발언(I
NFORMAL STATEMENT)으로 보며 특히 일본으로서는 정부 입장 변경시 당정협의를
거쳐 내각에서 공식 결정하여야 하는 과정이 필요한바, 이와같은 과정을 거치지 않는
것은 정부의 입장이 될수 없다고 함. 끝

　　　(대사 박수길-국장)

　　　예고:92.6.30 까지

통상국	장관	차관	1차보	2차보	외정실	분석관	청와대	안기부
경기원	재무부	농수부	상공부					

PAGE 1

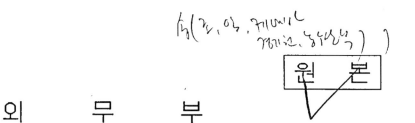

원 본

외 무 부

종 별 :

번 호 : JAW-0366   일 시 : 92 0122 1118

수 신 : 장관(통기)

발 신 : 주 일 대사(일정)

제 목 : UR/농산물 협상

대:WJA-0242

당관 김종주 농무관과 조태영 서기관은 1.21(화) "아즈마"농림수산성 국제부장을 면담, 표제건 의견교환한바, 동인의 발언요지를 다음 보고함.

1. 농업분야 협상 일정(양자 교섭관계)

0 농업분야의 양자간 교섭이 앞당겨져서 빠르면 1 월말부터라도 시작될 가능성이 있다고 봄.

0 크라우더 미 농무차관이 1.17 시와쿠 일 농수산심의관에게 "미국으로서는 던켈 합의초안의 확정을 기다리지 않고 동 초안을 토대로 양자간 교섭을 앞당겨서 행하는것을 제안할 생각이며, EC 도 이에 반대하지 않으리라고 생각함. 이와같이 양자간 교섭을 병해시 던켈합의 초안도 좀더 명확해 질것"이라고 발언한바 있음.

0 또한, 던켈 의장도 1.16 엔도오 국제무역담당 대사에대해 "상당수의 국가의 요망도 있으므로 3.1 의 농업관계자료 제출기한을 앞당기기 위한 TNC 회의의 소집을 고려하고 있으며, 제출기한을 앞당기는데 대해서는 EC 등도 문제없다고하고 있다는 감촉을 얻었다"고 발언한바 있음.

0 당기 던켈 의장 발언에 대해 언도오 대사는 일측으로서는 현재 3.1 을 목표로 작업중인바, 그 이전에 작업을 완료함은 무리라고 반론을 제기했음.

0 최종 합의 초안의 기본틀 속에서 어떤 품목의 보호조치를 몇% 삭감할것인가 검토되지 않는 상태에서는 양자간 교섭에 들어간다하더라도 일측으로서 구체적 반응을 보이기가 어렵다고 생각하나, 미국이 이를 적극 요구할 경우 거부하기는 어렵다고 생각되는바, 일단 미국측의 이야기를 들어보는 선에서 대응 할수 밖에 없을 것으로 봄.

2. EC 의 동정

통상국	장관	차관	1차보	2차보	아주국	경제국	외정실	분석관
청와대	안기부							

PAGE 1

0 EC 는 일단 집행위 차원에서 금주중 GATT 에 제출할 농업관계 자료를 작성할 예정인것으로 알고 있음.

0 그러나, 현재 수출 보조금 삭감에 있어 화란, 덴마크등 6 개국이 반대하고 있는것으로 알려지고 있는바, EC 집행위의 안이 그대로 확정 되기는 어려운 상황이라고 봄.

3. 향후 UR 협상 전망

0 현재 미국내 로비스트들 사이에서는 미국이 UR 협상의 종결을 대통령 선거시기인 금년 11 월 이후로 늦추려 한다는 것이 가장 유력한 관측으로 되어 있음(일본은 UR 관련 미.EC 내 로비스트를 활용중인것으로 알려지고 있음)

- 현재 미국내에는 금번 던켈 합의초안에 대해 세이프가드, 반덤핑, 섬유분야등을 중심으로 불만도 적지 않은바, 현재와 같은 상태로 UR 종결시 미대통령 선거에서 여당에게 불리한 상황이 되는바, 오히려 UR 을 종결시키지 않은채 계속보호주의 삭감을 위한 미국의 강경발언등 강한 모습을 보여주려할것이라는 관측임.

0 또한,"들로르" EC 집행위원장이 불란서 대통령 선거에 출마예정인 것으로알려지고 있는바, 이경우 동인으로서는 불란서 농민을 중심으로 강경한 불란서의 입장을 배려하지 않을수 없을 것인바, 이점도 UR 협상을 지연시키는 적지않은요인이 될것으로 보여지고 있음.

4. 최근 일본 국내 동정

0 와타나베 외상의 1.19 발언(대호 내용)은 외상이 1.20 당정 협의회에서도해명하였듯이, 부분개방과 관세화를 비교할때 차라리 고율의 관세가 붙은 관세화가 낫다(이경우 사실상 쌀의 수입이 없게 되므로)는 주장으로서 여러가지 선택지에 대한 이론적 의미에서의 해설내용이었으며, 관세화를 수용해야 함을 주장한것은 아님(외무성측에 확인결과 동일한 입장표명)

0 미야자와 수상등이 일본으로서도 어느정도 양보하지 않을수 없다고 언급 하고 있는것이 반드시 쌀시장 개방이라는 양보를 의미하는 것은 아니며, 각자가 가능한 분야에서 상응한 양보를 하여야한다는 의미로 해석되어야 함.

0 미야자와 내각발족후 UN 평화유지 협력법안, 국제공헌세등 주요 법률이 전부 국회에서 부결되는등 내각이 약한 상태로서, 오히려 자민당쪽이 발언권이 강한 성황인데 금년도 7 월의 참의원 선거등을 고려하여, 자민당에서 농민을 자극하는 조치는 취하기 어려운 형편임.끝

PAGE 2

0044

(대사 오재희-국장)

예고:92.6.30 일반

.

	분류번호	보존기간

발 신 전 보

WGV-0122   920122 1430 FL

번   호 : _____   종별 : _____

수   신 : 주   제네바   대사. 총영사

발   신 : 장   관 (통 기)

제   목 : UR 협상 대책 실무위 회의 결과

1.   1.21(화) 개최된 UR 대책 실무위 회의 결과를 아래 통보함.

    가. 시장접근 협상 대책

        1) 공산품 관세 및 비관세

            ㅇ 관 세

                - 기존 offer로 대처하되 협상 진전을 보아 일부 추가 양허 검토

            ㅇ 비관세

                - 수용 가능한 요청사항 중에서 양허(binding) 가능한 사항 확정

            ㅇ 한·일 양자협의 대책

                - 금번 일총리 방한시 일측이 UR 협상에서 고려키로한 대일 16개
                  관세인하 요청품목에 대하여는 적극 거론(talking points는
                  본부에서 작성, 송부)

        2) 농산물

            ㅇ 3.1이전 양허계획(list of commitments) 작성 추진

                - 동 양허계획 제출 이전에는 농산물 양허협상 추진 곤란

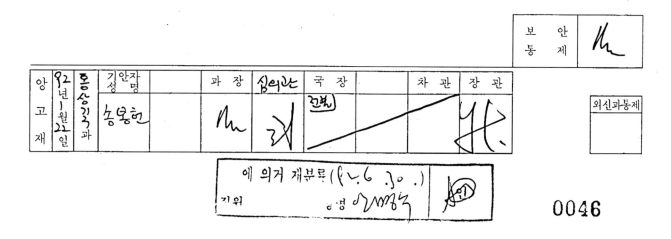

		보 안 통 제	

0046

o 작성 지침은 12.20자 Dunkel Paper에 기초하되 동 paper 수정이

필요하다는 아국 기본입장을 감안, 아래 아국 입장을 반영하여 작성

- 쌀등 기초식량은 관세화에서 제외

- 11조 2항 C에 근거한 생산 조절 품목도 관세화에서 제외

- 개도국 우대 적용(ceiling binding, 최소 시장접근 관련 선진국의

2/3 수준 허용 포함)

- 기준년도는 최근 년도 사용

3) 본부대표 파견 : 재무부, 상공부, 농림수산부 과장 또는 사무관 파견

나. Dunkel Paper 수정 협상(Track 4) 대책

o 관심국과의 공동 대응등 가능한 모든 대책 방안을 각부처에서 검토후

추가 협의

- 입장 유사국과의 공동 제안, 농수산부장관 명의 서한 발송, 주요국에

대한 지지 협상 방안등

다. 협정 초안 법적 정비작업 (Track 3)

o 협상 추진 절차 파악후 대처

2. 상기 관련, 아래 사항에 대한 귀관 의견 보고바람.

가. Track 4(협정 초안 수정) 관련 대책

o 관계부처간에는 상기 나항의 방안들이 거론되고 있는바, 아국이 전면에

나섬으로써 초래될 수 있는 부정적 이미지를 최소화하되, 국내 상황을

고려하고 아국 입장 반영에 도움이 될 수 있는 ~~협상 추진~~ 대처방 방안 및 (시기적

고려 포함)

나. Track 3(협정 초안 법적 정비작업) 관련 대책

o 향후 협상 추진 절차, 전망 및 본부 검토 필요사항

(본부대표 파견 필요성 포함)

3. 농산물 협상 시장접근, 국내보조 분야에 대한 기준년도를 최근년도 대신

'86-'88 평균을 사용할 경우 최고 30% 정도의 감축 의무가 추가 발생할 수

있으므로 앞으로 적절한 기회를 통하여 기준년도를 최근년도로 사용할 수

있도록 하는데도 중점을 두고 교섭바람.

4. 상기 UR 대책 실무위 자료는 파편 송부 예정임. 끝. (통상국장 김용규)

주 일 대 사 관

일본(농) 1176-4٢

1992. 1. 23

수신 : <u>외무부장관</u>

참조 : 농림수산부장관 (국제협력담당관)

제목 : UR 농산물협상

연 : JAW - 0366 (92.1.22)

별첨자료는 UR농산물협상에 있어서 주재국의 금후교섭 추진방향자료 (농상에게보고)이며, 특히 자료제공자는 2항의 (2)는 대외비로 취급해달라는 부탁이 있었음을 첨언합니다.

첨부 : 금후교섭 추진방향 1부. 끝.

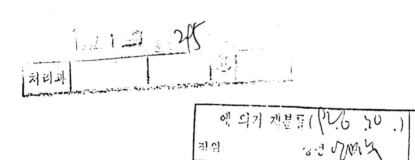

주 일 대

今後の交渉の進め方

１．市場アクセス非公式会合（１月１７日（金））の概要

（１）ドゥニ議長（カナダ）の冒頭発言

　　① 第１のトラック（路線）、即ち、市場アクセス・グループでは、農業の３分
　　　野での約束を含む、ＨＳ１類～９７類までのすべての物に対する関税・非関税
　　　措置を対象とする。

　　　（注）１月１３日のＴＮＣにおいて、ダンケル議長より、第１のトラック（市
　　　　　場アクセス交渉）では、農業における国内支持、輸出競争に関する約束も
　　　　　含まれるとの考え方が示されている。

　　② １月１３日以降、多くの参加国と非公式に協議を行ったが、３月１日までに、
　　　農業での場合を含め、タリフ・ラインごとの完全な譲許と約束の国別スケジュ
　　　ールを提出することが非常に重要であることについて、一般的同意があった。

　　③ 市場アクセス交渉を効果的に行うため、次の事項を提案する。

　　　ア．交渉を１月２８日（火）から２月６日（木）まで及び２月２０日（木）
　　　　から２月２８日（金）までの間、集中的な交渉を行う。
　　　　　交渉の進捗状況を点検するため、必要に応じ、２月７日（金）に非公式
　　　　会合を行う。

　　　イ．農業の場合を含め、タリフ・ラインごとの完全な譲許と約束の国別スケ
　　　　ジュールを、遅くとも３月１日までに提出する。その際、併せて、最終合
　　　　意文書案に基づく農業の国内支持及び輸出競争についての関連資料を提出
　　　　する。

　　　ウ．議定書（プロトコール）に添付する最終的な法的国別譲許表は、３月末
　　　　までに用意する。

（２）議長の発言に対し、主要先進国からの特段の発言はなかった。

２．今後のプロセスに関する関係者の発言

（１）ダンケル議長
　　　ダンケル議長より、１６日遠藤大使に対し、「かなりの国の要望を踏まえ、
　　３月１日の提出期限を前倒しするためのＴＮＣ会合の招集を考えている。ただ
　　し、ドゥニ市場アクセス議長とはまだ話していない。」との考え方が示された。

0049

- 1 -

<del>0048</del>

これに対し、大使より反論を行ったが、ダンケル議長より「ＥＣも含めて期限の前倒しは問題なしとの感触を得ている。」との再反論があった。

（２）クラウダー米国農務次官

　　クラウダー米国農務次官より、１７日塩飽審議官に対し、「米国としては、今般１週間か１０日のうちに、ダンケル案の最終確定を待つことなく、それをベースにしてバイの交渉を申し入れようと思っている。日本に対してもジュネーブで呼びかけることになろう。ＥＣも、ダンケル案を最終確定せずに、バイの交渉を行うことに反対しないと思われる。このようなバイ・プルリの話合いを通じて、ダンケル案もある程度は明確になってこよう。」との発言がなされている。

0050

면담 요록

1992. 1.23.
통상기구과

1. 면담일시 및 장소 : 92.1.23(목) 11:00-11:40, 통상기구과

2. 면 담 자 :

    ㅇ 홍종기 통상기구과장 (기록 : 송봉헌 사무관)

    ㅇ Wilson 주한 뉴질랜드 대사관 참사관, Smith 주한 호주 대사관 1등서기관

3. 면담요지

    가. 뉴, 호주측 질문요지

    ① four track approach의 개요

    ② track 4와 관련, 한국의 관심사항과 동 관심사항에 대한 입장의
       flexibility가 있는지

    ③ BOP 협의 결과와 UR 협상 연계 문제에 대한 한국측 입장 및 UR 협상
       연계시 93년도부터 자유화될 품목도 UR 협상 결과에 합치시키는지 여부

    ④ 쌀은 BOP 품목에 해당되는지 여부 및 BOP 품목이 아닌 경우 수입제한
       근거 국내법은 무엇인지

    ⑤ 농산물 양허 협상관련 한국측이 상대측에 request할 사항이 있는지

    ⑥ 농산물 양허협상 일정 연기를 요청할 예정인지

    ⑦ 정치적으로나 농민들을 고려할때 한국측이 green box의 범위 확대를
       통하여 시장개방과 관련한 국내적 우려를 경감할 수 있다고 보는지

    ⑧ 쇠고기 협상 일정에 대한 한국측 입장은 무엇인지

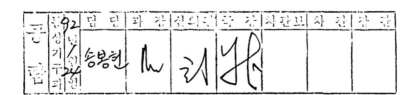

0051

나. 아측 답변요지

① four track approach 개요 설명

② track 4와 관련한 관심사항은 예외없는 관세화, 모든 해당품목에 대한
일률적인 최소 시장접근 허용 문제와 기준년도를 '86-'88 대신 통계자료가
있는 최근 년도를 사용하는 것임. 현재로서는 관심사항과 관련된 기존
입장 변경(flexibility) 여지는 없음.

③ BOP와 UR 연계 문제에 대한 기존 입장 변경은 없으며 93년도부터
자유화 하기로한 품목도 UR 결과에 합치시켜야 할 것임.

④ 쌀은 BOP 품목이 아니며 양곡관리법이 쌀 수입제한 근거 국내법임.

⑤ 농산물 양허 협상관련, 한국도 상대측에 request할 사항이 있을 것임.

⑥ 시장접근 분야 양허협상에 적극 참여한다는 것이 한국 방침임.
다만, 농산물 양허 계획 작성에 상당한 시일이 소요될 것으로 생각하며
track 4와 관련된 아국 관심사항 반영 문제등도 있으므로 동 계획 제출
이전에는 농산물 양허 협상 추진이 사실상 어려운 형편임. 그러나,
상대측 요청사항과 관심사항은 take note하여 가능할 경우 respond할
예정임. 농산물 양허계획은 기본적으로 Dunkel paper를 참고하여
3.1 이전 제출할 것임.

⑦ 식량안보 목적의 식량비축등 한국 관심사항이 green box에 많이
반영되어 있으나 기본적으로 green box의 범위와 시장개방 문제를
연계하여 검토하는 것이 국내 여론에 받아들여지기 어렵다는데 문제가
있음.

⑧ 쇠고기 협상 일정을 상대측이 제의해 오면 검토할 것임.　　　끝.

0052

발 신 전 보

분류번호	보존기간

번 호 : WJA-0341 920127 1449 FL 종별 : _____

WGV-0144

수 신 : 주   일   대사. 총영사//   (사본 : 주 제네바 대사)

발 신 : 장 관 (통 기)

제 목 : UR/농산물 협상

1.25자 외신은 '요미우리' 신문이 일 정부 고위 소식통을 인용, '미야자와' 일 총리가 관세부과(관세화)를 통한 쌀 수입 개방을 이미 결정했으며 동 관세 부과를 통한 쌀 수입은 관계법 개정을 통하지 않고서도 가능하다고 보도한 내용을 재인용 보도한 바, 동 내용 사실 여부 및 일 정부 입장 파악 보고바람.   끝.

(통상국장 김 용 규)

보 안 통 제	/\\\\

앙 고 재	92년 1월 2?일 통상기구과	기안자 성명 농봉헌	과 장	심의관	국 장 전결	차 관	장 관

외신과통제

0053

분류번호	보존기간

발 신 전 보

WGV-0159   920128 1801 DU

번   호 : _____   종별 : _____

WJA -0363   WUS -0408

수   신 : 주   제네바, 일본 대사. 총영사// (시본 독미. ElECCHl2035)

발   신 : 장 관 (통 기)

제   목 : UR/농산물 협상

1. 1.28 '시모코우지' 주한 일본 대사관 참사관은 본국 정부 훈령에 따라 본부
    통상국장을 면담, UR/농산물 협상 관련 일 정부 입장을 아래와 같이 전달
    하였으니 참고바람.

    o Dunkel paper상의 예외없는 관세화에 대한 수정(revision)을 계속 요청할
      예정

    o 한국이 농산물 협상에서 일측과 비슷한 입장을 취하고 있는데 대해 사의 및
      1.13 TNC 회의시 취했던 입장을 계속 견지해 줄 것을 희망

2. 동 참사관 언급내용중 기타 참고사항은 아래와 같음.

    o 상기 일 정부 입장은 카나다, 스위스, 이스라엘 및 멕시코에도 ㉑ 전달예정

    o 최근 '미야자와' 일 총리의 쌀에 대한 관세화 수용 언론 보도는 추측 기사에
      불과하며 일 정부 입장은 상금 불변

~~3. 동 면담요록은 파편 송부 예정임.~~   끝.   (통상국장 김 용 규)

					보 안 통 제

앙고재	92년 1월 28일	통상기구과	기안자 성명 동봉현	과 장	심의관	국 장 전결	차 관	장 관

외신과통제

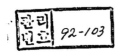

면 담 요 록

1. 면담일시 및 장소 : 1992.1.28(화) 15:30-15:50, 통상국장실

2. 면 담 자
    ㅇ 아 측 : 김용규 통상국장
    안명수 통상기구과 사무관
    ㅇ 일본측 : 주한 일본 대사관 경제참사관 시모코우지 슈지 외 1명

3. 면담내용 :

<u>참사관</u>

ㅇ Dunkel Paper와 관련 본국 정부 훈령에 따라 방문하게 되었으며 이에따라
귀측에 전달할 내용은 하기 3가지임.

   첫째, 한국이 UR 농산물 협상에서 일본과 동일한 입장을 취하고 있는데
   대해 사의를 표명함.

   둘째, Dunkel Paper에 포함된 예외없는 관세화에 대하여 일본으로서는
   계속해서 수정(revision)을 요청해야 한다는 것이 일본 정부 입장임.

   셋째, 일본으로서는 한국 정부가 1.13 TNC 회의시 취했던 입장을 계속
   견지하여 주기바람.

이상이 정부 훈령이며, 개인적으로 몇마디 덧붙이자면, 상기 일본의 입장은
카나다, 스위스, 이스라엘, 멕시코에도 보다 높은 레벨에서 전달 하였으며,
한국에 대해 낮은 레벨을 통해 전달하는 것은 관세화에 대한 예외 문제가
너무나도 민감한 사안이라는 점을 고려한 때문인바, 일본의 상기 입장을
상부에 전달하여 주시기 바람.

-1-

0055

통상국장

ㅇ 귀국의 입장을 전달해준데 대해 사의를 표명함.

최근 미야자와 수상의 쌀 관세화 허용 보도가 있던데, 일본 정부의 입장이
바뀐것이 아닌지 ?

참사관

ㅇ 그것은 신문보도에 불과하며, 일본 정부의 입장은 조금도 변화가 없음.

통상국장

ㅇ 그렇다면, 왜 일본이 쌀 관세화를 수용한다는 보도가 이처럼 광범위하게
퍼져 있는지 ?

일본이 쌀 관세화 방침을 이미 정해놓고 적절한 공포의 시기만을 기다리고
있다는 인상을 받았음.

참사관

ㅇ 일본으로서는 우루과이라운드의 성공을 바라고 있음. 일본 정부 내에서도
쌀 관세화 문제를 검토하고 있으며 정부와 정치권 일각에서 UR 협상에서
고립되는 것을 피하기 위해 쌀 관세화를 수용해야 한다는 의견도 있는것이
사실임. 그리고 동 문제가 워낙 민감한 사안이기 때문에 이러한 논의
과정에서 언론이 과장하여 마치 일본 정부가 입장을 변경 하였다는 보도를
하게 된것임. 지금 본인이 말할 수 있는 것은 일본 정부가 아무런 결정을
내린바 없으며 따라서 전과 동일한 입장이라는 것임.

통상국장

ㅇ 언론보도에 대해 일본 정부가 부인 하였는지 ?

참사관

ㅇ 부인하였음.

통상국장

ㅇ 주 제네바 대표부에도 동 입장을 통보 하였는지 ?

2

<u>참사관</u>

o 주 제네바 대표부에도 통보하였음. 다만 제네바에서는 현재 협상 과정에
  있기 때문에 외교적인 접근방법을 취해야 함. 과거 일본이 예외없는
  관세화를 수락할 수 없다는 입장을 여러차례 표명 하였으며 예외없는
  관세화에 대해 수정을 요청한 바 있음.

<u>통상국장</u>

o 오늘 방문의 주된 이유가 무엇인지 ?

<u>참사관</u>

o 일본은 전과 동일한 입장이며 한국도 마찬가지로 전과 동일한 입장을 취해
  주기를 바란다는 뜻을 전달하기 위해서임.

<u>통상국장</u>

o 아국 입장은 명확한바, 예외없는 관세화는 받아들일 수 없다는 것임.
  이러한 입장은 1.13 TNC에서도 확인 되었으며 이러한 입장을 계속해 나갈것임.
  제네바에서도 일본과 여타 몇개국과 협력 관계를 유지하고 있음.
  예외없는 관세화가 수정될 가능성에 대한 귀하의 견해는 ?

<u>참사관</u>

o 현재 4 track에 따라 협상이 진행중이며, 일본으로서는 예외없는 관세화에
  대해 수정을 요청할 것이나 상황이 유동적이어서 수정 가능성에 대해서는
  아무도 점칠 수 없을 것으로 생각함.

<u>통상국장</u>

o 부시 미 대통령 방일시 쌀 문제가 제기 되었는지 ?
  그리고 압력의 정도는 어떠했는지 ?

<u>참사관</u>

o 부시 대통령이 일본의 사정을 이해한 때문인지 예상보다 압력의 정도는
  약했음.

3

통상국장

o 며칠전 귀측의 입장에 변화가 있는지를 파악하도록 주일 대사관에 지시한 바
  있음.

참사관

o 일본 정부 입장에서는 하등의 변화가 없으며, 입장 변경이 있는 경우 사전에
  귀정부에 알려주겠음. 귀국 정부 입장에 변경이 있는 경우 우리에게**도**
  알려 주시기 바람.

통상국장

o 우리 입장에는 아무런 변화가 없을 것임.   끝.

외 무 부

종 별 :

번 호 : GVW-0195   일 시 : 92 0128 1000

수 신 : 장 관(봉기,경제기획원,재무부,농림수산부,상공부)

발 신 : 주 제네바 대사

제 목 : UR/농산물 협상

대: WGV-0144

대호 관련 당관 최농무관이 당지 일본대표부 하야시 참사관과 접촉 한바, 동인언급 요지 하기 보고함.

1. 최근 일본신문에 대호 내용이 보도된바 있으나 근거가 없는 것임.

가. 현행 식관법을 개정하지 않더라도 수입자동허가를 해주면 쌀수입 개방이 가능 하다는 일부 견해가 있으나

- 현재 일본의 쌀 수출입은 국영무역 토록되어있어 자동적인 허가 (AUTOMATIC PERMISSION) 자체가 불가능하고

- 정부가 매년 사전에 쌀 수급계획을 세워이에 따라 생산조정 (논면적의 1/3에해당하는 80만 HA의 휴경)을 하고 있기 때문에 자동수입허가 제도의 유지가 불가능함.

나. 또한 지난주 부터 개최된 정기 국회에서 미가야자와 총리가 현행 정부시책에 변화없음을 밝힌바 있음.끝

(대사 박수길-국장)

통상국   2차보   경기원   재무부   농수부   상공부

PAGE 1   92.01.29   08:07 WG

외신 1과 통제관

0059

報 告 畢

1992. 1. 29.
通 商 局
通 商 機 構 課(7)

長 官 報 告 事 項

題 目 : UR/農産物 協商 關聯 日 政府 立場

> 1.28(火) '시모코우지' 駐韓 日本 大使館 參事官은 本國 政府 訓令에 따라 김용규 通商局長을 面談, Dunkel Paper上의 例外없는 關稅化에 대한 修正이 必要하다는 日 政府 立場을 傳達한 바, 同 要旨를 아래 報告 드립니다.

1. Dunkel Paper 關聯 日本 政府 立場

   ○ 例外없는 關稅化에 대한 修正(revision)을 繼續 要請 豫定

   ○ 韓國이 農産物 協商에서 日側과 비슷한 立場을 취하고 있는데 대해 謝意 및
   1.13 TNC 會議時 취했던 立場을 繼續 堅持해 줄 것을 希望

2. 其他 言及事項

   ○ 上記 日 政府 立場은 카나다, 스위스, 이스라엘 및 멕시코에도 傳達예정

   ○ 最近 '미야자와' 日 總理의 쌀에 대한 關稅化 受容 言論報道는 推測 記事에
   불과하며 日 政府 立場은 尙今 不變

3. 國會 및 言論對策 : 別途 措置 不要

4. 措置事項 : 上記 內容을 關聯 公館 및 關係部處에 通報.   끝.

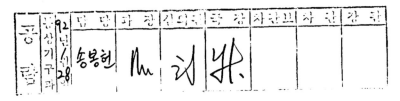

0060

관리 번호	92-112

외 무 부

종 별 :

번 호 : ECW-0130   일 시 : 92 0129 1830

수 신 : 장관 (통기, 경기원, 재무부, 농림수산부, 상공부)

발 신 : 주 EC 대사 사본: 주 미, 제네바대사중계필

제 목 : 갓트/UR 협상

연: ECW-0112

1. 1.29. DUNKEL 갓트 사무총장이 당지를 방문하여, ANDRIESSEN 대외다망 집행위원, MACSHARRY 농업담당집행위원과 회담을 가졌음. (PAEMEN 대외총국의 부총국장과 LEGRAS 농업총국장 배석) 등 회담후 DUNKEL 총장은 회담결과를 묻는 기자들의 질문에 일체 언급을 회피하고 회담장을 떠났으며, ANDRIESSEN 위원은 DUNKEL 총장과 농산물문제뿐 아니라 전체 UR 협상의 진행에 장애요소가 되고있는 전반문제에 대해 협의하였다고만 말하고 구체적인 언급을 회피함

2. 한편 집행위 대변인은 금번회담의 목적은 DUNKEL 협상안의 수정범위를 확인하기 위한 것이었다고 말하고 EC 로서 DUNKEL 협상안중 가장 받아드리기 어려운점은 CAP 개혁의 일환으로 추진중인 소득보조가 GREEN BOX 범주에서 제외되어 있는것과 물량기준한 수출보조금 감축폭을 제시하고 있는 내용이라고 언급함

3. 동건관련, 집행위 관계관들과 접촉후 추보하겠음. 끝

(대사 권동만-국장)

예고: 92.6.30 까지

통상국 안기부	장관 경기원	차관 재무부	1차보 농수부	2차보 상공부	구주국 중계	외정실	분석관	청와대

PAGE 1   92.01.30   08:04

외신 2과 통제관 BD

0061

외 무 부

종   별 :

번   호 : GVW-0206   일   시 : 92 0129 1200

수   신 : 장관(봉기, 경기원, 재무부, 농림수산부, 상공부)

발   신 : 주 제네바 대사

제   목 : UR/농산물 협상(감축 약속 계획표 작성 협의)

2.28(화) 최농무관은 갓트 농업국 ROGERSON 참사관을 면담 표제 협상 감축 약속 계획보 작성과 관련한 기술적 사항에 대하여 협의한바 요지 하기 보고함.

(농림수산부 배사무관 동석)

1. 농산물 분야 시장접근 협상 추진 방안

- 동인은 3.1 까지 감축 약속 계획표(LIST OF SPECIFIC COMMITMENTS)를 제출하는 것이 농산물 분야 협상의 1 차적이며 가장 기본적 단계(FIRST AND BASIC STEP) 가 될것이라고 하면서 3.1 까지 진행되는 양자 협상은 감축 약속 계획표 작성의 전단계(FOREPLAY)로서 각국이 동 계획표 작성을 위한 관심사항 교환 및 CLAIFICATION 등을 위해 필요한 절차로 평가하였음.

- 또한 감축 약속 계획표는 제한된 범위(던켈 총장 초안에 언급된 사항)에서 일종의 NATIONAL OFFER 로 해석할수도 있다고 하였음.

2. 시장접근 분야 최저 삭감율에 대한 개도국 우대 적용 여부

- 평균 삭감율 (36 %) 에만 개도국 우대를 적용하고 최저 삭감율 (15 %) 에 대해서는 개도국 우대를 적용하지 않는 것이 작성 취지라고 하면서 문안 해석상 이견이 있을수 있음을 인정하였음.

3. 시장접근 분야 삭감 대상 관세

- 관세화 대상 품목의 경우 TE 가 삭감 대상이며, TQ 내의 적용관세(실행관세)는 삭감 대상이 아니라고 함.

4. 국내 보조 삭감 약속 불이행

- 국내 보조 삭감 약속이 양허표로 첨부되게 되므로 불이행시는 일반적인 양허 위반과 동일하게 취급되어 갓트 23 조등 분쟁해결의 대상이 된다고 함.

5. 감축 약속 계획표 작성

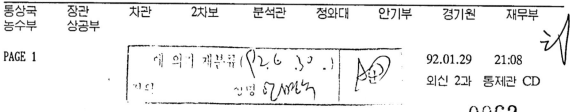

통상국 농수부	장관 상공부	차관	2차보	분석관	정와대	안기부	경기원	재무부

PAGE 1   92.01.29   21:08

외신 2과 통제관 CD

0082

- 동 계획표 작성을 위해 사무국이 작성한 참고자료 (INFORMAL TECHNICAL NOTE)를 별첨 FAX 송부함.

첨부: 감축약속 계획표 작성 참고 자료 1 부 끝 ──

(GVW(F)-55)

(대사 박수길-국장)

92.6.30 까지

PAGE 2

주 제 네 바 대 표 부

번 호 : GVE(F) - 0055   년월일 : 2014   시간 : 1800

수 신 : 장   관(동기、경기원、상공부、재무부、농림수산부)

발 신 : 주 제네바대사

제 목 :   " 첨 부 "

총 43 매(표지포함)

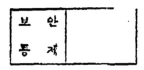

보 안	
통 재	

외신과	
통 재	

55 - 43 -1   0064.

102
27.1.1992

        This informal technical note by the Secretariat is intended to assist
in the preparation of the initial lists of specific binding commitments
under the agriculture reform programme. It has been prepared with
particular regard to the requests for technical assistance which have been
received from a number of developing countries. The explanations in the
note relate to the text on agriculture contained in the Draft Final Act
Embodying the Results of the Uruguay Round of Multilateral Trade
Negotiations (MTN.TNC/W/FA), which is the only authoritative document.

55 - 43 —2

0065

27.1.92

EXPLANATORY NOTES ON THE FORMATS FOR THE ESTABLISHMENT OF LISTS OF SPECIFIC
BINDING COMMITMENTS UNDER THE AGRICULTURE REFORM PROGRAMME

Informal Technical Note by the Secretariat

Introduction

1.   This note sets out explanations to assist in the completion of lists
of commitments in agriculture as specified in the 'Draft Final Act
embodying the Results of the Uruguay Round of Multilateral Trade
Negotiations' (MTN.TNC/W/FA pages L.1-74). It has been prepared
particularly having in mind the need for technical assistance for
developing countries.

2.   Relevant portions have been taken from that text and in addition,
further clarification and examples have been given. It should be noted
that the text itself is the authoritative document. This note does not
attempt to interpret the text in any way, but to give further clarification
where possible. It does not constitute a basis for evaluating or assessing
specific binding commitments by any participant.

3.   The ordering of tables in this note (see page 3) differs from the
draft final agreement in order to facilitate the presentation of data
requirements and the calculations necessary to establish the lists of
specific commitments.

4.   Reference to an Annex, Article or paragraph of the text on agriculture
in MTN.TNC/W/FA is made by referring only to the relevant part of that
text, e.g. (B: Annex 3, paragraph 1) refers to the first paragraph of Annex
3 of Part B of the agricultural text (the Agreement on Modalities for the
Establishment of Specific Binding Commitments under the Reform Programme).

General points

5.   In all Supporting Tables, there are two general columns, 'data
sources' and 'comments'. The listing of data sources should be explicit
enough to allow other participants to examine the data fully. Generally,
national data sources will be used although some of the data may come from
international sources. Data sources should also include the method of
calculation used to obtain any coefficients such as quality adjustments.
Any comments a participant wishes to make concerning the calculation should
appear in the comments column.

6.   The Supporting Tables also have horizontal rows under the headings.
In the market access and domestic support tables, these are rows (a) to
(d), and in the case of export competition, rows (a) to (f). The rows
indicate that for each product entered into the table, data for each of the
years included in the average (1986 to 1988 for market access and domestic
support and 1986 to 1990 for export competition) should be presented as
well as the average.

7.   Some tables also require participants to indicate annual commitment
levels representing the maximum level of the parameter concerned for each
year of the six-year implementation period (up to 10 years for developing
countries; B: paragraphs 5, 8, 11 and 15). The years shown in the
respective headings of the tables should be 1993 to 2003 (with the years
2000 to 2003 relating only to developing countries). If a calendar year is

55 - 43 ~7

0066

- 2 -

being used, the relevant years are 1993 to 1999 (1993 to 2002 for developing countries) and 1999 (2003) should be left blank. If a financial or marketing year is used which incorporates part of two calendar years, e.g a "crop year" may run from 1 July to 30 June, the 1993 year may not have an entry, but the years 1999 and 2003 would (A: Article 1(h)).

8.   The product coverage for the lists of commitments on all aspects of the agriculture reform programme other than the Sanitary and Phytosanitary agreement is as follows (A: and B: Annex 1):

    (i)   HS Chapters 1 to 24 less fish and fish products, plus

(ii)	HS Code	29.05.43	(manitol)
	HS Code	29.05.44	(sorbitol)
	HS Heading	33.01	(essential oils)
	HS Headings	35.01 to 35.05	(albuminoidal substances, modified starches, glues)
	HS Code	38.09.10	(finishing agents)
	HS Code	38.23.60	(sorbitol n.e.p.)
	HS Headings	41.01 to 41.03	(hides and skins)
	HS Heading	43.01	(raw furskins)
	HS Headings	50.01 to 50.03	(raw silk and silk waste)
	HS Headings	51.01 to 51.03	(wool and animal hair)
	HS Headings	52.01 to 52.03	(raw cotton, waste and cotton carded or combed)
	HS Heading	53.01	(raw flax)
	HS Heading	53.02	(raw hemp)

    (iii) Any participant may extend its commitments to include additional products to those listed above, provided that other participants agree.

9.   Particular tables need only be completed if a participant uses a particular measure. For example, Supporting Tables 1 and 2 need only be completed for those products to which border measures other than ordinary customs duties apply. Supporting Tables 6 to 8 need only be completed where products receive product-specific support at the 'basic product' level, i.e. as close as practicable to the point of first sale, etc. Also, as explained below, the level of product aggregation among specific commitments may differ. Accordingly, information need only be provided for the relevant level of aggregation.

- 3 -

10. The order of the tables in this paper is as follows:

0068

Supporting Table 1
(MTN.TNC(W)FA page L.64)

AGRICULTURAL NEGOTIATIONS: SUPPORTING DATA

MARKET ACCESS: name of country

Tariff Equivalents: Tariff Equivalents Calculated Directly from Price Comparisons

Tariff item number	Description of products	Current rate of duty (U(8)	Non-tariff measure(s) tariffied	Internal price	External price	Quality/ variety adjustment	Tariff Equivalent specific ad valorem	Tariff Equivalent ad valorem (0(6)% by 7)	Data sources	Comments
1	2	3	4	5	6	7	8 (5-6 adjusted	9 (0(6)% by 7)	10	11

(a) 1986 data used in columns 5 to 9
(b) 1987 data used in columns 5 to 9
(c) 1988 data used in columns 5 to 9
(d) average for product used in columns 5 to 9

- 5 -

Supporting Table 1

This table (or Supporting Table 2) should be completed for all tariff lines
(i.e. all items of the tariff schedule to which one single duty is attached) to
which border measures other than ordinary customs duties, such as quantitative
restrictions or non-tariff measures maintained through state trading
enterprises etc. currently apply. This requirement does not apply to those
non-tariff measures maintained for balance-of-payments reasons or under general
safeguard and exception provisions, i.e. Articles XII, XVIII, XIX, XX and XXI
of the General Agreement (B: Annex 3, paragraph 1 including footnote).

The distinction between Supporting Tables 1 and 2 is the method of calculation
of the tariff equivalent. If the calculation is made via a price comparison,
Supporting Table 1 should be used. This method of calculation will generally
apply to products at the four-digit level of the HS or in the case of
individual fruits and vegetables, etc. at a more detailed level. If the
calculation is made via the use of coefficients applied to other tariff
equivalents (generally transformed or processed products based on inputs for
which tariff equivalents have been calculated by direct price comparisons),
Supporting Table 2 should be used (B: Annex 3, paragraph 3).

Columns 1 and 2 - tariff item number and product description as in
     participants' tariff schedules.

Column 3 - current rate of duty as in participants tariff schedules for the
     product concerned, with an indication of its status, i.e. "B" for bound
     tariffs and "U" for unbound tariffs.

Column 4 - listing of the type of non-tariff measure(s) currently applying to
     the tariff line.

Column 5 - generally, a representative wholesale price ruling in the domestic
     market (or an estimate of that price where adequate data is not available;
     B: Annex 3, paragraph 6). The most important aspect of the internal price
     is that the price is, as close as possible, for the same quality and form
     (e.g. processing level and form of packaging) as the external price (see
     column 6).

Column 6 - generally, the actual average c.i.f. unit value. Where average
     c.i.f. unit values are not available or appropriate, the external price
     can be estimated from either the c.i.f. unit value of a near country or
     from average f.o.b. unit values of (an) appropriate major exporter(s)
     adjusted by adding an estimate of insurance, freight and other relevant
     costs to the importing country. Where the external price is not already
     in domestic currency, it should be converted to domestic currency using
     the annual average market exchange rate (B: Annex 3, paragraphs 4 and 5).

Column 7 - if the internal and external prices are not for the same quality of
     product, it may be considered necessary to adjust the tariff equivalent to
     take account of any differences (to ensure that the tariff equivalent
     represents the same initial level of protection as the current measures).
     The method used should be shown in column 10 or 11 (B: Annex 3,
     paragraph 7).

Column 8 - calculated: (internal less external price), adjusted to take
     account of quality.

Column 9 - calculated: (specific tariff equivalent divided by the external
     price), expressed as a percentage.

0070

Supporting Table 2
(MTN.INC/W/FA page L.65)

AGRICULTURAL NEGOTIATIONS: SUPPORTING DATA

MARKET ACCESS: name of country

Tariff Equivalents: Derived Tariff Equivalents for Transformed and Processed Products

Tariff item number	Description of products	Current rate of duty (1/8)	Non-tariff measure(s) tariffied	Component product(s) tariff equivalent(s)	Proportion(s) of component product(s)	External price of derived product	Tariff Equivalent specific $\{5(s)*6(s)\}$	Tariff Equivalent ad valorem $(8/7)*$	Additional industrial protection	Data sources	Comments
1	2	3	4	5	6	7	8	9	10	11	12

(a) 1986 data used in columns 5 to 9
(b) 1987 data used in columns 5 to 9
(c) 1988 data used in columns 5 to 9
(d) average for product used in columns 5 to 9

0071

Supporting Table 2

In general, the tariff equivalents calculated in this table will be those of transformed or processed products, calculated by multiplying the tariff equivalent(s) for input(s) into the product (e.g. wheat and sugar in biscuits) by the proportion of those input(s) in the transformed or processed products (B: Annex 3, paragraph 3(iii)). As noted above, this table should be completed for all such tariff lines to which border measures other than ordinary customs duties currently apply.

Columns 1 and 2 - tariff item number and product description as in participants' tariff schedules.

Column 3 - current rate of duty as in participants tariff schedules for the product concerned, with an indication of its status, i.e. "B" for bound tariffs and "U" for unbound tariffs.

Column 4 - listing of the type of non-tariff measure(s) currently applying to the tariff line.

Column 5 - tariff equivalent(s) of the input(s) into the transformed or processed product, e.g. wheat and sugar (these tariff equivalent(s) will generally have been calculated in Supporting Table 1).

Column 6 - the proportions of these input(s) in the transformed or processed product, e.g. biscuits may contain 20 per cent wheat and 10 per cent sugar. The proportion(s) may be derived in terms of physical quantities or in value terms (B: Annex 3, paragraph 3(iii)). Whether the former or latter proportion is used, it should be noted in the comments column.

Column 7 - the external price of the transformed or processed product (defined in Column 6 of Supporting Table 1) is only needed where the resultant tariff equivalent is to be expressed in ad valorem terms.

Column 8 - calculated: by multiplying the tariff equivalent(s) in column 5 by the relevant proportion(s) in column 6 and summing them into a total for each transformed or processed product.

Column 9 - calculated: (specific tariff equivalent divided by the external price), expressed as a percentage.

Column 10 - where the calculation of the tariff equivalent includes the effect of any industrial protection, e.g. where it is calculated through direct price comparisons at the level of processed products, the industrial protection should not be listed separately since to do so would be to double count it. Where coefficients are used in this table however, it may be necessary to add the additional protection (tariffs) currently provided to the manufacture of the transformed or processed product. For example, a product may currently have both an ordinary tariff plus a variable component. In this case, the variable component would be tariffied in columns 5 to 9, but, in order to maintain the current situation, the ordinary tariff would also be listed and added to arrive at the base rate of duty which will be included in Table 1 of the list of commitments (Table 1) (B: Annex 3, paragraph 3(iii)).

0072

Table 1
(MTN.TNC/W/FA page L.55)

AGRICULTURAL NEGOTIATIONS: LIST OF COMMITMENTS

MARKET ACCESS: name of country

__Lists Relating to Ordinary Customs Duties, Including those Resulting from Tariffication__

Tariff item number	Description of products	Base rate of duty (Supporting Tables 1 and 2)	Bound rate of duty	Other charges and duties	Year of Implementation of final tariff	Percentage reduction applied	Special safeguard (Y/N)
1	2	3	4	5	6	7	8

0073

- 9 -

Table 1

Columns 1 and 2 - tariff item number and product description as in participants' tariff schedules.

Column 3 - the base rate of duty for those tariff lines currently subject to ordinary customs duties only will be the bound duty rate, or for unbound tariff lines, the level applied as at 1 September 1986 (B: paragraph 3). The only exception to this is in the case of tariff lines subject only to unbound ordinary customs duties in developing countries (on which products the country may choose to offer ceiling bindings to which the reduction will apply; B: paragraph 14). For those tariff lines currently subject to border measures other than ordinary customs duties, the base rate of duty will be the tariff equivalent (in either specific or ad valorem terms) calculated in Supporting Tables 1 and 2 above (B: paragraph 4). There are however, two exceptions to this: (i) where such a tariff equivalent is negative or lower than the current bound rate (in which case this column may contain the current bound rate or a tariff resulting from an offer for that product; B: Annex 3, paragraph 8); and, (ii) where an adjustment is made to the level of a tariff equivalent which would have resulted from the guidelines (in which case this column may contain the adjusted tariff equivalent and the participant concerned should afford full opportunities for consultation; B: Annex 3, paragraph 9).

Column 4 - the bound rate of duty refers to the level to which the base rate will be reduced over the implementation period. This will be at least a 15 per cent reduction from the base rate, with the simple average of all reductions equalling 36 per cent (24 per cent for developing countries; B: paragraphs 5 and 15). Developed countries should take fully into account the particular needs and conditions of developing countries in the size of reduction for each tariff line (B: paragraph 17). Account may also be taken of guidelines relating to concessions and other liberalization measures implemented by developing countries (B: paragraph 17).

Column 5 - other duties and charges, i.e. those under Article II:1(b) of the General Agreement.

Column 6 - the year of implementation of the (final) bound rate of duty (column 4), i.e. the end of the six-year implementation period (up to 10 years for developing countries). The year will be not later than 1998 for developed countries (B: paragraph 5) and not later than 2002 for developing countries (B: paragraphs 5 and 15).

Column 7 - the percentage reduction of the base rate of duty that results in the bound rate of duty (as noted under column 4 above).

Column 8 - "Y" indicates a product subject to tariffication (Supporting Tables 1 and 2), on which a participant may therefore take recourse to the special safeguard provision (A: Article 5). "N" indicates that the special safeguard provision is not applicable, either because the tariff line concerned is currently subject to ordinary customs duties only, or because the participant decides not to invoke such a provision for a product subject to tariffication.

0074

0075

Table 2
(MTN.TNC/W/FA page L.57)

AGRICULTURAL NEGOTIATIONS: LIST OF COMMITMENTS

MARKET ACCESS: name of country

Lists Relating to Current Access

Tariff Item number	Description of product	Initial tariff quota quantity	In-quota tariff rate	Final tariff quota quantity	Other terms and conditions
1	2	3	4	5	6

55-(6) -/2

- 11 -

<u>Table 2</u>

This table applies to tariffied products, i.e. those for which tariff
equivalents have been calculated in Supporting Tables 1 and 2. For these
products current access opportunities are to be maintained on terms at
least equivalent to those existing and increased over the implementation
period (B: paragraph 6 and Annex 3, paragraph 11). However, in relation to
the expansion of current access, due account is to be taken of reduction
commitments in the export competition area (B: paragraph 6).

<u>Columns 1 and 2</u> - tariff item number and product description as in
  participants' tariff schedules.

<u>Column 3</u> - the initial tariff quota quantity reflects current import
  levels, but in no case less than the average quantity during the 1986
  to 1988 period. For global or country-specific quantitative
  restrictions, voluntary restraint agreements, etc., the quantity is
  defined as that permitted to be imported under those measures, whether
  or not that quantity was imported (where imports exceeded the quantity
  of product permitted to be imported the actual imported quantity is
  considered to be the current access opportunity; B: Annex 3,
  paragraph 12). For existing non-automatic import licensing,
  non-tariff measures maintained through state trading enterprises,
  etc., the quantity is defined as no less than that imported during the
  base period (B: Annex 3, paragraph 13).

<u>Column 4</u> - the in-quota tariff rate, reflecting the commitment to maintain
  the access on terms at least equivalent to those existing, will
  generally be the duty level applied (B: Annex 3, paragraph 11).

<u>Column 5</u> - the final tariff quota quantity reflects the possibility of an
  increase in current access opportunities (B: paragraph 6). Where
  there is no increase, the figure in column 5 will be the same as in
  column 3.

<u>Column 6</u> - other terms and conditions that may be listed are the country
  specificity of all or part of the imports (reflecting the current
  situation), particular quality or other standards that currently
  exist, etc. While existing current access opportunities may be
  maintained on a country-specific basis, any expansion of current
  access should be provided on an m.f.n. basis.

<u>Note:</u> While this table only reflects tariff quotas, current access
opportunities may be maintained by other means as long as they remain on
terms at least equivalent to those existing.

0076

0077

Supporting Table 3
(MTN.TNC/W/FA page L.66)

AGRICULTURAL NEGOTIATIONS: SUPPORTING DATA

MARKET ACCESS: name of country

Minimum Access Commitments

Description of products	Tariff (item number(s) encompassed in product description	Current access (product equivalent)	Consumption quantity	Initial new access quantity	Final new access quantity	Data sources	Comments
1	2	3	4	5	6	7	8
				(4*3%)-3	(4*5%)-3		

(a) 1986 data used in columns 3 and 4
(b) 1987 data used in columns 3 and 4
(c) 1988 data used in columns 3 and 4
(d) average for product used in columns 3 and 4

.(5-A) -/4

Supporting Table 2

This table applies to the tariffied products, i.e. those for which tariff equivalents have been calculated in Supporting Tables 1 and 2. For these products, where there are no significant imports, minimum access opportunities should be established. (Where imports of any product are greater than 5 per cent of domestic consumption, the table need not be completed for that product). The new access opportunities are to ensure that in the first year of the implementation period access opportunities representing not less than 3 per cent of corresponding domestic consumption in the 1986-88 base period are provided, and new access opportunities should be expanded to reach 5 per cent of that figure by the end of the implementation period (B: paragraph 5).

The commitment for minimum access is, in general, at the four-digit level of the HS, or wherever appropriate, at a more detailed level. However, depending on factors such as data availability, another level of aggregation may be used to implement the commitment (B: Annex 3, paragraph 15). In relation to transformed and processed products, new access opportunities need not be established, but the imports of the products included therein e.g. wheat in respect of biscuits, can be taken into account in the calculation used to determine whether the thresholds have been met.

Column 1 - the product description in this case is generally for products at the four-digit level, e.g. wheat and beef, but also for individual fruits and vegetables at the appropriate level.

Column 2 - includes the tariff item numbers for both the product in column 1 and any processed products in which that product is incorporated, e.g. pasta, biscuits or sausages.

Column 3 - current access for each of the products in column 1 is the total of imports of the product itself and, where appropriate, the product-equivalent level of imports of any products whose tariff item numbers are listed in column 2. For example, 200 tonnes of pasta would have, in product-equivalent terms, 100 tonnes of wheat if the coefficient was 50 per cent. (It is not essential to add up the various derived products, especially where the imports are at low levels. If only the imports of the product in column 1 are taken into account, however, current access would appear to be at lower levels than is actually the case).

Column 4 - the consumption quantity (of the products in column 1) may be directly available, or, as is often necessary, may be derived from domestic production figures plus imports and less exports (and adjusted for changes in stock levels if appropriate and practicable).

Column 5 - calculated: (domestic consumption times 3 per cent) less current access (product-equivalent terms) at the product level shown in column 1.

Column 6 - calculated: (domestic consumption times 5 per cent) less current access (product-equivalent terms) at the product level shown in column 1.

0078

55-83 - 15

0079

Table 3
(MTN.TNC/W/FA page L.5B)

AGRICULTURAL NEGOTIATIONS: LIST OF COMMITMENTS

MARKET ACCESS: name of country

Lists Relating to Minimum Access

Description of Products	Tariff item number(s) encompassed in product description	Initial tariff quota quantity (Supporting Table 3)	In-quota tariff rate	Final tariff quota quantity (Supporting Table 3)
1	2	3	4	5

55-43 -16

- 15 -

Table 3

This table applies to the tariffied products with no significant imports (i.e. where imports are less than 5 per cent of consumption as calculated in Supporting Table 3). New minimum access is to be provided via tariff quotas allocated to internationally traded products and be provided on an m.f.n. basis (B: Annex 3, paragraphs 14 and 15).

Column 1 - as with Supporting Table 3, the product description will depend on the level of aggregation used.

Column 2 - includes the tariff item numbers for the product in column 1, e.g. wheat and beef. Tariff quotas may also be established for any processed products incorporating the product in column 1, e.g. pasta, biscuits and sausages. The tariff item numbers for these products should be shown in this column.

Column 3 - the initial tariff quota quantity for each of the products listed in column 1 in product-equivalent terms. Tariff quotas should equal the level of new minimum access opportunities derived in Supporting Table 3, column 5.

Column 4 - the duty rate to apply to such access (a low or minimal rate; B: Annex 3, paragraph 14).

Column 5 - the final tariff quota quantities reflecting the expansion of such access from 3 to 5 per cent of domestic consumption (from Supporting Table 3).

0080

55-43-17

0081

Supporting Table 4
(MTN.TNC/W/FA page L.67)

AGRICULTURAL NEGOTIATIONS: SUPPORTING DATA

DOMESTIC SUPPORT: name of country

Measures Exempt from the Reduction Commitment

Measure name	Measure type	Description (including reference to criteria where appropriate)	Monetary value of measure	Data sources	Comments
1	*2*	*3*	*4*	*5*	*6*
(a) "general services"					
(b) "public stockholding for food security purposes"					
(c) "domestic food aid"					
(d) "decoupled income support"					
(e) "income insurance and income safety-net programmes"					
(f) "payments for relief from natural disasters"					
(g) "structural adjustment assistance provided through producer retirement programmes"					
(h) "structural adjustment assistance provided through resource retirement programmes"					
(i) "structural adjustment assistance provided through investment aids"					
(j) "environmental programmes"					
(k) "regional assistance programmes"					
(l) "other"					

- 17 -

Supporting Table 4

This table should be completed if a participant considers that some of its measures fall into the 'green box'. The requirements for such measures are defined in Annex 2 to Part A of the agriculture text. While the notification will by necessity be concise, it should include an adequate description to allow other participants to assess the appropriateness of such measures' placement in the green box. This is especially relevant for those measures in rows (d) to (l) which require certain policy-specific criteria to be fulfilled (A: Annex 2, paragraphs 6 to 13) in addition to the general criteria (A: Annex 2, paragraph 1).

Column 1 - the measure name, i.e. the title of the measure as it is known in the participant's legislation.

Column 2 - the type of measure, e.g. product inspection or a disaster relief payment.

Column 3 - a brief description of the measure allowing other participants to assess the measures effects, especially relative to the criteria in the Annex.

Column 4 - the monetary value or cost of implementing the measure.

The rows (a) to (l) reflect the breakdown of measures as they appear in Annex 2 to Part A of the agriculture text. Based on the criteria in that Annex, the participant concerned should make the decision as to which category the measure fits into.

The measures of developing countries, which in some cases may fit under categories in both this table and Supporting Table 5, could appear in either table. The main difference is that measures appearing in this table, i.e. those maintained in conformity with the green box criteria, are considered as non-actionable for the purposes of countervailing measures (A: Article 7, paragraph 3), while those in Supporting Table 5 are exempt from reduction, but remain in the 'amber' category.

0082

0083

Supporting Table 5
(MTN.TNC/W/FA page L.68)

AGRICULTURAL NEGOTIATIONS: SUPPORTING DATA

DOMESTIC SUPPORT: name of country

Measures Exempt from the Reduction Commitment - Special and Differential Treatment

Measure name	Measure type	Description	Monetary value of measure	Data sources	Comments
1	2	3	4	5	6
(a)	"Investment subsidies generally available to agriculture"				
(b)	"Support to encourage diversion from the cultivation of illicit narcotics"				
(c)	"Import subsidies generally available to low-income or resource poor producers"				

- 19 -

Supporting Table 5

This table should be completed if a developing country participant
considers some of its measures fall into the list of those exempt from the
reduction commitment. The requirements for such measures are defined in
paragraph 18 of Part B of the agriculture text. While the notification
will by necessity be concise, it should include an adequate description to
allow other participants to assess the appropriateness of the placement of
such measures, i.e. their coverage under paragraph 18 of Part B.

Column 1 - the measure name, i.e. the title of the measure as it is known
     in the participant's legislation.

Column 2 - the type of measure, e.g. farm investment aid.

Column 3 - a brief description of the measure allowing other participants
     to assess the measure's effects, especially with respect to
     agricultural and rural development programmes in the developing
     country concerned (B: paragraph 18).

Column 4 - the monetary value or cost of implementing the measure.

The rows (a) to (c) reflect the breakdown of measures as they appear in
paragraph 18 of Part B of the agriculture text. Based on that paragraph,
the participant concerned should make the decision as to which category the
measure fits into.

The measures of developing countries, which in some cases may fit under
categories in both this table and Supporting Table 4, could appear in
either table. The main difference is that measures appearing in Supporting
Table 4, i.e. those maintained in conformity with the green box criteria,
are considered as non-actionable for the purposes of countervailing
measures (A: Article 7, paragraph 3), while those in this table are exempt
from reduction, but remain in the 'amber' category.

0084

- 20 -

Supporting Table 6
(MTN.TNC/W/FA page L.69)

AGRICULTURAL NEGOTIATIONS: SUPPORTING DATA

DOMESTIC SUPPORT: name of country

Aggregate Measurements of Support: Market Price Support

Description of basic products	Measure type(s)	Applied administered price	External reference price	Eligible production	Associated fees/levies	Total market price support	Data sources	Comments
1	2	3	4	5	6	7	8	9
						((3-4)*5)-6		

(a) 1986 data used in columns 3 and 5 to 7
(b) 1987 data used in columns 3 and 5 to 7
(c) 1988 data used in columns 3 and 5 to 7
(d) average for product used in columns 3, and 5 to 7

0085

Supporting Table 6

This table should be completed for each basic product receiving market price support (B: Annex 5, paragraph 1) and for which it is possible to calculate the amount of market price support. In this context, a basic product is defined as the product as close as practicable to the point of first sale, e.g. wheat, rice, milk and individual fruits and vegetables, rather than any products derived from these products. Market price support is deemed to exist where there is an administered price of some type, e.g. an intervention price or state purchasing price, that is higher than the world price for the same product (but excluding such support which may be exempt from the reduction commitment, i.e. that listed in Supporting Table 5 above). Market price support at both the national and sub-national levels should be included as should revenue foregone (B: Annex 5, paragraphs 2 and 3). Support should be included to the extent that it benefits the producers of the basic products (B: Annex 5, paragraph 7).

Column 1 - description of the basic product, i.e. the product as close as practicable to the point of first sale or at the 'farmgate' level (B: Annex 5, paragraph 1).

Column 2 - the type of measure in operation, e.g. an intervention scheme or compulsory crop purchase scheme.

Column 3 - the average administered price applied to the basic product in the 1986 to 1988 period.

Column 4 - generally the average, for the years 1986 to 1988, of the f.o.b. unit value for the product concerned in a net exporting country, or the average c.i.f. unit value for the product concerned in a net importing country. The fixed reference price may be adjusted for quality differences as necessary (B: Annex 5, paragraph 9). The details of any quality adjustment should be shown in the data sources or comments column.

Column 5 - the average of the production eligible to receive the price in column 3 in the 1986-88 period (B: Annex 5, paragraph 8). For an open-ended intervention or buy-in scheme, this may be total production. If the scope of the measure is limited to a particular quantity, it is this limited quantity that should be used.

Column 6 - specific agricultural levies or fees paid by producers in relation to the market price support, e.g. co-responsibility levies, should appear in this column (B: Annex 5, paragraph 4).

Column 7 - calculated: (the administered price less the external reference price) multiplied by eligible production. From this figure, levies or fees may be deducted.

0086

Supporting Table 7
(MTN.INC(W)FA page L.70)

AGRICULTURAL NEGOTIATIONS: SUPPORTING DATA

DOMESTIC SUPPORT: name of country

Aggregate Measurements of Support: Non-Exempt Direct Payments

Description of basic products	Measure type(s)	Applied administered price	External reference price	Eligible production	Total price-related direct payments	Other non-exempt direct payments	Associated fees/levies	Total direct payments	Data sources	Comments
1	2	3	4	5	6	7	8	9	10	11
					((3-4)*5)			(6+7-0)		

(a) 1986 data used in columns 3 and 5 to 9
(b) 1987 data used in columns 3 and 5 to 9
(c) 1988 data used in columns 3 and 5 to 9
(d) average for product used in columns 3 and 5 to 9

(55 -43 -24

0087

Supporting Table 7

This table should be completed for each basic product (defined as the product as close as practicable to the point of first sale), receiving non-exempt direct payments (B: Annex 5, paragraph 1). These may be the same products as those in Supporting Table 6 and/or different products. Such payments include both those that are based on internal or external prices, e.g. deficiency payments, and those that are unrelated to price, e.g. a non-exempt per hectare payment. Support which may be exempt from the reduction commitment, i.e. that listed in Supporting Tables 4 or 5 above, would be excluded. Payments at both the national and sub-national levels should be included as should revenue foregone (B: Annex 5, paragraphs 2 and 3). Support should be included to the extent that it benefits the producers of the basic products (B: Annex 5, paragraph 7).

Column 1 - description of the basic product, i.e. the product as close as practicable to the point of first sale or at the "farmgate" level (B: Annex 5, paragraph 1).

Column 2 - the type of measure in operation, e.g. a deficiency payment scheme or per hectare scheme.

Column 3 - where the payments are based on internal or external prices, the average administered price that is applied to the basic product in the 1986 to 1988 period.

Column 4 - where there is an administered price in column 3, the fixed reference price will generally be the actual price used for determining payment rates for the years 1986 to 1988 (B: Annex 5, paragraph 11). If this is not available or appropriate, the external reference should be defined as in Supporting Table 6 (column 4).

Column 5 - the average of the production eligible to receive the price in column 3 in the 1986 to 1988 period (B: Annex 5, paragraph 8). For an open-ended deficiency payment scheme, this may be total production. If the scope of the payments is limited to a particular quantity, it is this limited quantity that should be used.

Column 6 - calculated: (the administered price less the external reference price) multiplied by eligible production. Alternatively, this column could contain the budgetary outlays on such support (B: Annex 5, paragraph 10).

Column 7 - non-exempt direct payments which are based on factors other than price should be measured using budgetary outlays (B: Annex 5, paragraph 12).

Column 8 - specific agricultural levies or fees paid by producers in relation to non-exempt direct payments, e.g. levies to fund research, etc. should appear in this column (B: Annex 5, paragraph 4).

Column 9 - calculated: (total price-related direct payments plus other non-exempt direct payments) less related levies or fees.

0088

- 24 -

0089

Supporting Table 8
(MTN.TNC/W/FA page L.71)

AGRICULTURAL NEGOTIATIONS: SUPPORTING DATA

DOMESTIC SUPPORT: name of country

Aggregate Measurements of Support: Other Product-Specific Support and Total AMS

Description of basic products	Measure type(s)	Other product-specific budgetary outlays	Other product-specific support (include calculation details)	Associated fees/levies	Total other product-specific support	Market price support (Supporting Table 6)	Non-exempt direct payments (Supporting Table 7)	Total AMS	Data sources	Comments
1	2	3	4	5	6 (3+4-5)	7	8	9 (6+7+8)	10	11

(a) 1986 data used in columns 3 to 9
(b) 1987 data used in columns 3 to 9
(c) 1988 data used in columns 3 to 9
(c) average for product used in columns 3 to 9

Supporting Table 8

This table should be completed for each basic product receiving market price support (Supporting Table 6), non-exempt direct payments (Supporting Table 7), and/or other product-specific support ("other non-exempt policies"; B: Annex 5, paragraph 1). Other product-specific support could include crop-specific input subsidies such as fertiliser subsidies, or investment aids linked to the establishment of specific crop or livestock products (but excluding such support which may be exempt from the reduction commitment, i.e. that listed in Supporting Tables 4 or 5 above). Subsidies provided at both the national and sub-national levels should be included as should revenue foregone (B: Annex 5, paragraphs 2 and 3). Support should be included to the extent that it benefits the producers of the basic products (B: Annex 5, paragraph 1).

Column 1 - description of the basic product, i.e. the product as close as practicable to the point of first sale or at the "farmgate" level (B: Annex 5, paragraph 1).

Column 2 - the type of other product-specific support measures in operation.

Column 3 - budgetary outlays on such support, e.g. crop-specific fertiliser subsidies, where such outlays reflect the full extent of the subsidy (B: Annex 5, paragraph 13).

Column 4 - the full extent of the subsidy where this is not reflected in budgetary outlays in column 3. For example, a crop-specific investment aid which is given in the form of an interest concession may have no budgetary outlays associated with it, but is a subsidy to the producer. In this case, the rate of interest paid by the producer should be compared to a representative market interest rate and the difference, multiplied by the amount of lending, included in this column. The calculation details should be shown either in this column or in column 10 or 11 (B: Annex 5, paragraph 13).

Column 5 - specific agricultural levies or fees paid by producers in relation to the other non-exempt product-specific support, e.g. product-specific fertiliser taxes, should appear in this column (B: Annex 5, paragraph 4).

Column 6 - calculated: (budgetary outlays plus other subsidies) less related levies or fees.

Column 7 - taken from Supporting Table 6, column 7.

Column 8 - taken from Supporting Table 7, column 9.

Column 9 - calculated: (total other product-specific support plus market price support plus non-exempt direct payments).

0090

- 26 -

0091

Table 4
(MTN.TNC/W/FA page L.59)

AGRICULTURAL NEGOTIATIONS: LIST OF COMMITMENTS

DOMESTIC SUPPORT: name of country

Product-Specific Aggregate Measurements of Support

Description of basic products	Calendar/ marketing year applied	Base product-specific AMS (Supporting Tables 4 to 8)	Annual commitment levels			
1	2	3	4	5	6	7...

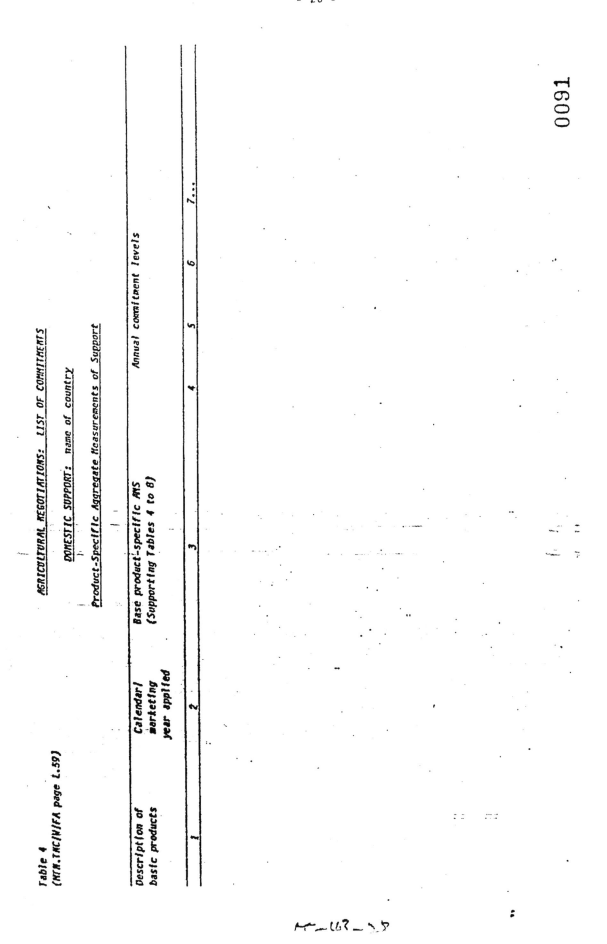

- 27 -

Table 4

This table should be completed for all basic products receiving market
price support, non-exempt direct payments, or any other product-specific
subsidy not exempted from the reduction commitment except those basic
products covered by equivalent commitments, i.e. for which it is not
practicable to calculate market price support (B: paragraph 8 and Annex 5,
paragraph 1). The data in column 3 comes from the Supporting Table 8
above, but may be expressed in either domestic currency or another currency
and credit is allowed in respect of actions undertaken since the year 1986
(B: paragraph 6).

Column 1 - description of the basic product, i.e. the product as close as
            practicable to the point of first sale or at the 'farmgate' level (B:
            Annex 5, paragraph 1).

Column 2 - the "calendar/marketing year applied" in this context refers to
            the calendar, financial or marketing year on which basis the AMS has
            been calculated, e.g. a "crop year" may run from 1 July to 30 June
            while a "financial year" may run from 1 April to 31 March
            (A: Article 1(h)).

Column 3 - based on Supporting Table 8, column 9.

Annual commitment levels - these will be the base product-specific AMS
            levels reduced in each of the 6 years (up to 10 years for developing
            countries) of the implementation period. The reductions, totalling 20
            per cent for developed countries and at least 13.3 per cent for
            developing countries, are to be undertaken in equal instalments (B:
            paragraphs 8 and 15). "4 5 6 7 ..." in the table's heading should be
            replaced by each of the years of the six-year (up to 10-year for
            developing countries) implementation period.

De minimis - as long as the product-specific AMS does not exceed 5 per
            cent of the total value of production of the basic product concerned
            for developed countries (or 10 per cent for developing countries),
            there is no requirement to undertake the reduction of that support (A:
            Article 6, paragraph 4 and B: paragraphs 10 and 19). Nevertheless,
            this table should also be completed for those products. The
            completion of the table would not imply that the AMS concerned has to
            be reduced; it could even be increased up to the de minimis level.

0092

K-43-2β

Supporting Table 9
(MTN.TNC/W/FA page L.72)

AGRICULTURAL NEGOTIATIONS: SUPPORTING DATA

DOMESTIC SUPPORT: name of country

Equivalent Commitments

Description of basic products	Measure type(s)	Applied administered price	Production eligible to receive the applied administered price	Market price support budgetary outlays	Non-exempt directs payments	Other product-specific support	Data sources	Comments
1	2	3	4	5	6	7	8	9

(a) 1986 data used in columns 3 to 6
(b) 1987 data used in columns 3 to 6
(c) 1988 data used in columns 3 to 6
(d) average for product used in columns 3 to 6

0093

- 29 -

Supporting Table 9

Where the calculation of the market price support component of an AMS is
not practicable, this table should be used to set out the data necessary to
make equivalent commitments (B: paragraph 8 and Annex 6, paragraph 1).
This may be the case where no appropriate reference price is available to
use in the market price support calculation. The table should be completed
for each such basic product. In this context, market price support is
deemed to exist where there is an administered price of some type, e.g. an
intervention price or state purchasing price, that is higher than the world
price for the same product. Market price support at both the national and
sub-national levels should be included (B: Annex 6, paragraph 1). Support
should be included to the extent that it benefits the producers of the
basic products (B: Annex 6, paragraph 4).

Column 1 - description of the basic product, i.e. the product as close as
          practicable to the point of first sale or at the "farmgate" level (B:
          Annex 6, paragraph 2).

Column 2 - the type of measure in operation, e.g. an intervention scheme
          or compulsory crop purchase scheme.

Column 3 - where there is a defined administered price, the average
          administered price applied to the basic product in the 1986 to 1988
          period.

Column 4 - the average of the production eligible to receive the price in
          column 3 in the 1986 to 1988 period (B: Annex 6, paragraph 2). For an
          open-ended intervention or buy-in scheme, this may be total
          production. If the scope of the measure is limited to a particular
          quantity, it is this limited quantity that should be used.

Column 5 - if the market price support in question does not involve a
          defined administered price, the budgetary outlays involved to maintain
          the system, e.g. buying or storage costs, should be listed in this
          column. This column could also contain (expressed as a negative
          amount) any specific agricultural levies or fees paid by producers in
          relation to the market price support (B: Annex 6, paragraph 4).

Column 6 - taken from Supporting Table 7, column 9 for the product
          concerned (B: Annex 6, paragraph 3).

Column 7 - taken from Supporting Table 8, column 6 for the product
          concerned (B: Annex 6, paragraph 3).

0094

Table 5
(MTN.GNG/FA page L.60)

AGRICULTURAL NEGOTIATIONS: LIST OF COMMITMENTS

DOMESTIC SUPPORT: name of country

Equivalent Commitments

Description of basic products	Calendar/ marketing year applied	Base commitment parameter(s) (Supporting Tables 4,5 and 9)	Annual commitment levels			
1	2	3	4	5	6	7...

55-43-82

- 31 -

<u>Table 5</u>

This table should be completed for each basic product receiving market price support, but for which it is not practicable to calculate this type of support (B: paragraph 8 and Annex 6, paragraph 1). The data in column 3 comes from Supporting Table 9, but financial data may be expressed in either domestic currency or another currency in this table and credit is allowed in respect of actions undertaken since the year 1986 (B: paragraph 8).

<u>Column 1</u> - description of the basic product, i.e. the product as close as practicable to the point of first sale or at the "farmgate" level (B: Annex 6, paragraph 2).

<u>Column 2</u> - the "calendar/marketing year applied" in this context refers to the calendar, financial or marketing year on which basis support has been calculated, e.g. a "crop year" may run from 1 July to 30 June while a "financial year" may run from 1 April to 31 March (A: Article 1(h)).

<u>Column 3</u> - based on Supporting Table 9, this column should show the parameter(s) on which the commitment is to be undertaken. This will be either the administered price and the production eligible to receive that price (columns 3 and 4 of Supporting Table 9) or the budgetary outlays involved in maintaining the market price support (column 5 of Supporting Table 9). Where there are non-exempt direct payments and/or other product-specific support for these products, it should also be included as one of the parameters on which commitments will be made.

<u>Annual commitment levels</u> - these will be the base parameters reduced in each of the 6 years (up to 10 years for developing countries) of the implementation period. The reductions of those parameters that provide equivalent commitments to market price support commitments undertaken in Table 4 should result in a reduction of support totalling 20 per cent for developed countries and at least 13.3 per cent for developing countries, and be undertaken in equal instalments. The actual reduction of these parameters may not equal these percentages, but the effect on support should do so. For the non-exempt direct payments and/or other product-specific support parameters, the reductions should total 20 per cent for developed countries and at least 13.3 per cent for developing countries, and also be undertaken in equal instalments (B: paragraphs 8 and 15). "4 5 6 7 ..." in the table's heading should be replaced by each of the years of the six-year (up to 10-year for developing countries) implementation period.

<u>De minimis</u> - as long as the product-specific support in this table does not exceed 5 per cent of the total value of production of the basic product concerned for developed countries (or 10 per cent for developing countries), there is no requirement to undertake the reduction of that support (A: Article 6, paragraph 4 and B: paragraphs 10 and 19). Nevertheless, this table should be completed as specified for those products. The completion of the table would not imply that the support concerned has to be reduced; it could even be increased up to the <u>de minimis</u> level.

0096

15 - 43 - 33

Supporting Table 10
(MTN.TNC/W/FA L.73)

AGRICULTURAL NEGOTIATIONS: SUPPORTING DATA

DOMESTIC SUPPORT: name of country

Non-Product-Specific AMS

Measure type(s)	Non-product-specific budgetary outlays	Other non-product-specific support (include calculation details)	Associated fees/levies	Total non-product-specific support	Data sources	Comments
1	2	3	4	5 (2+3-4)	6	7

(a) 1986 data used in columns 2 to 5
(b) 1987 data used in columns 2 to 5
(c) 1988 data used in columns 2 to 5
(c) average for measures in columns 2 to 5

55-43-34

0097

Supporting Table 10

A non-product-specific AMS should be calculated where there are
non-product-specific measures that are not exempt from the reduction
commitment (i.e. not included in the listing in either Supporting Table 4
or 5). Such support should be totalled into one non-product-specific AMS
in total monetary terms (B: Annex 5, paragraph 1). Subsidies provided at
both the national and sub-national level should be included as should
revenue forgone (B: Annex 5, paragraphs 2 and 3). Support should be
included to the extent that it benefits producers of basic products
(whether or not such products are included in Supporting Tables 6 to 9;
B: Annex 5, paragraph 7).

Column 1 - this column should list the measures for which a calculation is
   being made.

Column 2 - budgetary outlays on such support, e.g. widely available
   fertiliser subsidies, where such outlays reflect the full extent of
   the subsidy (B: Annex 5, paragraph 13).

Column 3 - the full extent of a subsidy where this is not reflected in
   budgetary outlays. For example, irrigation subsidies provided through
   reduced water charges may have no budgetary outlays associated with
   them, but are a subsidy to the producer. In this case, the water
   charge paid by the producer should be compared to a representative
   market water charge (e.g. the charge paid by factories or households)
   and the difference, multiplied by the amount of water used on farms,
   included in this column. The calculation details should be shown
   either in this column or in column 6 or 7 (B: Annex 5, paragraph 13).

Column 4 - specific agricultural levies or fees paid by producers in
   relation to other non-product-specific support, e.g. environmental
   taxes applied to fertilisers, should appear in this column (B: Annex
   5, paragraph 4).

Column 5 - calculated: (budgetary outlays plus other subsidies) less
   related taxes or levies.

0098

6699

table 6
(MTN.TNC/W/FA page L.61)

AGRICULTURAL NEGOTIATIONS: LIST OF COMMITMENTS

DOMESTIC SUPPORT: name of country

Non-Product-Specific AMS

Base AMS (Supporting Tables 4,5 and 10)	Calendar/ marketing year applied	Annual commitment levels			
1	2	3	4	5	6...

55-43-36

- 35 -

Table 6

This table should be completed for each participant for which
non-product-specific support has been calculated in Supporting Table 10.
The data in column 1 comes from Supporting Table 10, but may be expressed
in either domestic currency or another currency and credit is allowed in
respect of actions undertaken since the year 1986 (B: paragraph 8).

Column 1 - based on Supporting Table 10 column 5, this column should show
the base AMS level.

Column 2 - the 'calendar/marketing year applied' in this context refers to
the calendar, financial or marketing year on which basis the AMS has
been calculated (A: Article 1(h)).

Annual commitment levels - this will be the base non-product-specific AMS
level reduced in each of the 6 years (up to 10 years for developing
countries) of the implementation period. The reductions, totalling 20
per cent for developed countries and at least 13.3 per cent for
developing countries, are to be undertaken in equal instalments (B:
paragraphs 8 and 15). "3 4 5 6 ..." in the table's heading should be
replaced by each of the years of the six-year (up to 10-year for
developing countries) implementation period.

De minimis - as long as the non-product-specific AMS does not exceed 5 per
cent of the total value of agricultural production (at the basic
product level) for developed countries (or 10 per cent for developing
countries), there shall be no requirement to undertake the reduction
of the AMS (A: Article 6, paragraph 4 and B: paragraphs 10 and 19).
Nevertheless, this table should be completed as specified. The
completion of the table would not imply that the AMS has to be
reduced; it could even be increased up to the de minimis level.

0100

55-43-37

Supporting Table 11
(MTN.TNC/W/FA page L.74)

AGRICULTURAL NEGOTIATIONS: SUPPORTING DATA

EXPORT COMPETITION: name of country

Export Subsidies: Outlay and Quantity Reduction Commitments

Description of products	Direct export subsidies	Sales of stocks	Producer financed subsidies	Cost reduction measures	Internal transport subsidies	Total product specific export subsidies	Quantity of subsidized exports	Data source	Comments including measure description
1	2	3	4	5	6	7	8	9	10
(a) 1986 data used in columns 2 to 8									
(b) 1987 data used in columns 2 to 8									
(c) 1988 data used in columns 2 to 8									
(d) 1989 data used in columns 2 to 8									
(e) 1990 data used in columns 2 to 8									
(f) average for product used in columns 2 to 8									

0101

- 37 -

Supporting Table 11

This table should be completed for any product, including agricultural primary products incorporated in exported products, for which export subsidies as listed in the text (A: Article 9, paragraph 1 and B: Annex 6) are provided.

Column 1 - the products to be listed in this column should correspond to the level of specificity shown in Part B: Annex 8, paragraph 7. This level of specificity does not preclude listing particular products within these groups (B: Annex 8, paragraph 8). The list should also include a row in respect of aggregate subsidies on agricultural primary products incorporated in exported products (B: Annex 8, paragraph 9). This does not preclude listing particular incorporated products (B: Annex 8, paragraph 9).

Column 2 - this column should include, for each of the products in column 1, direct subsidies contingent on export performance (A: Article 9 and B: Annex 7, paragraph 1(a)).

Column 3 - this column should include, for each of the products in column 1, subsidies resulting from the sale or disposal for export of non-commercial stocks of agricultural products at a price lower than the comparable price charged for the like product to buyers in the domestic market (A: Article 9 and B: Annex 7, paragraph 1(b)).

Column 4 - this column should include, for each of the products in column 1, payments on the export of an agricultural product that are financed by virtue of governmental action including payments that are financed from the proceeds of a levy imposed on the agricultural product concerned (A: Article 9 and B: Annex 7, paragraph 1(c)).

Column 5 - this column should include, for each of the products in column 1, subsidies to reduce the costs of marketing exports of agricultural products (A: Article 9 and B: Annex 7, paragraph 1(d)). During the implementation period, developing countries are not required to undertake commitments in respect of these subsidies (B: paragraph 20).

Column 6 - this column should include, for each of the products in column 1, internal transport and freight charges on export shipments on terms more favourable than for domestic shipments (A: Article 9 and B: Annex 7, paragraph 1(e)). During the implementation period, developing countries are not required to undertake commitments in respect of these subsidies (B: paragraph 20).

Column 7 - calculated: (the sum of columns 2 to 6).

Column 8 - this column should include, for each of the products in column 1, the quantity exported with the aid of subsidies.

Column 10 - in addition to any other comments, this column should include a brief description of the measure(s) concerned.

0102

55-43-3P

Table 7
(MTN.INC/W/FA page L.62)

AGRICULTURAL NEGOTIATIONS: LIST OF COMMITMENTS

EXPORT COMPETITION: name of country

Export Subsidies: Budgetary Outlay and Quantity Reduction Commitments

Description of products	Calendar/ marketing year applied	Base outlay level (Supporting Table II)	Base quantity (Supporting Table II)	Annual outlay commitment levels			Annual quantity commitment levels			
1	2	3	4	5	6	7 8...	9	10	11 12...	

0103

55-43-40

- 39 -

<u>Table 7</u>

This table should result from Supporting Table 11 and be completed for any product, including agricultural primary products, incorporated in exported products, for which export subsidies as listed in the text (A: Article 9, paragraph 1 and B: Annex 7) are provided.

<u>Column 1</u> - as with Supporting Table 11, the products to be listed in this column should correspond to the level of specificity shown in Part B: Annex 8, paragraph 7 and will include a row in respect of aggregate subsidies on agricultural primary products incorporated in exported products (B: Annex 8, paragraph 9).

<u>Column 2</u> - the "calendar/marketing year applied" in this context refers to the calendar, financial or marketing year on which basis the data has been calculated (A: Article 1(h)).

<u>Column 3</u> - taken from Supporting Table 11, column 7.

<u>Column 4</u> - taken from Supporting Table 11, column 8.

<u>Annual commitment levels</u> - this is the base outlay level and base quantity reduced in each of the 6 years (up to 10 years for developing countries) of the implementation period. The base outlay reductions must total 36 per cent for developed countries and at least 24 per cent for developing countries, and the base quantity reduction must total 24 per cent for developed countries and at least 16 per cent for developing countries (B: paragraphs 11 and 15). In the first year of the implementation period, base levels should be reduced by an amount corresponding to the reduction that would be applicable under implementation on the basis of equal instalments. Thereafter commitment levels for any year of the implementation period should be reduced by at least half the reduction applicable under implementation on the basis of equal annual instalments. Commitment levels in the final year of the implementation period should be established at levels that ensure that the overall reduction during the implementation period is no less than if annual commitment levels had been established on the basis of equal annual instalments (B: Annex 8, paragraph 5). "5 6 7 8 ..." and "9 10 11 12 ..." in the table's heading should be replaced by each of the years of the six-year (up to 10-year for developing countries) implementation period.

0104

0105

Table 8
[MTN.TNC/W/FA page L.63]

AGRICULTURAL NEGOTIATIONS: LIST OF COMMITMENTS

EXPORT COMPETITION: name of country

Other: Commitments Limiting the Scope of Export Subsidies

Description of products	Nature of commitments
1	2

55-4) ~42

- 41 -

Table f

This table should contain other commitments in the area of export
competition such as commitments limiting the scope of subsidies on exports
of agricultural products as regards individual or regional markets (B:
paragraph 12 and Annex 8, paragraph 10).

Column 1 - description of products at the appropriate level.

Column 2 - nature of commitments, e.g. the markets to which such
     commitments apply (B: paragraph 12).

0106

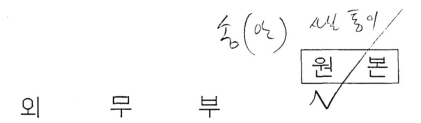

외 무 부

종 별 :

번 호 : GVW-0246   일 시 : 92 0131 1830

수 신 : 장 관(통기,경기원,재무부,농림수산부,상공부)

발 신 : 주 제네바 대사

제 목 : UR 농산물 협상 (한.카나다 양자협상)

1.31(금) 개최된 표제 협상 관련 카나다와 양자협의 결과 하기 보고함.

(아측: 최농무관, 농림수산부 배사무관, 카나다측:NORMAN (대외무역성), MCALPINE(대외무역성), DONAGHY (대표부 참사관), HANSEN(대표부 참사관참석)

1. 농산물 협상 동향 및 전망에 관한 의견교환

- 카나다는 갓트 11조 및 예외없는 관세화와관련 생산통제 품목의 생산자 단체로부터 던켈 초안 수정요구 압력이 있으나, 곡물, 쇠고기등 수출 관심품목 생산자 단체는 대체적으로 만족하고 있으며, 수출 보조 분야에대한 추가 삭감요구가 있다고 하였음.

0 현재 갓트 11조 개선에 관한 기존입장은 계속 유효하지만 생산 통제 대상품목도 일단 TE 를 계산하여 관련업계와 협의중에 있다고 하고, 감축 약속 계획서에 포함시킬 것인지 여부는 각료회의에서 결정될 것이라고 함

0 국내보조 분야는 허용대상 정책에 관심사항이 대체로 반영되어 있으며, 20 퍼센트 삭감율도 시행가능한 것으로 평가하였음.

0 카나다는 농산물 분야의 현 PACKAGE 가 줄어드는 것보다는 더 확대되기를 희망한다고 함.

- 아국은 이에 대하여 농산물 분야 던켈 초안에 대한 국내 불만이 크며 특히 예외 없는 관세화, 쌀에 대한 최저 시장접근, 기준년도 등에 어려움이 있다고 하고 던켈 초안이 개선되도록 노력할 것이라고 하였음.

0 아국 농업의 낙후성 때문에 개도국 우대 적용이 필요하다고 강조하고, 감축약속 계획서에 포함될 품목의 범위는 마지막 단계에서 결정될 것이라고 하였음.

2. 감축 약속 계획서 작성

- 카나다는 현재 기술적 작업이 진행중이며, 3.1까지는 제출할수 있을 것이라고함.

통상국   2차보   경기원   재무부   농수부   상공부

0 이와 관련 아국도 3.1 까지 가능한 한 완전한 감축약속 계획서를 제시해야 할것 이라고 하였음.

0 감축 약속 계획서는 사실상 마지막 OFFER 이며, 그 이후 협상의 여지는 매우 제한될수 밖에 없을 것이라고 함.

- 아국은 3.1 까지 감축 약속 계획서를 제출할수 있도록 국내에서 최선을 다해 작업중인바, 복잡한 국내 절차 때문에 시한을 맞추는데 다소 어려움이 있을수 있다고 하였음.

0 구체적인 협상은 감축약속 계획서가 제출된후에야 현실적으로 가능할 것이라고 하였음.

3. 카나다 관심품목 협의

- 카나다는 농산물에 대한 REQUEST 가 아국에기 전달되었음을 언급하면서 쇠고기, 돼지고기, 밀, 유채, 알팔파등이 아국의 감축 약속 계획서에 포함될 것인지 관심이 크다고 하였음.

- 아국은 이에 대하여 아직 품목별 입장이 정해지지 않았기 때문에 구체적으로 협의하기는 곤란하지만 양자간 문제를 개선하기 위한 노력은 꾸준히 진행될 것이라고 하 였음.

4. 기타

- 아직까지 미국과 이씨간의 구체적 협의는 없는것으로 보이나 2월 첫주간에는 양국간 실무급접촉이 예상됨 (EC 협상 담당자인 밀러부총국장이 2.4 당지 도착예정이며, 미국의 슈뢰터는 현재 당지 체재)

- 2월 첫주간에도 주요국간 농산물 분야 시장접근 양자 협상이 계속될 것으로 전망 됨. (미국, EC,카나다, 일본, 호주등) 끝

(대사 박수길-국장)

외 무 부

종   별 :

번   호 : GVW-0267   일   시 : 92 0203 1900

수   신 : 장관(봉기,경기원,재무부,농림수산부,상공부)

발   신 : 주 제네바대사대리

제   목 : UR/농산물협상

2.8(월) 최농무관은 일본 농림수산성 국제경제과장(일본 대표부 하야시 참사관 동석)과 오찬을 갖고 최근 표제협상 동향에 관하여 협의한바 동인언급 요지하기 보고함.

1. 미.일 양자협상 결과

- 1.31(금) 개최된 미.일 양자협상(미측은 슈뢰터 및 USDA 전문가들이 참석)에서 미국은 감축약속 계획서 작성을 원활히 하고, 던켈초안에 대한 각국의 이해를 명확히 하기위하여 주요국(국명은 거론되지 않았으나 G-8 으로 전망)이 참여하는 기술적 협의를 갖자고 제안하였음.

0 동 기술적 협의에서는 던켈초안의 내용보다는 국별감축 약속 계획서의 작성방법, 계산방법, 가격자료의 사용등이 주로 논의될 것으로 예상함.

0 일본은 이에대하여 동기술적 협의의 유용성을 인정하고 원칙적인 수용의사를 표명하면서, 주된 관심은 TRACK 4 에 있음을 제기하였음.

2. 일본의 던켈초안 수정추진

- 아직 공식적인 수정제안을 추진하고 있지는 않으며 EC 의 동향을 면밀히 살피고 있는 중임.

- 다만 던켈 초안에 대한 일본의 입장을 비공식 문서로 작성(별첨 FAX 송부), 갓트사무국에 전달한바 있음.(동 사안이 민감한 사항이며 TRACK 4 와 관련 오해를 불러일으킬 소지가 있어 여타 국가에는 배포되지 않았다고 하면서 동문서를 대외적으로 활용치 않도록 당부하였음)

0 수정제안의 추진은 시기가 중요한 변수임.

3. 국별 감축계획서 작성

- 국별 감축계획서 작성과 관련 한. 일간 실무협조가 유용하다고 생각하며 3.1

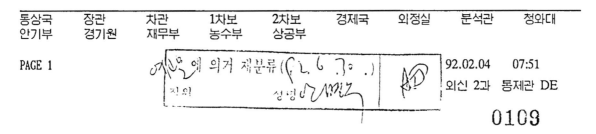

통상국	장관	차관	1차보	2차보	경제국	외정실	분석관	청와대
안기부	경기원	재무부	농수부	상공부				

PAGE 1

예 의거 재분류(92.6.30.)

92.02.04   07:51
외신 2과   통제관 DE

0109

제출 시한전에 양국실무자가 동경 또는 서울에서 접촉, 의견교환하는 방안을
본국정부에 전달하겠음.

　0 일부 TE 계산시 <u>조정계수 사용필요성</u>이 있으나 이를 사용할 경우는 사용국가가
그정당성을 입증해야 하므로 조심스럽게 검토하고 있음. 90 년 국별리스트 작성시
사용된 쌀에 대한 PSE 조정계수(0.66)와는 성격이 다르다고 봄.

　0 민감품목(쌀, 유제품, 전분)을 국별감축 약속계획서에 포함시킬 것인지는아직
결정된바 없음. 카나다, 스위스, 북구등이 감축 약속 계획서를 던켈 초안에 합치되게
낼수 있을 지는 두고봐야 할것임.

　첨부: 일본의 던켈초안에 대한 검토의견서(비공식 문서) 1 부
　(GVW(F)-0075). 끝
　(차석대사 김삼훈-국장)
　예고:92.6.30 까지

PAGE 2

0110

첨부는 지신의 관실

주 제 네 바 대 표 부

번 호 : GVR(R) - 0075   년월일 : 20203   시간 : 1800

수 신 : 장   관 (등기, 경기면, 상궁부, 재무부, 농림수산부)

발 신 : 주 제네바대사

재 목 : 첨부

총 2l 미 (표지포함)

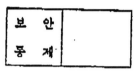

보 안 통 재	
외신과 뭄 재	

January 31, 1992

Japan's Comments to the Part A and Part B of the Draft Text on Agriculture (MTN.TNC/W/FA)

With a view to clarifying the positions of the Japanese Delegation, it wishes to make the following comments on the Draft Text on Agriculture (MTN.TNC/W/FA). This does not preclude the Japanese Delegation to make further comments and proposals in the course of negotiations.

The Japanese Delegation is of the view that, in agriculture of the Draft Final Act, there is lack of balance in the treatment of border measures, as compared with export subsidies. As one of the examples in that respect, the issues of the reduction rates and base periods should be readdressed so that reduction commitments of market access could be put in perspective in relation to those of export subsidies.

1.   Page L.2, Article 1, para (b):

     The following footnote should be added to para (b).
     ""basic product" includes a group of products."

     (Reason) Commitment on a group of products should be allowed not only for export subsidies but also for AMS.

2.   Page L.3, Article 4, para 2:

     Para 2 should be deleted or replaced with the following.

- 1 -

7521-2   0112

"Except as provided for in Article 5 below market access commitments and concessions shall be governed by the relevant provisions of the General Agreement."

(Reason) Without the deletion or replacement, the rights of participants to have recourse to GATT articles would be impaired.

3. Page L.4, Article 5, para 1(i), Footnote 1:

Footnote 1 should be deleted.

(Reason) "Commercially significant levels of imports" is not an objective concept. Such an additional criterion makes a trigger level of safeguard unclear and virtually obstructs smooth operations of volume-based special safeguard.

4. Page L.5, Article 5, para 4, first and second lines:

The words "shall only be maintained until the end of the year in which it has been imposed" should be replaced with "may be maintained for one year after it is imposed".

(Reason) Discipline imposed by the draft text is too stringent since safeguard application is required to be disinvoked at the end of the year, even if import levels remain high.

5. Page L.6, Article 5, para 7, fourth sentence:

The following fourth sentence of para 7 should be deleted.

- 2 -

"Participants undertake, as far as practicable, not
to take recourse to the provisions of paragraph 1(ii)
where the volume of imports of the products concerned
are declining."

(Reason) Price-based safeguard and volume-based safeguard
should be triggered separately and not be interlinked
together.

6.   Page L.7, Article 6, para 3:

Para 3 should be replaced with the following.

"Reduction commitments for any year of the implementation
period, as specified in Schedules, represent the maximum
level of AMS of an agricultural product or a group of
such products."

(Reason) Provisions of reduction commitments for internal
support should be the same as those for export subsidies.

7.   Page L.8, Article 9, para 3:

The following footnote should be added to para 3.

"The countries which implemented production control
and did not grant export subsidies during the base period
shall not be required to make commitments as specified
in para 3."

(Reason) The original text raises an issue of equity.
Credit should be given to production control measures
because such measures have contributed to avoiding
surplus production and resort to export subsidization.

- 3 -

가-21-다

0114

8.   Page L.9, Article 12:

(1) The words "and export subsidies" should be deleted.

(2) The following sentence should be added.

"Whether or not reduction commitments on export
subsidies are being applied in conformity with
the terms of this Agreement, serious prejudice
in the sense of Article XVI:1 of the General
Agreement shall be presumed to exist in the case
of "targeting practice"."

(Reason) In the case of "targeting practice", an
importing country should be allowed to take
countervailing measures without proof of serious injury.

9.   Page L.11, Article 17, para 4:

The words "of excessive rates" should be deleted.

(Reason) The influence of inflation should be adjusted
in reduction commitments on domestic support for any
country.

10. Page L.11, Article 19:

The whole paragraph should be replaced with the following
two paragraphs:

"1. Participants agree that the present Agreement
constitutes the initial step of a reform process
whose long-term objective, as agreed at the Mid-Term
Review Agreement, is to establish a fair and market-

- 4 -

15-21-5

0115

oriented agricultural trading system, noting that
commitments under the reform process should be
made in an equitable way among all participants.

2.   Participants shall accordingly meet at the
appropriate level one year before the end of the
implementation period to review the operation of
this Agreement and to consider a possibility for
maintaining and extending the reform process in
line with the long-term objective."

(Reason) The proposed paragraphs make it clear that
the main objective of the exercise in question is to
review the reform process.

11.   Page L.12, Annex 1, para 1(ii):

We propose to add the following products:

	2906.11	(Menthol)
	2918.14	(Citric acid)
ex.	2922.42	(Sodium glutamates)
	2923.20	(Lecithins and other phosphoaminolipids)
	2940.00	(Sugar ethers, sugar esters and salts, sorbose and other)
ex.	4601.20	(Mats, matting and screens of Igusa (_Juncus effusus_) or of Shichitoi (_Cyperus tegetiformis_))
ex.	4601.91	(Other products of Igusa (_Juncus effusus_) or of Shichitoi (_Cyperus tegetiformis_), bound together in parallel strand or woven, in sheet form, whether or not being finished articles)

- 5 -

/\℮ -2/-

12.   Page L.14, Annex 2, para 3, Chapeau, third line:

"a food security programme identified in national legislation" should be replaced with "a national food security programme".

(Reason) There is no need for distinction between a programme identified in national legislation and a budgetary programme since both legislation and budget are passed by the resolution of legislative body.

13.   Page L.14, Annex 2, para 4, Chapeau, second line:

The words "population in need" should be replaced with "population requiring special consideration".

(Reason) It is necessary to change the wording corresponding to the change from "related to need" to "related to nutritional objectives" as revised from the former draft text.

14.   Page L.15, Annex 2, para 6:

(1) Para 6 (ii), second line
     The words "the type or" should be deleted.

(2) Para 6 (iv)
     Para 6 (iv) should be deleted.

(Reason for (1) and (2)) In facilitating shift from price support to income support, there may be cases where linkage would not be avoidable between the amount of payments and the type or factors of production.

- 6 -

0117

(3) Para 6 (ii), fourth line
     "other than to reduce that production" should be
     added after "the base period".

(Reason) Due regard should be given to production
control.

(4) Para 6 (v)
     Para 6 (v) should be deleted.

(Reason) It is not appropriate to provide payments to
those who do not produce.

15. Page L.15-16, Annex 2, para 7:

(i) and (ii) of para 7 should be replaced with the
following.

"(i) Eligilibity for such payments shall be determined
     by an income loss, taking into account only income
     derived from agriculture, which exceeds a certain
     proportion of average gross income in a certain
     period to be defined by national legislation or
     programmes. Any producer meeting this condition
     shall be eligible to receive the payments.

(ii) The amount of such payments shall compensate for
     less than a certain proportion of average gross
     income in a certain period to be defined by national
     legislation or programmes."

(Reason) Specific figures of proportions should be left
to discretion of each participant, taking into account
situation specific to each country.

- 7 -

75-21-8

0118 .

16. Page L.16, Annex 2, Para 8 (i):

"30 per cent of the average of production in the
preceding three-year period or a three-year average
based on the preceding five-year period, excluding the
highest and the lowest entry" should be replaced with
"a certain proportion of the average of production in
a certain period to be defined by national legislation
or programmes".

(Reason) The same as 15.

17. Page L.17, Annex 2, para 11:

(1) (i), third line
     The words "restructuring of agricultural sector
     and" should be inserted between "assist" and "the
     financial or physical restructuring of a producer's
     operations".

(Reason) To implement agricultural restructuring as
a whole, it is not appropriate to limit the object of
investment aids to the financial or physical
restructuring of a producer's operation in response
to objectively demonstrated structural disadvantages.

(2) (i), fifth line
     The words "or necessity of facilitating efficient
     agricultural production" should be added after
     "structural disadvantages".

(Reason) The same as (1).

(3) (ii), second line
     The words "the type or" should be deleted.

- 8 -

가-21-P

0119 .

(Reason) In facilitating structural adjustment, commodity-specific investment may be necessary.

(4)   (v)
      Para 11 (v) should be deleted.

(Reason) The same as (3).

(5)   (vi), second line
      "compensate for the structural disadvantage" should be replaced with "compensate for the structural disadvantage and assist facilitation of efficient agricultural production".

(Reason) The same as (1).

18.   Page L.18, Annex 2, para 13:

(1)   (i), fifth line
      "spelt out in law or regulation" should be replaced with "spelt out in law, regulation, or other official document".

(Reason) The same wording is used in 8.2, (b) (ii) of the Draft Text on Subsidies and Countervailing Measures. The form of other official document should not be excluded.

(2)   (ii), second line
      The words "the type or" should be deleted.

(Reason) Payments under regional assistance programmes would be product-specific due to natural conditions of disadvantaged regions.

- 9 -

0120 .

(3) (v)

Para 13 (v) should be deleted.

(Reason) Payments to farmers in disadvantaged regions should not be degressive.

19. Page L.18, Annex 2, para 14 (new paragraph):

The following new paragraph should be added as Paragraph 14.

Compensation payments

(i)   Payments shall be made to offset negative effects caused by implementation of reduction commitments on border protection.

(ii) The criteria for establishing eligibility and for setting the payment rate shall be objective and clearly defined.

(iii) The support shall be provided to all farmers meeting the eligibility criteria.

20. Page L.18, Annex 2, para 15 (new paragraph):

The following new paragraph should be added as Paragraph 15.

Conversion payments

(i)   Payments shall be made for conversion in accordance with national programmes to reduce output of products under overproduction.

- 10 -

0121 .

(ii)   The support shall only be provided to farmers
         who have taken a commitment either to reduce
         production of products under overproduction or
         to replace production of those products with that
         of products not in surplus.

(iii)   The payments shall be limited to the amount of
         the loss of income due to conversion of the
         production.

21.   Page L.19, para 3:

"For agricultural products currently subject to ordinary
customs duties only", should be replaced with "For
agricultural products which were subject to ordinary
customs duties only at 1 September 1986".

(Reason) The products for which import quotas have been
eliminated since 1986 should be treated as proposed
in the paragraph 23 of this paper.

22.   Page L.19, para 4, third line:

A mark for footnote 1 should be placed after the words
"customs duties" and the following footnote should be ____
added.

"Footnote 1: In the case of state trading enterprises,
"customs duties" include the average mark-up charged
by the enterprises."

(Reason) It is to clarify the relationship between
tariffication and operations of state trading
enterprises.

23. Page L.19:

The following new paragraph should be added as paragraph
4-(2).

"4-(2). For agricultural products which are currently
subject to ordinary customs duties only and were subject
to border measures other than ordinary customs duties
at 1 September 1986, the reduction commitment shall
be implemented on

    (i)   the initial tariff rate established as the
            result of tariffication, or

    (ii)   the level of customs duties which would have
            resulted from conversion of non-tariff measures
            as at 1 September 1986, in accordance with
            Annex 3.

In the case of (ii), the level calculated in (ii) shall
be reduced to the level of customs duties offered as
the final rate for 1999, with the applied rate in each
year being the rate reduced according to the next paragraph from the level of (ii), or the rate of the customs
duties currently applied, whichever is the lower."

(Reason) It is necessary to reflect properly the level
of protection in the customs duties on the products
for which import quotas have been eliminated since 1986.

24. Page L.19, para 5:

(1) Third and fourth line
    The words "with a minimum rate of reduction of
    15 per cent for each tariff line" should be deleted.

- 12 -

(Reason) For extremely sensitive products, flexibility should be given to tariff reduction commitments.

(2) Last sentence
A mark for footnote 2 should be placed at the end of the last sentence of the paragraph 5 and the following footnote should be added.

"Footnote 2:

(i) Where the total imports of basic products and those incorporated in processed products exceed 3 per cent of corresponding domestic consumption in the base period, minimum access commitments shall not be required.

(ii) Where it is necessary to establish minimum access opportunities, total minimum access opportunities can be established for basic products and those incorporated in processed products."

(Reason) It should be allowed that establishment of minimum access opportunities covering basic products and the product-equivalent of those in processed products as a whole since this method provides a practical approach.

(3) The following sentences should be added at the end of the paragraph.
"Expansion of minimum access opportunities shall not be required for the products under production control. For exceptionally sensitive products to be carefully circumscribed, flexible treatment shall be admitted in regard to the starting year of tariffication, reduction rates of tariff equivalents and level of minimum access commitments."

(Reason) It is not practical to expand minimum access opportunities for products under production control. Also, flexibility should be allowed for exceptionally sensitive products as regards tariffication process.

25. Page L.19, para 6:

(1) Third line
     The words "and increased" should be deleted.

(Reason) Increase should not necessarily be required for the current access opportunities.

(2) A mark for footnote 3 should be placed after the words "the implementation period" and the following footnote should be added.

"Footnote 3:

Total current access opportunities can be established for basic products and those incorporated in processed products, where appropriate."

(Reason) The same as 24 (2).

(3) The second sentence should be deleted unless production control is treated in the same way.

(Reason) There should be no distinction for reduction commitments between export subsidies and internal support through production control since efforts for quantitative reduction must be needed in both cases and credit for these efforts should be given to both.

26.   Page L.19, para 7:

   (1)   The words "access opportunities" should be replaced
         with "minimum access opportunities".

   (Reason) Content of "access opportunities" should be
   clearly specified.

   (2)   "All customs duties" should be replaced with
         "Customs duties which are subject to reduction
         commitments".

   (Reason) The scope of binding should be limited to
   products on which reduction commitments will be made.
   It is not appropriate to bind customs duties of
   sensitive agricultural products. Furthermore, there
   is lack of balance between the treatment of industrial
   products and agricultural products because the different
   treatment is proposed for industrial products in regard
   to the scope of binding.

27.   Page L.19, para 7, second line and page L.20, para
      8, ninth line:

   (1)   The words "in equal instalments" should be replaced
         with "in accordance with the modalities prescribed
         in Annex 9".

   (Note) Annex 9 is attached.

   (Reason) Flexibility in implementing reduction
   commitments in the areas of internal support and market
   access should be allowed in the same manner as in the
   area of export competition.

- 15 -

15 -21 -16

0126

(2) The following sentence should be added at the
     end of the paragraph 8.

     "Due consideration shall be given to supply control
     and import ratio in calculation of AMS values
     or AMS reduction rates".

28. Page L.20, para 11, fourth line:

The words "the year 1990" should be replaced with "the
year 1988".

(Reason) The base period should be the same among the
three areas: internal support, market access, and export
competition.

29. Page L.20, para 12, fourth line:

(1) The words "may be negotiated to limit" should
     be replaced with "shall include undertakings
     to limit".

(Reason) The scope of subsidies on exports of
agricultural products as regards individual or regional
markets should be subject to binding commitments in
the same manner as these for new products.

(2) The following sentence should be added at the
     end of this paragraph.

     "The above undertakings shall not apply to export
     subsidies to be granted for the products for which
     production control was implemented during the
     base period."

- 16 -

0127

(Reason) Import control coupled with production control
should be maintained by which we can cope with the
issue of surplus production internally. If these import
control measures are not permitted, it would become
very difficult for us to address this problem.

30.   Page L.25, Footnote to para 1:

The footnote should be replaced with the following.

"Excluding measures maintained for balance-of-payments
reasons or under general safeguard and exception
provisions (Articles XI, XII, XVIII, XIX, XX, XXI and
Article concerning basic foodstuffs as proposed as
Article XXI bis of the General Agreement). Article
XI 2(c)(i) shall be reviewed and clarified."

(Reason) Non-tariff measures based on Article XI and
of basic foodstuffs should be exempted from
tariffication. The conditions for application of
Article XI 2(c)(i) should be reviewed and clarified.

31.   Page L.26, para 8:

The following sentence should be added at the end of
the paragraph.

"Where a tariff equivalent resulting from these
guidelines is higher than the current bound rate, the
initial tariff equivalent shall replace the current
bound rate without giving rise to any claim for
compensation."

(Reason) No compensation should be required if the

- 17 -

0128

new tariff rate would be higher than the current bound
rate because the current rate was bound on the premise
of continuation of the non-tariff measures.

32. Page L.26, para 11:

The words "average annual import quantities for the
years 1986 to 1988" should be replaced with "either
average annual import quantities for the years 1986
to 1988 or quantities obtained by multiplying domestic
consumption for the preceding year by the average ratio
of import quantities to corresponding domestic
consumption for the years 1986 to 1988".

(Reason) Commitments by percentage should be allowed
since it is not practical to make commitments on the
annual import quantities for products which are imported
in large quantities and products consumption of which
is unstable.

33. Page L.27, para 13, third line:

The words "the quantity of product imported during
the base period" should be replaced with "either the
quantity of product imported during the base period
or the quantity obtained by multiplying domestic
consumption for the preceding year by the average ratio
of import quantities to corresponding domestic
consumption for the years 1986 to 1988".

(Reason) The same as 32.

- 18 -

75-21-1P

0129

34.   Page L.27, para 14:

The words "a low or minimal rate" should be replaced
with "a low or appropriate rate".

(Reason) It should be allowed to establish within-quota
tariff at an appropriate level, provided that the
quantity of minimum access opportunity is fulfilled
with the actual imported quantity. Setting appropriate
level of tariff is essential in coping with the issue
of quota rent.

35.   Page L.29, Annex 5, para 9

The words "average f.o.b. unit value" and "average
c.i.f. unit value" should be replaced with "average
or estimated f.o.b. unit value" and "average or
estimated c.i.f. unit value", respectively.

(Reason) The estimated price should be also allowed
to use as the external reference price as is used for
calculating the tariff equivalents.

Annex 9

MODALITIES OF REDUCTION COMMITMENTS FOR MARKET ACCESS

AND DOMESTIC SUPPORT

1.   Commitments to reduce ordinary customs duties
and Aggregate Measurements of Suppport (AMS) shall be
established in accordance with this Annex.

Reduction commitments

2.   Base levels reduced in each year of the
implementation period in accordance with paragraph 3 below
shall constitute the annual commitment levels.

3.   In the first year of the implementation period
base levels shall be reduced by an amount corresponding
to the reduction that would be applicable under
implementation on the basis of equal instalments. Thereafter
commitment levels for any year of the implementation period
shall be reduced by at least half the reduction applicable
under implementation on the basis of equal annual
instalments. Commitment levels in the final year of the
implementation period shall be established at levels that
ensure that the overall reduction during the implementation
period is no less than if annual commitment levels had been
established on the basis of equal annual instalments.

4.   Base levels, as well as commitment levels for
each year of the implementation period, shall be specified
in Schedules of commitments of market access and domestic
support.

- 20 -

75 - 21 - 21

0131

외 무 부

종   별 :

번   호 : GVW-0287   일   시 : 92 0205 1800

수   신 : 장 관(통기, 경기원, 재무부, 농림수산부, 상공부)

발   신 : 주 제네바 대사대리

제   목 : UR 농산물협상

2.5(수) 카나다대표부에서 갓트 11조 개선관심국가 (아국, 일본, 스위스, 노르웨이, 이스라엘등 6개국) 회의가 개최되어 표제 협상 동향에 대한 논의가 있었는바 주요국 언급요지 하기 보고함.

　　1. 스위스

　- 기존입장에 변화가 없으며, 감축 약속계획서를 내부적으로 작성하고 있으며 이를 기초로 농산물 협상 결과가 국내에 미치는 영향을 분석할 계획임.

　- 감축 약속 계획서의 내용에 대하여 아직미정이며, 제출시기는 다른나라의 동향을 보아가며 정할 것임.

　- TRACK 4 도 중요하지만 TRACK 3 를 통해서도 기술적 개선 노력을 하겠음.

　　2. 일본

　- 기존 입장에 변화가 없으며 TRACK 4 를 통한 던켈 초안 조정작업이 필요함.

　- 3.1 까지 감축 약속 계획서를 제출할 수 있도록 국내에서 작성하고 있는바, 구체적인 내용은 아직 미정임. 삭감폭등에 대한 합의가 없는 단계이므로 COMPLETE OFFER 가 되기는 어려울 것임.

　　3. 노르웨이

　- 2.6(목) 의회에서 던켈 초안에 대한 논의가있을 예정이며 현재까지 기존 입장의 변화는없음.

　- 3.1 까지 감축 약속 계획서를 제출할 수있을지는 아직 알수 없음.

3.1 까지는 감축 약속계획서 제출이 부진할경우는 협상이 BLOCK 될 가능성이 있음.

　　4. 이스라엘

　- 기존 입장에 변화가 없으며, 감축 약속 계획서작성을 위해 각종 자료를 수집하고 있는 단계임.

- 구체적인 삭감 약속내용은 아직 미정이며, 앞으로 본질적인 내용에 대한 협상이 재개되어야 함.

5. 카나다

- 4월중순까지 협상이 타결되기 위해서는 미국과 이씨간의 타협이 절대 조건임.

양국간 타협 여부가 각국의 감축 약속 계획서의 질을 결정할 것임

- 카나다는 생산통제 품목을 제외하고는 대부분 던켈초안에 따라 감축 약속 계획서를 제출할 계획임.

생산통제 품목의 제시여부는 아직 미정임. 미.이씨간 타협이 이루어지면 기존 입장을 재평가할것임.

6. 아국

- 기존 입장에 변화가 없음.

던켈 초안에 대한 국내 불만이 크며 특히 예외없는 관세화에 대한 강한 반대가 있음. 따라서 TRACK 4 에 의한 던켈 초안 개선이 필요함. 갓트 11조 개선에도 적극동참 할 것임.

- 감축 약속 계획서는 국내에서 최선을 대해 준비중에 있음.

동 내용을 확정짓기 위해서는 복잡한 국내절차를 거쳐야 함. 제출시기는 여타국동향을 보아가며 정하게 될것임.끝

(차석대사 김삼훈-국장)

외 무 부

종   별 :

번   호 : JAW-0745

일   시 : 92 0208 1830

수   신 : 장 관(봉기,농수산부)

발   신 : 주 일본 대사(일경)

제   목 : UR/농산물 협상

　　"시와쿠" 농림수산성 심의관은 2.7(금) 동경주재 외교단을 대상으로 표제협상에 대한 일본의 입장을 다시한번 강조하기 위한 설명회를 갖었는바, 요지 아래 보고함.

　　1. 예외없는 관세화 문제

　　가. 91.12.20. 제시된 합의초안이 국경조치의 완전관세화를 주장하면서도 정작 농산물 왜곡의 주요원인인 수출보조금의 철폐를 언급하고 있지 않음은 형평의 원칙상 문제가 있음.

　　나. 기초식량 및 11 조(C)(I)는 관세화의 예외로서 인정되어야 하며 나아가 11 조 2 항(C)(I) 조항을 명확히 할 필요가 없음.

　　2. 삭감 기준연도 및 삭감율

　　가. 던켈 초안은 시장접근 삭감과 수출보조금의 삭감에 있어서 삭감 대상 산출 기준연도 및 삭감율에 있어서 형평을 잃고 있음.

　　나. 시장접근의 경우, 86-88 년이 삭감대상 산출 기준연도이나, 수출보조금의 경우에는 86-90 년간이 산출기준 연도가 되어 있는바, 이는 최근들어서의 수출 보조금의 급격한 증가를 반영키 위한 것으로서 상대적으로 수출보조금에 유리한 결과가 되어 있음.

　　다. 시장접근은 평균 36 프로 삭감케 되어 있음. 수출보조금도 예산면에서는 36 프로 삭감케 되어 있기는 하나, 물량면에서는 24 프로 삭감에 머물고 있는바, 이는 명백히 불공평한 대우임. UR 종료시 국제농산물 가격이 상승할 것으로 예상됨을 고려할때 의미가 있는 것은 물량기준 삭감임.

　　3. 허용가능 보조금(GREEN BOX) 의 범위

　　0 "생산량과는 직접 관계가 없는 소득보조(DECOUPLED INCOME SUPPORTS)"와 구조조정을 위한 지원이 일단 조건부로 GREEN 정책으로 인정되어 있기는 하나, GREEN

통상국	장관	차관	1차보	2차보	아주국	경제국	외정실	분석관
청와대	안기부	농수부						

92.02.08   20:54

외신 2과 통제관 BS

0134

정책으로 인정받기 위한 조건이 너무 엄격한바, 이의 완화가 필요

　4. 수출보조금

　0 던켈 초안은 신제품에 대한 수출 보조금의 금지 및 새로운 시장 진출시 수출 보조금의 제한을 규정하고 있으나, 지금까지 국내 생산 조정을 실시해 왔고, 수출보조금을 전혀 쓰지 않았던 국가에 대해서는 이와같은 금지 또는 제한이 적용되지 말아야 할 것임.끝.

　(대사 오재희-국장)

PAGE 2

0135

발 신 전 보

분류번호	보존기간

번   호 : WJA-0583   920211 1918 DU 종별 : _____

수   신 : 주   일   대사. 총영사///

발   신 : 장 관 (통 기)

제   목 : UR 농산물 협상관련 한.일 실무협의

    92.3.1 까지 UR 농산물 관련 감축 이행계획서를 갓트 사무국에 제출키로되어 있는 것과 관련, 하기 농수산부 실무자들이 92.2.13-15간 귀지를 방문하여 2.14일중 귀 주재국 농무성 관계자와 UR 농산물 협상에서의 상호 관심사항 협의를 희망하고 있으니 조속 일정 주선 후 결과 보고바람.

               - 아   래 -

      국제협력 담당관   손정수
      통상협력 1담당관실 사무관   정 승
      국제협력 담당관실 주사   최대휴
                            끝.

보안 통제						외신과통제
앙고재 92년 월 일 통상국과	기안자 성명 안병준	과장	국장	차관	장관	

0136

농 림 수 산 부

우 427-760 / 주소 경기 과천시 중앙동 1번지 / 전화 (02) 503-7227 / 전송 503-7249

문서번호 국협20644-140

시행일자 1992.2 .8 (년)

(경유)

수신 외무부장관

참조 통상국장

선결			지시	농임ㅣ으로써 팔바	
접수	일자시간	1992. 2. 11	결재공람		
	번호	4661			
처리과				바강	(서명)
담당자	(서명)				

제목 UR농산물협상관련 한.일 실무협의

───────────────────────────────────────

　　　　1. '92.3.1까지 GATT에 제출하여야 할 UR농산물협정 이행계획과 관련, 아직까지 감축원칙에 합의를 이루지 못한 단계에서의 각국의 이행계획수립은 각국의 기존입장에 크게 영향을 받을 것으로 예상되는바, 그동안 농산물협상에서 상당부분 입장을 같이해 왔고, 또 농업정책운용방식이 아국과 유사한 일본과 이행계획 수립이전에 상호 관심사항에 대한 협력방안 모색 및 기술적인 문제에 대한 협의가 아국의 이행계획 수립에 유익할 것으로 판단되어 다음과 같이 당부 실무자를 일본에 파견 코자 하오니 일본 농무성 관계자와의 실무협의가 원만히 이루어질 수 있도록 일정 주선등에 협조 하여 주시기 바랍니다.

　　　　　　　　　　　　　　- 다　음 -

　　가. 당부대표

소　　속	직　　위	성　　명	비　　고
국제협력담당관실	국제협력담당관	손 정 수	FAO 아.태지역총회 참석후 귀로에 실무협의 추진(2.14)
통상협력1담당관실	행정사무관	정　승	
국제협력담당관실	행정주사	최 대 휴	

　　나. 출장기간 및 출장지
　　　　0 '92.2.13-15(3일간), 일본동경
　　　　　- 실무협의 희망일시 : '92.2.14

　　다. 실무협의 대상자
　　　　0 일본 농무성 이행계획수립 관계실무자

0137

우 427-760 / 주소 경기 과천시 중앙동 1번지 / 전화 (02) 503-7227 / 전송 503-7249

라. 출장목적
　　0 UR농산물협상에 대한 상호 관심사항 협의
　　0 UR농산물협정 이행계획수립에 따른 기술적문제 협의

마. 소요경비 : 농림수산부 부담

마. 기　　타
　　0 구체적인 협의사항은 별도 준비, 출장예정

첨부 : 출장일정 및 소요경비내역 1부.　끝.

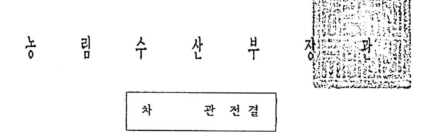

농 림 수 산 부 장　관

┌─────────────┐
│ 차　관　전　결 │
└─────────────┘

0138

출장일정 및 소요경비내역

가. 출장일정

'92. 2. 13(목) 09:30 서 울 발(KE 702)
                11:30 동 경 착

'92. 2. 14(금)   한.일 실무협의

'92. 2. 15(토) 15:50 동 경 발(KE 001)
                18:15 서 울 착

나. 소요경비 : $1,361 (1113-213)

	정 승 사무관	최 대 휴
항 공 료	$332	$332
일 비	$20 X 3일 = $ 60	$16 X 3일 = $ 48
숙 박 비	$83 X 2일 = $166	$75 X 2일 = $150
식 비	$48 X 3일 = $144	$43 X 3일 = $129
소 계	$370	$327
합 계	$702	$659

0139

UR/농산물 협상 감축 약속 계획서(country plan) 작성관련 비공식 회의

1. 일시 및 장소 : 1992. 2.11(화) 11:00-12:20, 농림수산부 제2차관보실

2. 참 석 자 : 농림수산부 제2차관보 (회의 주재)
   외무부 (통상국 심의관), 경기원, 상공부

3. 의   제 :

   O UR 농산물 협상과 관련, 국별 감축 약속 계획서 제출 시기와 NTC 15개 품목
   포함 여부에 대한 비공식 의견 교환

4. 부처별 의견 :

   O 농림수산부

   - 사안의 민감성을 감안할때 3.1까지 아국의 감축 약속 계획서를 제출하는
     것은 매우 어려우며, 특히 15개 NTC 품목과 관련하여 91.1.9 대외협력
     위원회에서 동 품목을 신축성있게 조절키로 하였으나, 상금 ~~이해~~ 농민
     단체
     당사자와의 공청회 및 당정협의 등의 절차를 거치지 않았기 때문에
     현재로서는 15개 NTC 품목을 감축 약속 계획서에 포함시키는 것이
     불가능함. 또한 현재 농산물 보조금 분야에서 미국과 이씨가 대립
     양상을 보이고 있는점등을 감안할때, 각국의 제출 동향을 보아 3.1
     혹은 3월중순에 NTC 이외의 품목에 대한 감축 약속 계획서를 우선
     제출하고 3월말경에 나머지 품목에 대한 계획서를 제출하는 방안도
     좋을 것으로 생각됨.

ㅇ 외 무 부

  - 아국이 UR 협상 과정에서 공표한 입장과 국내사정이 상충되는 어려움이
    있기는 하나, NTC 품목을 포함하여 3.10까지 감축 약속 계획서를 제출하는
    것이 바람직함. 아국이 NTC 품목이 제외된 계획서를 제출할 경우
    UR 협상에서의 부담이 더 클 것으로 예상됨.
    15개 NTC 품목이 제외된 계획서를 제출하느니 보다는 차라리 offer 없이
    협상과정에서 표명된 아국의 기본입장만을 기초로 양자협상을 진행시키는
    편이 더 나을지도 모름.

ㅇ 경제기획원

  - 아국 정부가 15개 NTC 품목을 철회한 것은 기정 사실이며, 대외협력위원회의
    결정은 존중되어야 함.
  - UR 협상이 타결되지 않을 것이라고 전망되더라도 협상 스케줄 및 절차는
    더 잘 지켜야 할 것인바, 계획서 제출을 늦추는 것은 바람직하지 않음.
  - 감축 약속 계획서 제출 자체보다는 계획서의 내용이 더 중요하므로 NTC
    15개 품목을 제외시키는 것은 아국의 입장을 더약화시킬 것임.

ㅇ 상 공 부

  - 91.1.9 대외협력위원회에서 결정된 입장을 기초로 감축 이행 계획서를
    작성해야 할 것임.

5. 결   론

ㅇ 감축 약속 계획서 제출 시기 및 NTC 품목 포함 여부에 대해 결론을 내리지
   못하였으며, 2.17 시작주초에 관계장관 비공식 간담회를 개최하여 그 결과에
   따라 대책을 협의키로 함.   끝.

0141

외 무 부

종 별 :

번 호 : ECW-0186   일 시 : 92 0211 1600

수 신 : 장관 (통기,경기원,재무부,농림수산부,상공부)

발 신 : 주 EC 대사 사본: 주 미,제네바대사-중계요망

제 목 : 갓트/UR 협상

2.10 당관 이관용농무관은 EC 집행위 대외총국의 GUTH 농산물협상 담당과장을 오찬에초대 표제관련 협의한바, 동인의 발언요지 아래 보고함

1. DUNKEL 협상안에 대한 EC 수정안과 미.EC 양자협상

가. DUNKEL 협상안 제시이후 EC 의 입장을 수차 밝힌바 있으므로 수정안을 마련하는 것은 어려운 작업이 아니며, 동 수정안은 이미 마련된 것으로 알고있고, 동 수정안에는 농산물문제 뿐 아니라 시장접근, 서비스등 기타 분야도 포함될것임

나. 미.EC 양자협상의 시기, 장소, 중점제기사항 등은 협상전략상 보안을 유지하고 있으며, 따라서 미측과의 협상중에는 동 수정안이 공개적으로 EC 이사회에서 논의될 것으로는 보지않음

다. OLIVEIRA 폴투갈 외무장관의 워싱턴방문은 표제협상 추진의 의미있는 계기로 보지 않으나 DUNKEL 총장이 설정한 협상시한 등을 고려할때 양측은 협상을 곧 개시하여야 할것으로 봄

라. 최근 ANDRIESSEN 위원 또는 QUAYLE 미 부통령등의 강경한 발언은 미측으로는 대통령선거, EC 로서는 회원국들간의 의견조정을 목표로 한 협상과정의 일환으로 보아야 함

2. 협상전망

가. EC 로서는 UR 협상에서 EC 농산물수출을 몇백만톤 더 확보하느냐 여부가 CIS 등 동구유럽문제 또는 EC 통합문제보다 중요하다고 판단하고 있지 않으며, 미국도 UR 협상 추진결과가 대통령선거에 미칠 영향등을 고려해야 한다는 점은 있으나, 양측은 동 협상의 조속한 종결을 원하고 있음

다. DUNKEL 총장이 설정한 협상종결 시한은 기술적및 정치적인 측면에서 지켜지기 어려울 것으로 전망되나, 미.EC 간의 대화가 원활히 추진된다면 동 시한까지

통상국	장관	차관	1차보	2차보	외정실	분석관	정와대	안기부
경기원	재무부	농수부	상공부	중계				

PAGE 1   92.02.12   04:44
외신 2과 통제관 FM

0142

기본골격에 대한 정치적 합의를 이룰수 있을것임

　3. 기타 농산물협상 관련사항

　가. EC 가 국내보조, 시장접근및 수출보조감축율을 동일하게 할것을 요구하고 있는것은 대내외적인 측면에서의 고려때문임. 즉 대내적으로 EC 회원국들은 각각 농산물협상에서의 관심분야가 다르고 (예, 불란서는 수출문제, 독일은 국내보조), 대외적으로는 EC 는 수출보조 감축율의 하향조정을 원하고 있기 때문임

　나. 86-90 기간중 EC 의 평균 CEREAL 수출물량은 18-19 백만톤 정도였으며 따라서 99 년도의 수출량이 15 백만톤 수준이면 수락 가능하다는 의미는 물량기준한 수출보조 감축율이 20% 정도를 의미하는 것임. 끝

　(대사 권동만-국장)

　예고: 92.6.30 까지

PAGE 2

0143

관리
번호 92-137

외 무 부

원 본

종 별 :

번 호 : GVW-0334   일 시 : 92 0211 1730

수 신 : 장관(봉기, 경기원, 재무, 농수산, 상공부)

발 신 : 주 제네바 대사대리

제 목 : EC 협상 담당관 접촉

1. 김삼훈 차석대사는 금 2.11. EC 대표부 JOHN BECK 차석대표 및 K.F.FALKENBERG
참사관과 오찬을 갖고 UR 협상 동향 및 전망에 관한 의견을 교환함.(최농무관
이참사관 동석)

2. 상기 양인은 전반적으로, 극히 신중한 태도를 유지하면서 협상 동향 및 전망에
관해 아래와같은 의견을 조심스럽게 피력함.

0 2.5. 개최된 QUAD 회의결과에 관심을 표명한바, 동인은 UR 협상 타결의 관건이
결국은 미.EC 간 이견 조정 및 타협성패 여부에 달려 있다고 보기 때문에 QUAD 회의가
큰 역할을 수행할 것으로는 보지 않는다는 견해를 표명하였음.

0 TRACK 4 협상 가동 전망에 관해서는 4 TRACK 방식이 1.13. 시점에서 GATT
사무국에게 유용한 동시 유일한 방편이긴 하였지만, 과연 액면 대로의 의미가
있는것인지의 여부에 대해서는 다소 회의적으로 본다하였으며, 미.EC 간 농산물
분야에서 TRACK 1 을 활용 사실상 문제를 해결할 수도 있을 것이라는 의견도 있는
것으로 안다는 질문에 대해서는 이를 부인치 않았음.

0 부활절 이전 협상 타결 전망에 대해서는 실무선에서 정확한 판단을 내리기는
어려운 상황임을 전제한후 약 50 퍼센트 정도의 확률이 있지 않겠느냐는 의견과 함께
협상 성패와는 관계없이 내주부터 실무진 바빠지게 될것으로 본다고 언급함.

3. 한편 EC LEGRAS 농업총국장 및 PAEMAN 부총국장이 2.13-14 워싱톤을 방문
미측과 협의를 갖는 것으로 확인됨. 끝

(차석대사 김삼훈-국장)

예고:92.6.30 까지

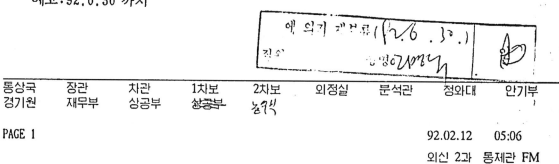

통상국	장관	차관	1차보	2차보	외정실	분석관	청와대	안기부
경기원	재무부	상공부	상공부	농수산				

PAGE 1   92.02.12   05:06
                                              외신 2과 통제관 FM

                                              0144

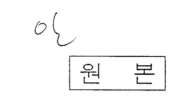

관리 번호	92-136

외 무 부

종 별 :

번 호 : GVW-0336 　　　　　　　　　일 시 : 92 0211 1830

수 신 : 장관(통기, 경기원, 재무부, 농림수산부, 상공부)

발 신 : 주 제네바 대사대리

제 목 : UR 농산물 협상

당관 최농무관은 UR 관련 2.11 주재국 일본 대표부 하야시 참사관과 접촉한바, 동인 언급 내용 하기 보고함.

1. 일본정부는 TRACK 4 의 조기가동등과 관련 주요국에 4 진의 대표단은 파견, 현재 아즈마 국제부장이 미국을 거쳐 카나다에서 협의중에 있으며 2 진은 호주, 뉴질랜드, 태국, 3 진은 멕시코, 아르헨티나, 브라질, 4 진은 EC 의 주요국을 방문할 예정임.

2. 금주 14 일 개최 예정인 농산물 비공식 G-8 회의는 미국의 주도로 열리게 되며 어디까지나 던켈 TEXT 상의 기술적인 의문사항에 대한 의견 교환등이 목적이지 농산물 협상의 위한 모임은 아님. 끝

(차석대사 김삼훈-국장)

예고 92.6.30 까지

대 의기 재분류 (92.6.3-.)	
지원	정영

통상국	장관	차관	1차보	2차보	외정실	분석관	청와대	안기부
경기원	재무부	농수부	상공부					

PAGE 1 　　　　　　　　　　　　　　　　　　　　92.02.12　05:15

　　　　　　　　　　　　　　　　　　　　　　外信 2과 통제관 FM

0145

발 신 전 보

	분류번호	보존기간

번 호 : WEC-0123 외 별지참조   종별 :

수 신 : 주   수신처 참조 대사. 총영사

발 신 : 장 관 (통 기)

제 목 : UR/농산물 감축 이행계획서 제출

1. 92.1.13 UR/무역협상위원회 (TNC) 회의시 던켈 갓트사무총장이 제시한 협상일정에
   따르면 각국은 농산물 분야에서의 관세및 관세상당치(tariff equivalent)의 인하계획,
   국내보조 감축계획, 수출보조 감축계획등 감축 이행 계획서 (list of commitments)를
   3.1까지 제출토록 되어있음.

2. 아국의 농산물 분야에서의 감축이행계획서 제출과 관련하여 참고코자 하니,
   귀 주재국의 상기시한내 감축이행계획서 제출가능 여부등에 관한 동향을 파악
   보고바람.   끝.   (통상국장 김 용 규)

수신처 : 주 EC, 카나다, 스위스, 스웨덴, 핀란드, 호주, 인도, 파키스탄, 멕시코,
         브라질, 알젠틴, 말련, 필리핀대사.

앙고재	기안자 성명	과장	국장	차관	장관	보안통제
92년 월 일	안명수		전결			
						외신과통제

0146

외 무 부

종 별 :

번 호 : CNW-0163   일 시 : 92 0211 1600

수 신 : 장 관(통기, 상공부, 농수산부)

발 신 : 주 캐나다 대사

제 목 : UR/농산물 감축 이행계획서 제출

대 : WCN-0113

1. 주재국은 UR/농산물 분야에서의 감축 이행계획서를 <u>3.1.</u> 까지 제출할 계획으로있음. 이를 위해 현재 주정부, 농업단체등과 협의를 진행중에 있으며, 내주중 각의심의를 준비중이라고 함.

2. 주재국내 농민 만여명은 2.21. 오타와에서 UR/농산물 협상 관련 대정부 시위를 벌일계획임. 이들은 대부분 낙농등 SUPPLY MANAGEMENT PROGRAM 에 의해 보호를 받고 있는 농민들로서 예외없는 관세화에 대한 주재국 정부의 확고한 반대 입장 견지를 촉구하는데 목적이 있다고 함.끝

(대사-국장)

통상국   2차보   농수부   상공부

                92.02.12   08:05 WG

외신 1과 통제관

0147

오2

외 무 부

종 별 :

번 호 : ECW-0194   일 시 : 92 0211 1730

수 신 : 장관 (통기, 경기원, 재무부, 농수산부, 상공부)

발 신 : 주 EC 대사 사본: 주미, 제네바대사-중계요망

제 목 : 갓트/UR 협상

2.10-11 개최된 EC/농업이사회는 CAP개혁방안과 갓트/UR 협상문제에 대해 논의한바, 표제관련 논의결과 아래 보고함

1. MAC SHARRY 위원은 1.29. 브랏셀에서 가진 DUNKEL 사무총장과의 협의시 동위원은 상당한 수정이 있기 전에는 EC 가 DUNKEL협상안을 받아드릴수 없다는 입장을 동총장에게 명백히 전달했다고 보고함. 또한 동위원은 DUNKEL 협상안은 EC 측에 특히불리 하도록 되어 있으며, 협상상대국들과의 부담 분담측면이 고려되어 있지 않음을지적하였다고 말하면서, 수정필요 항목으로서 GREENBOX, REBALANCING, 물량기준한 수출보조 감축문제와 국내보조등 <u>3개 분야의 감축율을 동일화하는</u> 문제들을 제시하였다고 보고함

2. 위와같은 MAC SHARRY 위원 보고에대해 동이사회는 구체적인 토의는 없었으나 (종전이사회에서 기히 공식입장을 천명하였기 때문임)불란서, 아일랜드는 DUNKEL 협상안에 대한 EC수정제안에 포함되어 있는 구체적인 숫자에대해 의문을 표시하면서 특히 113 위원회 개최시 토의된 숫자등과의 합치 여부에대해 문의한바, 동 위원은 언급을 회피했다고 함

3. 한편 1.27-28 이사회시 CAP 개혁과 UR농산물협상을 별개로 추진한다는 방침을다수결로 결정하고, CAP 개혁논의를 본격적으로 진행하고 있으나, 금번 이사회에서네델란드는 자국의 입장을 일부 수정하여 CAP 개혁과 UR협상문제는 별개로 논의는 하되, <u>UR 협상의 결론이 도출되기 전에 CAP 개혁문제를 결정할수 없다는</u> 의견을 제시한바, 다수의 회원국들이 동조함. 끝

   (대사 권동만-국장)

통상국   2차보   경기원   재무부   농수부   상공부   중계

92.02.13   08:19 DQ

외신 1과 통제관

0148

외 무 부

원 본

종 별 :

번 호 : ECW-0195

일 시 : 92 0212 1730

수 신 : 장관 (통상,통기,경기원,농림수산부)

발 신 : 주 EC 대사 사본: 주제네바대사-중계필 W

제 목 : EC/CAP 개혁

　2.10-11 개최된 EC/농업이사회는 CAP개혁내용에 대하여 중점적으로 논의한바, 결과하기 보고함

　1. CUNHA 농업이사회 의장은 지난 이사회 종료시 공약한바에 따라 집행위의 CAP개혁안에대한 WORKING PAPER 를 제출하고, 동 PAPER 를중심으로 논의를 진행함. 동 PAPER 의 요지는아래와같음

　가. CEREALS

　0 지지가격 인하와 소득손실 보상액간의 적절한관계가 설정되어야 하며, EC 곡물의국제경쟁력 확보방안이 강구되어야 함

　0 목표가격과 한계가격 (THRESHOLD PRICE) 의차액이 30 ECU 이상되도록 하여야 함

　나. 엽연초

　0 최대가격 보장량을 93 및 94년도 각각 370 및350천본으로 함

　0 회원국별 생산쿼타및 품종별 생산쿼타를현실성 있게 조정하며, 품종전환 대책을추진함

　다. 우유

　0 생산쿼타량은 CAP 개혁방안에서 결정할것이 아니라 시장상황, 지역여건 등을 감안하여집행위는 매년 생산쿼타의 감축방안을 마련하여 이사회에 제출함

　0 조방축산에 따른 보상기준을 당초 집행위안보다완화함

　라. 쇠고기및 양고기

　0 연간 쇠고기의 시장 개입 물량한도를 설정하고 개입기준을 완화함

　0 쇠고기의 개입가격 인하에따라 지급하는소득보상금의 지급기준을 완화함

　0 양고기의 경우, 농업환경 보존계획,조방화등에 따라 지급하는 소득보상금의지급기준완화및 지급액을 인상함

통상국　2차보　통상국　경기원　농수부　중계

PAGE 1

92.02.13　08:19 BD

외신 1과 통제관

0149

UR(우루과이라운드)-농산물 협상, 1992. 전4권(V.1 1-3월) 467

마. 부수조치

0 환경보전 관련조치에 따른 소득보상지급대상을 확대함. 즉 수질보전, 유기농법에따른 생산을 할 경우등도 소득보상대상으로 함.

0 농경지의 산림복구시 지급하는 보상액을 상향조정함

2. 금번 이사회에서도 CAP 개혁 내용에대한합의를 이룬 사항은 없으며, 위와같은의장WORKING PAPER 에대한 회원국 각료들의대체적인 반응은 아래와같음

가. 동 의장 PAPER 는 비록 각 회원국들간의 이견을 조정하는데 기여할수 있을것으로 보나,집행위 개혁안과 대동소이 하다는 반응을 보임

나. CEREALS 분야의 경우, 집행위 개혁안에 비하면 개선되었으며, 특히 휴경보상 대상의확대, EC 농산물 우선취급원칙을 확보하려는 시도에 대해서는 환영함. 그러나 일부회원국들은 소득보상 조치는 선별적,일시적이어야 한다는 점을 지적함

다. 쇠고기분야의 의장안에 대해 불란서,아일랜드는 지나치게 야심적이라고 비난함. 그러나우유분야에 대하여는 의장안이 집행위안보다 현실적이라는 평가를 받음

3. 동 이사회 종료후 MAC SHARRY 집행위원은 당초집행위가 제출한 CAP 개혁안을수정하려면이와 관련한 예산변경 조치도 고려되어야 하며,CEREALS 의 국제가격 경쟁력이 확보되려면개입가격은 최소 35프로 인하되어야 할 것이라고말함

4. 차기 이사회는 3.2-3 개최키로 함. 끝

(대사 권동만-국장)

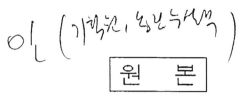

외 무 부

종 별 :

번 호 : FNW-0070   일 시 : 92 0213 1700

수 신 : 장 관(봉기,구이)

발 신 : 주 핀랜드 대사

제 목 : UR/농산물 감축 이행계획서

대:WFN-0050

1.92.1.13자 HELSINKI SANOMAT 신문보도에 의하면 주재국은 던켈 사무총장의 타협안에 대하여 다음 3가지 수정을 요구키로 하였음.

　가.86-89년의 농업보조금 준거년도 설정은 곤란함.

　-그 이유로 87년도가 주재국 농업의 최대 흉작년도임을 듬.

　나.수당 성격의 농업보조금(ALLOWABLE SUBSIDIES)의 신설 필요

　-주재국의 북극지방등 벽지인 경우 생산량과 관계없이 보조금을 지불하지 않을 경우 사람이 거주하지 않는 불모지가 될 우려가 있음.

　다.비교적 요소 추가

　-상기 보조금 규모 설정시 환경 및 서비스 이용가능성(SERVICE AVAILABILITY)등비교역적요속가 추가 고려되어야함.

2.이와 관련 당관 문창부 서기관은 2.13 주재국 외무부 HUHTANIEMI 대사와 접촉,대호 주재국 준비상황을 문의한바,동 대사 언급내용 아래보고함.

　가.주재국은 국내 유관기관의 전문가로 구성된 대책반을 구성,2.21.감축 이행계획서 초안을 마련할 예정이며,그후 미국.EC 간 협상추이에 따라 관계장관 회의에서 그 제출여부를 확정할 계획임.

　나.주재국은 우선 미국.EC 간 협상 진전상황을 주목하고 있으며,동 협상이 원칙적으로 수용가능한 합리적인 선에 타결될 경우,구체적인 이행계획서를 제출하고 국내농민 설득 및 이해 관계국간 공동노력 등을 추진할것이나,미국.EC간 협상이 여의치않을 경우에는 자국이 먼저 이행계획서를 제출키 어려움.

　다.HUHTANIEMI 대사는 EFTA 국간 관련 협의를 위해 2.24부터 제네바로 출장예정임.

통상국　　구주국

PAGE 1   92.02.14   02:16 FN

외신 1과 통제관

0151

3.동대사는 1항 신문보도 내용을 확인했으며,특히 1.나항의 GREEN SUPPORT 를강조
함.끝
   (대사 윤억섭-국장)

외   무   부

종   별 :

번   호 : ARW-0116   일   시 : 92 0213 1330

수   신 : 장관(통기)

발   신 : 주아르헨티나대사

제   목 : UR 농산물 보조금 감축이행 계획서

　　　대:WAR-53

　　당관 신공사가 2.13.주재국 외무부 다자경제국 UR담당관 LA GUARDIA 에 확인한바,
주재국은 담배 및 설탕 두 품목에만 보조금을 지급(생활조건 열악지역에서 재배)하고
있으며 요청대로 3.1.까지 보조금 감축 계획을 제출할예정으로 있다고 함.

　　　-담배:UR 과 별도로 1995년까지 완전제거 계획 기수립

　　　-설탕:농수산부와 협의중.

　　　(대사 김해선-국장)

통상국　　미주국

PAGE 1

관리
번호 *92-185*

외　무　부

원　본

종　별 :

번　호 : JAW-0849

일　시 : 92 0214 1139

수　신 : 장관(통기,농수부)사본:대통령비서실,국무총리실,경기원,US,GV,EC

발　신 : 주 일 대사(일경)

제　목 : 농림수산부 차관 방일

1. 이병석 농림수산부 차관은 인도에서 개최된 FAO 아. 태 지역 총회 일정을
마치고 예정대로 2.13 오전에 일본에 도착하여 다나부 농림수산대신, 하마구찌
농림수산성 사무차관 및 시와꾸 심의관등을 면담하여 UR, 농업구조조정 정책등 양국간
관심사항에 대하여 의견을 교환한바, 그 결과를 하기 보고함.

2. 다나부 대신 면담결과

가. 아측은 다나부 대신이 쌀에 대한 예외없는 관세화에 대하여 그간 반대입장을
표명해 준데 대해 사의를 표명한후 인도 FAO 지역총회에서 식량안보, 지역개발,
환경보전등 농업의 비교역적 기능의 중요성에 대해서 강조한바 있음을 일측에
전달하고 앞으로 계속 협조해 나갈것을 당부함.

나. 이에대해 일측은 FAO 지역총회 관련, 아측 수석대표 발언내용을 보도를통해
알고 있다고 언급하면서 예외없는 관세화는 절대 받아들일 수 없다는 입장을
관철하도록 노력하겠다는 의사표명과 함께, HILLS 미 USTR 대표 방일시에도인구증가로
인한 식량문제 해결등 농업문제는 단순한 상업적 차원에서 다루어서는 안된다는
입장을 표명하였음을 밝히고 이를 재강조하였음.

3. 시와꾸 심의관 면담결과(UR 관련)

가. 예외없는 관세화

1) 아측은 최근 일부 일본 언론보도를 통해 일본정부가 예외없는 관세화를 수용할
뜻을 시사했다는데 대해서 일본정부의 입장을 문의한바, 일측은 일부 정치권에서
그러한 논의가 있는것은 사실이나 일본입정부의 입장은 변화된 것이 없음을 분명히
밝힘.

2) 이에대해 아측에서는 기존 한. 일간의 협조체제를 계속 유지해 나가되 스위스,
멕시코, 이스라엘등 입장이 같은 나라들과 긴밀히 협력해야 할 것임을 강조하고 쌀에

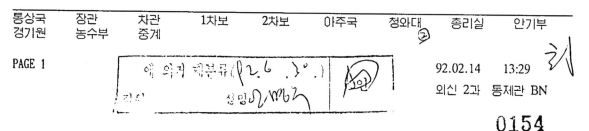

통상국	장관	차관	1차보	2차보	아주국	청와대	총리실	안기부
경기원	농수부	중계						

PAGE 1

92.02.14　13:29

외신 2과 통제관 BN

0154

대해서는 최소시장 접근도 불허한다는 아국입장을 강조함.

나. 국별 이행계획(COUNTRY PLAN) 제출에 대한 일본의 입장

1) 일측은 3.1 까지 일본정부가 이행계획서를 제출하는 것 자체는 틀림이 없음을 밝히고, 단 쌀에 대한 관세화 부문은 공란으로 제시할 가능성이 매우 높다는 의견을 제시함.

2) 11 조 2C, 국역무역등 제한품목에 대해서는 기존 일본입장을 그대로 제출할 것인지 일부수정을 할 것인지 계속 검토중이라고 말하면서 한국의 15 개 품목처리 문제에 대해 깊은 관심을 표명함(이에대해 아측도 역시 검토중이라고 답변)

다. 기준년도 문제에 대한 아측입장 전달

1) 국내보조, 시장개방의 기준년도가 '86-'88 로 되어 있는것은 수출보조 기준년도 '86-'90 과 균형이 맞지 않음을 언급.

2) 아울러, '89.4 중간평가시 개도국은 보조금 동결(STANDSTILL) 의무를 면제하기로 한 바 있음을 상기시키고 그간 계속 보조가 늘어난 한국등 개도국은 최근년도를 기준하여 감축하는 것이 불가피함을 강조

라. 기타 UR 관련 사항

1) 동 심의관은 미.EC 간의 의견접근 문제에 대해서는 양국의 정치적 여건등으로 상당히 어려움이 있을것임을 피력하고, 2.13-14 간 예정된 WASHINGTON 의미.EC 간 차관급 협의의 성과에 대해서는 의문을 나타냄.

2) 최근 미국.EC 및 DUNKEL 총장이 비밀리에 한국을 포함한 극히 제한된 국가에 예외없는 관세화에 DEROGATION 을 인정하기로 합의했다는 일부 루머가 있어일본측은 상당한 불안감이 있음을 설명하면서 동 루머의 진위여부는 미확인이라함.

3) 아측은 농업기반 조성등의 측면에서 미국, EC, 일본등과는 많은 차이가 있음을 지적하고, 한국은 반드시 개도국 우대를 받아야 하며 이를 위해 일측의 협조를 요청함.

4. 하마구찌 사무차관 면담결과

가. 아측과 일측은 그간의 일측의 구조조정 노력에 대한 의견을 교환하고, 특히 한국이 UR 등 개방화에 대응하기 위해서는 먼저 구조조정을 추진한 일본의 경험등에 대한 의견교환등 협조체제를 강화해 나가야 한다는데 인식을 같이함.

나. 또한 동 사무차관도 UR 쌀문제에 대한 일본의 입장에 변화가 없음을 아측에 강조한데 대해 아측도 남은 UR 협상에 공동대처하는 것이 바람직 하다는 의견을

피력함.

다. 동사무차관의 면담에 이어 운노 구조개선국장 등으로 부터 농어민 후계자,
농지 유휴문제등 일본 농업구조의 현상과 구조정책을 상세히 보고받았음. 끝
    (대사 오재희-국장)
    예고:92.6.30. 일반

외 무 부

종 별 :

번 호 : GVW-0366   일 시 : 92 0214 1900

수 신 : 장관(통기,경기원,재무,농수부,상공부)주미,EC-중계필

발 신 : 주 제네바 대사대리

제 목 : UR/농산물 협상

1. 당관 최농무관은 92.2.14(금) UR 스위스 농산물 협상대표인
MATYASSY(연방대외경제부 GATT 담당부대표)와 면담 UR 농산물 협상관련 의견을
교환한고 스위스의 입장등을 문의한바 동인 언급 요지 하기 보고함.

가. UR 협상 동향

- 전반적으로 시간이 부족한 것이 사실이나 미.EC간의 정치적 의지만 있으면
부활절까지 합의 가능할 것으로 봄. 다만 미.EC의 합의가 있더라도 이는 다른
나라들의 합의를 얻어야 하는 문제와 각기 국내적 동의(EC는 이사회, 미국은의회)를
얻어야 하는 문제가 남아있음.

- EC도 자체적으로 확실한 결정이 나있지 않은 것으로 전망

나. 스위스로서는 현재 3 가지 과정(TRACK)으로 추진하고 있음.

1) 제 1 과정

0 던켈 TEXT 상의 문제점에 대한 수정안을 준비하는 것으로 이미 준비는 되어
있으나 당분간은 서면제출은 유보하고 있으며 다음과 같은 문제점이 있음.

0 이행기간

- 93년초 이행은 국내법의 제정과정(각의, 상하양원, 국민투표)으로 볼때
불가능함.

- 만약 합의가 될 경우 현행정부 정책을 전면 수정 제시하여야 하므로
이를농민들에게 7 년동안 이행토록 하는데는 부족하기 때문에 10 년정도의 장기간
필요

0 관세화 예외문제

- 우선은 법적인 예외(GATT 조문 11 조 2C,33 조등)에 중점을 두고 있음.(11조 2
항 C 적용 가능 품목은 설탕과 신선우유뿐이므로 미흡함)

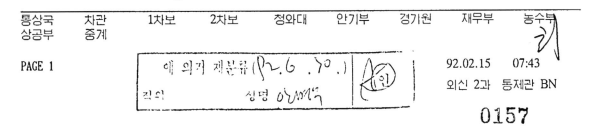

통상국	차관	1차보	2차보	정와대	안기부	경기원	재무부	농수부
상공부	중계							

PAGE 1

92.02.15   07:43
외신 2과 통제관 BN

0157

O 특별구제 조치(SPECIAL SAFEGUARD)

- 물량기준에 의한 발동 수준에는 개념상 문제가 있음. 특히 현행 소비 수준의 3-5 퍼센트 최소 시장접근은 문제가 안되지만 50 퍼센트의 시장접근(CURRENT ACCESS)이 되는 경우 25 퍼센트이상 수입이 증가될때만 발동하게 되어 이경우, 5-6 년후에는 동품목의 생산기반이 완전 붕괴될 가능성이 크므로 이는 보다 세분된 기준이 필요함.(동 부분 제안 초안을 내부자료로 사용할 것을 전제로 제공: 별첨)

O 수출보조분야

- 타분야와의 일관성(COHERENCE) 문제로 수출 보조분야에도 DI MINIMIS 개념의 도입이 필요함.

- 물량감축은 유보함.

O 기타

- CONTINUATION CLAUSE 도 수정되어야 함.

2) 제 2 과정

O 현행 던켈 TEXT 에 따라 그대로 작성하는 것으로 이는 GATT 제출용이 아니라 시안용으로 작성되는대로 정부에 제출하게 되며, 이를 토대로 각계 관련 단체, 기관과 협의예정임.

- 어제(2.13) 시안이 온료되어 일차적 내부 협의가 있었음.

3) 제 3 과정

O 이와같은 내부 협의를 거친 결과를 어떻게 제출할 것인가를 결정하는 과정임. 특히 현재 TRACK 4 가 가동되지 않고 있으나 가동시 자국의 입장 반영 정도 및 다른나라의 제출 내용에 따라 달라질수 있음. 다만 현재로서는 다음과 같은 가능성을 예견할 수 있음.

- 이행 년도는 94 년부터 10 년

- 일부 품목은 관세화에서 제외

- BASE DATA 만 제출

라. 국별 계획 제출시기는 국내과정을 거쳐야 함으로 3.1 일이 지난 가능성도 있으며 특히 다른나라의 제출 동향을 보아 중간정도 낼 것임.

마. 기타 작성상의 문제점

- 전농산물의 양허(BINDING)은 공산물이 모두 양허 가능할 경우에 한함.

- 품질계수는 자료 이용 가능한 한 활용함.

PAGE 2

0158

- 과수, 야채의 관세화는 계절성, 기후조건, 쿼타부여등에 상당히 영향을 받기 때문에 지극히 어려움

2. 최농무관은 아국은 구체적으로 결정된바는 없으나 쌀등 식량안보, 11조2 항 C 대상 품목을 관세화 대상에 포함시키기 어렵다고 하고 스위스의 관세화에의 가능 품목을 문의한바, 가장 어려운 품목은 우유, 유제품 및 쇠고기(농업소득의 70 퍼센트 점유)이며 과실, 야채는 기술적으로 어렵다고 하면서 결국 타국의 제출 수준에 따라 제외 품목의 범위를 결정할 것임을 시시함. 특히 EC 가감축 약속이 아닌 BASE DATA 만 제출할 경우 자국도 상당히 달라질수 있다고 첨언함.

첨부: 특별구제 조치 스위스초안(GVW(F)-0107). 끝

(차석대사 김삼훈-국장)

예고:92.6.30 까지

주 제 네 바 대 표 부

번 호 : GVW(F) - 0/07   년월일 : 2021/4   시간 : 0800
수 신 : 장   관 (통기, 경기원, 재무부, 농림수산부, 상공부) 사본: 주비·주EC대사
발 신 : 주 제네바대사
제 목 : ' 회복 '

총 3 매(표지포함)

보 안 봉 제	회
외신과 통 제	

0160

107-37

2.2 Safeguard

Switzerland proposes the following core amendments:

- Page L4, Article 5, Para 1 (i): This Para should read as follows:

  the volume of imports of that product entering the customs territory of the participant granting the concession during any year exceeds a trigger level equal to the corresponding average quantity during the five preceeding years for which data are available, increased by a fixed percentage depending from the market access opportunities as set out in sub-paragraph 4 below; or, but not concurrently

- Page L5, Article 5, Para 5 b: This Para should read as follows:

  if the difference between the import price and the trigger price (hereafter the "difference") is greater than 10 per cent but less or equal to 30 per cent of the trigger price, the additonal duty shall equal 50 per cent of the amount by which the difference exceeds 10 per cent.

- Page L6, Article 5, Para 9: This Para should be deleted.

Consecutive amendments to maintain the coherence of the Agreement:

- Page L4, Article 5, Para 1 (i): Footnote 1 should be deleted.

- Page L5, Article 5, Para 4: This Para should be amended as follows:

  Any additonal duty imposed under subparagraph 1 (i) above shall only be maintained until the end of the year in which it has been imposed, may only be levied at a level which shall not exceed 100 per cent of the level of the ordinary customs duty in effect in the year in which the action is taken, and shall be set according to the following schedule:

  a) if the market access opportunities for a product are less than or equal to 10 per cent of the corresponding domestic consumption in the base period, the additional duty imposed under sub-paragraph 1 (i) above may be invoked if the volume of imports of that product entering the customs territory of the participant granting the concession during any year exceeds a trigger level equal to 125 per cent;

  b) if the market access opportunities for a product are greater than 10 per cent but less than or equal to 30 per cent of the corresponding domestic consumption in the base period, the additional duty imposed under sub-paragraph 1 (i) above may be invoked if the volume of imports of that product entering the customs

107-3-2

0161

territory of the participant granting the concession during any year exceeds a trigger level equal to 110 per cent;

c) if the market access opportunities for a product are greater than 30 per cent but less than or equal to 60 per cent of the corresponding domestic consumption in the base period, the additional duty imposed under sub-paragraph 1 (i) above may be invoked if the volume of imports of that product entering the customs territory of the participant granting the concession during any year exceeds a trigger level equal to 105 per cent;

d) if the market access opportunities for a product are greater than 60 per cent of the corresponding domestic consumption in the base period, the additional duty imposed under sub-paragraph 1 (i) above may be invoked if the volume of imports of that product entering the customs territory of the participant granting the concession during any year exceeds a trigger level equal to 102 per cent.

- Page L5, Article 5, Para 5c: This Para should read as follows:

  if the difference between the import price and the trigger price is greater than 30 per cent but less or equal to 60 per cent of the trigger price, the additional duty shall equal 75 per cent of the amount by which the difference exceeds 30 per cent, plus the additonal duty allowed under (b).

- Page L5, Article 5, Para 5d: This Para should read as follows:

  if the difference between the import price and the trigger price is greater than 60 per cent, the additonal duty shall equal 100 per cent of the amount by which the difference exceeds 60 per cent, plus the additonal duties allowed under (b) and (c).

- Page L5, Article 5, Para 5e: This Para should be deleted.

10 7 - 3 - 2 7

0162

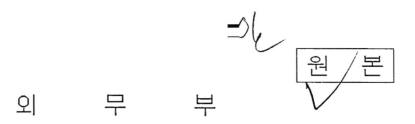

외 무 부

종 별 :

번 호 : GVW-0375

일 시 : 92 0217 1800

수 신 : 장 관(통기,경기원,재무부,농림수산부,상공부)

발 신 : 주 제네바 대사

제 목 : UR/농산물 협상

당관 최농무관은 당지 일본대표부 하야시 참사관과 접촉 2.13-14 개최 농산물 G-8 (미국, EC, 일본, 카나다, 호주, 뉴질랜드, 알젠틴,북구) 실무급 기술회의 내용을 문의한바 동인 언급 요지 하기 보고함.

1. 동 회의는 2.13-14 양일간 8개국 실무대표가 참석 진행 (미국은 USDA 슈로터 해외농업처부처장, USTR 챠틴과장, EC는 농업총국의 올슨과장, 일본은 농림수산성 기타 하라가트 실장등 참석) 되었는바, 주로 DUNKEL TEXT상의 기술적인 문제점의 명료화를 위한 회의였음.

   - 정치적 문제인 관세화의 범위, 전품목 양허, 감축율, 기준년도등에 대한 논의는 일체없었음.

   - 최소시장 접근 (MMA) 부여와 관련 TARIFF LINE별 소비통제 자료 미비문제가 제기되었는바, EC는 예를 들어 버터, 치즈등 주요품목은 산출가능하나 기타 품목 및 가공 품은 어려움을 표시함.

   - TC 산출관련 EC 는 개입가격에 10를 추가 (EC PREFERENCE)하는 기존 입장을 재 강조함.

   - 국내보조 관련 EC는 86-88 평균보다 86년도 AMS만 기준으로 사용할 것을 주장하였음.

   2. 동 회의는 각국이 가지고 있던 기술적의 문점만 제기되었을 뿐이며 어떠한 결론도 없었음. 향후 3.1 까지는 동 종류의 회의는 더이상 갖지 않을 전망임.끝.

   (대사 박수길-국장)

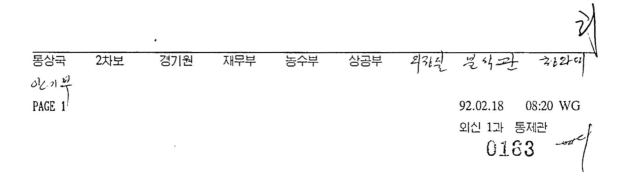

통상국   2차보   경기원   재무부   농수부   상공부   외기원   물식관   차1와대

안기부

PAGE 1

92.02.18   08:20 WG

외신 1과 통제관

0163

외 무 부

종 별 :

번 호 : SDW-0155

일 시 : 92 0217 1600

수 신 : 장 관(통기)

발 신 : 주 스웨덴대사

제 목 : URI 농산물 감축이행계획서

대:WSD-0078

대호관련, 당관 정의민 참사관이 금 2.17.외무부 PER WALLEN 통상2국 UR 담당과장을 접촉한 바, 주재국은 농산물의 감축이행 계획서를 신중하게 작성중이며 기한내 제출할 계획이라 함.끝

(대사 최동진-국장)

통상국   2차보

외 무 부

관리
번호 92-15

종 별 :

번 호 : ECW-0230   일 시 : 92 0217 1800

수 신 : 장관 (통기,경기원,농림수산부)

발 신 : 주 EC 대사

제 목 : 갓트/UR 협상

대: WEC-0123

1. 2.17. 당곤 이관용농무관은 대호관련, OLSEN EC 농업총국 담당관을 접촉한바
아래 보고함

가. EC 는 감축이행 계획서를 기한내에 제출한다는 기본방침하에 관계부서간의
협의를 갖고, 동 계획서를 작성중에 있으며 금주말경 회원국 실무담당관회의,
집행위원회의 등을 개최하여 확정할 예정임

나. DUNKEL 협상안 내용중 EC 가 수락할수 없는 사항, 즉 GREEN BOX,
REBALANCING, 수출보조금 감축문제등을 동 감축계획서에 어떻게 반영할 것인가에
대하여도 금주말 개최되는 관련회의에서 확정하게 될것임

다. 2.13-14 워싱턴에서 개최된 미.EC 고위급협상 결과에대해 언급할 입장은
아니나, 양측간의 상황이 호전 또는 악화된바도 없으며 양자간 협의를 계속할 것으로
알고있음

2. 2.24. 동인과 오찬협의후 동건 추보하겠음. 끝

(대사 권동만-국장)

예고: 92.6.30 까지

통상국   차관   2차보   구주국   외정실   분석관   안기부   경기원   농수부

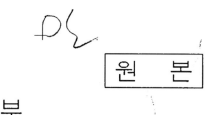

```
관리
번호  9ㅗ-154
```

외 무 부

종   별 :

번   호 : CNW-0201   일   시 : 92 0218 1710

수   신 : 장 관(통기,상공부,농수산부)

발   신 : 주 캐나다 대사

제   목 : UR 농산물 협상관련 주재국 동향

연 : CNW-0163

하상무관이 주재국 외무무역부 MARIO STE-MARIE 부조정관(MTN BRANCH 농산물 담당)으로부터 탐문한 UR 농산물 협상관련 주재국 동향을 아래와 같이 보고함.

1. 주재국 정부는 UR 농산물 협상관련 자국 입장에 대한 지지확보를 위해 WILSON 산업과기 장관겸 통상장관, MCKNIGHT 농무장고나 및 BLAIS 농무담당 국무상등 정부인사와 주요 농업단체 대표등으로 구성된 대표단(약 30 여명)를 구성, 2.19. 유럽에 파견할 계획이라고 함. 금번 유럽 방문에 포함될 지역은 브랏셀, 본 및 제네바인바 방문 기간중 EC 및 서독 정부인사 및 DUNKEL 총장등과 만나 주재국의 낙농 및 가금류에 대한 SUPPLY MANAGEMENT PROGRAM 지속을 위한 관세화에대한 예외 인정과 곡물, 유체 및 가축류에 대한 수출 보조금 감축의 확대등을 역설, 이에 대한 지지를 확보하는데 노력할 것이라고 함.

2. MULRONEY 수상은 금일 25 명의 낙농대표와 만나 UR 농산물 협상문제 특히 낙농 수입개방문제에 관해 협의할 계획이며, 이에 400 여명의 MARKETING BOARD(낙농, 가금류 공급 통제제도 관리기구)간부들에게 연설할 계획임.

3. 주재국내 농문(주로 낙농농가) 2 만 여명은 2.21. 오타와에서 UR 농산물관련 시위를 벌일 계획인바, 동 시위대상에는 주재국 정부는 물론 미국, 호주등 예외없는 관세화를 지지하고 있는 국가의 대사관도 포함될 가능성이 크다고 함. 끝

(대사-국장)

예고문 :92.12.31 까지

검 토 필 (199ㅗ. 6 3ㅇ.)

통상국 상공부	차관	1차보	2차보	외정실	분석관	청와대	안기부	농수부

외 무 부

관리
번호 [P2 - /53]

종 별 :

번 호 : USW-0791   일 시 : 92 0218 1546

수 신 : 장관(통기,통이,경기원,농수산부,상공부,재무부)

발 신 : 주 미 대사

제 목 : UR/ 농산물 협상

　　당곤 이영래 농무관은 2,18 미 농무부 SCHROETER 처장보를 면담하고 표제 관련 사항을 협의한 바, 요지 하기 보고함.

　1. 미.EC 간 고위 실무협상결과

　. 동 처장본 지난 2.13-14 동안 EC 집행위원 농업총 국장원 GUY LEGRAS 와 UR 고위협상 대표인 HUGO PUEMEN 이 워싱톤을 방문, 미 농무부의 RICHAR CROWDER 차관과 USTR 의 JULLIUS KATZ 부대표를 면담하고, UR 농산물 관련 사항등을 집중 협의하였으나 별다른 진전이 없었다고 함.

　. 특히 금번 협의는 EC 측의 요청에 의해서 이루어졌으나 WEC 측은 계속하여 종전과같이 REBALANCING 과 CAP REFORM 의 직접소득 보조에 대한 GREEN BOX 인정, 수출보조에서 24%의 물량감축 조치에 대한 완화등을 요구하고 특별한 새로운 대안제시도 없었다고 하며, 양측은 내주중에 유럽에서 다시 협상키로 하고 금번 협의를 끝냈다고 함.

　2. 앞으로의 전망

　. 동처장보는 미국과 EC 간의 농산물 분야에 대한 미합의로 MARKET ACCESS 등 타분야의 협상에 지장을 초래하고 있음을 인정하면서 미국과 EC 간에 내주에 협상을 재개하겠지만 당분간 EC 측으로 부터 새로운 대안제시도 기대해 어려울 것으로 전망하고 있음.

　. 또한 미측의 입장과 관련하여 농산물 분야에 대한 DUNKEL TEXT 는 미의회와 업계가 수락할수 있는 MINIMUM POSITION 이라고 설명하면서 교착상태에 빠진 미.EC 간에 협상 돌파구를 열기위해서는 정치적 결단이 필요한데 현재 미국이 경제적으로 어렵고 NEW HAMPSHIRE 예비선거 실시등 선거철로 들어감에 따라 현실적으로 얼려운 상황에 있다고 함.

통상국	장관	차관	1차보	2차보	통상국	외정실	분석관	정와대
안기부	경기원	재무부	농수부	상공부				

PAGE 1

. 따라서 DUNKEL 사무총장이 제시한 4.15 까지의 협상완료 시한은 특별한 변화가 없는한 지키기 어려울 것으로 전망하면서 일단 5,6 월 이후로 연기될 것이지만 개인적으로는 미국과 EC 측이 모두 협상의 성공 필요성을 잘 알고 있으므로 종국적으로는 합의가 이루어 질수 있을 것이라고 말함.

(대사 현홍주-국장)

92. 6. 30 까지

외 무 부

종 별 :

번 호 : SZW-0090   일 시 : 92 0218 1720

수 신 : 장 관(봉기)

발 신 : 주 스위스 대사

제 목 : UR 농산물 감축이행 계획서

대: WSZ-0060

1. 본직은 2.17. 주재국 경제성 GATT문제담당 GIRARD 대사와 오찬중 대호관련 주재국의 추진 계획을 타진한바, 동인에 의하면 주재국은 던켈 GATT 사무총장이 제시한 DEADLINE 을 존중하여 감축이행 계획서는 대체로 3.1. 시한에는 맞추어 제출할것이나 최종 순간까지 유보적 태도를 보일것으로 감지되며 내용은 상당히 수정된 것으로서 제시기준과는 거리가 있을 것으로 보임.

2. 본건 관련 계속 경제성 GATT 관계관과 접촉, 진전동향 보고위계임.끝

(대사 이원호-국장)

통상국

PAGE 1   92.02.19   13:46 WG

외신 1과 통제관

0189

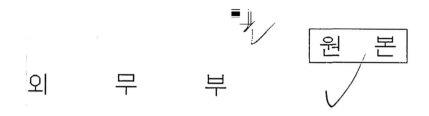

외 무 부

종 별 :

번 호 : CNW-0210   일   시 : 92 0219 1800

수 신 : 장 관(봉기,상공부)

발 신 : 주 캐나다 대사

제 목 : UR 농산물 협상 관련 주재국 동향

연 : CNW-0201

1. 멀루니 수상은 2.18. 400 여명의 MARKETING BOARD간부들에게 행한 연설에서 주재국 정부는 낙농, 계란 및 가므류 분야의 농민 보호를 위해 UR 농산물 협상에서 모든 노력을 경주할것이라고 하였음. 주재국의 SUPPLY MANAGEMENT PROGRAM의 존속을 위해서는 선진 공업국들의 지지를 확보하는것이 최선의 방법이며, 이를 위해 동수상은 미국 BUSH 대통령 및 독일 KOHL수상등에게 금주중 전화로 협조를 요청할 계획이라고 언급 하였음.

2. 그러나 동 수상은 최종 UR 협정안이 SUPPLY MANAGEMENT PROGRAM 을 허용하지 아니하는 경우 이를 거부할 것인지는 확약할수 없다고 하면서 카나다가 UR 에서 탈퇴하는 것은 카나다와 반대입장을 가진 국가들에 손에 놀아나는 결과에 불과하다고 주장하였음.끝

(대사-국장)

통상국   2차보   미주국   상공부   청와대   안기부

PAGE 1   92.02.20   10:03 WG

외 무 부

종 별 :

번 호 : AUW-0134   일 시 : 92 0220 1100

수 신 : 장 관(봉기)

발 신 : 주 호주 대사

제 목 : UR/농산물감축 이행계획서 제출

대:WAU-0097

대호 주재국 외무.무역부 DEADY GATT 농업담당과장에 의하면, 주재국은
표제계획서를 3.1까지 제출할수 있도록 최대한 노력중이며, 기한내 제출이 가능할
것으로 본다고함.끝.

(대사 이창범-국장)

통상국

PAGE 1   92.02.20   10:06 WG

외신 1과 통제관

0171

외 무 부

종 별 :

번 호 : MAW-0184   일 시 : 92 0220 1200

수 신 : 장 관(통기)

발 신 : 주 말련 대사

제 목 : UR/농산물 감축 이행계획서 제출

WMA-0119

　　대호 관련 주재국 상공부 및 농수산부등에 확인한 바, 3.1 시한전 제출을 위해 최대한 노력하고 있으나 많은 기술적 어려움때문에 시한내 제출을 낙관할 수 없다 함.그러나 늦어도 3월 첫주내 제출하는 것이 목표라 함.끝

　　(대사 홍순영-국장)

통상국

PAGE 1

외   무   부

종   별 :

번   호 : CNW-0215   일   시 : 92 0220 1700

수   신 : 장 관(통기, 상공부, 농수산부)

발   신 : 주 캐나다 대사

제   목 : UR/ 농산물 감축 이행계획서 제출

    대: WCN-0113

    연: CNW-0163

    WILSON 산업과기장관 겸 통상장관은 3.1 까지 제출키로 되어 있는 UR/농산물분야감축이행 계획서중 SUPPLY MANAGEMENT PROGRAM 에 의해 보호를 받고 있는 우유, 치즈, 버터, 계란, 칠면조 및 닭고기등 품목에 대해서는 이를 제출하지 않을것이라고 2.19 하원에서 밝혔음. (대사- 국장)

통상국   농수부   상공부

PAGE 1   92.02.21   10:11 WH
                                                외신 1과 통제관
                                                0173

외 무 부

종 별 :

번 호 : NDW-0293

일 시 : 92 0220 1900

수 신 : 장 관(통기)

발 신 : 주 인도 대사

제 목 : UR/농산물 감축 이행계획서 제출

대:WND-0112

1. 대호, 당관 임재홍서기관이 2.19.RANDHAWA 상무부 부국장과 접촉, 확인한 바, 동 부국장은 현재 표제작업을 진행중에 있으나, 제출기한인 3.1 까지 감축계획서 제출이 가능할 것 같지는 않다고 언급함.

2. 또한 동 부국장은 인도는 농산물분야에 있어서는 관세및 관세상당치 인하 대상국이 아니며, 단지 국내보조분야(비료분야)만이 감축대상이 될 것이나, 현 RAO 정부가 경제개방화정책에 따라 비료보조금 삭감정책을 취하고 있기때문에감축계획작성에 큰 어려움은 없을 것으로 전망됨. 다만 덴켈협정안에 대한 야당등의 반대와 비료보조금 삭감의 정치적 민감성을 고려할때는 다소 시간이 걸릴것으로 보인다고 첨언함.

(대사 이정빈-국장)

통상국

PAGE 1

92.02.20   22:52
외신 2과   통제관 CH

0174

외　무　부

종　　별 :

번　　호 : ECW-0255　　　　　　　　　일　시 : 92 0220 1840

수　　신 : 장 관 (통기,경기원,재무부,농수산부,상공부)

발　　신 : 주 EC 대사　사본: 주제네바-직송필

제　　목 : 갓트/ UR 협상

　　1. 2.20. 카나다의 WILSON 무역장관과 MAKNIGHT농무장관은 당지에서 MAC SHARRY 집행위원과 회담후 가진 기자회견에서 카나다가 제안한바 있는 갓트 제11조 2항 C 개정문제에 대해 EC 측의 지지를 요청하였다고 밝힘. KCKINGHT 농무장관은 금번회담에서 동 문제에 대한 양측의 입장을 이해하게 되었으며 자국은 어느정도 EC로부터 고무를 받기는 하였으나 전폭적인 지지를 약속받았다고 말하기는 어렵다고 말함.

　　2. 한편, EC 집행위의 한 관계관은 동 회담에서 MAC SHARRY 집행위원은 EC는 예외없는 관세화가 기본입장임을 재천명하고, 특별 SAFEGUARD 조항을 가지고 급격한 대량의 농산물유입에 대처하기 어려운 경우에 대비하기 위해 갓트 11-2- C 를 존치하는 방법을 고려하고 있으나, 동조항의 개정을 지지하기는 어렵다는 입장을 취하였다고 전언함.

　　3. 2.21. WILSON 무역장관은 제네바에서 DUNKEL총장과, MCKNIGHT 농무장관은 본에서 KIECHLE 독일 농무장관과 각각 회담을 가질 것으로 알려짐. 끝

　　(대사 권동만-국장)

통상국　　경기원　　재무부　　농수부　　상공부

PAGE 1　　　　　　　　　　　　　　　　　　92.02.21　　09:45 WH

외신 1과 통제관

0175

외　무　부

종　별 :

번　호 : GVW-0411
일　시 : 92 0221 1200

수　신 : 장관(통기, 경기원, 재무부, 농림수산부, 상공부)사본:주미, 주EC대사-직송필

발　신 : 주제네바대사

제　목 : UR/농산물 협상

　　1. 표제협상 최근 동향 관련 BROADBRIDGE 갓트 사무차장보에 의하면 EC 의 113위원회가 2.21-22개최 되며, 동 회의는 EC의 UR농산물협상 입장 조정과 관련 중요한성격을 갖는 것으로 알고 있다함.

　　2. 동 차장보에 의하면 2.24 주간중 워싱턴에서 미-EC간 양자협의가 재개될 것이라고 함.

　　(1.13-14 개최되었던 양자협의와 동일한 FORMAT이 될것으로 전망 .끝

　　(대사 박수길-국장)

통상국　　경기원　　재무부　　농수부　　상공부

PAGE 1

92.02.22　　07:17 DQ

외신 1과 통제관

0176

외 무 부

종 별 :

번 호 : CNW-0235   일 시 : 92 0224 1630

수 신 : 장 관(통기,상공부,농림수산부)

발 신 : 주 캐나다 대사

제 목 : UR/농산물 협상 관련 주재국 동향

연:CNW-201

UR 농산물 협상관련 주재국 입장에 대한 지지확보를 위해 파견된 관민 사절단 (단장 :WILSON 산업과기장관 겸 통상장관) 의 유럽방문 성과등에 대해 GLOBE MAIL 지등 당지언론에 보도된 내용에 대해 하기와 같이 보고함.

1. EC 농업위원장 (MACSHARRY) 대변인 및 EC 농업단체등은 카나다 측 주장대로 MARKETINGBOARD 의 존속을 고집하는 것은 현재 협상이 진행중인 UR협상 자체를 결렬 시킬 가능성이 있기 때문에 카측입장을 거부하였음.

2. WILSON 장관도 동문제 관련 EC 측과의 COMMON GRUND 모색을 위해 전문가팀이이에 대해 연구해 나가기로 하였다고 언급하였음.

3. MULRONY 수상은 KOHL 독일수상, MAJOR 영국수상 및 DELORS EC 위원장관 전화협 의를 통해 카나다의 SUPPLY MANAGEMENT PROGRAM 이 국제 무역에 있어 왜곡을 초래하는 보조금 성격이 없다는 점과 동 PROGRAM 폐지가 카나다 가계농업(FAMILY FARM) 에 미칠 심각한 영향에 대하 강조를 하였던 바, 이에 대해 이들 EC 지도자들이 약간의 동정을 갖고 있다는 인상을 받았으며, HOHL 수상은 카측 입장을 검토키로 동의 하였다고 MULRONEY 수상은 발언하였음.

4. 2.21. 주재국 농민 2만 5천 - 3만명(경찰추정)은 낙농, 계란, 가금류에 대한예외 없는 관세화를 반대하는 시위를 오타와에서 벌였음.

5. GLOBE MAIL 및 OTTAWA CITIZEN 지등 주요언론은 사설을 통해 카나다 정부가예외없는 관세화에 대한 GATT 협상안을 수락하는 것이 세계 농산물 교역은 물론 카나다에도 이익이 될 것이라고 주장하고 관련 농민들은 국제적인 무역자유화 조류로 부터 야기되는 도전을 직시, 이에 대처해 나가야 할 것이라고 하였음.

(대사 - 국장)

통상국   2차보   농수부   상공부

외신 1과 통제관

0177

```
관리
번호  82-168
```

외 무 부

종   별 :

번   호 : ECW-0267   일   시 : 92 0225 1600

수   신 : 장관 (통기,경기원,재무부,농림수산부,상공부,기정동문)

발   신 : 주 EC 대사 사본: 주 미, 제네바대사-중계요망

제   목 : 갓트/UR 농산물협상

   연: ECW-0230

   2.24. 당관 이관용농무관은 EC 농업총국의 OLSEN 담당관을 오찬에 초청, 표제협상 전망등에 대해 협의한바 동인의 발언요지 아래 보고함

   ① 감축이행계획서 제출

   가. EC 집행위는 3.1. 까지 제출토록 되어있는 국내보조등 감축이행 계획서를 2.21. 개최된 113 위원회에서 사실상 확정한바 있음

   나. 동 감축이행 계획서 작성과 관련하여 GREEN BOX 등 EC 가 수정을 요구하고 있는 사항을 처리함에 있어 큰 문제점은 없었으며, 부분적인 문제에 대하여는 조건부 또는 주 (FOOT NOTE) 를 붙여 제출할 것으로 알고 있음. 다만 113 위원회에서 몇몇 회원국들이 동 계획서 내용중 일부사항은 순수한 기술적인 내용이 아니라는 이유를 들어 농업이사회에 회부하여 결정할 것을 제안함. 동 의견에대해 집행위와 이사회간의 견해차이가 예상되나, 현재 이견을 조정중에 있으므로 3.2-4 중에 감축이행 계획서를 갓트에 제출할 것으로 보임 (다만, 3.2-3 예정인 농업이사회에서 동 문제가 토의될 경우 제출시기가 약간 지연될 가능성도 있음)

   ② 미.EC 간 양자협상

   가. 금주중 미.EC 양자협상을 가질 것이며, 동 협상은 정치적인 수준의 협상보다는 2.13-14 워싱턴에서 개최된 수준의 고위급협상이 될 것으로 알고 있음

   나. 2.21. DELORS 위원장이 언급한바와 같이 미국은 UR 협상 추진에대해 상당히 소극적인 입장으로 임하고 있는것은 사실이며, 그 이유는 미국 국내 정치일정뿐 아니라 미국은 DUNKEL 협상안에 대해 대체적으로 만족하고 있어 적극적인 타협 필요성을 느끼고 있지 않은 것으로 판단됨

   다. 미.EC 간 양자협상 추진과 관련하여 마지막 단계에서는 미측의 입장이 어렵게

통상국	차관	2차보	외정실	분석관	안기부	경기원	재무부	농수부
상공부	중계							

PAGE 1   92.02.26   01:25

                                                   외신 2과 통제관 FM

                                                        0178

될것으로 보며, 그 이유는 DUNKEL 협상안의 촛점은 시장접근 분야에 있으며 미측은 동분야에는 어려움이 없으나, 국내보조 감축분야에 국내적인 어려움이 있기 때문임. 또한 EC 가 국내보조와 시장접근 감축율을 동일하게 하자는 강한 입장을 제시할 경우, 미측은 국내 보조감축율을 상향 또는 시장접근 감축율을하향 조정하는 선택을 강요받게 될것임

　　3. 협상전망

　　가. 주요 협상국들의 감축이행 계획서 제출여부 또는 제출된 내용 (즉, 품목범위등) 정도는 협상진전에 큰 영향을 미칠 것으로 보며, 일례로 2.21 WILSON 카나다 무역장관이 제네바에서 언급한바와 같이 카나다가 낙농제품, 가금류를, 일본이 쌀등 주요품목을 감축 이행대상에서 제외할 경우, 이러한 사실은 협상추진의 장애요소로서 미.EC 등 주요협상 참여국들의 강한 비난의 표적이 될것임

　　나. 부활절휴가 이전에 협상이 종결될 가능성은 현실적으로 희박하다고 보며, 기술적 또는 정치적 타협이 필요한 내용이 정리되어 표출되는 정도가 될것으로 봄

　　4. EC 회원국 동향

　　가. 최근 독일의 경우 업계의 압력, 경제상황의 악화등으로 인하여, UR 협상의 조속한 종결을위해 상당한 노력을 기울이고 있으며, 특히 농업보조금 감축협상에서 양보하는 대신에 타분야에서 유리한 결론을 도출하려는 의지를 보인바 있고 최근 KOHL 수상이 MITTERAND 불 대통령과 접촉하는 한편, 금명간 BUSH 대통령과도 접촉할 예정인 것으로 알고 있음

　　나. 불란서가 이제까지 보여온 강한 입장은 협상전략및 국내문제 때문인 것으로 해석하여야 하며, 최종단계에 가서는 불란서가 협상결과를 긍정적으로 받아드릴 준비를 갖추어가고 있는것으로 알고 있음. 끝

　　(대사 권동만-국장)

　　예고: 92.6.30 까지

외 무 부

종 별 :

번 호 : MXW-0196

일 시 : 92 0225 1200

수 신 : 장관(봉기,미중)

발 신 : 주 멕시코 대사

제 목 : UR/농산물 감축이행 계획서

대:WMX-0062

1. 대호 당관 추서기관은 금 2.25(화) DR.HECTOROLEA 주재국 상공성 GATT 및 국제기구담당과장을 접촉, 대호건에 대해 문의한바,동과장은 우선 던켈 사무총장이 제시한 협상일정 및 농산물 감축 이행계획서 기준 및방법등이 융봉성을 결여하고 있음을 지적하면서 멕시코측은 이미 상기계획서를 시장접근,국내보조 및 수출 보조항목으로 나누어 작성 하였으며 현재 제네바 GATT 내 분위기를 예의주시 하면서 제출 시기를 고려 하고 있다함.

2. 한편, OLEA 과장은 동 계획서 제출시기관련, 주제네바 자국대사가 현지에서 일본,카나다,스위스등 국가와 긴밀한 협의를 갖고있으며 공동조치를 강구하고 있다고 언급함.

(대사 이복형-국장)

통상국   2차보   미주국

PAGE 1

92.02.26   07:47 FE

외신 1과 통제관

0180

외 무 부

종 별 :

번 호 : BRW-0231   일 시 : 92 0225 1740

수 신 : 장 관(통기)

발 신 : 주 브라질 대사

제 목 : 브라질 UR 농산물 감축 계획서 제출

대:WBR-0087

1. 당관 임참사관은 2.25 주재국 외무부 기초제품과 JOSE AMIR 과장 차석을 방문, 표제감축 계획서 제출 가능 여부를 문의한바, 동인은 현재 농무부에서 기술적인 부문을 검토중이며, 3.1 시한내 제출 가능한 것이라 하고 언급함.

REZEK 외무장관도 기일내 제출하도록 지시한바 있다함.

2. 동인은 CAIRNS 그룹 국가들도 동일한 입장의 감축 계획서를 제출 할것으로 본다고 하면서 브라질 정부는 DUNKEL 안을 내용 그대로 수용하고 있는 입장이며, 동 안이통과 안될시 GATT가 입는 손상은 클것이라고 예상함.

3. 한편 동인은 지난주 일본 관계부처 공무원2명이 자신을 방문, 일본의 입장을설명하면서 일본 정부는 동 감축 계획서를 제출하기가 어려울것이라고 설명하였다함.끝

(대사 한철수-국장)

통상국   2차보   미주국

PAGE 1   92.02.26   07:54 FE

외신 1과 통제관

0181

원 본

외 무 부

종 별 :

번 호 : SZW-0102   일 시 : 92 0225 1200

수 신 : 장관(통기)

발 신 : 주 스위스 대사

제 목 : UR/농산물 감축 이행계획서

대:WSZ-0060

연:SZW-0090

1. 당관이 연호와 관련 주재국 경제성 GATT 국 담당관에게 2.24 재확인한 바에 의하면 주재국은 대호 갓트 사무총장 제시 일정보다는 좀 늦게 제출될 것이라고 함.

2. 동 담당관에 의하면 주재국은 작년 12.20 이후 내부목적을 위한 기준 수립을 하여 놓은바 이결과 금주중에는 최소한 실무선에서는 계획서 작성이 가능한것으로 보고 있으나, 국내 경제단체와의 조정등을 거친후 정부의 최종적이며, 공식적인 결정은 내주중에나 가능할 것이라고 함. 끝

(대사 이원호-국장)

예고문: 92.12.31 까지

검 토 필 (1992. 6. 30.)

통상국

외 무 부

종 별 : 지 급

번 호 : PAW-0166

일 시 : 92 0227 1800

수 신 : 장 관(통기)

발 신 : 주 파키스탄 대사

제 목 : U/R 농수산물 감축이행 계획서

대 WPA-70

대호,주재국은 표제계획서에 대한 관계부처및 이해기관과의 협의문제로
3.1시한까지 동계획서를 제출하기 어렵다고함.끝.

(대사 전순규-국장)

통상국   구주국

92.02.27   20:49 FN

외신 1과 통제관

0183

외 무 부

종 별 :

번 호 : JAW-1108

일 시 : 92 0227 2145

수 신 : 장 관(봉기,통일,경일,농수산부)

발 신 : 주 일 대사(일경)

제 목 : 일본의 쌀시장 개방문제

주재국 정부는 2.26 미야자와 수상 주재의 관계각료협의에서 쌀의 관세화 반대 방침을 관철한다는 방침을 결정하였는바, 언론보도를 중심으로 동 관련 주요내용 아래 보고함.(관련 특이동향 있을시 추보예정임)

1. UR 국별보호 삭감표의 쌀에 관한 표기에대해, 쌀의 관세화를 받아들이지 않는다는 기본입장에서 아래와 같이 관세율을 명시하지 않기로 결정

가. 쌀, 맥, 전분, 유제품등에 대해서는 관세율도 관세삭감율도 명시않음.

나. 덩켈 합의안에 명시된 국내보호 20 퍼센트 삭감은 원칙적으로 받아들임.

다. 이미 관세화된 품목에 대해서는 합의안에 명시된 36퍼센트의 삭감폭을 축소, 평균 24퍼센트의 삭감에 그침.

2. 일정부결정의 배경

가. 현재 국별 보호 삭감표 제출기한이 임박한 상황에서 미. EC 간의 대립이 심각하여 타협이 대폭 늦춰질 공산이 커졌음.

나. 미야자와 수상은 쌀생산지인 미야기현의 보궐선거를 앞두고 있어 쌀시장 개방 문제결단을 뒤로 미루지 않을수 없었음.

3. 상기결정 관련 가또 관방장관 기자회견(2.26)언급내용

가. 금후 교섭전망이 이전보다 더 불투명해지고있으며 일본은 농업교섭에서 쌀을포함한 농산물의 포괄 관세화에 반대할 방침임.

나. 일본의 국별표 제출시기는 3월1일 시작하는주가 될것임.끝

(대사 오재희-국장)

통상국   2차보   경제국   통상국   청와대   안기부   농수부

PAGE 1

92.02.27   23:35 FN

외신 1과 통제관

0184

관리번호 92-1커

분류번호	보존기간

발 신 전 보

WGV-0337   920228 1856 ED

번   호 : _____   종별 : _____

수   신 : 주 제네바 대사. 총영사 /

발   신 : 장 관 (통 기)

제   목 : UR/농산물 국별 이행계획서

대 : GVW-0410

1. UR/농산물 국별 이행계획서 제출 문제를 협의하기 위한 관계장관 회의가 2.26(수)
   경제 부총리 주재로 개최된바 결과 요지 아래임 (외무부, 농수산부, 상공부장관,
   경제수석, 행조실장 참석)

   가. 쌀을 제외한 관세화 예외품목(1-2개의 식량안보 품목과 11:2(C)에 해당되는
       ~~6개 경도와~~ 생산 통제품목) 선정을 포함한 어려운 결정은 3.24 총선후 3월말
       또는 4월초에 함.

   나. 3월초이후 예상되는 농산물 양자협상에 참여할 수 있도록 3월초에 협상자료를
       제출함.

       ○ 구체적인 제출일자는 여타국 동향을 보아 결정함.

       ○ 협상자료는 90.10월 C/L 제출시 관세화 대상에서 제외한 15개 NTC 품목에
         대해서는 협상 기초자료(품목별 관세율, 관세 상당치, 국내 및 수출보조치)를
         제시하고, 여타품목에 대해서는 감축 계획도 제시토록 구체적인 내용은
         농수산부가 외무부와 협의하여 결정함.

       ○ 정리된 국별 감축 계획을 제출할 수 없는 사정은 미국에 사전 설명하여
         이해를 얻도록 함 (알파 품목을 결정하여 발표하는 것이 어려운 입장 설명)

보안통제	

앙고재	92년 월 28일	통상기구과	기안자 성명 안명수	과장	국장 신의관	차관	장관	외신과통제

에 의거 재분류 (92. 6. 30.)
직위

다. 양자협상에서는 이미 관계국에 설명하고 협상 과정에서 밝힌대로 15개 품목에
   융통성이 있으며 쌀 및 알파 품목에 대한 관세화 예외가 아국 입장임을 밝히고,
   감축 계획을 협상토록 함.

라. 새로운 수정 이행 계획서는 상기 3월말, 4월초 관세화 예외품목 결정후 필요시
   제출토록 함.

2. 상기 나항 협상자료의 구체적 내용에 관해 현재 협의중인바, **쌀**에 대하여는 TE를
   포함한 관련자료를 모두 공란으로 남겨두는 방안을 검토중에 있음.

3. 시장접근 분야 양허표 제출과 관련, 농산물을 제외한 공산품 분야는 이미 결정한대로
   3.1경 먼저 제출하고, 농산물 분야는 여타국 동향을 보아 추후 제출코자 하는바,
   이에 관해 특별한 의견이 있으면 회시바람.

4. 대호 3항 농산물 아국 입장 지지 교섭 관련, 현재 협상 추이에 비추어 일단 양자
   협상을 통한 아국 입장 반영이 중요하다고 보며, 쌀등 기초식량에 대한 예외 인정등
   핵심사항 반영 위하여는 Track 4의 활용도 중요하므로, Track 4가 가동되는 경우
   주요국 수도 및 귀지에서의 지지 교섭 추진, 수정안 제출등 가능한 방안을 검토할
   예정이니 참고바람.   끝.   (통상국장 김 용 규)

외 무 부

원 본

종 별 : 지 급

번 호 : GVW-0480

일 시 : 92 0228 2300

수 신 : 장관(통기, 경기원, 재무부, 농수산부, 상공부)

발 신 : 주 제네바 대사

제 목 : UR/농산물 국별 이행 계획서

대: WGV-0337

1. 3 월 이후의 양자 협상에 참여하고, 아국의 진지한 협상 자세를 표시하기 위해서도 대호 1 항 "나"와 같은 협상 자료를 3 월중 적절한 시점에 제출하는것이 중요하며, 동 구체시기는 아래 같은 당지 사정을 고려 3.10 이후에는 하시라도 제출할수 있도록 준비가 완료되어야 할 것으로 판단됨.

가. DENIS 의장은 이미 국별 양허 계획 제출시기를 10 여일 연기하겠다는 뜻을 밝힌바 있고, 동 의장은 이를 위해 각 지역 그룹과의 별도 접촉(아주그룹 10개국 회의 3.4 소집 예정)을 거쳐 3.5 로 예정된 공식회의에서 이문제를 거론할 예정임.

나. 지난 2.13-14 워싱톤에서 미.EC 접촉이 개시된 이래 양측은 계속 접촉(금 2.28 에도 브랏셀에서 협의중인바, 오전에는 농산물, 오후에는 여타분야를 협의하였으며, CROWDER 농무차관은 명일 귀국하고 KATZ 및 LAVOREL 부대표는 브랏셀에 잔류 LEGRAS, PAEMAN 대표등과 계속 협상 예정인 것으로 파악됨)을 해 왔으며, 동 결과는 내주중 좀더 가시화 될것이라는 당지의 일반적 관측임.

다. 상당수 국가가 이미 국별 계획을 제출할 준비가 되어 있는 것으로 파악되고 있고, 특히 일본의 경우 당초 예정된 일정을 중시하여 내주중 국별 계획을 제출할 것이라고 말하고 있음. (농산물 포함)

라. 미.EC 도 합의에 도달하는 시점에서는 최단시일내 국별 계획을 제출할 것으로 예상되며, 합의이전이라고 불완전한 형태의 협상자료를 제출할 가능성이 있음.

2. 3.10 까지 농산물 분야 협상 자료의 제출이 필요하다고 판단되는 이상, 공산품 분야와 농산품 분야는 동시에 제출하는 것이 효과적이라고 봄.

3. 당지 사정을 보아 실기하지 않고 제출할수 있도록 대호 1 항 "나" 농산물 협상 자료를 당관에 송부해 줄것을 건의함. 끝

통상국	장관	차관	1차보	2차보	외정실	분석관	청와대	안기부
경기원	재무부	농수부	상공부					

PAGE 1

이 의기 재분류 (92. 6. 30.)

92.02.29 07:49

외신 2과 통제관 BX

0187

(대사 박수길-국장)
예고 92.6.30 까지

0188

외 무 부

종 별 :

번 호 : ECW-0301

일 시 : 92 0304 1600

수 신 : 장관 (통기, 경기원, 재무부, 농림수산부, 상공부, 제네바대사-직송필)

발 신 : 주 EC 대사대리   사본 권동만 주 EC 대사

제 목 : 갓트/UR 협상

표제협상 관련 최근 당지의 동향을 아래 보고함

1. 농산물협상 감축이행 계획서 제출

가. 3.3 EC 집행위 고위관계관은 EC 의 농산물관세 상당치등 감축이행 계획서를 3.4 갓트에 제출할 것이라고 말함. 동인은 동 문서가 관세상당치, 수출보조금에 대한 통계자료등을 포함 400 여 페이지에 달하며 지속적인 협상추진 기초자료로서 활용될 것이라고 부언함

나. 한편, 3.2 부터 계속중인 농업이사회에서 불란서와 독일은 동 이행계획서에 포함될 내용에대해 이견을 보인 것으로 알려짐. 불란서는 물량기준한 수출보조금 통계자료를 동 이행계획서에 포함시키는 것은 EC 가 수출물량을 감축할 용의가 있음을 표명하는 것으로 이해될 수도 있을 것이라고 지적하면서 이에 반대한 반면, 독일은 동 자료를 제출함으로서 EC 가 UR 협상에 탄력적으로 대처하고 있음을 보여주어야 할 것이라고 주장함

2. 비공식 무역및 농업이사회 결과

가. 3.2 개최된 무역및 농업연석이사회에서는 표제협상이 지연되고 있음에 우려를 표명하고 특히 DUNKEL 협상안은 UR 협상이 균형되고 실질적인 결과를 조기에 도출하는데 적절한 협상안이 될수 없다는 점을 재천명함

나. 동 이사회는 표제협상의 조속한 종결이 세계 경제발전에 기여할 것이라는 점을 강조하면서 모든 협상참여국들은 협상에 적극적으로 참여할 것으로 촉구하면서 동 이사회가 UR 협상을 충분히 평가할수 있는 기회를 마련할수 있도록 EC 집행위측에 UR 협상 평가보고서를 조속 제출할 것을 지시함

3. 당초 3.2-3 기간중 예정이었던 농업이사회는 3.4 까지 연장하여 개최할 것임. 동건 추보하겠음. 끝

통상국	차관	1차보	2차보	구주국	구주국	분석관	경기원	재무부
농수부	상공부							

(공사 정의용-국장)

0190

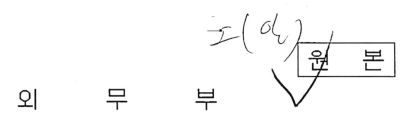

외 무 부

종 별 :

번 호 : ECW-0318   일 시 : 92 0306 1700

수 신 : 장관 (봉기,경기원,재무부,농림수산부,상공부), 권동만대사

발 신 : 주 EC 대사대리   사본: 주제네바대사-직송필,

제 목 : GATT/UR 협상

표제협상 관련한 최근 당지동향을 아래 보고함

1. EC 감축이행 계획서

가. 3.5 EC 집행위 관계관은 EC 는 DUNKEL타협안을 원안대로 수락할수 없다는 기본입장을 수차 천명한바 있으므로 최근 갓트에 제출한 농산물 보조등 감축이행 계획서는 EC의 감축이행 공약은 아니라고 밝힘

나. 동 관계관이 설명한 EC 의 감축이행계획서의 골자는 아래와 같음

1) 시장접근

0 관세상당치는 DUNKEL 타협안을 기초로 하지않고, EC 의 OFFER 를 기초로 하여산정했으며, 바나나는 동 이행계획서에서 제외하고 추후 제출키로 함 (제외이유등은 추후 별도보고)

0 현행 시장접근 (CURRENT MARKET ACCESS) 의 경우 92년도 수입을 기초로 하되,다만 수량제한이 적용되는 품목은 DUNKEL 협상안에 따라 86-88 평균치를 사용했음

2) 국내보조

0 CAP 개혁안에서 제시한 소득보조등이 협상에서 GREEN BOX 로 수락된다는 조건하에 국내보호감축계획은 DUNKEL 협상안에 의거 작성했음)

0 86-90 기간중에 보조를 받아 수출된 물량과 수출보조 금액을 제시했음

2. 회원국 동향

가. DUMAS 불란서 외무장관은 EC 의 농산물 감축이행 계획서는 EC 집행위안에불과 하며, 이사회가 공약한 것은 아니라고 말하고,불란서는 이사회에 다른 회원국들과 같이 명백히 유보의사를 밝힌바 있다고 말함

나. LATTANZIO 이태리 무역장관은 자국은 갓트협상 결과를 받아드릴수 <u>없는</u> 상황이

롱상국   2차보   구주국   외정실   분석관   경기원   재무부   농수부   상공부

발생될수 있다고 말하였으며, GORIA 농무장관은 3.3 이사회에서 검토된
감축이행계획서는 수락할수 없는 내용이었으며, 집행위는 부여된 권한을 초월하여
행사하고있다고 비난함

　　다. MOLLEMAN 독일 경제장관은 CAP개혁에 대한 합의없이 UR 협상의 합의는
불가능할 것이라고 말하고, 독일은 미국과 불란서간의 중재역할을 할 것이며,
UR협상문제는 농업각료 수준이 아닌 EC 정상들이 직접 결정하여야 할 것이라고 말함.
끝

　　(공사 정의용-국장)

우루과이 라운드 농산물 협상관련 국별 감축 약속 이행 계획표 제출에관한 일본 농림수산성 입장

===

1. 91.12.20 배포된 농산물 관련 최종협정문 초안 (던켈 paper)에 협상 참가국은 농산물 협상의 각 분야별 협상방식에 근거하여 감축 약속에 관한 계획표를 제출키로 되어있음.

2. 지금까지 일본은 1) 농산물 보조 및 보호의 삭감 방법으로 AMS 를 채택하며, 2) 기초 식량 및 갓트 11조 2항 Ci에 해당하는 수량 제한 품목은 관세화 해서는 아니됨 등을 협상의 기본 방침으로 해오고 있음.

3. 일본으로서 계속 협정문 초안의 수정을 요구해갈 생각이며 일본의 지금까지의 주장에 입각하여 하기 내용의 국별 감축 약속 이행계획표를 제출키로 함.

   가. 국내 보조관련 약속

   하기 품목에 대하여는 품목별 AMS를 표시함. 단, 밀, 보리 및 쌀등 3개 품목에 대하여는 곡물 섹터로하여 계상함.

   - 밀, 보리, 쌀 콩, 사탕, 우유 및 유제품, 소고기, 돼지고기, 닭고기, 야채 및 과일.

   나. 국경조치 관련 약속

   1) 관세화

   일본은 기초식량인 쌀 및 갓트 11조 2항 Ci 대상품목에 대해서는 관세화의 대상에서 제외해야 하며, 포괄적인 관세화 개념에 문제가 있다고 보며, 이들 품목에 대하여는 관세 상당치를 제시하지 않을것이며 이들 품목에 관한 감축율 등의 기재를 하지않음.

   한편, 86.9월 이후에 자유화를 결정한 품목에 대하여는 관세 상당치등을 제시함.

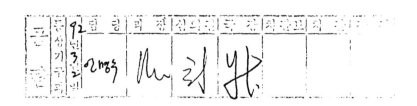

0193

2) 시장접근 약속

갓트 11조 2항 Ci 대상 품목에 대해서는 동조항의 요건을 명확하게 하는
견지에서 현행 시장접근 기회의 유지를 제시함.

3) 관세율 인하

농산물 협정문 초안에는 총관세의 평균 인하율이 36%로 되어 있어 수출보조
대상 수량의 삭감율과의 사이에 격차가 있음을 감안하여 하기 방침에 따라
관세율 인하를 행함. 그리고 상기 에도 불구하고 이와같은 관세 인하에
의해서도 아직 실행세율과 괴리가 있는 것에 대해서는 실행세율 까지의
인하를 행함.

가. 각 품목의 인하율에 대해서는 재작년 브랏셀 회의에서 일본이 제출한
offer상의 인하율 30%를 기본으로함.

나. 그렇지만 국내산업 보호를 위해 관세의 인하가 곤란한 품목에 대해서는
농업에 관한 합의문의 최저 삭감율을 참고로하여 인하율 15%로 함.

다. 단, 수입수량제한 품목에 밀접하게 관련된 품목, 할당관세 품목등
제도 관련 품목에 대해서는 인하율을 0으로 함. 이 경우 86년이후
자유화한 품목이면서 동시에 별도의 관세율에 관한 약속이 있는 품목에
대해서는 당해 관세율을 최종 세율로 함.

다. 수출 보조금에 관한 약속

일본은 기준 기간에 있어서 수출보조금의 공여를 행하고 있지않고 있으므로
삭감약속을 기입하지 않음.   끝.

0194

長官報告事項

報 告 畢

1992. 3. 9.
通 商 局
通 商 機 構 課(17)

題 目 : 我國의 UR 農産物 履行 計劃表 提出 方針

1. 3.9(月) UR 實務 對策委員會, 表題件 關聯 下記와 같이 暫定 決定

 (經企院 對調室長 主宰, 外務部 通商局 審議官 參席)

 가. 履行 計劃表의 內容

  o 15개 NTC 品目以外의 品目에 대해서는 具體的 減縮 約束(offer) 提示

  o 15개 NTC 品目中 쌀 以外의 品目에 대해서도 最小 및 現行 市場接近,

   總量 보조치를 提示하되 關稅 상당치(TE)만은 減縮 約束이 아닌 基礎

   資料로 提出 (이와관련 農林水産部는 關稅 상당치를 提示하는데 留保

   立場)

  o 쌀에 대해서는 基礎資料도 提出치 않음.

  o 全體的인 我國 立場을 cover note에 明示

   - 我國 履行 計劃表의 暫定的 性格, NTC 品目의 調整 可能性等

 나. 提出 時期

  o 3.16 제네바 代表部에 송부할 수 있도록 農林水産部가 作成

  o 제네바 代表部가 各國 動向을 考慮하여 提出 時期를 本部에 청훈한후

   갓트사무국에 提出

 다. 其 他

  o 農林水産部가 上記 事項을 農民團體 및 與黨에 대해 事前 說明

2. 言論 對策 : 제네바 代表部에서 履行 計劃書를 갓트사무국에 提出하는 싯점에

   맞추어 農林水産部가 報道資料 配布.   끝.

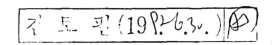

0195

長官報告事項

1992.　3.　9.
通　商　局
通商機構課(17)

題　目 : 我國의 UR 農産物 履行 計劃表 提出方針

3.9.(A)

1. UR 實務 對策委員會, ~~92.3.9(月) 經企院 對調室長 主幸로 開催되며~~ 表題件 關聯
   下記와 같이 決定 (경기원 대조실장 주제, 외무부 통상국 심의관 참석)

   가. 履行 計劃表의 內容

   o 15개 NTC 品目以外의 品目에 대해서는 ~~offer~~ 提示　　구체적 감축 약속 (offer)

   o 15개 NTC 品目中 쌀 以外의 品目에 대해서는 ~~基礎資料(關稅 상당치,~~
      最小 및 現行 市場接近, 總量 보조치)를 ~~別途로~~ 提出 (이와관련 農林水産部는
      關稅 상당치를 提示하는데 留保 立場 ~~表明~~)　　제시하되 관세 상당치(TE)만은
      　　　　　　　　　　　　　　　　　　　　　　　간축약속이 아닌 기초자료로

   o 쌀에 대해서는 基礎資料도 提出치 않음.

   o 全體的인 我國 立場을 cover note에 明示
      - 我國 履行 計劃表의 暫定的 性格, ~~15개~~ NTC 品目 調整 ~~豫定~~等
      　　　　　　　　　　　　　　　　　　　　　　안　　　　　가능성

   나. 提出 時期

   o 3.16 제네바 代表部에 송부할 수 있도록 農林水産部가 作成

   o 제네바 代表部가 各國 動向을 考慮하여 提出 時期를 本部에 청훈한후
      갓트사무국에 提出

   다. 其　他

   o 農林水産部가 上記 事項을 農民團體 및 與黨에 대해 ~~非公式으로~~ 事前 설명
      ~~briefing~~

      검 토 필 '1992.6.30.)

2. 言論 對策 : 제네바 代表部에서 履行 計劃書를 갓트사무국에 提出하는 싯점에
      맞추어 農林水産部가 報道資料 配布.　　　끝.

통 상 기 구 과	92 3 9	담 당	곡 장	심의관	국 장	차관보	차 관	장 관
		안병두						

0196

長 官 報 告 事 項

1992. 3. 9.
通　商　局
通 商 機 構 課 (15)

題 目 : 日本의 UR/農産物 履行 計劃書의 內容

1.　日本은 3.4 下記 要旨의 UR/農産物 履行 計劃書(cover note 包含)를 갓트事務局에
　　提出

　　가.　前提條件 : 餘他 協商 參加國들의 適切하고 형평에 맞는 감축 約束 履行이
　　　　前提되어야 함.

　　나.　關稅化 例外 認定 要求

　　　　○ Track 4를 통한 追加 協商이 必要하며, 특히 食糧安保 및 갓트 11조
　　　　　2항 C(i)을 關稅化에 대한 例外로 認定해야 함 (農産物 交易 歪曲의
　　　　　主原因인 輸出補助를 完全히 撤廢치 않으면서 例外없는 關稅化를 要求하고
　　　　　있는 農産物 協定案은 不合理)

　　다.　履行 計劃表 (country plan)의 主要內容

　　　　1) 市場接近 : 基礎食糧인 쌀 및 11조 2항 C(i) 品目에 대한 關稅 상당치
　　　　　및 減縮率을 공백으로 남겨둠.

　　　　2) 國內補助 : 곡물류, 콩, 설탕, 우유, 쇠고기, 돼지고기, 계급류, 달걀,
　　　　　야채 및 과일에 대해서는 品目別 총량 보조치(AMS) 提示

　　　　3) 輸出補助 : 없 음.

2.　國會 및 言論對策 : 別途 措置 不要.　　　　　끝.

공 람	92 년 3 월 9 일 무 역 위 과 장 인	담 당	과 장	심의관	국 장	차관보	차 관	장 관
		안명수						

0197

長官報告事項

題 目：日本의 UR/農産物 履行 計劃書의 內容

---

1. 日本은 3.4 下記 要旨의 UR/農産物 履行 計劃書(cover note 包含)를 갓트事務局에
    提出

    가. 前提條件 : 餘他 協商 參加國들의 適切하고 형평에 맞는 감축 約束 履行이
        前提되어야 함.

    나. 關稅化 例外 認定 要求

    ○ Track 4를 통한 追加 協商이 必要하며, 특히 食糧安保 및 갓트 11조
        2항C(i)을 關稅化에 대한 例外로 認定해야 함 (農産物 交易 歪曲의
        主原因인 輸出補助를 完全히 撤廢치 않으면서 例外없는 關稅化를 要求하고
        있는 農産物 協定案은 不合理)

    다. 履行 計劃表 (country plan)의 主要內容

    1) 市場接近 : 基礎食糧인 쌀 및 11조 2항 C(i) 品目에 대한 關稅 상당치
        및 減縮率을 공백으로 남겨둠.

    2) 國內補助 : 곡물류, 콩, 설탕, 우유, 쇠고기, 돼지고기, 계금류, 달걀,
        야채 및 과일에 대해서는 品目別 총량 보조치(AMS) 提示

    3) 輸出補助 : 없 음.

2. 國會 및 言論對策 : 別途 措置 不要.   끝.

0198

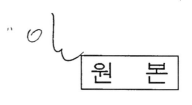

외 무 부

종 별 :

번 호 : ECW-0325   일 시 : 92 0309 1800

수 신 : 장 관 (봉기, 경기원, 재무부, 농림수산부, 상공부)

발 신 : 주 EC 대사대리 사본: 주제네바대사-직송필, 주 EC 권동만 대사

제 목 : EC/바나나 수입제도와 갓트/UR 협상

　　최근 EC 는 93.1. 시행예정인 시장통합및 갓트/UR 농산물협상 (관세화대상
포함여부)과 관련하여 EC 의 바나나 수입제도의 재정립방향에 대해 검토하고 있는바
동향은 아래와 같음

　　1. 문제제기 경위

　　가. EC 는 세계 제 2위의 바나나 수입국 (90 소비량-3.3백만톤) 이며, 회원국별로
수입제도를 달리하고 있음. 즉 독일은 수입제한이 없어 가격이 저렴한 중미지역
(DOLLAR ZONE) 산의 바나나를 주로 수입하고 있으나, 불란서, 스페인등은 LOME
협정에따라 ACP 국가에서 생산되는 바나나를 비교적 고가로 수입하고 있음

　　나. 따라서 93.1. EC 시장이 통합되어, 역내 바나나 유통이 자유로와 지고,
갓트/UR 농산물 협상결과에 따라 관세화및 점진적인 관세 인하원칙이 바나나에 적용될
경우, EC 회원국 해외영토 (예: 불령 GUADELOUP) 또는 ACP국가들의 주소득원인
바나나생산기반이 붕괴되어, 정치적.사회적 문제가 발생될 것을 우려하고 있음

　　2. EC 의 대책가. EC 집행위는 88년도에 바나나 대책그룹을 설치, EC 회원국, EC
및 ACP 의바나나 생산자 단체, 바나나 수입상및 중미국가들의 의견을 청취하여,
93년이후 제기될 문제와 갓트 관련사항의 처리대책을 검토하여 왔음

　　나. 동 그룹은 아래와 같은 대안을 마련하여 EC집행위에 회부한바, 집행위는 3.18
동 제안에 대해 부표로서 방향을 결정할 것임

　　1) EC 영토및 ACP 국산 바나나에 대하여는 자유로운 시장접근을 허용하고, DOLLAR
ZONE 바나나는 수입쿼타를 적용하되 상황변화에 따라동 수입쿼타를 증대할수
있는장치를 마련함

　　2) 매년 EC 바나나 소비량등 시장여건을 평가하여 공급원별로 수입허용량을 설정함

　　3) EC 영토및 ACP 국산 바나나 생산여건에 따라 바나나 수입상별로 수입허가 쿼타

통상국 　2차보 　　　　　　外정실 　분석관 　청와대 　안기부 　경기원 　재무부
농수부 　상공부

PAGE 1   92.03.10   07:03 DS

를 유지함

　3. 회원국및 ACP 국들의 최근동향

　가. 독일과 불란서, 영국, 스페인등 여타 회원국간 의견대립뿐 아니라 집행위내에서도 시장통합및 자유무역 추진을 희망하는 그룹과 바나나에 대한 예외인정이 필요하다는 상반된 의견이 표면화 되고 있음

　나. 특히 불란서는 바나나 관세화에 반대하고 회원국별 수입쿼타제를 유지하여 줄 것을 요청하고 있으며, 스페인, 폴투갈, 영국등이 이에 긍정적인 입장을 보이고 있음

　다. EC 및 ACP 바나나 생산자 연합 (EABP) 은 EC 가 바나나 문제에 대한 해결방안을 마련하기 전까지는 바나나는 관세화 대상에서 제외되어야 한다는 성명을 발표함

　라. 최근 CHARLES 도미니카 수상은 브랏셀과 제네바를 방문하여 바나나를 관세화대상에서 제외하여 줄것을 요청하면서 바나나가 관세화대상이 될 경우 세계 바나나시장은 미국계 다국적기업들의 독과점 상태에 처하게 될 것이라고 말함

　4. 상기 문제점을 감안하여, EC 는 갓트에 제출한 농산물 감축이행 계획서에서바나나를 제외한바 있는바 동건은 향후 갓트/UR 농산물협상 결과에도 영향을 미칠 것으로 전망됨. 3.18 EC 집행 위 결정내용등 계속파악 보고하겠음. 끝

　(공사 정의용-국장)

이씨의 공동 농업정책 (CAP) 개혁동향

1. EC 농업 이사회 (3.2-4)

   - 3.2-4간 개최된 이씨 농업 이사회는 의장의 CAP 개혁안을 검토함.

   - 동 이사회시 영국, 덴마크, 화란이 UR 협상 종료 이전에 CAP 개혁 내용을
     확정 하는데에 반대함에 따라 차기 이사회 (3.30-31)시 재론키로함.
     (영국, 덴마크, 화란은 91.11 이씨 집행위원회의 CAP 개혁안의 대체적인 내용을
     원칙적으로 수락한 바 있음.

2. 의장안 주요내용

   가. 기본방향

   의장안은 지지 가격을 대폭 인하하고 소득보조 제도를 도입하는 것을 골자로
   하고 있음 (이에대해 영국. 벨지움, 화란, 이태리가 반대입장)

   나. 분야별 주요내용

   1) 곡 물

   o CAP 개혁안중 곡물 분야가 핵심적인 요소인바, 의장안은 3년동안
     지지가격을 30% (당초 35%) 인하하고 소득 손실보상액을 톤당 45ECU로
     조정
     (이에 대해 대부분 회원국들이 가격인하율이 너무 높다는 점 지적)

   2) 축 산 물

   o 쇠고기 가격 하락시 시장개입 요건을 시장 가격이 개입 가격의
     " 75% 이하 " 로 부터 "55% 이하 " 로 떨어지는 경우로 변경
     (이에 대해 대부분 회원국들이 개입가격 인하율이 너무 높다고 지적)

   o 수출용 쇠고기 비축 한도를 93-97간 단계적으로 80만 톤에서 30만
     톤으로 감축

0201

○ 방목지 면적당 소사육 두수 한도를 hectare당 2마리로 제한

○ 소의 두당 생산보상금을 3년간 분할 지급하는 대신 특정 1년내에 두당 120ECU만 지급

3) 우 유

○ 생산쿼타를 4% 감축하고 가격을 10% 인하하되 생산쿼타 감축분중 1%에 해당하는 부분에 대해서는 회원국이 감축 여부를 결정

3. CAP 개혁과 UR 협상과의 관계

- 지난 1월에 개최된 이씨 농업이사회는 UR 협상과 관련없이 CAP에 개혁 논의를 계속키로 결정한바 있으나 영국, 덴마크, 화란등이 UR 협상이 종료되기 이전에 CAP 개혁내용을 확정하는데 강한 반대 의견을 표명함으로써 금번 농업이사회에서도 CAP 개혁에 대한 논의가 활발하게 이루어지지 않음.

- 동 문제는 차기 이사회 (3.30-31)시 재론키로 하였으나, UR 협상에서 합의가 이루어지기 전에 EC회원국간에 CAP 개혁에 대한 실질적인 결론이 도출되기 어려울 것으로 예상됨

4. 이씨 집행위의 입장

이씨 집행위는 92/93 농산물 가격 Package에 대해 3.31 이전에 합의가 이루어져야 하며, UR 협상을 CAP 개혁과 별개로 추진해야 UR 협상에 탄력적으로 대처할수 있다는 고려에서 농업이사회의 조속한 CAP 개혁 문제 해결을 희망.   끝.

0202

주 제 네 바 대 표 부

제네(경) 20644-260   1992. 3. 6.

수신 : 외무부장관

참조 : 통상국장, 농림수산부장관

제목 : UR/농산물 C/S 송부

EC 및 일본의 농산물 C/S를 별첨 송부합니다.

첨부 : UR/농산물 C/S (EC 및 일본) 각 1부.   끝.

주 제 네 바 대

접수일시 1992. 3. 10

14218

0203

COMMISSION
OF THE EUROPEAN
COMMUNITIES

Geneva, 4/3/92

Permanent Delegation to the
International Organizations in Geneva

The Head of Delegation

i43

Dear Chairman,

In pursuance of paragraph 21 of Part B of the text on agriculture of the Draft Final Act, I herewith transmit the draft lists of commitments (schedules) of the European Community, together with supporting tables, for the establishment of final schedules. The submission is without prejudice to the position of the Community on the Draft Final Act.

Any final commitment on the draft schedules is dependant upon final agreement on the Draft Final Act and the schedules submitted in pursuance of it. Therefore, the Community reserves the right to modify the draft schedules if the course of the negotiations makes those modifications necessary in order to achieve a balanced result.

The draft schedules do not indicate to what extent the Community will take reduction commitments in the three areas of the negotiations, as this remains to be negotiated.

In this context, the Community recalls that it has proposed a lesser rate of reduction for a number of products which in the past have not created major problems of surplus production. The Community maintains this position.

On bananas, the Community will communicate its position at a later stage.

Supporting table 4 is being submitted on the assumption that an agreement can be reached on the Final Act by which

- per hectare and headage payments will not be subject to a commitment of reductions if they are linked to measures to limit production and

- payments for set-aside will not be subject to a reduction commitment.

./.

Mr Arthur DUNKEL
Director-General GATT
Chairman of the TNC (Official Level)
Centre William Rappard
Rue de Lausanne, 154
1211 GENEVA

0204

Address: Post Box 195, 37-39, rue de Vermont, CH - 1211 GENEVA 20
Tel: 734 97 50   - Fax: 734 22 36   - Telex: 414165 and 414186 ECO CH

522   우루과이라운드 농산물 협상 4

Of course, the precise definition of per hectare and headage payments which will not be subject to reduction commitments remains to be determined.

On export competition, the Community has not included the volume of sugar corresponding to its imports of sugar from ACP countries. The Community will not take commitments on this part of its sugar exports.

Furthermore, in table 7, the break-down of products is without prejudice to a possible regrouping for reduction commitments.

Finally, the base rates of duty in table 1 and any reductions of these rates will be applied in Spain and Portugal without prejudice to the temporary mandatory measures resulting from the Accession Treaties to the EC.

I would like to ask you to distribute this letter together with the draft schedules to the participants of the Uruguay Round.

Trân Van-Thinh
Ambassadeur-Représentant Permanent auprès du GATT

0205

이씨의 UR/농산물 관련 기초자료 제출

1. 이씨는 3.4 농산물에 대한 기초자료를 갓트사무국에 제출 (공산품에 대한 이행 계획서는 협상이 진행중임을 이유로 추후 제시 예정)

2. 이씨는 동 기초자료에 관세 상당치, 보조총량을 표시 하였으나, 구체적인 감축 약속은 제시치 않음.

3. 주 제네바 이씨 대표부는 상기 기초자료에 대한 cover note에서 하기 사항 지적

   가. 기초자료 제출이 최종의정서안에 대한 이씨의 입장에 영향을 미치지 않음.

   나. 균형된 결과 도출을 위해 필요한 경우 수정할 권리를 유보함.

   다. 금번에 제출하는 기초자료가 이씨의 감축의무의 정도를 표시하는 것은 아님.

   라. 기 타
      ○ 바나나에 대한 입장은 추후 통고 예정
      ○ 국내보조 관련 기초자료는 하기사항에 대한 합의가 이루어진다는 전제로 작성
        - 단위면적 및 두당 직접보조는 생산 감축 조치와 연계된 경우 감축 의무 대상에서 제외
        - 휴경 보조는 감축 의무 대상에서 제외.   끝.

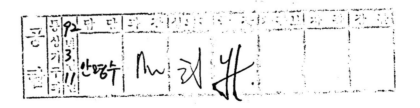

0206

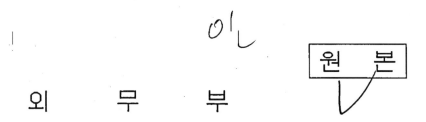

외 무 부

종 별 :

번 호 : USW-1221　　　　　　　　　일 시 : 92 0311 1123

수 신 : 장 관 (통기,통이,농림수산부) 사본: 주미대사

발 신 : 주 미 대사대리

제 목 : DUNKEL TEXT 에 대한 미국 농업(품목별) 영향분석

　1. UR/ 농산물 협상과 관련하여 지난해 12.20.DUNKEL TEXT 가 발표된 이래 미 의회의 요구에 따라 미 농무부는 최근 별첨 FAX 와 같이 DUNKEL TEXT가 미국 농업에 미치는 영향을 품목별로 분석제시하였음.

　2. 동 PAPER 의 주요 골자는 UR 협상이 성공적으로 종결되어 1993년 부터 발효된다는 가정하에서 1998년에는 미국의 농산물 총수출이 40-50억불 증가하고 농가 총수익도 약 50억불 (정부지불 감소, 생산비 증가등 감안시 순수익은 10억불수준)이 증가될 것으로 보았으며 품목별로는 땅콩, 낙농제품, 돼지공기등 일부 품목을 제외하고는 밀, 옥수수등 사료곡물, 육류제품과 과채류등에서 농가 소득이 증가되는 것으로 분석하였음.

　첨부: USW(F)-1408(21 매).끝.

　(대사대리 김봉규-국장)

통상국　　미주국　　통상국　　농수부

김 (안색어느 협의,
토약 브레이?범)
✓

주 미 대 사 관

USW(F) : 1408   년월일 : 92. 3. 11   시간 :

수 신 : 장 관 (통, 동, 농림수산부)

발 신 : 주미대사

제 목 : Dunkel Text에 대한 미 농업(통요부) 영향분석 (출처 :   )

(총 21매)

배부처	경기보고실	장관보고실	그그보실	국기실	그그실	국장	그주국	그주국	경아기국	국제국	경제국	민상국	민감국	영과국	총무과	감시관	공과관	기언원	경회대	동기신	동기부	경기기	성공부	농수부
											10											1

(1408   1   )

0208

PRELIMINARY ANALYSIS OF THE ECONOMIC IMPLICATIONS
OF THE DUNKEL TEXT FOR AMERICAN AGRICULTURE

Office of Economics
United States Department of Agriculture
March 1992

The Uruguay Round of Multilateral Trade Negotiations, under the auspices of the General Agreement on Tariffs and Trade (GATT), has been underway for more than 5 years. After proposals from many countries, including the United States, a Draft Agreement was released at the end of 1991.

The Director General of the GATT, Mr. Arthur Dunkel, released the text of a proposed agreement for the Uruguay Round before Christmas. [1] This report analyzes the economic implications of the Uruguay Round for U.S. agriculture based on this so-called Dunkel Text. Potential economic effects are estimated for major agricultural commodities and for aggregate U.S. farm product exports and farm income.

The potential effects of a GATT agreement on U.S. agriculture are estimated using economic models and analysts' judgements. [2] Because countries can adjust policies in several ways to meet GATT commitments, this analysis must also be based on judgements about how specific policies would evolve in the United States and elsewhere.

The economic effects are measured against the President's budget baseline extended to marketing year 1998. The effects would continue past 1998, but this date is used as a convenient point for an assessment. The baseline reflects a continuation of current trends and likely policy and technical developments, excluding trade reform. If the Uruguay Round fails, however, world agricultural trade will likely become more protectionist, causing world markets and prices to deteriorate from baseline levels. Therefore, the estimates of the benefits from a successful Uruguay Round presented below are likely understated.

---

[1] Uruguay Round Draft Final Act, Text on Agriculture, GATT Secretariat, Geneva, December 20, 1991.

[2] For details on the analytical approach and other background information, see Economic Implications of the Uruguay Round for U.S. Agriculture, Office of Economics, United States Department of Agriculture, May 1991.

USW(5) - 1408-21-2

KEY FEATURES OF THE DUNKEL TEXT

The Draft Final Act is over 400 pages long and deals with essentially all international trade. The agricultural part is itself a long and complex document. Here we highlight key features that were particularly important for our quantitative assessment.

- The value of export subsidies is reduced by 36 percent and the quantity of subsidized exports is reduced by 24 percent.

    -- The annual average over the period 1986-1990 is used as a base for the reductions.

    -- Reductions are on a commodity by commodity basis.

    -- In this analysis, the quantity discipline is key.

- All non-tariff import barriers are converted to bound tariffs.

    -- Domestic and world market prices over the 1986-1988 period are used to calculate the tariff equivalents.

    -- This tariffication will likely result in high levels of initial tariff equivalents so that little increased imports over the new tariff walls are anticipated for these products.

- All tariffs (continuing and newly created) are reduced by an average of 36 percent.

    -- For simplicity, we use the 36 percent cut for all tariff lines in this analysis.

- For all commodities with non-tariff barriers in all countries, a minimum import access of 3 percent of domestic consumption is required. In addition, access must be maintained equal to that of the 1986-88 base period for all products that had non-tariff barriers.

1408 - 3

• Internal production subsidies must be reduced by 20
percent as measured by an Aggregate Measure of Support
(AMS).

-- This reduction is calculated from a 1986-88 base but
credit is provided for subsidy cuts since 1986.

-- Only trade-distorting support is included in the
subsidy cuts.

-- No reduction is required if support is less than 5
percent of the value of output for a commodity or
for the sum of sector-wide programs.

The Dunkel Text also includes many caveats and safeguards that are
too numerous to list here. For more details, readers are referred
to the Text itself.

0211

AGGREGATE EFFECTS

The most important summary measures of broad effects on American
agriculture are exports and farm income. If started in 1993 and
completely implemented by 1998, the Dunkel Text would result in
higher U.S. exports and farm income in 1998 compared to baseline
levels.

A summary of the export effects are listed in the Table 1 below.
Added exports in grains account for about half of the total $4 to
$5 billion in export expansion over the 6-year period.

TABLE 1. PROJECTED U.S. AGRICULTURAL EXPORTS IN 1998--DUNKEL
          TEXT [1]

Commodity	Change from baseline in 1998
	Bil. $
Grains	2.40-2.80
Cotton	0.30-0.40
Meat	0.40-0.50
Poultry and eggs	0.10-0.15
Tobacco	0.30-0.40
Fruits and tree nuts	0.30-0.50
Vegetables & greenhouse/nursery	0.20-0.30
Total [2]	4.00-5.00

[1] Valued at point of export.
[2] Additional imports of about $600 million--dairy products, fruits
and vegetables, peanuts, etc. are also likely.

0212

O

Farm income gains are made up of several items. The increase in
cash receipts is about $5 billion. However, lower government
outlays and higher production costs caused by expanded output and
higher prices mean that with no re-orientation in farm programs,
net cash farm income goes up by about $1 billion.

TABLE 2. PROJECTED CASH FARM INCOME IN 1998--DUNKEL TEXT

Item	Change from baseline in 1998
	Bil. $
Market receipts	+4.6 to +5.2
Government payments 1/	-2.6 to -2.7
Cash production expenses 2/	+1.2 to +1.3
Net farm income with no reallocation of payment savings to agriculture	+0.8 to +1.2

1/ Due mainly to higher crop prices.
2/ Due to increased planted acreage and higher input prices, etc.

DOMESTIC SUPPORT POLICIES

For most U.S. commodities, no changes would be required to meet
internal support cuts of 20 percent by 1998. Policy changes
authorized by the 1985 and 1990 Farm Bills and budget legislation
have already reduced support substantially for most commodities.
The principal exceptions are peanuts, sugar, and wool (see Table
3).

COMMODITY ANALYSIS

The remainder of this report reviews the outcome on a commodity by
commodity basis. Readers should recognize that these projections
are based on the standard assumptions used in economic baseline
projections such as normal weather and other market conditions.
Deviations from these trends would certainly be expected in any
given year. Therefore these projections are not forecasts of
specific outcomes for 1998.

1408-6

0213

TABLE 3. UNITED STATES AGGREGATE MEASURES OF SUPPORT (AMSs): 1966-88 BASE PERIOD AND 1991

YEAR [1/]	1986-88 [2/]	1991E
		(Mil $) (Percent)
WHEAT		
AMS	4,073	2,004
% CHANGE FROM BASE PERIOD	NA	-51
CORN		
AMS	7,838	3,095
% CHANGE FROM BASE PERIOD	NA	-61
SORGHUM		
AMS	957	303
% CHANGE FROM BASE PERIOD	NA	-68
BARLEY		
AMS	336	134
% CHANGE FROM BASE PERIOD	NA	-60
COTTON		
AMS	2,348	1,184
% CHANGE FROM BASE PERIOD	NA	-50
RICE		
AMS	980	648
% CHANGE FROM BASE PERIOD	NA	-34
SOYBEANS [3/]		
AMS	248	-19
% CHANGE FROM BASE PERIOD	NA	-108
OATS [3/]		
AMS	21	11
% CHANGE FROM BASE PERIOD	NA	-48
RYE [3/]		
AMS	1	0
% CHANGE FROM BASE PERIOD	NA	-100
TOBACCO [3/]		
AMS	45	-5
% CHANGE FROM BASE PERIOD	NA	-111
SUGAR		
AMS	1,047	1,098
% CHANGE FROM BASE PERIOD	NA	5
PEANUTS		
AMS	347	405
% CHANGE FROM BASE PERIOD	NA	17
HONEY		
AMS	55	15
% CHANGE FROM BASE PERIOD	NA	-72
WOOL		
AMS	73	83
% CHANGE FROM BASE PERIOD	NA	14
MOHAIR		
AMS	46	33
% CHANGE FROM BASE PERIOD	NA	-28
DAIRY		
AMS	5,766	4,116
% CHANGE FROM BASE PERIOD	NA	-29
BEEF [3/]		
AMS	375	0
% CHANGE FROM BASE PERIOD	NA	-100

[1/] The year used is the appropriate crop year or fiscal year for each commodity or policy. [2/] 1986-88 base period adjusted for credit to 1986. [3/] Not subject to reduction because support is less than 5 percent of the value of production.

(408-5)

0214

O

WHEAT

The United States would benefit from expanded export opportunities for wheat that would lead to larger exports and higher prices. The major factor affecting the world wheat market through 1998 would be a reduction in subsidized wheat exports.

The United States would be in a good position to improve its world market share which now stands at about ⃝31 percent. Other efficient exporters would also increase their foreign sales. Reductions in U.S. export subsidies would likely have little effect on U.S. exports as other countries also reduce subsidies. By 1998, U.S. wheat exports are projected to rise 10-12 percent above baseline levels.

This boost in exports would raise farm prices by 17-19 percent and production would increase 1-3 percent. Wheat producers' gross income from wheat production would increase 3-4 percent, with market receipts rising and deficiency payments falling because of higher prices. Because the U.S. wheat program was adjusted between 1986 and 1990 and again by the 1990 Farm Bill and budget legislation, no additional program changes would be required to meet the cut in internal support.

WHEAT SECTOR EFFECTS--DUNKEL TEXT

Item	1998 Projections	Percentage change from baseline in 1998
		Percent
Farm price ($/bu)	3.40 - 3.45	17 - 19
Target price ($/bu)	4.00	0
Production (bil. bu)	2.78 - 2.82	1 - 3
Domestic use (bil. bu)	1.20 - 1.19	-5 to -6
Exports (bil. bu)	1.57 - 1.60	10 - 12
Producer revenue (bil. $):		
Market receipts	9.45 - 9.60	19 - 21
Government payments 1/	1.10 - 1.02	-52 to -56
Total	10.55 - 10.62	3 - 4

1/ The government payment figures reflect a reduction in deficiency payments based on higher market prices.

0215

O

FEED GRAINS

The United States would benefit from increased demand for U.S. feed grain exports and higher prices. Changes in world feed grain markets would result mainly from reduced subsidized feed grain exports, increased market access opportunities, and increased world feed use to meet growing global animal product consumption.

The United States could readily meet additional world feed grain import demand. Other exporters would also benefit from higher feed grain prices. By 1998, U.S. corn exports are projected to rise 5-6 percent above the baseline level.

Larger exports would raise farm prices by 4-6 percent and production would increase a little. Domestic feed use would decline slightly but higher livestock and poultry prices would generally offset increased feed costs. Corn producers' gross income would increase 1-2 percent with corn market receipts rising more than the decline in government payments for corn. The same general results hold for grain sorghum and barley.

Because the U.S. feed grains program was adjusted between 1986 and 1990 and again by the 1990 Farm Bill and budget legislation, no additional program changes would be required to meet the internal support commitment.

CORN SECTOR EFFECTS--DUNKEL TEXT

Item	1998 Projections	Percentage change from baseline in 1998
		Percent
Farm price ($/bu)	2.45 - 2.50	4 - 6
Target price ($/bu)	2.75	0
Production (bil. bu)	9.25 - 9.34	0 - 1
Domestic use (bil. bu)	7.17 - 7.07	0 to -1
Exports (bil. bu)	2.18 - 2.20	5 - 6
Producer revenue (bil. $):		
Market receipts	22.66 - 23.00	4 - 6
Government payments [1]	1.34 - 1.20	-40 to -45
Total	24.0 - 24.2	1 - 2

[1] The government payment figures reflect a reduction in deficiency payments based on higher market prices.

1408-9

O

BARLEY SECTOR EFFECTS--DUNKEL TEXT

Item	1998 Projections	Percentage change from baseline in 1998
		Percent
Farm price ($/bu)	2.20 - 2.25	2 - 5
Target price ($/bu)	2.36	0
Production (bil. bu)	0.520 - 0.535	0 - 3
Domestic use (bil. bu)	0.430 - 0.425	0 to -1
Exports (bil. bu)	0.093 - 0.097	3 - 8
Producer revenue (bil. $):		
Market receipts	1.15 - 1.20	2 - 8
Government payments 1/	0.070 - 0.047	-30 to -49
Total	1.22 - 1.25	1 - 3

1/ The government payment figures reflect a reduction in deficiency payments based on higher market prices.

GRAIN SORGHUM SECTOR EFFECTS--DUNKEL TEXT

Item	1998 Projections	Percentage change from baseline in 1998
		Percent
Farm price ($/bu)	2.20 - 2.30	3 - 6
Target price ($/bu)	2.36	0
Production (bil. bu)	0.740 - 0.755	0 - 2
Domestic use (bil. bu)	0.465 - 0.455	0 to -2
Exports (bil. bu)	0.250 - 0.255	4 - 6
Producer revenue (bil. $):		
Market receipts	1.63 - 1.74	3 - 8
Government payments 1/	0.22 - 0.14	-18 to -43
Total	1.85 - 1.88	0 - 2

1/ The government payment figures reflect a reduction in deficiency payments based on higher market prices.

1408-A

O

RICE

The United States alone, among major rice producers, would have the technical- and resource capability to meet a large part of the additional demand for japonica rice that would result from increased market access. World demand for rice would increase, particularly for japonica rice (medium-grain) in East Asian countries. The demand for indica rice (long-grain) would also rise in East Asia, the EC, and Latin America. World prices for japonica would increase more than for indica.

U.S. rice exports in 1998 would be. up 9-12 percent, compared with baseline levels. Japonica-like rice exports will rise and domestic indica rice will be devoted more to the domestic market. The U.S. prices for japonica-like rice would increase as would indica prices. Overall, the average U.S. farm price for rice in 1998 would rise 14-17 percent compared to baseline levels. Rice producers' total revenues would be up 3-4 percent. Because the rice program was changed by 1985 and 1990 legislation, no additional policy adjustments would be necessary to meet the GATT commitment.

RICE SECTOR EFFECTS--DUNKEL TEXT

Item	1998 Projections	Percentage change from baseline in 1998
		Percent
Farm price ($/cwt)	8.80 - 9.00	14 - 17
Target price ($/cwt)	10.71	0
Production (mil. cwt)	172 - 174	1 - 2
Domestic use (mil. cwt)	112 - 110	-2 to -4
Exports (mil. cwt)	64 - 66	9 - 12
Producer revenue (bil. $):		
Market receipts	1.51 - 1.57	15 - 19
Government payments 1/	0.33 - 0.29	-36 to -44
Total	1.84 - 1.86	3 - 4

1/ The government payment figures reflect a reduction in deficiency payments and marketing loans based on higher market prices.

1408-70

0218

O

COTTON

World cotton trade would be affected by several factors. Global textile use would increase due to economic growth stimulated by an overall GATT agreement and by increased market access to textiles. Foreign cotton production would likely fall due to cuts in internal support and some shift of acreage from cotton to grain because of higher grain prices.

With a GATT agreement, U.S. cotton exports are projected to rise by 7-9 percent by 1998, compared with the baseline.

Reform of textile and apparel trade policies is expected to leave U.S. cotton mill use slightly below the level projected under a continuation of current policies. A GATT textile agreement would allow further reductions in trade barriers, with a modest increase in U.S. cotton textile imports. Stronger income growth under overall trade reform would raise cotton textile consumption in the United States and worldwide. Income growth abroad and improved market access in foreign markets for U.S. cotton textiles would lead to a projected slight increase in U.S. cotton textile exports.

Total use of U.S. cotton is projected to increase. No significant increase in U.S. cotton imports is projected as a result of the tariffication of import quotas. Larger U.S. cotton exports are projected to increase farm prices by 4-6 percent by 1998. Production would rise by 1-3 percent. With higher prices and increased production, producers' gross income would be 2-3 percent larger. No additional changes would be needed in the cotton program because of program changes under 1985 and 1990 legislation.

COTTON SECTOR EFFECTS--DUNKEL TEXT

Item	1998 Projections	Percentage change from baseline in 1998
		Percent
Farm price ($/lb)	1/	4 - 6
Target price ($/lb)	0.729	0
Production (mil. bales)	18.0 - 18.4	1 - 3
Domestic use (mil. bales)	10.3 - 10.1	-1 to -3
Exports (mil. bales)	8.0 - 8.2	7 - 9
Producer revenue (bil. $):		
Market receipts	6.3 - 6.4	5 - 7
Government payments 2/	0.34 - 0.29	-35 to -45
Total	6.64 - 6.69	2 - 3

1/ USDA is prohibited from publishing cotton price projections.
2/ The government payment figures reflect a reduction in deficiency payments based on higher market prices.

1408-12

0219

'92-03-12 02:07

O

OILSEEDS

Oilseeds have little support and protection in the United States or other exporting countries. A major exception is the European Community where high support prices have stimulated production, leading to a displacement of imports. A GATT panel found the EC oilseed regime to be inconsistent with its GATT commitments. However, this analysis does not include EC program changes that would occur as a consequence of the GATT panel rather than of the Uruguay Round.

U.S. oilseed policies would likely be little affected by a Uruguay Round agreement itself. Imports are subject to generally low tariffs while exports of soybeans and meal are made without subsidies. The U.S. vegetable oil exports receive assistance under the Export Enhancement Program and other programs. Reductions in U.S. export subsidies would likely have little effect on the U.S. industry as other countries also reduce subsidies. Support for soybeans is less than 5 percent of the value of production and therefore not subject to reduction under the Dunkel Text. However, marketing loans for soybeans and minor oilseeds authorized by the 1990 Farm Bill would be subject to cuts if outlays exceeded 5 percent of the value of production.

Overall, a GATT agreement would have small effects on U.S. oilseeds. A slight price increase is projected as protein meal and vegetable oil demand increase due to higher global incomes and livestock product consumption. U.S. oilseed price also will be influenced by higher prices for grains and cotton.

SOYBEAN SECTOR EFFECTS--DUNKEL TEXT

Item	1998 Projections	Percentage change from baseline in 1998
		Percent
Farm price ($/bu)	6.07	1
Production (bil. bu)	2.08	*
Domestic use (bil. bu)	1.37	*
Exports (bil. bu)	0.72	*
Producer revenues (bil. $)	12.63	1

* Less than 1 percent.

(40-13

0220

O

PEANUTS

The United States is in a position to take advantage of any
enhanced export opportunities under a GATT agreement. The United
States produces peanuts that generally sell at a premium to other
peanuts.

Internal support commitments could be met in several ways. A
reduction could be made in the quota loan rate, the marketing
quota or some combination of these two mechanisms. Alternatively,
assessments or other policy measures could be introduced. One
option is a reduction in the loan rate by 1998 to $0.26 to $0.27
per pound, with the marketing quota adjusted only to account for
additional imports.

Imports under the minimum access provision would rise to about 156
million pounds by 1998, but no other imports would be likely
because the tariff level would be high enough to maintain an
advantage for U.S. peanuts.

The main effect of reform would be a reduction in the value of
peanut marketing quotas. Under the above option, peanut prices and
production would decline 4-6 percent from 1998 baseline levels.
Production costs would decline because of lower seed costs (about
25 percent of variable cash expenses) and declining quota rents for
producers. Producer revenues would decline 8-14 percent from
baseline levels.

PEANUT SECTOR EFFECTS [IN SHELL]--DUNKEL TEXT [1]

Item	1998 Projections	Percentage change from baseline in 1998
		percent
Farm price ($/lb)	0.315 - 0.308	-4 to -6
Loan rate ($/lb)	0.270 - 0.260	-28 to -32
Production (bil. lbs)	4.61 - 4.53	-4 to -6
Domestic use (bil. lbs)	3.76 - 3.68	-4 to -6
Exports (bil. lbs)	0.935 - 0.952	5 - 7
Imports (bil. lbs)	0.156	[2]
Producer revenue (bil. $)	1.45 - 1.40	-8 to -14

[1] Commitments under the Dunkel Text could be met with several
different changes to the peanut program. These projections reflect
one option.
[2] 0.002 billion pounds of imports in baseline.

(4:8-14

TOBACCO

The United States is the world's largest exporter and importer of tobacco. Under a GATT agreement, the United States would expand exports of U.S. leaf and cigarettes containing U.S. leaf. These export opportunities will occur for several reasons: reduced export subsidies, cuts in production subsidies, conversion of non-tariff barriers to tariffs, and lower tariffs. In addition, higher income growth means increased tobacco consumption in many countries as well as a shift to higher quality tobacco products, either U.S. cigarettes or cigarettes using U.S. leaf. Overall exports of leaf, including that contained in cigarettes, are projected to increase by 14-16 percent by 1998 under reform.

The United States tobacco policies would face no substantial change under a GATT agreement. The domestic tobacco program would not have to be modified because support is less than 5 percent of the value of production and expected to decline. Most imported tobacco enters the United States at low tariff levels amounting to 10 percent of the import value or less for most products. Moreover, most tobacco tariff collections are refunded through the duty drawback program that allows firms duty credit when they reexport tobacco and tobacco products.

Higher U.S. leaf exports would result in slightly higher farm prices and higher tobacco production. Producer revenues would increase by 5-9 percent.

TOBACCO SECTOR EFFECTS--DUNKEL TEXT

Item	1998 Projections	Percentage change from baseline in 1998
Farm price ($/lb)	1.96 - 1.98	1 - 2
Production (bil. lbs)	1.56 - 1.60	4 - 7
Consumption (bil. lbs)	0.94 - 0.96	0
Exports (bil. lbs)	0.63 - 0.66	14 - 16
Imports (bil. lbs)	0.192 - 0.198	0
Producer revenue (bil. $)	3.0 - 3.2	5 - 9

O

SUGAR

Nearly all national governments intervene in sugar markets,
including the United States. A GATT agreement would make sugar
production and consumption more responsive to market forces,
causing world prices to increase.

The United States could meet the internal support commitment by
reducing the loan rate for raw sugar. Depending on production
levels, the loan rate for cane sugar would have to be cut from the
current $0.18/lb to $0.155-$0.165/lb by 1998 with a similar
reduction in the beet sugar loan rate. Access to the U.S. market
would be determined annually. Imports beyond the level permitted
at low tariffs would be subject to an initial tariff of $0.16/lb.

A GATT agreement and domestic sugar policy used in this analysis
would result in imports, domestic prices, and production that are
similar to the levels expected under the baseline. While the sugar
loan rate would be reduced 8-14 percent from baseline levels by
1998, imports would be the key factor affecting domestic prices and
production. A more expansive import policy would be a matter of
domestic policy choice not a GATT requirement.

SUGAR SECTOR EFFECTS--DUNKEL TEXT [1]

Item	1998 Projections	Percentage change from baseline in 1998
		Percent
Domestic price ($/lb) [2]	0.2256	0
Loan rate ($/lb)	0.1580	-10
Production (mil. st)	7.97	0
Domestic use (mil. st)	9.72	0
Imports (mil. st)	1.74	0
Producer revenue (bil. $)	2.16	0

[1] Commitments under the Dunkel Text could be met with little effect
on U.S. sugar prices and production as compared to the baseline.
[2] Number 14.

$1408 - 16$

0223

The strong growth in U.S. exports of fruits, tree nuts, and wine has been due in large part to the opening of markets and reductions of tariff and non-tariff barriers. A GATT agreement will open up additional export opportunities for U.S. producers. Overall, U.S. fruit and tree nut exports would increase by 4-7 percent, adding $310-$480 million to export values by 1998. Because of the variety of commodities in this category and the importance of export growth, the summary table below focuses only on exports.

New markets, particularly for apples, pears, nuts, and grapefruit, will open in many developing countries that have been closed by import bans or severely restrictive licensing arrangements. In the already important markets of Japan, Taiwan, and Korea, U.S. fresh oranges, table grapes, wine, and other products will encounter reduced tariffs. Tariff barriers for most fruits will be reduced in Korea and Taiwan as well as much of Latin America.

Reduction in U.S. import protection would have mixed effects. Tariff reductions for many products with already low tariffs are unlikely to have much effect on trade. For some U.S. products such as frozen orange juice concentrate, lower tariffs would lead to lower domestic prices. Income growth and import increases in Asia and Europe will raise world prices and help to offset U.S. tariff reductions for frozen orange juice concentrate. U.S. exports of high quality juice will increase.

The GATT disciplines on sanitary and phytosanitary measures would benefit U.S. exports of fruits and tree nuts by preventing the use of unjustified import barriers under the guise of food safety or plant and animal health. Imports into the United States would continue to meet all standards applicable to U.S. domestic production.

FRUITS AND TREE NUTS EXPORTS--DUNKEL TEXT [1]

Item	1998 projected export revenues change from baseline	
	Mil. $	Percent
Grapes, fresh	10 - 20	5
Apples	30 - 60	15
Other fruits	140 - 220	12
Wine	20 - 30	8
Fresh oranges	30 - 60	15
Orange juice concentrate	5 - 10	6
Other citrus	10 - 20	4
Almonds	30 - 50	5
Other tree nuts	12 - 20	5
Total[2]	310 - 480	4 - 7

[1] Tariff cuts of 36% for every tariff line.
[2] Total is not a simple sum of the components to reflect across category adjustments.

(408-79)

VEGETABLES AND NURSERY AND GREENHOUSE PRODUCTS

The strong growth in U.S. exports of vegetables and nursery and greenhouse products has been due in large part to the opening of markets and reductions of tariff and non-tariff barriers. A GATT agreement would create additional export opportunities. The U.S. vegetable, greenhouse, and nursery product exports would increase by 5-7 percent in 1998. Because of the variety of commodities in this category and the importance of export growth, the summary table below focuses only on exports.

Reduction in U.S. import protection would have mixed effects in vegetable markets. Tariffs for many fresh vegetables are already low or zero, and tariff reductions are unlikely to have much effect on trade. Major competitors in Central America and the Caribbean already have access to the U.S. markets for fresh vegetables and many greenhouse and nursery products through the Caribbean Basin Initiative and the General System of Preferences. For other U.S. products such as frozen broccoli, cauliflower, and canned tomato products, lower tariffs would lead to lower prices. Mexico could increase its share of the U.S. market for some fresh vegetables.

The GATT disciplines on sanitary and phytosanitary measures also would benefit U.S. exports of vegetables by preventing the use of unjustified import barriers under the guise of food safety or plant and animal health. Imports into United States would continue to meet all standards applicable to U.S. domestic production.

VEGETABLES, GREENHOUSE & NURSERY PRODUCTS EXPORTS--DUNKEL TEXT [1]

Item	1998 projected export revenues change from baseline	
	Mil. $	Percent
Dried beans, peas, lentils	30 - 60	10
Potatoes, inc. products	10 - 20	5
Tomatoes, inc. products	5 - 13	9
Other vegetables	140 - 170	6
Total vegetables	180 - 240	5 - 7
Greenhouse and nursery	20 - 30	5 - 7
Total[2]	200 - 270	5 - 7

[1] Tariff cuts of 36% for every tariff line.
[2] Total is not a simple sum of the components to reflect across category adjustments.

(444-18   0225

○

MILK

Reform of world dairy trade would lead to <u>an increase in world prices for dairy products</u>. By 1998, world dairy product prices are projected to increase 10-15 percent compared with prices if current global trends were to continue.

U.S. quotas on dairy product imports would be converted to tariffs. Because the tariffs would be relatively high, imports would occur only under the access provisions. By 1998 the access commitments would be the equivalent of an additional 2.6 billion pounds (milk equivalent, fat basis).

U.S. dairy policy would probably not have to be changed to meet internal support commitments by 1998. Support prices have been reduced since the base period and other actions have resulted in additional credits for policy changes.

The key factor affecting U.S. dairy prices and production by 1998 would be additional imports of dairy products under the access provisions. The effect on milk prices and production, however, would be small compared to baseline levels. Government purchases would increase moderately.

DAIRY SECTOR EFFECTS--DUNKEL TEXT

Item	1998 Projection	Percentage change from baseline in 1998
		Percent
All milk price ($/cwt)	13.00 - 12.75	0 to -2
Support price ($/cwt)	10.10	0
Production (bil. lbs)	162 - 160	0 to -1
Domestic use (bil. lbs)	157	*
Exports (bil. lbs ME)	2.0	0
Imports (bil. lbs ME)	5.2	100
Producer revenue (bil. $)	21.0 - 20.4	0 to -3

* Less than 1 percent.
ME: Milk equivalent, milk fat basis.

(斗부-1張)

O

POULTRY AND EGGS

A GATT agreement will lead to increased broiler and egg trade. Trade would be boosted by increased market access in developed and rapidly growing countries by the late-1990s, while income growth would spur longer-term demand in developing countries. Reductions in subsidized EC exports of broilers and eggs would also create trade opportunities for U.S. and other exporters.

Domestic producers would benefit from larger exports that would offset lower domestic use, and higher prices would partially offset higher grain prices. Overall, U.S. poultry and egg production by 1998 would be down a little from baseline levels.

POULTRY AND EGGS EFFECTS--DUNKEL TEXT

Item	1998 Projection	Percentage change from baseline in 1998
		Percent
Poultry		
Production (mil. tons)	13.70 - 13.66	-2 to -3
Consumption (mil. tons)	13.07 - 13.03	-2 to -3
Exports (mil. tons)	0.62 - 0.66	2 - 9
Imports (mil. tons)	NA	NA
Price ($/lb.) [1]	0.58 - 0.62	2 - 8
Value of production (bil. $)[2]	19.10 - 19.5	0 - 3
Eggs		
Production (bil.)	70.2 - 69.5	0 to -1
Consumption (bil.)	69.3 - 68.6	0 - -1
Exports (bil.)	1.3 - 1.4	8 - 12
Imports (bil.)	0.1	0 - 1
Price ($/doz) [3]	0.79	0 - 1
Value of production (bil. $)[2]	5.6 - 5.7	0 - 3

[1] 12 city broiler price. [2] Valued at wholesale. [3] New York wholesale.

SHEEP AND WOOL

Government policies affecting U.S. sheep and angora goat producers are support payments for wool and mohair, tariffs on some wool, lamb, and mutton products, and import quotas on mutton. The principal effect of trade reform would be a reduction in wool payments. The support price for wool would have to be reduced about 15 percent from the current level or wool production eligible for support could be reduced by about 30 percent. Mohair support is already below the cut required by the Dunkel Text.

/   (४ ॱ५-२ ⊘

O

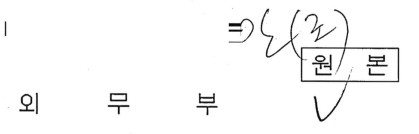

외 무 부

종 별 :

번 호 : ECW-0345
일 시 : 92 0311 1900

수 신 : 장 관(봉기,경기원,재무부,농림수산부,상공부,기정동문)

발 신 : 주 EC대사대리(권동만) 사본:주미,주제네바대사(중계요망)

제 목 : 갓트/UR 협상

연: ECW-0307

표제 관련한 최근의 미.EC 양자협상 동향등을 아래 보고함

1. NATO/NACC 회의참석차 당지방문중인 BAKER 미 국무장관은 3.10 DELORS EC 집행위원장을 만나 UR 농산물협상과 관련한 미측의 새로운 입장을 전달한 것으로 알려짐. 한편, 상기제안과 관련 금 3.11 당지에서 미.EC 고위급협상이 개최되었는 바, 동협의내용은 상금 파악되지 않고 있음 (미.EC 양측은 동 협의 진전사항에 관해 당분간 보안 유지키로 한 것으로 보도되고 있음)

2. 이와관련, 당지 전문가들은 최근 BUSH대통령이 DELORS 위원장에게 보낸 서한에서 농산물 보조감축 문제에 대해 미국은 탄력성있는 입장을 취한다는 입장을 전달한바 있음을 상기시키면서, 금번 고위협상에서 미측은 EC가 CAP 개혁의 일환으로 시행코자 하는 직접소득보조를 감축대상 보조에서 제외하는 방법을 제시한 것으로 추정하고 있으며 그 구체적 방법으로 EC의 직접 소득보조를 GREEN BOX 에 포함하는 것이 아니라 BLUE BOX를 새로이 설정하고 이의 정확한 개념 및 운영방법을 협의할 것으로 보고 있음. 그러나 REBALANCING 문제에 대해서는 미측의 입장이 변경된바 없는 것으로 보임.

3. ANDRIESSEN 집행위원은 3.11 미측의 새로운 제안내용을 신중히 검토한후 자신의 입장을 밝힐수 있을 것이라는 반응을 보였으며, MACSHARRY 집행위원은 CAP 개혁안에 제시된 소득보조가 감축대상에서 제외될수 있는 제안이라면 이를 환영한다고 말함. 끝

(공사 정의용-국장)

| 통상국 | 안기부 | 경기원 | 재무부 | 농수부 | 상공부 | 2차42 | 구국중 | |

관리 번호	92-203

외 무 부

종 별 :

번 호 : ECW-0357   일 시 : 92 0312 1900

수 신 : 장관 (통기, 경기원, 재무부, 농림수산부, 상공부, 기정동문)

발 신 : 주 EC 대사대리   사본:주미, 제네바대사(중계필), 주EC대사(봉삼경유)

제 목 : 갓트/UR 협상

연: ECW-0345

표제협상 관련 당지동향을 아래 보고함

1. 3.11. 개최된 미.EC 양자협상 결과와 관련 EC 집행위의 관계관들은 미측이 새로운 입장을 제시함으로서 대통령선거 이전이라도 UR 협상 추진하겠다는 의지를 보여주었다는 점을 평가하면서도, 국내 보조분야 이외에 물량기준한 수출보조 감축, REBALANCING 및 PEACE CLAUSE 문제에대한 새로운 입장이 제시되지 않은것에 대해 실망을 표시하고 있음. 이와관련 당관이 접촉한 대부분의 EC 관계관들은 미. EC 간 UR 관련 주요 현안가운데 아직 한가지도 합의된 것이 없음을 지적, 4 월중순 시한까지의 UR 협상 타결전망에 대해 부정적인 견해를 보이고 있음

2. 한편 DELORS 위원장은 금 3.12 BUSH 대통령의 서한에 대한 답신을 보낸 것으로 알려졌으며, 동 답신에서 양측간의 농산물 현안사항에 대한 EC 측의 입장이 전달된 것으로 전망되고 있어 내주 개최예정인 미.EC 양자협상 결과가 주목되고 있음. 끝

(공사 정의용-국장)

예고: 92.6.30 까지

통상국	장관	차관	1차보	2차보	통상국	분석관	청와대	안기부
경기원	재무부	농수부	상공부	중계				

PAGE 1

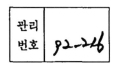

외　무　부

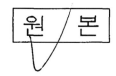

종　별 :

번　호 : GVW-0600　　　　　　　　　　일　시 : 92 0318 1830,,

수　신 : 장관(통기,경기원,재무부,농림수산부,상공부)

발　신 : 주　제네바 대사대리

제　목 : UR 농산물 협상 최근 동향

　　표제 협상 관련 당관이 파악한 최근 동향을 하기 보고함.

　　1. 미.이씨 협의

　- 3.19-20 기간중 워싱턴에서 양국간 차관급 협의가 개최될 예정이고, 3.20콜 독일수상 방미시 부시 대통령과 UR 협상에 관한 협의가 있을 것으로 알려짐.

　　0 동 정상회담시 콜 수상은 미국이 곡물 대용품(콘글루텐, 타피오카, 시트러스 펠렛등)의 이씨에 대한 수출을 현 수준으로 동결할 경우, 이씨는 수출 보조물량 감축을 수용하는 타협안을 제시할 것으로 관측(F.T 지 3.18 자 보도)

　　2. 시장접근 협상 동향

　- 3.19(목) 15:00 시장적븐 그룹 비공식 회의 개최 예정

　- 3.23(월) 12:00 이씨 요청으로 아국 및 인도, 파키스탄등이 참여하는 다자협의 예정

　- 3.23 주간중 G-8 회의 개최 예상(기 제출된 농산물 C/S 평가 회의전망)

　- 3.25(수) 15:00 미국 요청으로 한. 미간 농산물 분야 양자 협의 예정

　　(미측은 슈퇴터 FAS 처장보가 수석 대표)

　　0 미측 요청에 대해 아측은 동 양자 협의는 아국이 농산물 분야 C/S 를 동일까지 제출할 경우 응할수 있을 것이라고 답변해 두었음.

　　3. 주요국의 C/S 제출 동향

　- 노르웨이는 3.19-20 중 제출 예정임. 농산물 분야는 이씨와 같이 기초 자료만 제출하고 생산통제 품목(일부 유제품)은 TE 를 제시핳 않을 것으로 알려짐.

　- 멕시코는 금주중 제출 예정인바, 민감품목(옥수수, 닭고기, 계란, 설탕, 콩, 일부 유제품)에 대한 TE 는 제시하지 않을 것으로 알려짐.

　- 이스라엘은 아직 작성이 완료되지 않은 상태이며, 생산통제 품목(닭고기)은 TE

통상국 상공부	장관	차관	2차보	분석관	안기부	경기원	재무부	농수부

PAGE 1　　　　　　　　　　　　　　　　　　　　　　92.03.19　05:42

　　　　　　　　　　　　　　　　　　　　　　　　외신 2과　통제관 FM

0230

를 제시하지 않을 계획으로 알려짐.(3 월말경 제출을 목표로 추진중) 끝

(차석대사 김삼훈-국장)

예고 92.6.30 까지

관리번호 ~A-222   외 무 부   원 본

종 별 :

번 호 : GVW-0614   일 시 : 92 0319 1900

수 신 : 장 관 (봉기,경기원,재무부,농림수산부,상공부)

발 신 : 주 제네바 대사

제 목 : UR 농산물 (한,미 양자 협의)

대: WGV-0428

대호 관련 당관 최농무관이 당지 USTR 의 BYLENGER 농무관을 접촉한 결과 하기 보고함.

1. 미측이 요청한 한, 미 양자 협의 관련 현재 농산물 분야 C/S 를 작성중에 있으나 3.25 까지 가스에 제출할 가능성은 높지 않다고 하고 이러한 경우 의미있는 양자 협의가 어려울 것이므로 아국의 농산물 분야 C/S 제출 이후에 동 양자 협의를 갖는 것이 좋겠다고 하였음.

- 동인은 이에 대하여 긍정적으로 답변하였음.

2. 미측대표단은 3.23(월) 부터 개최되는 G-8 평가회의에 참석하는데 주목적이 있다고 하며, 현재로서는 여타국과의 양자 협의 계획이 정해진바는 없다함.

- G-8 회의 진행중 시간사정 여하에 따라 여타국과의 협의를 추진할 것임. 서자

- 동 미측 대표단은 내주말까지 당지 체재 여정이나 경우에 따라서는 월말이후 까지 있을 계획이라고 함. 끝

(대사 박수길-국장)

예고: 92.6.30 까지

통상국   장관   차관   1차보   2차보   분석관   청와대   안기부   경기원
재무부   농수부   상공부

PAGE 1   92.03.20   18:44
                                                   외신 2과 통제관 DV

0232

550 우루과이라운드 농산물 협상 4

관리
번호 *92-219*

분류번호	보존기간

발 신 전 보

WGV-0428   920319 1909 CJ

번   호 : _____   종별 : **지급**

수   신 : 주   제네바   대사. 총영사/

발   신 : 장   관 (통 기)

제   목 : UR 농산물 한.미 양자협의

대 : GVW-0600

　　대호 미측의 양자협의 요청과 관련 참고코자하니, 미측이 아국이외에 일본, EFTA

국가등과도 양자협의를 요청 하였는지 여부 및 3.25 경에는 농산물 양자협의가 본격으로

개시될 것인지 등을 파악, 보고바람.　　끝.

　　　관련동향을

　　　　　　　　　　　　　　　　　　　　　　(통상국장 김 용 규)

에 의거 재분류 (92.6.30.) 지 ✗ 성명 이재희		보 안 통 제	〰

앙고재	92년 3월 19일	통상국 기 통상기획과 안명수	기안자 성명	과 장 〰	심의관	국 장 전결	차 관	장 관 〰	외신과통제

0233

외　무　부

증　별 :

번　호 : ECW-0387   일　시 : 92 0319 1700

수　신 : 장관 (통상, 정보, 통기) 경기원, 농림수산부)

발　신 : 주 EC 대사대리 사본: EC주재국대사, 주제네바, 직송필

제　목 : EC의 92/93 농산물 가격안(자료응신 제 92-15)

．3． 18 EC 집행위는 92/93 시장년도 의농산물가격안을 확정하여 농업이사회에제출하였는바 요지 아래 보고함

1. 가격안

가． 91.92년도에 적용하던 지지가격, 과잉생산에대한 공동책임 부과금, 생산및 가격안정장치에 대한 협정, 즉 BUDGET-STABILIZER 등을유지함

나． 올리브유, 면화, 엽연초및 토마토 가공품에대하여는 CAP 개혁안과 현행규정을연결시키는 잠정조치 (예, 엽연초의 경우 품종별로생산쿼타량을 조정등) 를 실시할수 있도록 함

다． 따라서 금반 EC 집행위의 가격수준과 가격안정장치 관련 협정을 고수한다는방침이 농업이사회 (3.30-31, 개최) 에서 확정될 경우 지난해에는 CEREAL 의 경우 MGQ (즉 최대가격보장량) 160백만본을 초과한 169백만본이 생산(동독지역을 포함할 경우 180백만본) 된 것으로집계되었기 때문에, 92/93년도의 CEREAL가격은 전년대비 3프로 자동인하될 뿐만 아니라 공동책임부과금 (CO-RESPONSIBILITY LEVY) 도지난해 부과되었던 5프로 이외에 3프로를 추가납부하게 되어, CEREAL 의 농민수취가격은전년대비 6프로가 순수하게 감소되며, 기존의공동책임 부고금까지 포함될 경우 개입가격 대비11프로 적제 받게됨

2. 92/93 농산물가격안 제안배경 (요약)

가． 92/93 농산물 가격 지지예산은 89년 대비 43프로가증가된 350억 ECU 가 소요될 전망임 (91/92-330억 ECU)

나． 주요농산물 수급추정

ㅇ CEREALS: 수요는 계속 감소되고 있으나, 91년도의생산량이 89년보다 6백만본이증가한180백만본에 달해 자급도는 130프로 (91수출량-33백만본) 이며,

| 통상국 | 2차보 | 통상국 | 외정실 | 경기원 | 농수부 | 본과관 |

금년말 재고량은25백만본이 될것으로 전망됨

　　0 MILK:　84년부터　시행하고　있는　생산쿼타제에불구하고　우유생산량은　계속
증가하여,　91 자급도는125프로 이며,　버터및 탈지분유의 재고량은700천본이나 재고량
처분전망은 매우 불투명함

　　0 쇠고기:　소비는　감소추세이나　91생산은　89대비10프로가　증가되어　1백만본의
수출에도 불구하고,91년말 재고량은 800천본임

　　0 양고기: 91 생산과 소비량은 89대비 공히 16프로증가함

　　3. MAC SHARRY 집행위원은 표제가격안 발표후가진 기자회견에서 EC 농산물
시장상황이 매우악화되었음에도 불구하고 가격수준 등을 동결한것은 농업이사회에서는
CAP개혁과 갓트/UR협상 문제를 집중 논의함으로서 적절한시한내에 합의가 도출되기를
희망하기 때문이라고설명함. 끝

　　(공사 정의용-국장)

PAGE 2

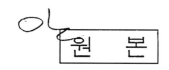

외 무 부

종 별 :

번 호 : ECW-0388   일 시 : 92 0319 1730

수 신 : 장관 (통기, 경기원, 재무부, 농림수산부, 상공부)

발 신 : 주 EC 대사대리   사본: 주제네바대사(직송필)

제 목 : 갓트/UR 협상과 EC/바나나 수입제도

연: ECW-0325

1. EC 집행위 대변인은 당초 3.18 EC집행위원회는 바나나의 관세화 수용등 EC바나나 수입제도의 재설정 문제를 결정할 예정이었으나, 집행위원간의 의견조정,관계단체 들의 의견수렴 필요성을 감안하여, 3.25까지 연기하였다고 발표함

2. 이와 관련, 최근 유럽의회는 EC 해외영토와ACP 국들의 바나나 생산기반과 농가소득을보호하기 위해 현행 바나나 수입제도, 즉 ACP바나나의 무관세 수입과 달라 바나나 수입에대한쿼타및 관세부과를 유지하는 한편, 바나나는갓트/UR 협상의 관세화대상에서 제외할것을 요구하는 결의문을 채택함

3. 한편, 유럽 바나나 수입상들은 DELORS위원장에게 보낸 서한에서 영,불,스페인등의수입제한 정책을 비난하고 소비자보호,라틴아메리카의 취약한 경제구조및 EC 시장통합기본정신 등을 고려하여 달라 바나나에 대한수입 제한을 철폐하여 줄것을 요청 함. 끝

(공사 정의용-국장)

통상국   2차보   경기원   재무부   농수부   상공부

PAGE 1   92.03.20   22:44 FE

외신 1과 통제관

0236

외 무 부

종 별 :

번 호 : FRW-0579   일 시 : 92 0320 1630

수 신 : 장 관(통기,통삼)

발 신 : 주 불 대사

제 목 : 미-EC간 농산물 논쟁

1. 91.12월 미측의 제소로 EC의 식용유작물(콩,해바라기등)생산
농민(40만명)에대한보조금 지급 정책의 위법 여부를 심의한 GATT PANEL 은 최근 미측의
제소가 이유있다는 결정을 내리고 EC측 에게 대미 보상 또는 보조금삭감을 제안
하였는바, 금번결정 은 EC 공동농업 정책 개혁 및 UR 의 조기 타결을 더욱 어렵게
만들것으로 전망되고 있음.

2. EC 는오는 3.30 브라셀 관계 장관 회의에서 상기결정에 대한 불복입장을
공식화하는 한편 이를계기로 세계 무역 중재자로서의 GATT 역할강화론에 대한 반대를
강화 할것으로 보임.

3.이와 관련 주재국 언론은 GATT 가 UR협상을 위요한 미-EC 간 갈 등을
더욱심화시키고 있다고 지적하고, EC 의 GATT PANEL판결불복시 미국의 무역 보 복
조치를 초래할가능성을 우려하면서도 GATT 와 미 불공정무역법간 냉혹한 연대로부터
EC 가 벗어나야 하며이를 위해 역내 결속과 정치적 용기를 강조함.

4.금번 미-EC 간 갈등은 금주말 미-독 정상회담을 통해 미국의 곡물 대체
산품의수출 동결과 EC의 수출 물량 감축등 상호양보를 통해 교착상태의 UR 을
타개코자 하는 KOHL 독일 총리의 교섭 전망을 어둡게 할것으로 우려됨.

(대사 노영찬- 국장)

통상국   2차보   구주국   통상국

PAGE 1

외 무 부

종 별 :

번 호 : ECW-0405   일 시 : 92 0323 1900

수 신 : 장 관 (봉기, 경기원, 농수산부, 상공부)

발 신 : 주 EC 대사 사본: 주미, 제네바대사(중계요망)-중계필

제 목 : BUSH-KOHL 회담

KOHL 독일수상이 연호 BUSH 대통령과 미국에서 가진 회담을 마치고 귀국하여 가진기자회견 내용을 아래 보고함

1. 미.EC 는 교착상태에 빠진 UR 협상을 4월말까지 마감한다는데 원칙적인 의견의 일치를 보았으나 주요 핵심문제에 대한 타협에는 상당한 견해차이가 상존함

2. 미국이 요구하고 있는 농산물 보조금 감축, 특히 물량기준 감축과 관련 가장큰 저항을 보이고 있는 불란서로 하여금 양보하도록 압력을 가하는 문제와 관련, 이는 불란서 정치의 속성상 아주 위험한 일임

3. 금번 회담에서 아래 3가지 분야에서 진전을 보임

가. EC 측의 소맥수출 감축

나. EC 에로의 저가의 대체곡물 수입제한

다. EC 의 농가소득 보조계획 보장

4. 현싯점에서 양측간에 UR 협상의 성공을 위하여 가장 필요한 것은 타협 (COMPROMISE) 이며 타협이란 양측 모두의 양보 (CONCESSION) 를 의미하는바, 문제는 어느측도 양보없이 타협만을 모색하고 있는 것임. 현재로서 협상의 성공을 보장할수없으며 아직도 협상은 진행중이므로 비관론에 빠질 필요는 없음

5. 자신이 의장을 맡게될 7월 뷘헨 정상회담전까지 UR 협상이 타결되지 않을 경우, 동 정상회담에서 타결을 기대하는 것은 현실적으로 불가능 할 것인바 그 이전에협상타결을 위하여 미.EC 양측의 정치적 의지를 가지고 최선을 다해야 할것임. 금주중 주요 회원국 정상및 DELORS 집행위원장과 미국방문 결과및 향후대책을 협의할 것임. 끝

(대사 권동만-국장)

통상국   경기원   농수부   상공부   외신1과   장관

92.03.24   05:09 DS

외신 1과 통제관

0238

관리 번호	JU-23P

외 무 부

종 별 :

번 호 : USW-1450   일 시 : 92 0323 1610

수 신 : 장관(봉기,봉이,경기원,상공부,농수산부)사본:주제네바,EC대사-중계필

발 신 : 주 미 대사

제 목 : UR/농산물 협상동향

1992.12. 지 예스에서
의기 일반문서로 재분류됨

1. 당관 이영래농무관은 3.24 GRUEFF 미농무부 해외 농업 다자협력과장과 면담, 미.독일 정상회담 및 미-EC 고위 실무협의 결과등을 문의한바 동결과 및 당지언론 보도등을 종합한 UR 농산물 협상 관련 동향을 하기 보고함.

가. 미-독일 정상회담 결과

0 3.21-22 CAMP DAVID 에서 개최된 BUSH 대통령과 KOHL 독일 수상간의 UR 관련 협상은 현재 교착상태에 빠져있는 UR 농산물 협상에 아무런 돌파구를 찾지못한것으로 알려지고있음.

0 특히 KOHL 수상은 기자회견에서 미국과 EC 간 합의 도출을 위하여는 양자가 공히 움직여야한다고 강조하면서 금번 정상 회담의 결과를 EC 지도자들에게 알리겠다고 하고 다시 한번 협상을 모색해야할것이라고 말하면서 금년 7 월 독일MINICH 개최되는 G-7 정상회담에서도 GATT/UR 협상이 주요의제가 될것것 같다고함.

0 GRUEFF 과장은 KOHL 수상이 제의할 것으로 알려진 CORN GLUTEN FEED 의 대 EC 수출 동결과 수출보조의 물량기준 감축과의 연계는 미측으로서는 받아들일수없는 사항인 REBALANCING 과 동일한 효과를 가져오므로 당초부터 양국정상회담결과를 크게 기대하지는 않았다고 말하면서 DUNKEL TEXT 에서 제시된 수출보조의 물량기준 24 프로 감축은 미측으로서도 고수해야할 최소한의 수준이라고 강좋아였으.

나. 미-EC 고위 실무 협의 결과

0 3.19-20 워싱본에서 개최된 미-EC 간 고위 실무협의회에서는 종전과 같이미측에서 KATZ USTR 부대표, CROWDER 노무부 차관과 JOE OMARA, ZOELICK 국무차관등이 참석하고 EC 측에서 LEGRAS 농업총국장 및 PEAMEN 대외담당 부총국장등이 참석하여 협의를 진행하였다고함.0 GRUEFF 과장은 금번에 CAP REFORM 의 GREEN BOX 문제에 집중적인 협의가있었다고 하면서 그동안 미측에서 SET ASIDE 20

통상국	장관	차관	1차보	2차보	통상국	분석관	청와대	안기부
경기원	농수부	상공부	중계					

PAGE 1

검 토 필 (1996.3.)

92.03.24 07:38
외신 2과 통제관 BX

0239

프로 부여등 여러조건을 붙여 SAFE BOX(BLUE BOX)를 제시해왔으나 EC 측에서 미측조건들에 대하여 새로운 제안을 하지 않으므로 합의도출에 어려움이 많다고 하면서 CAP REFORM 에서 직접소득 보상의 GREEN BOX 인정문제는 앞으로 미.EC 상호간에 조건드을 합의하면 인정될수있을것이라고 말함.(REBALANCING 문제는 MACSHARRY EC 농업담당 집해위원이 크게 강조하지 않고있다고함).

2. 앞으로의 계획과 전망

O GRUEFF 과장은 현재 제네바에서 COUNTRY PLAN 의 기술적인 사항에 대하여양자협상이 진행주이라고 하면서 우리측도 COUNTRY PLAN 을 국회의원 선거후에조속히 제출해줄것을 요청하였음.

O 동인은 또한 앞으로의 UR 협상타결은 전적으로 EC 측 특히 불란서와 독일등의 입장에 달려있다고 하면서 EC 내부의 합의도출을 강조하고 미측으로서는 DUNKEL TEXT 를 계속 지지한다고 하면서 4 월중 UR 협상의 성공으 불투명한상태(CARLA HILLS 도 3.17 의회증언에서 UR 의 성공적인 협상을 OPTIMISTIC 이아니고 HOPEFUL 로 표현)라고 전망하면서도 미.EC 간 정치적인 협상은 4 월에도 계속될것이라고 말함. 끝

(대사 현홍주-국장)

예고문: 92.12.31 까지

관리번호	RL-240

외 무 부

종 별 :

번 호 : USW-1473   일 시 : 92 0323 2034

수 신 : 장관(통기,통이,경기원,농수산부,상공부,),사본:주제네바,

발 신 : 주미대사   EC대사(중계필)

제 목 : UR 협상 동향

대 WUS-1286

1. 당관 장기호참사관은 3.23 USTR 의 SUSAN EARLY 대표보를 면담, 3.21-22 간의 미.독 정상회담 결과등 최근 UR 협상동향에 대해 문의한바 결과 하기 보고함(김중근 서기관 배석)

1. BUSH-KOHL 회담결과와 관련, 동대표보는 본인으로서는 언론에 보도된 내용 이외에는 아는바가 없다고 언급하면서 양국정상이 기자회견에서 4 월중순까지 UR 타결전망을 낙관 한다고 발표한것은 정상회담을 장식하는 수사학적인 의미 정도일 것이라는 반응을 보였음.

2. 콜수상이 금번 회담에서 '미국이 대 EC 대체곡물 (CEREAL SUBSTITUTE) 수출을 동결한다는 조건으로 EC 측이 수출물량 감축을 받아들이겠다'는 제안을 하였는가 하는 장참사관의 질문에 대해 동대표보는 콜수상이 이를 제안 하였는지의 여부는 알수없으니 이러한 제안은 REBALANCING 과 동일한 효과를 가져오므로미국으로서는 결코 받아들일수 없는 제안이라고 일축하였음.

3. 국내보조문제와 관련동인은 미측이 기간 및 감축폭에 조건을 붙여 보조금 지급을 허용하는 SAFE BOX(BLUE BOX)를 제시한데 대해, EC 측이 아직도 구체적대안을 제시하지 않고 있는등 미.EC 간 교섭에서 '볼'은 EC 측에 넘어가 있다고 강조하였음.

4. 향후 UR 타결전망에 관한 동대표보의 개인적 의견을 문의한데대해 동인은 최근 EC 와의 협상에 진전이 없어 비관적인 의견이 대두될수도 있겠으나 미.EC 고위층에서 아직도 UR 의 성공적인 타결을 기대하고있으므로 자신으로서는 아직 희망을 버리지 않고있다 하였음.

또한 UR 협상이 타결될 경우에도 의회 동의를 위해서는 최소한 11 개월이 소요되므로 EAST TRACK 만료일의 93.6.30 인점을 감안할때 4 월말까지 협상이

통상국 안기부	장관 경기원	차관 농수부	1차보 상공부	2차보 중계	경제국	통상국	분석관	청와대

PAGE 1   92.03.24   13:15

외신 2과 통제관 BZ

검 토 필 (19 . .)

0241

타결되어야만 의회동의가 가능하리라 보여진다고 전망하였음. (의회의 심의에는 행정부와 의회의 비공식 협의기간 90 일 (CALENDAR DAYS)과 UR 협정과 관련 법안에 대한 심의기간 60 JAULUKUV (LEGISLATIVE DAYS)이 소요되는 바 금년의경우 선거준비를 위한 조기 회기종료 (10.2. 예정)및 하계휴회를 감안하면 60 일 회기일은 실제로 약 8 개월에 해당될 것이라함).

5. 또한 동대표보는 농산물 협상과 관련 일본을 포함 현재 28 개국이 COUNTRY PLAN 을 제출하였다고 설명하고 한국도 조속히 COUNTRY PLAN 을 제시하여 줄것을 요청하였음.

이에 대해 장참사관은 한국의 농업여건을 감안할때 아직 미.EC 간에 기본적인 문제도 타결되지 않은 시점에서 한국이 협상을 주도해 나갈 입장이 되지 않으며 미.EC 협상의 진전을 보아 대응해 나갈것이라고 하고 UR 협상의 성공적인 타결을 기대한다고 언급하였음. 끝

(대사 현홍주-국장)

예고:92.12.31 까지

대 한 민 국
외 무 부

92 -   1992. 3. 23.

아래 문건을 수신자에게 전달하여 주시기 바랍니다.

제 목 : UR / 농산물 C/S cover note

수 신 : 농림수산부 국제협력과 (배종하 사무관님)

(FAX NO : 503-7249, 7247)

발 신 : 외무부 통상기구과

(총 7 매)

1. Korea has prepared the attached Lists of commitments on the basis of the relevant provisions of the draft Text on Agriculture and, for certain aspects where Korea's position is not consistent with the provisions, in line with its standing position in the agricultural negotiations.

2. These Lists are presented not in their final form, since the draft Text on Agriculture does not provide an agreed guideline for reduction commitments.

3. Korea takes the view that the draft Text failed to balance the interests of net agricultural importing and exporting countries. Accordingly, the draft Text should be modified through negotiations under the Track 4 which have yet to be activated and Korea's view on the draft Text on Agriculture is attached.

4. In line with this position, Korea submits the attached Lists with the understanding that further improvements would be achieved in the draft Text through the Track 4 negotiation. At the same time, Korea reaffirms its statement made at the 15 January 1991 TNC meeting that Korea will table a more flexible offer depending upon further developments in the agricultural negotiations.

5. The outlines of Korea's Lists of commitments are as follows :

   a. Market Access

      - 1988-1990 are taken as the base period in the belief that it would be reasonable to take the most recent years and the most recent data available in calculating reduction commitments.

      - Because of its serious difficulties with the idea of comprehensive tariffication with regard to basic foodstuffs and other items covered by the GATT Article XI. 2(c), specific commitments are not provided for a certain number of products.

/   0244

- In determining the level of reduction commitments and the minimum market access, the element of special and differential treatment was incorporated.

- For certain number of products that have been liberalized since 1986, the base rates are bound at ceiling level rather than that applied in September 1986.

- For the products subject to tariffication, current market access is guaranteed at the annual average level over the period 1988-1990.

b. Domestic support

- 1989-1991, the most recent years for which statistics are available, are used as base period for the same reasons stated above under market access.

- While reduction commitments on barley, soybean, corn and rapeseed are provided, other products are exempt from these commitments since the AMS for these products and non-product specific AMS are well below 10% of total value of production.

c. Export competition

- As Korea does not maintain export subsidy programmes which fall under the reduction commitments as defined in Article 9 of Part A of the draft Text on Agriculture, no schedule of reduction commitments on export competition is provided.

0245

Korea's view on the draft Text on Agriculture

1. Comprehensive Tariffication

- Korea continues to have serious difficulties with regard to the idea of comprehensive tariffication because it tends to ignore the specific characteristics of agriculture in the individual food importing countries and further fails to safeguard the fragile agricultural production base against collapse. Since export subsidies practiced by certain countries are widely recognized as the major factor distorting agricultural trade, it is less than fair that the draft Text has put unjustifiably strong commitments in the area of market access by prescribing comprehensive tariffication.

- For this reason, it is Korea's considered view that a carefully defined exception from tariffication for the basic foodstuffs vital for food security should be established. In addition, products subject to production controls under the Article XI : 2(c) of the General Agreement should not be tariffied.

2. Special and Differential Treatment

- In line with the basic guideline of S & D treatment, and in consideration of the disadvantageous situation in which developing countries find themselves, minimum access opportunities should be set at 2%, two thirds of that specified in paragraph 5 of Part B of the draft Text.

3

0246

3. Base Period

- Despite the fact that under the Mid-term Agreement the commitment on standstill of domestic support and market access did not apply to the less developed countries, using 1986-1988 as the base period for the calculation of commitments in the market access and domestic support would in fact impose greater burden on the less developed countries than on the developed ones.

- Therefore, in the case of less developed countries, it would be more reasonable to take as the base period the most recent year for which statistical data are available.

4. Current and Minimum Market Access

- Korea believes that current market access should be maintained at the average annual level of imports over the base period. The increase of current maket access should not be obligatory, but subject to negotiations among interested parties.

- In the first year of implementation, minimum access opportunities should be set at 2% for developing countries, in line with the special and differential treatment applying two thirds of that specified in paragraph 5, part B of the draft Text.

- Korea has serious difficulties in permitting the minimum market access to all products across the board.

5. Binding of Ordinary Customs Duties and Tariff Equivalents

- The draft Text provides that all ordinary customs duties and tariff equivalents should be bound. Due to the special characteristics of agricultural products, however, it is extremely difficult for developing countries to bind all ordinary customs duties and tariff equivalents. In this regard, it should be pointed out that even the customs duties of the manufactured products are not fully bound.

6. Credits for Measures Implemented since the Punta del Este Declaration

- According to the Mid-term Review agreement, credit should be given for measures implemented since the Punta del Este declaration which have contributed positively to agricultural reform. The draft Text should be revised to introduce concrete methods which would reflect these credits.

7. Green Box

- Because the criteria for the Green Box is set according to the policies of developed countries, many criteria are too strict for developing countries to observe. Therefore, the conditions for certain policies in the Green Box should be revised to be more practicable.

8. Inflation

- Not just excessive inflation but all inflation rates should be reflected in determining the level of annual commitment. The level of commitment should be adjusted every year to take into account the level of inflation as well. Unless inflation is reflected, the real rates of reduction will be much higher than the nominal rates.

ſ   0248

9. Export Subsidy

- Product coverage should not be limited to 22 product groups as is
  suggested in the Draft. To be consistent, all products in the product
  coverage in Annex I of Part A should be subject to reduction commitments
  if there are export subsidies listed in Annex 7 of Part B. In addition,
  the reduction rates in budgetary outlays and in quantities should be
  the same. Circumventions of export subsidies such as export credit and
  export credit guarantees should be under strict scrutiny.

6

0249

외 무 부

종 별 :

번 호 : ECW-0407　　　　　　　　　　　일 시 : 92 0324 1800

수 신 : 장 관 (봉기, 경기원, 농림수산부, 상공부)

발 신 : 주 EC 대사　사본: 주미, 제네바대사(중계필)

제 목 : 갓트/UR 협상

　　연: ECW-0405

　　BUSH 대봉령과 KOHL 수상의 표제 관련한 회담결과에 대한 당지의 동향을 아래 보고함

　　1. DELORS 위원장은 파리에서 가진 기자회견에서 KOHL 수상은 BUSH 대봉령에게 EC 의 입장을 명백히 전달한 것으로 평가한다고 말하고, KOHL 수상이 표제협상과 관련미. EC 간의 협의에 노력을 기울인 것은 불란서와 EC회원국 그리고 개도국 모두의 이익을 대변하기 위한 것이었으며, 단지 어떤 합의를 도출하기 위한 것은 아니었다고말함

　　2. 한편, 당지 전문가들은 회담에서 KOHL 수상이 제시한 입장 (즉 EC 의 보조수출 물량 제한에 대하여 미국은 곡물소비 대체품의 대 EC 수출량을 동결) 은 미국뿐 아니라 EC 내의 농민들로서도 받아드리기 어려운 제안이라고 평가하고 있음. 끝

　　(대사 권동만-국장)

롱상국　　2차보　　　　　　　　　-　　　경기원　농수부　상공부

PAGE 1　　　　　　　　　　　　　　　　92.03.25　　05:11 FN

　　　　　　　　　　　　　　　　　　　외신 1과　통제관

　　　　　　　　　　　　　　　　　　　0250

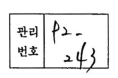

외 무 부

종 별 :

번 호 : GVW-0652

일 시 : 92 0324 1930

수 신 : 장관(봉기, 경기원, 재무부, 농림수산부, 상공부)

발 신 : 주 제네바 대사

제 목 : UR/시장접근 협상

　　1. 3.24 갓트 사무처 WOLTER 농업국장은 3.26(목) 개최 예정인 공식회의에 앞서 조만간 C/S 를 제출할 예정이라고 한 국가들의 현재의 입장을 확인하기 위한 목적이라고 하면서 당관 김대사에게 전화로 아국의 농산물 C/S 를 언제 제출할수 있는지와 특히 금주중 제출이 가능한지 여부를 문의하여 왔음. 이에 김대사는 가급적 조속히 제출하고자 하는 것이 아국의 기본입장이긴 하나 국내적 절차등이 있으므로 금주중 제출은 곤란할 것이라 답변함.

　　2. 또한 금일 오후 3.26(목) 공식회의에 앞서 3.25(수) 11:30 15 개국을 DENIS 의장이 초청하여 공식회의 준비 및 향후 협상 진행 방향등을 논의하기 위한비공식 협의가 있을 예정이라고 통보하여 왔음.

　　3. 당관으로서는 현재의 협상 진행상황으로 보아 아국 농산물 C/S 를 조속히 제출하는 것이 필요할 것으로 사료되는바, 그 제출 가능시기를 회보 바람. 끝

　　(대사 박수길-국장)

　　예고 92.6.30 까지

통상국	차관	2차보	안기부	경기원	재무부	농수부	상공부

長官報告事項

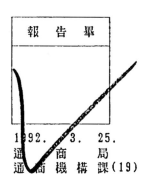

報告畢

1992. 3. 25.
通商局
通商機構課(19)

題目 : 美 議會 內에서의 韓.日 쌀 市場 開放法 推進 動向

1. 韓.日 쌀 市場 開放法案 美 議會 提出

○ 92.3.25字 外信 報道에 따르면, 페이지오 美 下院 議員(民主)이 3.23
   我國, 日本等의 쌀 市場 開放을 要求하는 下記 要旨의 法案을 議會에 提出
   - USTR이 일정 期限을 두고 韓國, 日本等과 쌀 市場 開放 交涉
   - 同 期限內에 쌀 市場開放이 이루어지지 않을 境遇, 美 通商法 301조에 따라
     相對國에 대해 高關稅 賦課等 報復措置 發動

2. 評價

○ 現在 UR 農産物 協商이 進行中에 있으며, 또한 同 法案의 內容(美 通商法
   301조에 따른 一方的인 報復措置 發動)이 UR 紛爭解決 協定案中 一方措置
   抑制 및 갓트 紛爭解決 節次 遵守 條項에 正面으로 背馳되기 때문에 議會
   通過가 어려울 것으로 展望

3. 措置事項 : 駐美 大使館에 上記 法案 內容 및 推進 動向 把握 指示

4. 國會 및 言論對策 : 別途 對策 不要.   끝.

0252

長官報告事項

報告畢

1992. 3. 25.
通 商 局
通商機構課(19)

題 目：美 議會 內에서의 韓·日 쌀 市場 開放法 推進 動向

1. 韓·日 쌀 市場 開放法案 美 議會 提出

  O 92.3.25字 中央經濟新聞 報道에 따르면, 페이지오 美 下院 議員(民主)이 3.23
    我國, 日本等의 쌀 市場 開放을 要求하는 下記 要旨의 法案을 議會에 提出
    - USTR이 일정 期限을 두고 韓國, 日本等과 쌀 市場 開放 交涉
    - 同 期限內에 쌀 市場開放이 이루어지지 않을 境遇, 美 通商法 301조에 따라
      相對國에 대해 高關稅 賦課等 報復措置 發動

2. 評 價

  O 現在 UR 農産物 協商이 進行中에 있으며, 또한 同 法案의 內容(美 通商法
    301조에 따른 一方的인 報復措置 發動)이 UR 紛爭解決 協定案中 一方措置
    抑制 및 갓트 紛爭解決 節次 遵守 條項에 正面으로 背馳되기 때문에 議會
    通過가 어려울 것으로 展望

3. 措置事項 : 駐美 大使館에 上記 法案 內容 및 推進 動向 把握 指示

4. 國會 및 言論對策 : 別途 對策 不要.   끝.

	분류번호	보존기간

발 신 전 보

WUS-1336   920325 1132 DQ

번 호 :   종별 :

WGV -0457

수 신 : 주   미   대사. 총영사 (사본 : 주 제네바 대사)

발 신 : 장 관(통 기)

제 목 : 현~~물~~ 쌀 개방법 추진

1. 국내언론 보도(3.25자 중앙경제신문)에 따르면 페이지오 미 하원의원(민주)이

    3.23 한국~~과~~ 일본의 쌀시장 개방을 요구하는 새로운 법안을 의회에 제출 하였다 함.

2. 동 법안은 USTR이 일정 기한을 두고 상대국과 쌀시장 개방 교섭을 한뒤, 동 기한내에

    시장개방이 이루어지지 않을 경우 미 통상법 301조에 기초한 고관세 부과등 보복

    조치를 취할 수 있도록 한다는 내용이라 하는바 관련 동향 및 동 법안 채택 전망등을

    파악 보고바람.   끝.   (통상국장   김 용 규)

예규에 의거 재분류(92.6. 30 .)

직위   성명 이재욱

	기안자 성명	과 장	심의관	국 장	차 관	장 관
앙 고 재 92 년 3 월 25 일 통상기구과 안명수				전결		

보 안 통 제	

외신과통제

0254

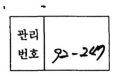

외 무 부

종 별 :

번 호 : USW-1519

수 신 : 장관(통기)통이,미일,경기원,농수산부

발 신 : 주 미 대사   재무부,상공부) 사본:주제네바대사-본부중계필

제 목 : 쌀 시장개방 법안

일 시 : 92 0325 1907

대 : WUS-1336

1. 대호, VIC FAZIO 하원의원 (민주-캘리포니아)은 3.20 한국, 일본, 홍보대만의 쌀 및 쌀제품 (RICE AND RICE PRODUCTS) 시장개방을 위해 USTR 이 한국, 일본, 대만 정부와 미 통상법 301 조에 의한 협상을 개시할 것을 요구하는 아래 요지의 법안 (H.R. 4533) 을 제출함. (동 법안 별첨 팩스 송부)

가. 일본, 한국, 대만의 미국산 쌀 수입금지와 관련한 301 조 적용

(1) 미국산 쌀의 시장접근에 영향을 주는 일본, 한국, 대만의 모든 행위, 관행, 정책은 74 년 미 통상법상의 정당화 할수 없는 (UNJUSTIFIABLE), 미국의 교역을 제한하고 부담을 주는 행위, 관행, 정책으로 간주함.

(2) USTR 은 상기 외국의 행위, 관행, 정책을 철폐하기 위하여 통상법 301 조 (C)항 (보복 또는 협상개시 규정)에 의거 보복조치를 취하거나 또는 해당국과의 협상을 개시함.

나. 협상의제 및 의무적 조치

(1) 통상법 301 조(C)(1)(C) 항에 의한 외국과의 협상시 협상 의제에는 아래 내용이 포함됨.

. 미국산 쌀의 수입금지 철폐

. 미국산 쌀의 가격, 이용, 판매, 유통에 대한 정부의 제한 및 통제 철폐

. 미국산 쌀에 대한 제한적인 수입허가조건 철폐

. 미국산 쌀이 유통과정에서 제한없이 IDENTITY 를 유지할수 있도록 보장

. 쌀에 대한 국제가격 (WORLD MARKET PRICES) 설정

0 상기 가(1)의 행위, 관행, 정책이 없었을 경우 미국산 쌀이 차지했을시장 점유율에 해당하는 물량의 미국산 쌀판매 보장.

통상국 정와대	장관 안기부	차관 경기원	1차보 농수부	2차보 중계	미주국	통상국	~~외정실~~	분석관

PAGE 1

검 토 필 (19ㅣㅣ6.30.)

92.03.26   11:17
외신 2과 통제관 BX

0255

0 미국과 해당국가간의 정확한 쌀 교역 평가를 위해 정부기관간의 정보교환체제 확립.

(2)의무 조치

0 USTR 은 아래의 경우를 제외하고는 93.3.1 또는 동 법제정 이후 6 개월 이 되는 날짜중 나중의 시한 이내에 통상법 301 조 (C)(1)(A) 및 (B) 에 따른 조치 (해당국가와의 협정상 이익 부여 중지 또는 수입규제 부과등 보복 조치) 를 취함.

- USTR 이 동법제정 이후 6 개월 되는 날짜 또는 93.3.1 중 내중의 시한내에 협정을 체결할 경우.

- USTR 이 93.3.1 이전에 GATT 의 일부로서 쌀 교역에 대한 협정을 체결한다는 의사를 통보할경우(UR 타결의미).

2. 상기 법안 입법추진 동향 및 법안 채택 전망등은 FAXIO 의원실등을 접촉, 추보 여정임.끝

(대사 현홍주-국장)

예고문: 92.12.31 까지

PAGE 2

0256

주 미 대 사 관

USW(F) : *1830*   년월일 : *0321*   시간 : *1909*

수 신 : 장   관(통기.통아.이민.경기원.재무우.상공부)

발 신 : 주 미 대 사   상: 주제네바 대사

제 목 : 첨부

보통   안제

(출처 :   )

(*1830 - 5 - 1*)

의신 1과
등제

102D CONGRESS
2D SESSION

H. R. 4533

To require the United States Trade Representative to take action authorized
under section 301 of the Trade Act of 1974 against certain foreign
countries in retaliation for the imposition by such countries of a ban
on the importation of rice and rice products of the United States,
and for other purposes.

IN THE HOUSE OF REPRESENTATIVES

Mr. FAZIO introduced the following bill; which was referred to the Committee
on _____

A BILL

To require the United States Trade Representative to take
action authorized under section 301 of the Trade Act
of 1974 against certain foreign countries in retaliation
for the imposition by such countries of a ban on the
importation of rice and rice products of the United
States, and for other purposes.

1   *Be it enacted by the Senate and House of Representa-*

2 *tives of the United States of America in Congress assembled,*

0258

1 SECTION 1. "301" ACTION WITH RESPECT TO JAPAN'S BAN

2   ON THE IMPORTATION OF UNITED STATES-

3   PRODUCED RICE.

4   (a) IN GENERAL.—On the date of the enactment of

5 this Act, all acts, practices, and policies of a foreign coun-

6 try described in subsection (b) that affect the access to

7 the foreign country's market of rice and rice products of

8 the United States shall, for purposes of title III of the

9 Trade Act of 1974, be considered as being acts, practices,

10 and policies of a foreign country that are unjustifiable and

11 burden or restrict United States commerce. Subject to sec-

12 tion 2, the United States Trade Representative (in this

13 Act referred to as the "Trade Representative") shall im-

14 mediately proceed to determine, in accordance with section

15 304(a)(1)(B) of such Act, what action to take under sec-

16 tion 301(c) of such Act to obtain the elimination of such

17 acts, practices, and policies.

18   (b) FOREIGN COUNTRIES.—For purposes of this Act,

19 the term "a foreign country described in subsection (b)"

20 includes—

21   (1) Japan;

22   (2) the Republic of Korea; and

23   (3) Taiwan.

24 SEC. 2. NEGOTIATION AGENDA; MANDATORY ACTION.

25   (a) IN GENERAL.—If the Trade Representative de-

3

1   the Trade Act of 1974 with respect to an act, practice,

2   or policy referred to in section 1, the agenda for negotia-

3   tions shall include, but not be limited to—

4   (1) the elimination of all bans or embargoes

5   against rice and rice products of the United States;

6   (2) the elimination of all government limitations

7   on, or control of, the pricing, use, marketing, and

8   distribution of rice and rice products of the United

9   States;

10   (3) the elimination of restrictive import licens-

11   ing requirements with respect to rice and rice prod-

12   ucts of the United States;

13   (4) guarantees that rice and rice products of

14   the United States will maintain their identity

15   throughout the distribution system without restric-

16   tions;

17   (5) the establishment of world market prices for

18   rice and rice products;

19   (6) guarantees for sales in the foreign country's

20   market of rice and rice products of the United

21   States in an aggregate amount equal to the percent-

22   age of such market that would be held by rice and

23   rice products of the United States in the absence of

24   the acts, practices, and policies described in section

25   1(a); and

1   (7) the establishment of procedures for the ex-

2 change of information between the appropriate agen-

3 cies of the United States and of the foreign coun-

4 try's government that will permit the accurate as-

5 sessment of the trade in rice or rice products be-

6 tween the United States and the foreign country.

7   (b) MANDATORY ACTION.—On or before March 1,

8 1993, or the date which is 6 months after the date of the

9 enactment of this Act, whichever is later, the Trade Repre-

10 sentative shall initiate action in accordance with subpara-

11 graph (A) or (B) of section 301(c)(1) of the Trade Act

12 of 1974 unless the Trade Representative—

13   (1) enters into an agreement in accordance with

14 subsection (a)—

15   (A) within 6 months after the date of the

16   enactment of this Act; or

17   (B) on or before March 1, 1993,

18 whichever is later; or

19   (2) notifies Congress on or before March 1,

20 1993, of the intent to enter into an agreement on

21 rice trade as part of the General Agreement on Tar-

22 iffs and Trade.

외   무   부

종   별 :

번   호 : FRW-0616   일   시 : 92 0325 1000

수   신 : 장 관 (통기)

발   신 : 주 불 대사

제   목 : UR 협상 동향

연:FRW-0505

1. KOHL 독일 총리는 3.23 연호 BUSH 대통령과의 정상회담을 통해 UR 협상 타결을 위한 어느정도의 진전은 있었으나 타결에 이를 수준은 아니었다고 말하고, 앞으로도EC 의 이익을 보전토록 노력할 것이나 UR 타결을 위해 불란서의 양보를 강요할 의향은 없다고 밝힘.

2. 또한 총리는 7월이전에 UR 이 타결되지 않을 경우 7.6-7, 뮌헨 개최 G-7 정상회담에서 동건이 해결될수는 없을것임을 지적함으로써 G-7정상회담이 UR 문제로 영향을 받아서는 안된다는 입장을 강력히 표명함.

3. 상기와 같이 미.독간 UR 타결을 위한 막후협상이 전개되고 있는 가운데 당지유력 경제일간지 'LA TRIBUNE D'EXPANSION'은 불란서가 EC 공동농업정책(CAP)에 있어 독일로부터 보상을 받는 댓가로 UR 타결 필요성을 강조하는 아래 내용의 논평기사를 3.23 게재함.

가. UR 농산물 분야 협상이 시작될때부터 그기능이 문제시 될것으로 예상된 CAP가 30년간 회원국에 대한 기여후 재검토되는 것은 당연함.

나. 그간 EC 는 CAP 개혁의 자체적 당위성에도 불구하고 회원국 특히 불란서의반대로 집행위가 준비한 최소한의 이니시어티브 조차 수용치 못한 결과,EC 는 농산물 문제에 있어 거부할줄만 알지 제안할줄은 모른다는 국제적비난에 봉착하였음.

다. 이러한 가운데 EC 자체간 분열이 노정되어 독일은 최소한 2회에 걸쳐 불란서와 합의한'농산물 협약'을 위반하였으며, 미국은 독일(농산물의 자급자족 목표)과 불란서(농산물 수출 추진)간 상이한 이해관계를 이용하여 독일을 회유하고 있는바, 불란서는 점차 EC 내외에서 고립되고 있음.

라. 4월중 타결코자 하는 농산물 협상결과는 EC와 불란서 입장에서 보면

통상국   2차보

PAGE 1   92.03.25   20:01 DS
                                                   외신 1과 통제관

                                                   0262

불만족스런 내용이 될것이며, CAP 는 미국으로로부터 상응할만한 진정한 보상없이 그 중요한 부분을 상실하게 될것임.

    마. 한편, 불란서의 경우 자국의 반대로 농산물협상이 타결되지 않을 경우, 곡류.설탕등 주요농산물 교역의 새로운 전쟁에 있어 최대의 피해자가 될 가능성이 큼.

    바. 불란서로서는 UR 이 타결되든 안되든 농산물분야의 손익계산서는 적자가 분명한바, 현재로서 유일한 대안은 불란서를 이탈한 독일로 하여금 CAP 개혁에 있어 값비싼 댓가를 치루도록 하는 방법뿐 임.끝.

    (대사 노영찬-국장)

외 무 부

종 별 :

번 호 : ECW-0427

일 시 : 92 0326 1730

수 신 : 장 관 (봉기,농림수산부)

발 신 : 주 EC 대사

제 목 : 갓트/UR 협상

표제 관련한 최근 당지의 동향을 아래 MOEL가 MANN 독일경제장관 (자민당) 은 농업 보조금 감축문제가 표제협상 타결의 장애요소가 되어서는 안된다고 말하고, 동 보조금감축과 관련된 독일의 제안을 마련하기 위해 4월초에 농업전문가 회의를 개최하겠다고 말함. 이에대해 종전 보조금 감축문제에 대해 반대하는 입장을 취해온 기독민주당 출신 KIECHLE 농무장관도 MOELLEMANN 장관제의에 반대하지 않는다는 의사를 표명함

2. BRITTAN EC 경쟁담당 집행위원은 런던의 미상공회의소에서 가진 연설에서 표제 협상의 돌파구를 마련하기 위해서는 EC 뿐 아니라 미국도 탄력적인 입장을 취해야할 것이라고 말하고, 미.EC 양측은 실무적인 차원의 협상에 주력하는것이 바람직하며, G-7 정상회담에서 UR협상 문제를 논의하는 것은 바람직하지 않다고 말함

3. DE CLERCQ 구주의회 대외경제관계 위원장은 4.15. 브랏셀에서 DUNKEL 갓트 사무총장과 회담할 것이라고 발표함. 끝

(대사 권동만-국장)

통상국   농수부   그러선

PAGE 1

92.03.27   06:38 FN

외신 1과 통제관

0264

외 무 부

종 별 :

번 호 : GVW-0679

일 시 : 92 0326 1930

수 신 : 장관(봉기, 경기원, 재무부, 농림수산부, 상공부, 경제수석)

발 신 : 주 제네바 대사

제 목 : UR/시장접근(농산물 C/S 제출 건의)

대: WGV-0337

1. 최근 국제 언론의 일부 및 갓트 사무국, 외교계에서는 UR 부진의 주된 책임은 미국 및 이씨에 있다는 사실을 인정하면서도 부수적으로 일본과 아국도 협상진전에 다소 부정적인 영향을 주고 있다는 인상을 갖고 있음에 비추어 내실있는 농산물 C/S 의 조속한 제출이 필요한 것으로 사료되는바 가능하면 내주중 이를 제출할수 있도록 필요한 조치를 취하여 주실것을 건의함.

2. 금 3.27 (목) 현재 농.공산품 전부 또는 일부라도 제출한 국가는 30 개국, 조속한 제출을 약속하고 있는 국가수는 20 여개임.

3. DENIS 시장접근 분야 협상 그룹 의장 주재하에 금일까지 개최된 3 월중 공식, 비공식 회의는 6 회에 이르며, 동 회의시마다 C/S 미제출국가의 조속한 제출 요구와 제출하였으나 그 내용이 부실한 나라(미, EC, 일, 카 등)에 대한 비판이 커지고 있는 실정이며 TNC 개최 필요성도 대부되고 있음.

4. 우리는 지난 3 월초 공산품 C/S 제출시 농산물 C/S 도 가능한 빠른 시일내 제출 하겠다는 약속을 서면 및 구두로 한바 있음. 특히 금주에 개최된 비공식회의(3.25 , 수)및 금일 공식회의(3.26, 목)에서 이제 기술적 문제점이 거의 해결 되었으므로 필요한 국내절차를 거쳐 조만간 농산물 C/S 를 제출하겠다는 입장을 표명한바 있으며, 동 기회에 UR 이 실패해서는 안되며, 조속한 성공을 위해서는 협상 참여국이 모두 성의를 가지고 기여해야 할 것이라는 입장을 표명한바 있으며, 사무국 당국자도 비공식적으로 아국의 총선이 끝난만큼 조속한 농산물 C/S 제출을 종용하고 있음.

5. 미.EC 간 막후 협상이 상당한 진전을 보이고 있음에도 불구하고 일부 핵심 쟁점에 대한 합의가 이루어지지 않고 있는 가운데 UR 협상의 조기 타결 가능성이 불투명한것이 사실이나 미.EC 간 막후 협상이 계속 되고 있는점, UR 의 성공적 타결에

통상국	장관	차관	1차보	2차보	분석관	정와대	정와대	안기부
경기원	재무부	농수부	상공부					

PAGE 1

92.03.27 06:54
외신 2과 통제관 BX
0265

기여하겠다는 확고한 우리 의지의 표명 필요성등을 감안할때, 이러한 시점일수록 내실있는 농산물 C/S 제출이 긴요하다고 판단함.

6. 농산물 C/S 를 작성함에 있어서는 91 년 1.15 TNC 회의시 밝힌 아국의 입장 및 현재 제출된 일본 농산물 C/S 가 비판의 대상이 될수 밖에 없을 것이라는 점을 감안 하여야 할 것이며, 이렇게 볼때 대호 1 항과 같이 품목별 정부 입장(쌀 프러스 알파 등)을 확정하여 C/S 를 제출하는 것이 가장 바람직 스럽다고 사료됨. 끝

(대사 박수길-국장)

예고 92.6.30 까지

長 官 報 告 事 項

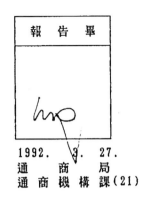

報 告 畢

1992. 3. 27.
通 商 局
通 商 機 構 課(21)

題 目 : UR/農産物 國別 履行 計劃 提出 準備

주 제네바 大使는 2.26 我國의 UR/農産物 國別 履行 計劃(country schedule)을 早速 提出할 것을 건의해 온바, 關聯 動向을 아래 報告 드립니다.

---

1. 現 況

   ㅇ 市場接近 分野(工産品 및 農産物) 讓許 計劃書 提出 國家 : 30個國(3.26 現在)

   ㅇ 我國은 3.5 工産品 讓許 計劃書만 提出, 農産物 履行 計劃은 조만간 提出 豫定임을 表明

2. 我國 農産物 履行 計劃 提出 準備 動向

   ㅇ 農水産部에서 履行 計劃書 試案 作成 完了

   ㅇ 4月初 提出을 目標로 UR 對策 實務委, 農産物 輸入開放 對策委, 黨政 協議等 國內節次 推進中

   ㅇ 15개 NTC 品目 處理 問題와 關聯, 關係部處間 協議中

      - 農水産部는 15개 品目 全部에 대하여 協商 資料만 提出할 것을 希望

      - 經濟企劃院은 總選이 終了 되었으므로 차제에 15개 品目을 縮小 調整, 이에 의거 履行 計劃書를 作成할 것을 主張

3. 當部 措置事項 : 農水産部와 經濟企劃院의 早速한 意見 調整 促求

4. 國會 및 言論對策 : 該當事項 없음.   끝.

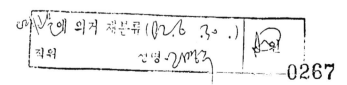

에 의거 재분류(92.6.30.)
직위   신명

-0267

報 告 畢

長 官 報 告 事 項

1992. 3. 27.
通 商 局
通 商 機 構 課 (21)

題 目 : UR/農産物 國別 履行 計劃 提出 準備 動向

주 제네바 大使는 2.26 我國의 UR/農産物 國別 履行 計劃(country schedule)을 早速 提出할 것을 건의해 온바, 關聯 動向을 아래 報告 드립니다.

1. 現 況

   ㅇ 市場接近 分野(工産品 및 農産物) 讓許 計劃書 提出 國家 : 30個國(3.26 現在)

   ㅇ 我國은 3.5 工産品 讓許 計劃書만 提出, 農産物 履行 計劃은 조만간 提出 豫定임
   意思 表明

2. 我國 農産物 履行 計劃 提出 準備 動向

   ㅇ 農水産部에서 履行 計劃書 試案 作成 完了

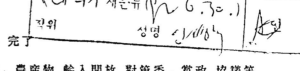
에 의거 재분류(92. 6.30.)
직위   성명 신내수

   ㅇ 4月初 提出을 目標로 UR 對策 實務委, 農産物 輸入開放 對策委, 黨政 協議等
   國內節次 推進中

   ㅇ 15개 NTC 品目 處理 問題와 關聯, 關係部處間 協議中

      - 農水産部는 15개 品目 全部에 대하여 協商 資料만 提出할 것을 希望

      - 經濟企劃院은 總選이 終了 되었으므로 차제에 15개 品目을 縮小 調整,
        이에 의거 履行 計劃書를 作成할 것을 主張

3. 措置事項 : 농수산부 및 경기원의 의견조정 촉구

4. 國會 및 言論對策 : 該當事項 없음.   끝.

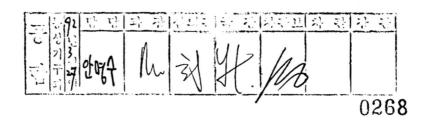

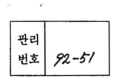

외　무　부

종　별 :

번　호 : USW-1559　　　　　　　　　　일　시 : 92 0327 1848

수　신 : 장관(통기,통이,미일,경기원,농수산부,재무부,상공부)

발　신 : 주 미 대사　　　　사본:주제네바 대사 - 본부중계필

제　목 : 쌀 시장개방 법안

연: USW-1519

1. 당관 조일환 참사관은 금 3.27 미하원 VIC 노탈 의원 사무실의 TIME TERRY 보좌관을 면담(안총기 서기관 배석), 연호 FAZIO 의원의 쌀 시장개방 법안 제출과 관련, 협의하였는 바, 동 보좌관의 언급요지 아래 보고함.

　가. 법안 제출 배경

　. SACRAMENTO 를 중심으로 하는 FAZIO 의원 선거구 지역은 캘리포니아 쌀의90 %를 생산하고 있는 바, 쌀 시장개방 법안 제출은 FAZIO 의원 지역구민의 의사를 반영한 것임.

　. 또한 UR 협상이 성공하지 못할 경우에 대비하기 위한 것임. 현재 UR 타결여부는 매우 불확실한 상황이고, 설사 타결되더라도 쌀 문제가 포함되지 않을 가능성이 있으므로, 이에 대비하여 USTR 로 하여금 미 통상법 301 조에 의한 양자협상을 개시토록 하려는 것임.

　나. 여타 의원 지지여부

　. 현재 BILL ALEXANDER(민주-아칸소), JACK BROOKS(민주-텍사스), JIMMY HAYES(민주-루이지아나), WALLY HERGER(공화-캘리포니아), CLYDE HOLLOWAY(공화루이지아나), RAY THORNTON(민주-알칸소)등 의원이 공동 제안자로 가담하였는바, 동 의원들은 모두 미국의 주요 쌀 생산지역 출신 의원임.

　다. 입법추진 계획

　. 쌀 시장개방 법안 자체를 위해 청문회가 계획되어 있지는 않으나 현재 의회에 계류중인 SUPER 301 조 부활법안 및 자동차 경쟁력 제고 법안등 심의시 함께 논의될 가능성이 있음.

　. 또한 GEPHARDT 등 무역 분야에 관심이 많은 의원들이 상기 기존의 개별 법안등을

통상국	장관	차관	1차보	2차보	미주국	통상국	분석관	청와대
안기부	경기원	재무부	농수부	상공부	중계			

PAGE 1　　　　　　　　　　　　　　　　　　　　　92.03.28　10:19

종합하여 단일 법안을 제출할 가능성도 없지 않으며, 이경우 쌀 시장개방 법안도 포함되어 검토될 것임.

라. 행정부와의 협의 여부

. 동 법안과 관련 행정부와 협의한바는 없으나 행정부에서는 반대입장을 갖고 있을 것으로 생각함. 일반적으로 행정부는 의회가 외국과의 협상을 강요하는 것을 좋아하지 않으며, 쌀 문제도 UR 을 통해 해결하는 것이 바람직 하다는 입장을 보일 것임.

2. 조 참사관은 한국이 분단국가로서 안보적으로 특수한 상황에 처해 있기 때문에 한국인이 주식으로 하는 쌀에 대한 식량안보가 절대 필요한 상화이며, 인구의 16%가 종사하고 있는 농업분야가 산업화 과정에서 상대적으로 혜택을 받지 못했기 때문에 쌀 시장개방 문제는 농민 보호라는 차원에서도 매우 민감한 정치적 문제라는 점을 미 의회 인사들도 이해해야 할 것이라고 설명함.

3. 관찰 및 평가

. FAZIO 의원 및 동 법안의 공동제안 의원들이 모두 쌀 생산지역 출신이라는점과 FAZIO 의원이 3.23 자신의 선거구인 캘리포니아 SACRAMENTO 에서 동 법안제출 사실을 발표한 점등을 감안할 때 동법안 제출은 금년 11 월 선거에서 지역구민의 지지를 획득하기 위한 선거전략의 일환인 것으로 판단됨.

. 현재 동 법안 입법추진을 위한 청문회등의 구체적 계획이 없고, 미 의회가 최근 미국 경제 침체와 관련하여 대외무역문제 보다는 주로 예산안, 세금등과관련한 국내 관련 대책 마련에 주력하고 있는 만큼 동 법안이 조만간 입법화될가능성은 많지 않은 것으로 보이나, 11 월 선거와 관련하여 대외무역 문제가 또다시 쟁점으로 부각될 경우 동 법안이 여타 법안들과 함께 논의될 가능성을 배제할 수는 없음.

4. 동 법안 심의동향 관련 진전사항 있을 경우 추보 예정임.

예고:일반 92.12.31.

(대사 현홍주-국장)

PAGE 2

외 무 부

종   별 :

번   호 : FRW-0655   일   시 : 92 0329 1200

수   신 : 장관(경일, 통기) 사본: 농림수산부

발   신 : 주불 대사

제   목 : OECD 농업 각료 회의 결과

. 3.26-27 간 스웨덴 OLSSON 농업장관 주재, 표제 회의 결과 아래 보고함 (
COMMUNIQUE 전문 기송부)

1. 농업 정책 조정

0 1987 농업 개혁 원칙 재확인

0 우루과이 협상의 조기, 성공적 타결을 위해 새로운 정책적 IMPETUS 가 필요함을
강조

0 농업 부문이 우루과이 협상의 주요 해결 사항임을 인식하고, 우루과이
협상이조기 타결되지 않을 경우, 국제 무역 체계가 악화될것을 우려

0 농업, 농식량 부문이 경제 전반에 이바지 하기위해, 농업 정책의 조정이
필요한바, 농업 정책의 조정은 고품질 제품을 생산하는 시장 경제확대, 무역 자유화
및환경 보호 증대 차원에서 이루어져야 함.

0 최근 농업 부문에서 수급 균형 조짐을 보이고 있지만, 중기적 전망시 OECD역내
국가의 많은 농산품이 공급 초과 현상을 보일것으로 전망, OECD 를 중심으로농업 정책
조정이 조기 이루어 져야 함.

2. 구조 조정

0 농업 부문의 지속적 성장을 위하여 왜곡된 시장 구조의 점진적 교정,
생산자에대한 보조지원 감소등 시장 경제 원리의 확대 적용이 요구 되며, 이러한 구조
조정실현을 위하여 OECD지원을 강화 함.

3. 농업과 환경

농.임업 부문이 환경과 밀접한 관계가 있음에 비추어, 농업정책 조정할경우 생태계
보존, 농업자원보호 및 환경 보호 등을 고려해야 하며, POLLUTER PAYS 원칙이보다 폭
넓게 적용되어야 함.

경제국   통상국   농수부

PAGE 1   92.03.29   21:04 DW
                                                외신 1과 통제관
                                                  0271

4. 농촌 개발

농촌 개발 정책을 단순 농업 정책이 아닌 경제, 사회 문제를 포함한 종합적 정책으로 이루어 져야 하고 농촌 경제의 지속적 성장 활동을 저해 하는 요소를 제거함을골자로 해야 할것임.

5. 역외국과의 관계

0 역외국에 대한 식량 원조, 기술 및 농업정책 조정 지원을 위하여 역외국과의대화를 증대하고, 역외국의 OECD 시장 접근을 촉진함.

 0 시장 경제에로의 전환을 추진중인 동구국가들(CEECS) 과 농업 부문 협력강화

0 CIS 및 발틱 국가에 대한 식량 원조 필요성 인식. 끝

(대사 노영찬- 국장)

관리
번호 92-28P

외 무 부

종 별 :

번 호 : GVW-0713　　　　　　　　　　일 시 : 92 0331 1600

수 신 : 장관(통기, 경기원, 재무부, 농림수산부, 상공부)

발 신 : 주 제네바 대사

제 목 : UR 농산물 협상

3.23-27 기간중 당지에서 개최된 G-8 회의 관련 최농무관이 일본 및 카나다대표부 관계관을 접촉 탐문한 요지 하기 보고함.

1. 회의 개요

- 미국 USDA FAS 슈뢰터 처장보 주재로 미국, 이씨, 일본, 카나다, 호주, 뉴질랜드, 알젠틴, 핀랜드, 노르웨이, 스웨덴 등 10 개국 참석(아이슬랜드만 미제출)

- 기 제출된 농산물 C/S 에 대한 기술적 문제 중심으로 논의

- 분야별, 국별로 차례대로 논의

2. 논의 요지

- 각국 C/S 의 던켈 초안 합치 여부가 주로 논의되었음.

케언즈 그룹 국가, 미국, 스웨덴 등의 C/S 는 대부분 던켈 초안에 합치하지만 일부 불합치하는 부분도 있음.

0 미국의 낙농 제품 TE 계산시 국제가격 CIF 가격대신 MINIMUM PRICE 를 적용하였고, 국내 가격은 도매 가격대신 생산자 가격 더하기 수송비를 적용하여 TE를 높게 책정하였음. WAIVER 적용 품목의 TE 가 90 년 C/L 제출시 보다 높게 제시된 경우가 상당수 있음.

0 호주는 일부 품목 양허 관세를 조정하였는바, 이씨는 28 조 해당 사항이라고 문제를 제기하였으며, 이에 대하여 호주는 대체적인 공감을 표명함.

- 일본, 카나다, 노르웨이등은 예외없는 관세화에 대한 기존 입장을 표명함.

0 노르웨이는 유제품 및 사슴을 관세화 예외 대상 품목으로 제시(C/S 에 이들 예외 품목의 TE 는 제시하였으나 삭감 약속은 하지 않았음)

0 핀랜드는 기초 자료를 제시(모든 품목의 TE 를 제시하였으나 삭감 약속은하지 않았음.)

통상국　장관　　차관　　1차보　　2차보　　외정실　　분석관　　경기원　　재무부
농수부　상공부

PAGE 1　　　　　　　　　　　　　　　　　　　　　　　　　　92.04.01　　00:05

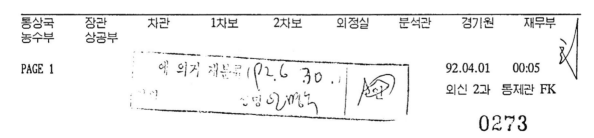

외신 2과 통제관 FK

0273

UR(우루과이라운드)-농산물 협상, 1992. 전4권(V.1 1-3월)　591

- 일본은 다수 품목을 관세화 예외 품목이라 하여 TE 등 기초자료를 제시하지 않은점, 던켈 초안에 합치 하지 않는 내용이 많은점, 86 년 이후 자유화 품목의 CREDIT 를 요구한 점등에 대하여 상대국으로부터 강한 문제 제기가 있었음.

3. 차기 회의 일정등에 대한 논의는 없었음. 끝

(대사 박수길-국장)

예고 92.6.30 까지

외교문서 비밀해제: 우루과이라운드2 14
우루과이라운드 농산물 협상 4

초판인쇄 2024년 03월 15일
초판발행 2024년 03월 15일

지은이 한국학술정보(주)
펴낸이 채종준
펴낸곳 한국학술정보(주)
주 소 경기도 파주시 회동길 230(문발동)
전 화 031-908-3181(대표)
팩 스 031-908-3189
홈페이지 http://ebook.kstudy.com
E-mail 출판사업부 publish@kstudy.com
등 록 제일산-115호(2000. 6. 19)

ISBN   979-11-7217-116-2 94340
        979-11-7217-102-5 94340 (set)